MARTIAL

Epigrams
Book Two

MARTIAL

Epigrams
Book Two

Edited with
Introduction, Translation, and Commentary
by
Craig A. Williams

OXFORD
UNIVERSITY PRESS

2004

OXFORD
UNIVERSITY PRESS

Oxford   New York
Auckland   Bangkok   Buenos Aires   Cape Town   Chennai
Dar es Salaam   Delhi   Hong Kong   Istanbul   Karachi   Kolkata
Kuala Lumpur   Madrid   Melbourne   Mexico City   Mumbai   Nairobi
São Paulo   Shanghai   Taipei   Tokyo   Toronto

Copyright © 2004 by Oxford University Press, Inc.

Published by Oxford University Press, Inc.
198 Madison Avenue, New York, New York, 10016
www.oup.com

Oxford is a registered trademark of Oxford University Press

Library of Congress Cataloging-in-Publication Data
Martial.
[Epigrammata. Liber 2. English & Latin]
Epigrams. Book two / Martial ; edited with introduction, translation,
and commentary by Craig A. Williams.
p.   cm.
Includes bibliographical references and index.
ISBN 0-19-515531-9
1. Martial—Translations into English.   2. Epigrams,
Latin—Translations into English.   3. Epigrams, Latin.   I. Williams,
Craig A. (Craig Arthur), 1965–   II. Title.
PA6502.W55 2003
878'.0102—dc21   2003004244

1 3 5 7 9 8 6 4 2

Printed in the United States of America
on acid-free paper

PREFACE

lector, opes nostrae: quem cum mihi Roma dedisset,
  "nil tibi quod demus maius habemus" ait.
                                        (10.2.5–6)

O reader, my treasure! When Rome gave you to me,
she said, "I have nothing greater to give you."

"illa tamen laudant omnes, mirantur, adorant."
  confiteor: laudant illa sed ista legunt.
                                        (4.49.9–10)

"But everyone praises, admires, and reveres that [mythological]
poetry!" Yes, I admit it, they praise that kind of poetry. But
what they *read* is this.

Martial's epigrams display a remarkable interest in what we would now call
their own reception by readers. But while this poet self-consciously distances
himself from arcane mythological poetry and boasts that his readers should
have no need of learned commentary (10.21.5–6: "mea carmina, Sexte, /
grammaticis placeant, ut sine grammaticis"), it is precisely because he so
firmly anchors his epigrams in the Rome of his day that readers of the early
twenty-first century need assistance. The central goal of this commentary is

to help contemporary readers, both those who have previous experience reading Martial and those who do not, deepen their understanding of the text in front of them by locating the epigrams in the cultural and literary contexts in which they arose and by drawing attention to specific features that are characteristic of author and genre.

Thus, in this commentary, the first specifically dedicated to Martial's second book, I have offered grammatical discussion, lists of ancient parallels, and references to scholarship less in the interests of compiling and epitomizing per se and more in hopes of contributing to a greater appreciation of a given epigram or of the corpus as a whole, or where there has been disagreement or controversy. I have presented fairly generous lists of parallels within Martial, and especially within Book II, in order to give a sense of the techniques characteristic of this poet, who frequently reuses and recasts linguistic and thematic material. My references to other ancient texts are selective and representative, but the prominence of Juvenal will be clear: working in a closely related genre, Martial's younger contemporary sometimes takes on similar topics in a strikingly different manner.

My emphasis on certain interpretive aspects will be most noticeable in the introductory analyses of each epigram's themes and structure. These discussions make no claim to offer an "exhaustive reading," especially elusive in the case of short poems that emphasize irony, wit, and double meaning; with respect to these aspects of Martial's work I have been mindful of Freud's warning that analysis and enjoyment of a joke may necessarily be mutually exclusive. I am also interested in the implications of a sequential reading of the book, and thus, at the beginning of each of my thematic discussions I offer brief remarks regarding each epigram's relationship with the poems that have preceded it in the collection. It must be emphasized that these remarks are meant to be suggestive rather than definitive and that this is hardly the only way to read Martial's book. Indeed, such a collection of independent poems raises complex questions of reading in general, but a commentary does not seem the most effective context in which to make a sustained contribution to that theoretical debate.

My translations—in prose because I can make no claim to being a poet—attempt above all to reflect the tone of the original, as expressed, for example, in word choice, which ranges from the poetic and elevated to the prosaic and chatty to the earthy and obscene. I have stayed as close as English permits to Martial's syntactic structures and word order, paying attention to such things as the positioning of the nearly ubiquitous vocative addressee, the repetition of key terms, and variations in sentence length and complexity, since these are often important for certain effects. My translations are intended to be accessible to Latinless readers, but I have generally left unchanged names of people and places, units of currency, and the like, as well as certain terms so laden with specifically Roman ideology as to be untranslatable (e.g., *cinaedus*). I have explained such terms in the accompanying notes, where I have also indicated significant variations among modern translations. For the text printed in this edition, see the Introduction, section 5.

For their concrete help and suggestions or more general support I wish to thank Widu-Wolfgang Ehlers, Marco Formisano, Ralph Hexter, and Elena Merli. I owe special thanks to the anonymous readers for Oxford University Press, whose comments and criticism were extremely helpful; one in particular was quite rigorous, and I am grateful for it. I was able to bring this project to completion thanks to two generous research fellowships, one from the Ethyle R. Wolfe Institute for the Humanities of Brooklyn College and another from the Alexander von Humboldt Foundation (Bonn), which allowed me to take advantage of the considerable resources and pleasant atmosphere of the Seminar für Klassische Philologie at the Freie Universität Berlin.

CONTENTS

ABBREVIATIONS

ANRW   H. Temporini, ed. *Aufstieg und Niedergang der römischen Welt.*
       Berlin, 1972–.

CEG   P. A. Hansen, ed. *Carmina epigraphica Graeca*. 2 vols. Berlin,
       1983–1989.

CGL   Georg Goetz, ed., *Corpus glossariorum Latinorum*. 7 vols. Leipzig,
       1888–1923.

CIL   *Corpus inscriptionum Latinarum*. Berlin, 1863–.

CLE   F. Bücheler and E. Lommatzsch, eds. *Carmina Latina epigraphica.*
       Leipzig, 1895–1926.

FLP   Edward Courtney, ed. *The Fragmentary Latin Poets*. New York
       and Oxford, 1993.

Forcellini   Egidio Forcellini, *Totius Latinitatis lexicon*. 6 vols. Prato, 1858–
       1875.

FPL   Jürgen Blänsdorf, ed. *Fragmenta poetarum Latinorum epicorum
       et lyricorum praeter Ennium et Lucilium*. 3rd ed. Stuttgart, 1995.

GLK   Heinrich Keil, ed. *Grammatici Latini*. 7 vols. Leipzig, 1857–1870.

KS   Raphael Kühner and Friedrich Holzweissig. *Ausführliche Gram-
       matik der lateinischen Sprache*, 2 vols. (vol. 2 by Raphael Kühner
       and Carl Stegmann). 2nd ed. Hannover, 1912–1914.

LHS   Manu Leumann, J.B. Hofmann, and Anton Szantyr, *Lateinische
       Grammatik*. 2 vols. Munich. (Vol. 1: M. Leumann, *Lateinische
       Laut- und Formenlehre*, 1977; vol. 2: J.B. Hofmann and Anton
       Szantyr, *Lateinische Syntax und Stilistik*, 1965).

LSJ   Henry George Liddell and Robert Scott. *A Greek-English Lexi-con*. Revised by Sir Henry Stuart Jones and Roderick McKenzie. 9th ed. Oxford, 1940.

OCD   Simon Hornblower and Anthony Spawforth, eds. *The Oxford Classical Dictionary*. 3rd ed. Oxford and New York, 1996.

OLD   P. G. W. Glare, ed. *Oxford Latin Dictionary*. Oxford, 1982.

PHI   Packard Humanities Institute CD-ROM #5 (Latin Texts).

PIR   *Prosopographia imperii Romani saeculorum I II III*. 2nd ed. Berlin, 1933–.

RE   *Paulys Realencyclopädie der classischen Altertumswissenschaft*. Munich, 1894–1980.

TLL   *Thesaurus linguae Latinae*. Leipzig, 1904–.

Abbreviations for ancient authors and texts are generally those found in LSJ and *OLD*. Editions, commentaries, and translations of Martial (see the Bibliography for a list) are referred to by the author's last name only (e.g., "Friedlaender"; references to "Merli" are to the notes accompanying the translation by Scandola). References to "the *variorum* commentary" are taken from the compilation of scholarly comments presented in Schrevelius' 1670 edition. Works of modern scholarship are cited by last name and year of publication (e.g., "Sullivan 1991").

MARTIAL

Epigrams
Book Two

INTRODUCTION

1. MARTIAL'S LIFE AND WORKS

The only external ancient evidence regarding Martial is limited but valuable: Pliny the Younger's letter to Cornelius Priscus, datable to no later than A.D. 105, records Martial's death and reveals a few precious details (*Epist.* 3.21). Otherwise, as is the case with most ancient authors, our knowledge is fairly sketchy and largely dependent upon inferences drawn from the poet's own work. It has long been recognized that we must approach the latter with great skepticism in view of the fact that epigram is not autobiography; the relationship between poetic persona and the historical figure of the poet himself is particularly complex in the case of Martial.

On such an apparently straightforward point as whether or not Martial ever married, for example, the epigrams themselves offer conflicting perspectives: sometimes he speaks as a married man, sometimes as a bachelor (see on **2.91.5**, **2.92.3**). Yet there are certain basic facts about himself to which he alludes in a consistent manner and which have generally been taken to be autobiographical: his name and that of his hometown, his approximate age, and the facts that he had the status of "knight," or *eques,* and had been awarded the *ius trium liberorum.* Exercising due caution, we can thus reconstruct a bare outline of the poet's life. His name was Marcus Valerius Martialis (1.5, **2.praef**; Plin. *Epist.* 3.21); his parents were almost certainly named Valerius Fronto and Flaccilla (5.34); he was born in Bilbilis in Spain

3

(1.49, 1.61, etc.) between A.D. 38 and 41 (10.24, 12.60) in the month of March (see 9.52.3: *nostras Martias Kalendas;* comparing 8.64 and 10.87, Lucas 1938 convincingly reconstructs a Roman practice of observing birthdays on the first day of the month in which they fell); he came to Rome around 64 (10.103) and spent most of his life thereafter in Rome, with the exception of a stay of about a year's length in Forum Cornelii (modern Imola) around 87 (Book III passim); sometime between 98 and 101 he returned to Spain (Book XII passim), where he died before 105.

These bare bones can be fleshed out to a certain extent. It is clear, for example, that he had received a respectable education in Spain (9.73); that he did not pursue the obvious career path in rhetoric, whether in the schools or in the courtroom (**2.30, 2.90**); that once in Rome he sought and obtained the friendship and patronage of such well-known men as Decianus (**2.praef.**), Regulus (**2.74.2**), Atedius Melior (**2.69.7**), and L. Arruntius Stella (1.7, 7.14, 12.2); that through his poetry he had some access to, but apparently no close relationship with, the emperor (**2.91**); that, despite complaints (and occasional boasts) of modest means, he was never desperately poor but owned slaves and an estate at Nomentum (**2.38**) and eventually obtained the status of *eques,* which required a fortune of at least 400,000 sesterces; that he was awarded the *ius trium liberorum* by the emperors Titus and Domitian (**2.91–92**); and that at Rome he lived for some years in a third-floor apartment on the Quirinal (1.108, 1.117) but eventually acquired a house (9.18, 9.97, 10.58, 11.1).

The activity for which Martial won fame both in his own lifetime and afterward was the writing and publishing of epigrams (see below), and indeed his decision to publish *only* in this genre—as opposed, for example, to his contemporary Statius, who in addition to the occasional poetry known as the *Silvae* published an epic *Thebaid* and a partial *Achilleid*—seems to have been fairly unusual, even bold. The publication itself of these poems would have taken various forms, but the most common pattern is clear: individual epigrams were circulated informally and later gathered together in collections, or "books," which the poet himself published by giving to a bookseller, who then copied the manuscripts and sold them to the public (**2.1, 2.6**).

The chronology of this publication is in its general outlines fairly clear; for more detailed argumentation, see the introduction to Friedlaender. The earliest extant book, transmitted with the generic title *Epigrammaton liber* but usually referred to as *Liber de spectaculis* or *Liber spectaculorum,* celebrates the opening of the Flavian Amphitheater, or "Colosseum," in A.D. 80 and must have been published soon thereafter. Next come two collections of poems on the subject of gifts and food items at the Saturnalia, which call themselves the *Xenia* and *Apophoreta* but which are labeled Books XIII and XIV respectively in our manuscripts; on internal grounds it has been argued that these came out, probably separately, in 84–85. Thereafter, beginning with Book I in early

86, Martial published single books of epigrams at approximately one-year intervals (10.70); with the exception of Books XIII and XIV, Martial himself assigned the books the numbers they still bear—itself a novel practice (see on **2.93**). Book II probably appeared in late 86 or early 87; we cannot know, of course, how much earlier the individual poems themselves were written.

We also know that Martial published at least one revised edition of his works, as Ovid had done with his *Amores*. Book X originally appeared in A.D. 95 in a form now lost to us, followed by Book XI in December of 96, a few months after the death of Domitian. But after the death of Domitian's successor Nerva in 98, Martial published a revised edition of Book X (see 10.2), which is the version transmitted to us in the manuscripts. It is also likely that Martial brought out a revised edition of Book I in codex form at some later date (see 1.1–2).

Indeed, many scholars have been struck by the contrast between the defensive stance adopted in certain epigrams of Book II (e.g., **2.1**, **2.6**, **2.8**) and the confidence of such pieces as 1.praef., 1.1 ("toto notus in orbe Martialis"), 1.2, and **2.22**. One possible explanation (Citroni; Nauta 2002: 93, 132–133) is that the latter poems had not appeared in the original editions of Books I and II and were composed only later, for a hypothetical second edition of Martial's epigrams brought out around A.D. 93 and containing the present Books I-VII (for this "revised edition," see Schneidewin, Dau 1887, Immisch 1911, Prinz 1911). Lehmann 1931: 36 proposes a more extreme hypothesis: that the present Book II was actually the first book of epigrams published after the *Liber de spectaculis, Xenia,* and *Apophoreta,* and that the present Book I was published for the first time in the "second edition" (see further on **2.93**). If Martial did publish a revised collection of Books I–VII, our current text of Book II may derive from the revised version, the earlier version, or just possibly a collation of both effected by a later editor (see below, section 5).

2. EPIGRAM BEFORE MARTIAL

Although he often uses vague terms like *libelli, nugae,* and *ioci* to refer to his poems, Martial clearly understands himself as writing poetry belonging to a specific genre, and the name he gives to it—and perhaps he was the first literary writer in Latin to do so—is the Greek *epigramma* (**2.praef.**, **2.1**, **2.7**, **2.77**, etc.; cf. Pfohl 1969, Puelma 1996). The genre had a long history reaching back to early Greek texts that, as the name suggests, had the nature of inscriptions: ἐπιγράμματα were originally texts *written on* such objects as statues or tomb markers and thus from the beginning tending toward brevity, clarity, and focus. Already by the fifth century B.C., however, *epigrammata* had begun to detach themselves from this concrete function and to take on a literary form, exploring not only funerary but also symposiastic and erotic topics and showing a strong predilection for one meter in particular: the elegiac couplet. The epigram in this sense saw something of an explosion beginning in the Hellenistic period. Important names include Asclepiades, Callimachus, and Posidippus; especially influential on Martial was Lucillius, active in the period of Nero. Two major anthologies, or "garlands," of Greek epigrams were those of Meleager (ca. 100 B.C.) and of Philip (probably in the age of Nero, though perhaps earlier in the first century A.D.). Much later, in the tenth century A.D., poems from these anthologies were selected and combined with later epigrams to form the large extant collection now known as the *Palatine Anthology*.

The Latin epigram likewise has its roots in early metrical inscriptions and above all epitaphs—such as those for the Scipios from the late third century B.C.—but the influence of the Greek literary epigram and its characteristic themes soon made itself felt, as did the predilection for the elegiac couplet, apparently introduced to Roman poetry by Ennius. Important figures in the history of Latin epigram before Martial include Q. Lutatius Catulus, Helvius Cinna, C. Licinius Calvus, Domitius Marsus, Albinovanus Pedo, Cornelius Lentulus, and above all Catullus, whose influence on Martial is pervasive (see below). The date at which a collection of epigrams known as the *Carmina Priapea* was published is unknown, but if they predate Martial, they too exerted a clear influence on both his subject matter and his language. Most of these predecessors, above all Catullus, display characteristics fundamental to Martial's epigrams: these include a strong inclination (shared with the quintessentially Roman genre of *satura*) toward making social commentary, both in general and with regard to specific individuals, along with a propensity for blunt descriptions of sexual and scatological situations, the use of open obscenity being considered a characteristic privilege of the genre (**2.praef.**).

The influence of Catullus will be evident from his frequent appearance in this commentary (see, e.g., **2.6**, **2.14**, **2.22.3–4**, **2.23.4**, **2.41**, **2.50**, **2.65.3**, **2.71**). But it will also be seen that the language and thematic concerns of two other authors who worked in quite different genres were noticeably influential on Martial: Ovid (**2.22**, **2.25.2**, **2.29.4**, **2.35.1**, **2.36.1**, **2.41.8**, **2.46.1**, **2.47.2**, **2.61.1**, **2.84.1**, **2.94.4**; cf. Williams 2002a) and Seneca (**2.4.1–3**, **2.5**, **2.7**, **2.25–26**, **2.41.13**, **2.53.1**, **2.68.6**, **2.80**, **2.91.1–2**).

3. CHARACTERISTICS OF MARTIAL'S EPIGRAMS

A brief survey of some of the most salient traits of Martial's epigrams follows; see Mendell 1922, Kruuse 1941, Seel 1961, Citroni 1969, Sullivan 1991, and Holzberg 1986 and 2002 for more detailed discussion.

Particularly characteristic of Martial's epigrams are their satiric approach and ironic commentary on social practices and typical individuals, along with a type of wit that tends toward the concrete and the use of a sharp point. They tend to be brief, they are written in a limited variety of meters (see below), and they have the nature of "occasional poetry." A late-antique definition of the genre seems to have been specifically influenced by Martial's practice: epigrams are "pleasing not because of their quantity but because of their sharpness" (*non copia sed acumine placent,* Sidon. Apollin. *Epist.* 8.11.7). Centuries later, Coleridge speaks of "a dwarfish whole, / its body brevity, and wit its soul" (*On Epigram*), and Klopstock's lengthier description is also worth quoting:

> Bald ist das Epigramm ein Pfeil,
> > Trifft mit der Spitze;
> > Ist bald ein Schwert,
> > Trifft mit der Schärfe;
> Ist manchmal auch (die Griechen liebten's so)
> Ein klein Gemäld', ein Strahl, gesandt
> Zum Brennen nicht, nur zum Erleuchten.
> > > *(Epigramme, Vorrede)*

Sometimes the epigram is an arrow: it hits the mark with its point. Sometimes it is a sword: it hits the mark with its sharp blade. Sometimes too—the Greeks loved it like this—it is a small painting, a beam sent out not to burn but only to enlighten.

3.1. Themes

Thematic variety is central to Martial's work, but certain clear predilections emerge, and the range of subject matter of Book II is typical. Predominant is the satiric epigram, offering commentary on social relations in general or on particular individuals. Recurring themes include the following: masculine friendship (**2.5**, **2.24**, **2.43**, **2.46**) and patron-client relationships (**2.18**, **2.32**, **2.55**, **2.68**; for the overlap between the two see on **2.55**); dinner parties and various kinds of undignified and unfitting behavior associated with them, including the hunting for invitations, cheap hosts, and badly behaved guests (**2.11**, **2.14**, **2.19**, **2.27**, **2.37**, **2.40**, **2.69**, **2.79**); legacy hunting (**2.26**, **2.76**); moneylending, seen from both sides of the phenomenon (**2.3**, **2.30**, **2.44**); the extravagant lifestyle of wealthy ex-slaves and their occasional attempts to disguise their origins (**2.16**, **2.29**); physical peculiarities and unattractive women and men (**2.35**, **2.41**, **2.52**, **2.87**); marriage and its attendant oddities (**2.54**, **2.65**, **2.83**); mistreatment of slaves (**2.66**, **2.82**); sexual relationships and practices, wheter desired or consummated, acceptable or unacceptable (**2.4**, **2.9**, **2.25**, **2.28**, **2.31**, **2.34**, **2.47**, **2.49–51**, **2.56**, **2.60–63**, **2.73**, **2.84**, **2.89**); and images of "the good life" and other philosophical reflections (**2.48**, **2.53**, **2.90**). We also find epideictic pieces describing objects, places, or events (**2.59**, **2.75**, **2.80**) or praising the emperor (**2.2**, **2.91**). Finally, a not insignificant number of epigrams reflect on poetic practice and the life of the poet, both in general and in Martial's own case, with an emphasis on such questions as the length of individual poems and whole books, the risk of plagiarism, and the relatively limited financial rewards of the profession (**2.1**, **2.6**, **2.8**, **2.20**, **2.71**, **2.77**, **2.86**, **2.88**, **2.93**).

3.2. Characters

A reader of Martial will be struck by the recurring presence of specific persons. His satiric pieces most often do not speak of human accomplishments, desires, or foibles in general terms but name names, sometimes of well-known contemporaries. In Book II, for example, apart from the emperor Domitian (**2.2**, **2.91**, **2.92**), there are Quintilian (**2.90**) and Atedius Melior (**2.69.7**). But scattered programmatic statements on Martial's part make it clear that epigrams attacking or satirizing individuals do not use real names: *parcere personis, dicere de vitis* (10.33.10; cf. also 1.praef. with Citroni, 5.12, 7.12 with Galán Vioque). Zoilus, Postumus, Sextillus, Galla, and others like them may thus reasonably be called "fictional" characters. A more difficult question is whether or not any of these names are pseudonyms for specific real people: in **2.23** and elsewhere Martial implies the existence of individuals behind some of the characters of his poetry; in 9.95 he asserts that "Athenagoras" is not a *verum nomen;* in 4.31 he tells us that his addressee's name cannot fit the meter. Yet it is quite possible that the motif of refusing to reveal a name is itself a literary game— that there is, in other words, no specific man directly corresponding to Zoilus, Postumus, and the others, just as there may have been no single woman behind Ovid's Cynthia, despite the poet's occasional claims to the contrary (e.g., *Trist.* 4.10.59–60). Obviously, the question cannot be settled definitively; see further on **2.11.1**, **2.16.1**, **2.69.6**.

What is clear, however, is that some of the fictitious characters have an *internal coherence,* in the sense that a given name repeatedly refers to a character portrayed in the same way; Zoilus is a particularly good example (see on **2.16**). It is also clear that, despite some scholars' assumptions to the contrary, this continuity in some cases stretches over a period of years, from one book to another: see on **2.25.1** (Galla), **2.33.1** (Philaenis), **2.35.2** (Phoebus), **2.57.4** (Cordus), **2.82.1** (Ponticus), **2.77.1** (Cosconius). On the other hand, some of Martial's fictional names, often quite common in any case, do *not* refer to a single coherent figure, and indeed some of them are clearly attached to more than one character; see, for example, on **2.10.2** (Postumus).

3.3. Formal Features: Point, Bipartite Structure, Length, and Meter

Perhaps the best-known formal feature of Martial's epigrams is their tendency to culminate in a tightly worded, often quite sharp "point" (Kruuse 1941: 286–294). For examples of especially compressed one- or two-word points from Book II, see the endings of **2.11**, **2.17**, **2.33**, **2.39**, **2.40**, **2.47**, **2.56**, **2.79**. Whether sharply pointed or not, many of his epigrams also end with such rhetorical features as *sententiae* (maxims cast in universalizing terms; e.g., **2.4**, **2.12**, **2.18**, **2.68**) or paradoxical formulations (e.g., **2.32**, **2.37**, **2.44**, **2.77**, **2.80**). In all of this Martial is typical of Latin literature of the first century A.D. (Hutchinson 1993).

Another renowned trait of Martial's epigrams is their bipartite structure, and various ways of describing the two halves have been proposed. Among the most influential has been Lessing's division into an *Erwartung,* or "expectation," created by the opening and the *Aufschluss,* or "information," conveyed at the end; later variations have included Kruuse's distinction between *exposition* and *conclusion* and Barwick's division (taken up by Laurens) into an *objective* and a *subjective* half; Marion Lausberg suggests *Bericht* ("report") and *Kommentar* ("commentary"); Siedschlag proposes *Ereignis* ("event") and *Kommentar;* in English we might speak of *situation* and *response.* It is worth emphasizing, however, that, as with the sharp point, a bipartite structure hardly characterizes every poem in Martial's corpus; Kruuse 1941 observes, for example, that in some cases it is best to speak of a one-unit (*unicellulaire*) structure; in others, of a tripartite structure.

The epigrams of Book II are characteristic with respect to poem length, ranging from one (**2.73**) to twenty-three lines (**2.41**), the average length being about six verses per poem. The number of meters they use is limited, and in this too they are typical of Martial's overall practice. There is a noticeable preponderance of elegiac couplets (seventy out of ninety-three poems): otherwise, there are seventeen poems in hendecasyllabics, five in scazons (choliambics), and one in pure hexameters. Martial's metrical techniques are essentially traditional, one exception being the relaxation of the earlier, especially Ovidian tendency to end pentameters of elegiac couplets with disyllabic words: Martial's pentameters not infrequently end in three-, four- or even five-syllable words, and not just in the case of intractable proper names (see **2.7.4**, **2.7.8**, **2.10.2**, **2.10.4**, **2.14.6**, **2.16.2**, **2.24.6**, etc.). In the hendecasyllabic poems Martial's most notable departure from the practice of his predecessor Catullus is that he invariably begins the verse with a spondee. For a detailed discussion of Martial's meters, see Marina Sáez 1998.

3.4. Book Structure

Martial himself was keenly aware of what may be the greatest risk in publishing a substantial collection of short poems: that the reader will quickly become tired or bored (**2.1**). His response was to rely on the principle of *variety*. Anyone who reads Book II in sequence, whether beginning from the first poem and continuing onward or beginning somewhere in the middle of the book (Merli 1998, Scherf 2001), will instantly be struck by the constant shifts in subject matter and in form: shorter poems alternate with longer, and subject matter and meter vary unpredictably as well.

A number of scholars have spoken of *cycles* (the term was popularized by Barwick 1958) or groups of poems that are usually not contiguous but that are nonetheless closely related in subject matter. A good example is the "Postumus cycle" in Book II, for which see on **2.10**. Barwick and others have analyzed these cycles as independent units, and some patterns have indeed emerged, although in view of the fact that these poems are often separated from each other by considerable gaps, these patterns do not perhaps urge themselves on readers as directly as those emerging from a *sequential* reading. In my introductory discussion of most of the epigrams, I have hinted at the possibilities of such a reading, comparing each poem to its predecessors in terms of content and/or form in remarks that are deliberately brief and suggestive.

Here I offer some further examples of suggestive sequences, well aware that the degree of subjectivity is higher than usual. Some may be coincidental; some may have contributed to the poet's arrangement of the poems in the sequence we have before us; in some cases it might even be that he composed the poems in question more or less together.

1. The word *cena* figures in the opening line of both **2.18** and **2.19**.
2. Epigrams **2.33–36** present a series of Greek names beginning in *Ph-* and *P-*: Philaenis, Phileros, Phoebus, Pannychus.
3. At **2.37.4** two prized types of fish, the *mullus* and the *lupus*, are mentioned together in a single line, as they are once again three poems later (**2.40.4**).
4. Epigram **2.51** ends with the clause *ille vorat;* **2.52** ends with the metrically equivalent *illa dedit*.
5. Epigram **2.64** contains the verb *sperabimus* in its final couplet, while **2.65** contains *cernimus* in its first line. These are two of the very few epigrams in Book II in which the poet uses a first-

person plural to explicitly mark himself as part of a larger group ("us") watching, observing, or commenting.

6. The penultimate line of **2.71** contains a question followed by *credimus istud;* the penultimate line of **2.72** contains a question (*vis hoc me credere?*) followed by *credo.*

4. *NACHLEBEN* AND RECEPTION

Martial's contemporary Pliny was skeptical as to whether his friend's poetry would survive him, noting that although the epigrams will perhaps not last forever, he wrote them as if they would (*Epist.* 3.21: "'at non erunt aeterna quae scripsit'; non erunt fortasse, ille tamen scripsit tamquam essent futura"). Martial would have been glad to know that Pliny's fears proved unfounded. Indeed, Martial's fundamental contributions to the history of Latin and, indeed, European epigram are unquestioned. For a detailed survey of his reception from antiquity to modernity, see Sullivan 1993; studies of particular periods or authors include Whipple 1925, Giulian 1930, Nixon 1963, and Humez 1971. Here I offer a brief sketch of the history of Martial's reception, and in the commentary on individual epigrams I occasionally quote later imitations or translations.

The epigrams were well known throughout antiquity. Martial's influence on Juvenal is massive (Wilson 1898, Colton 1991); the emperor Hadrian's adopted son Aelius is said to have called the epigrammatist "my Virgil" (SHA *Ael.* 5.9); late-antique poets like Ausonius, Sidonius Apollinaris, and Luxorius frequently imitated him. Nor did his influence abate in the literature of the Middle Ages (for his importance to the poetry of Godfrey of Winchester, for example, see Maaz 1992), and the Italian humanists knew Martial well. It is surely not insignificant that Martial was among the first classical authors to receive a printed edition (Rome, 1470–1471). He was particularly valued in sixteenth- and seventeenth-century England, France, and Spain, all of which witnessed a flowering of the epigrammatic form. Thus, the poet and translator Thomas Bastard (1566–1618) exclaims: "Martiall, in sooth none should presume to write / Since time hath brought thy Epigrams to lighte" (1.17), while Sir John Harrington (1560–1612) expresses the opinion that "of all poems, the Epigram is the pleasantest, and of all that write epigrams, Martial is counted the wittiest."

A distinct downturn in Martial's fortune is detectable beginning with the advent of the Romantic movement and its emphasis on sincerity and emotion; at the same time, the increasingly prudish culture of the nineteenth century was increasingly scandalized. A bias against Martial on the grounds of his obscenity on the one hand and his servile flattery of the powerful on the other had a strongly negative impact on his reception. Macaulay complains that "besides his indecency, his servility and his mendicancy disgust me," while in the 1882 edition of his history of Roman literature, W. S. Teuffel comments: "This is a great talent, but repulsive in its lack of feeling for what is morally and aesthetically permissible, or compatible with manly dignity" ("Es ist ein großes Talent, aber abschreckend durch die Abwesenheit von Gefühl für das was sittlich und ästhetisch zulässig oder mit Manneswürde verträglich sei"; Teuffel 1882: 728). One of the central aims of Spiegel's 1891 monograph is to acquit Martial on charges of servility and hypocrisy, although the editor of a 1908 anthology concludes that "nothing can serve to render the more objectionable pieces tolerable to the modern reader" (Post, p. xxviii).

Such biases, albeit in subtler form, continued to exert influence well into the twentieth century. For English readers, a striking illustration is offered by the Loeb translation of Walter C. A. Ker, published in 1919 and, until the appearance of Shackleton Bailey's new Loeb edition in 1993, the only accessible modern English translation of the entire corpus of Martial's epigrams. In his introduction, Ker declares that "the poet's adulation of Domitian sounds to modern ears shameless and disgusting" (xvi), and he sets out a policy of not giving an English translation of "the obscene epigrams," providing for these the Italian version of Giuspanio Graglia (London, 1782 and 1791). It is interesting to observe that Ker does not consistently carry out this policy: in Book II, **2.51**, **2.61–62**, and **2.84** are not rendered into English, but many other epigrams containing blunt obscenities are, albeit with bowdlerism. These include **2.28** (*pedico, fututor*), **2.31** (*futui*), **2.33** (*fellat*), **2.34** (*cunno*), **2.45** (*mentula*), **2.47** (*pedico, irrumat, futuit*), **2.50** (*fellas*), **2.60** (*futuis*), **2.70** (*mentula*), **2.73** (*fellat*), **2.83** (*irrumare*), **2.89** (*fellas*).

Recent decades have seen a return of interest in Martial, accompanied by a willingness to view his obscene pieces and his flattery of the emperor in a more historically informed light and by a renewed appreciation of his mastery of the epigrammatic form. "The impression left by Martial's couplets," notes one critic, "is a rare thing: that a metrical form has at last found its ideal content" ("Rarement comme devant les distiques de Martial on a l'impression qu'une forme métrique a enfin trouvé son contenu idéal"; Laurens 1989: 287–288).

5. MANUSCRIPT TRADITION

The text of Martial is, in general, in good state, and the manuscript tradition has been carefully described by Friedlaender and Citroni; see further Lindsay 1903a, Lehmann 1931, Reeve 1983, and Schmid 1984. A brief summary follows.

Since Schneidewin it has been recognized that our MSS of Martial belong to three separate families—usually identified by means of the sigla α, β, and γ—which seem to have remained independent until fairly late in the tradition, perhaps the twelfth century. Each of them derives from an archetype now lost to us (A^A, B^A, and C^A respectively) but datable to the period between the eighth and tenth centuries. These archetypes in turn were directly descended from late-antique MSS; family β, for example, derives from an edition by Torquatus Gennadius in A.D. 401.

The families and their principal MSS may be summarily described as follows.

Family α: Represented by three MSS (H, T, and R) containing anthologies and dating from the eighth to tenth centuries, this family has a noticeable tendency to bowdlerize, that is, to consciously and carefully—though not consistently—replace obscenities with metrically equivalent alternatives (see on **2.31.1**). This is also the only family to preserve the *Liber de spectaculis*. Well more than half of the epigrams of Book II are included in the anthologies of family α, but the following thirty-six poems are omitted: **2.3–6, 2.13–15, 2.17, 2.23, 2.25, 2.27–29, 2.34, 2.39, 2.43–44, 2.48, 2.50, 2.52, 2.54–55, 2.57, 2.59, 2.61, 2.63, 2.65, 2.68, 2.70, 2.73–74, 2.83–84, 2.86, 2.91–92.**

Family β: Descended from Torquatus Gennadius' edition of A.D. 401, this family is represented by MSS L (twelfth century), P, Q, and f. Peculiarities in its text of Book II include the conflation of **2.48** and **2.49**, of **2.72** and **2.73**, and of **2.91** and **2.92**.

Family γ: Represented by the largest number of extant MSS, this family includes MSS E (ninth century), X, V, A, and others. It omits **2.praef.**; other peculiarities include the fact that it places **2.28.5–6** after **2.29.8** (Lindsay suggests that the verses had been found at the very bottom of the page in the archetype) and treats **2.84.3–4** as a separate epigram.

Especially interesting are those occasions on which two families are in agreement against the third (or, when family α is not represented, when the other two families disagree), but linguistic and literary arguments may be made for both alternatives and modern editors have not been unanimous: see, for example, **2.1.5, 2.5.3, 2.7.1, 2.18.8, 2.30.3, 2.55.2, 2.57.7, 2.61.1, 2.79.1**. How might these alternatives have arisen? Since we know that Martial published a revised edition of at least one book, he might have done so on other occasions as well (see above, section 1), and some have argued that these alternatives, especially when it is a question of personal names, are due to author variants (Lindsay 1903a, Heraeus 1925). Others are skeptical, suggesting instead that the shared errors may be traced back to a point very early in the tradition but not necessarily to the author himself (Kay, p. 4; Schmid 1984 posits a late-antique corrector; see further on **2.18.8**). Indeed, cases in which all extant MSS and/or families *agree* in what is obviously an erroneous reading are fairly rare but significant: in Book II, see

2.praef. (*verbis; dein toga saltanti*), **2.60.2** (*puer Hylle* or *puer ille*), **2.83.2** (*e se* or *et si*), **2.84.4** (*ab hoc*), and perhaps also **2.46.8** (*times*). This consideration suggests that these variants, and indeed the existence of three MS families, cannot be traced back to the poet himself (Reeve 1983).

I have used Lindsay's 1929 Oxford edition as my text of reference, introducing slight changes in punctuation and orthography here and there; all other departures from his text are discussed in the relevant notes. I have constantly taken Shackleton Bailey's 1991 Teubner text into consideration, noting every occasion on which its reading differs from that of the OCT and sometimes following it. The appended list offers an overview of the passages in question.

	Lindsay (*OCT*)	Shackleton Bailey (*Teubner*)	*This edition*
2.1.5	peragit	peragit	peraget (γ)
2.5.3	disiungunt	distinguunt	disiungunt
2.7.1, 5	Attice	Attale	Attice
2.14.13	iterumque iterumque	iterum ternis	iterumque iterumque
2.24.6	multum est?	"multum est."	multum est?
2.27.4	"facta . . . tace."	"facta . . . tace."	facta . . . tace.
2.29.5	Marcelliano	Marcellano	Marcelliano
2.30.3	felixque	fidusque	fidusque
2.35.1	similent	simulent	similent
2.36.3	nec tibi mitrarum	nec mitratorum	nec tibi mitrarum
2.40.5	saccentur	saccantur	saccentur
2.40.6	condantur	conduntur	condantur
2.42.1	quid . . . perdis?	quod . . . perdis,	quid . . . perdis?
2.43.1	Κοινὰ φίλων	"Κοινὰ φίλων."	"Κοινὰ φίλων."
2.43.2	sonas:	sonas?	sonas.
2.46.5	atque unam	†atque unam†	atque unam
2.46.8	times	tui	tui
2.46.10	renuis	metuis	renuis
2.53.7	vincitur	iungitur	vincitur
2.55.2	colere	coleris	coleris
2.73.1	Lyris:	Lyris?	Lyris.
2.76.2	dedit?	dedit.	dedit.
2.84.4	abs hoc occisus	alter ab hoc caesus	esse huic occisus (*Rooy*)
2.86.6	tam	iam	tam
2.91.3	tibi lecta	collecta	tibi lecta

TEXT, TRANSLATION,

AND COMMENTARY

2.praef.

VAL. MARTIALIS DECIANO SVO SAL.

"Quid nobis" inquis "cum epistola? parum enim tibi praestamus, si legimus epigrammata? quid hic porro dicturus es quod non possis versibus dicere? video quare tragoedia atque comoedia epistolam accipiant, quibus pro se loqui non licet; epigrammata curione non egent et contenta sunt sua, id est mala, lingua. in quacumque pagina visum est, epistolam faciunt. noli ergo, si tibi videtur, rem facere ridiculam et in toga saltantis inducere personam. denique videris an te delectet contra retiarium ferula. ego inter illos sedeo qui protinus reclamant."

puto me hercules, Deciane, verum dicis. quid si scias cum qua et quam longa epistola negotium fueris habiturus? itaque quod exigis fiat. debebunt tibi, si qui in hunc librum inciderint, quod ad primam paginam non lassi pervenient.

VALERIUS MARTIALIS SENDS GREETINGS
TO HIS FRIEND DECIANUS.

"What do we need an introductory epistle for?" you ask. "Have we not done enough for you by reading your epigrams? Besides, what will you say here that you couldn't say in the poems themselves? I can see why tragedy and comedy receive a prose introduction, since they cannot speak for themselves; but epigrams have no need of a herald, as they are quite content to speak up using their own—indecent—language. Indeed, on whatever page they have seen fit they offer an epistle. So, if you please, don't be so absurd as to bring on a character dressed in a toga and dancing. In short, think about whether you really want to fight against a gladiator with a stick. You will find *me* seated among those who cry out in protest right away."

My God, Decianus, I think you're right. If only you knew what kind of preface you would have had to deal with, and how long! So, then, your request is granted. If anyone happens upon this book, he will owe it to you that he does not reach the first page already tired.

Themes. The book opens with characteristically light play on the grand tradition of *recusatio,* as Martial announces in a prose preface that he is not going to offer a prose preface. Representing himself as having been talked out of writing such a thing by his friend Decianus, he offers a brief substitute in the form of an imagined dialogue. In the course of this he manages to slip in his core message, effectively placed in Decianus' mouth rather than his own and structured around several key points: epigram has a *mala lingua* and speaks for itself (i.e., is blunt and clear); there is the risk of boredom or satiety; but Martial has taken countermeasures. With the theme of potential boredom Martial picks up where he had left off at the end of the previous book (1.118: "Cui legisse satis non est epigrammata centum, / nil illi satis est, Caeciliane, mali"). The theme continues in **2.1**, is strategically resurrected in **2.6**, and indeed is characteristic of Martial's early books.

For prose prefaces and dedications in Latin literature in general and Martial in particular, see Immisch 1911: 488–489, Janson 1964, White 1974, Citroni ad 1.praef., Citroni 1988, Merli 1993, and Nauta 2002: 113–120, 281–283; for the subgenre of the epistolary prose preface, see on *epistola* below; for this preface in particular, see Borgo 2001. Martial's defensive tone here implies that the use of such prefaces with collections of poetry was controversial or not yet established in this genre (Janson 1964: 111). All five of Statius' books of *Silvae* but only five of Martial's twelve books (I, II, VIII, IX, XII) come with epistolary prefaces, and the two poets use the technique quite differently. Statius' prefaces essentially summarize the contents of the book, thus serving as a descriptive index; nearly all of Martial's take on larger questions of epigrammatic technique and style. Some (e.g., Fontán Pérez 1987: 353 n. 11) have speculated that each of Martial's books, if in fact they were published separately, originally had a prose preface, but there is no good reason to think so. Perhaps taking Martial too literally, White 1974: 58 suggests that "the letter to Decianus was originally just a private letter, not intended to form part of the text of the second book, but . . . Martial eventually set it in its present place, without revision, or concern for self-consistency."

In view of this preface's ironic hand-wringing about its own appropriateness, it is amusing to see that MSS of family γ omit it entirely, as also the preface of Book IX (family β omits the preface of Book VIII). Lindsay 1903a: 15–17 observes that "the prose prefaces to various books of the epigrams must have been a stumbling-block to scribes, who would be liable, after copying page upon page of poetry, to regard these pieces of prose as alien matter." Lehmann 1931: 56–57 suggests that Martial himself omitted this preface from his revised edition (see Introduction, section 1).

VAL. MARTIALIS DECIANO SVO SAL[VTEM DICIT]: A standard opening formula for letters; see below on *epistola*.

DECIANO SVO: We have no external evidence regarding this man, but Martial provides some basic information. Like Martial, he came from Spain (Emerita, modern Merida), a fact that provokes Van Stockum 1884: 13 to speculate that his success in Rome, like that of his fellow Spaniards Seneca, Lucan, Quintilian, Licinianus, and Canius Rufus, might have contributed to Martial's decision to move to the capital. He was a Stoic writer and busy lawyer (1.61.10, **2.5**), and in Book I Martial follows up warm praise of Decianus (1.39.1: "si quis erit raros inter numerandus amicos") with an epigram alluding to malicious critics (1.40: "qui ducis vultus et non legis ista libenter"); see also 1.8, 1.24.

The fact that Martial opens Book II with a preface dedicated to him obviously signals a desire to advertise their friendship or, better, Decianus' patronage. Yet Decianus is never mentioned again after Book II, and scholars have asked why. The most obvious explanation is that he died. But Citroni ad 1.8 and Sullivan 1991: 16–17 find it significant that we have no epigram commemorating his death and speculate that Decianus fell into disgrace, possibly becoming too deeply involved in the Stoic resistance, or that Martial felt himself otherwise compelled to distance himself from him. This hypothesis rests on the questionable assumption that the extant books of epigrams function as a more or less thorough documentation of Martial's relationships and experiences. If Decianus in fact died, it is not clear that Martial *must* have composed a eulogy on his friend *and* included it in the published collection we now have.

For the use of *suo* as a greeting in epistolary format, see 14.11.2: "omnes ista solet charta vocare *suos*."

1 nobis . . . praestamus . . . legimus: Decianus presents himself as one among many readers, before turning to himself in particular (*video*). Alternatively, the plurals refer to Decianus himself (see on **2.3.1**, *fatemur*).

1 inquis: The technique of quoting or paraphrasing the interlocutor's words and marking this with *inquis, dicis, quaeris,* and the like is found in a number of epigrams; see on **2.21.2**.

1 epistola: The earliest extant example of using an epistolary format, with opening salutation (*salutem dicit*) and/or closing *vale*, as a dedication or preface to a larger work in Latin is Hirtius' introduction to the eighth book of *De bello Gallico* (cf. Sen. *Contr.* 1.praef.). Greek precedents go back to Archimedes (ca. 287–212 B.C.). Martial and Statius are the first attested Latin authors to use such prefaces with collections of poetry. See further Peter 1901: 242–249, Janson 1964: 106–112, Borgo 2001: 498–499.

2 versibus: Either "in the poems themselves" or perhaps more generally "in verse." The MSS read *verbis,* but this makes no sense and was emended by Italian humanists to *versibus,* which has won acceptance. Cases in which the universal MS reading is clearly false (see also below, *in toga saltantis*) are rather rare in Martial: see Introduction, section 5.

2–3 quare tragoedia atque comoedia epistolam accipiant: Apart from this passing remark, there is little evidence for the practice of introducing dramatic texts with prose prefaces. Quint. *Inst.* 8.3.31 reports that Pomponius Secundus and Seneca discussed stylistic issues *etiam praefationibus,* but this may refer to spoken introductions to recitations rather than epistolary prose prefaces (Nauta 2002: 282 n. 91). On the basis of *Silv.* 4.pr. ("epistola, quam ad illum [sc., Maximum Vibium] de editione Thebaidos meae publicavi") Janson 1964: 109 speculates that Statius accompanied his epic *Thebaid* with an epistolary preface, but he admits the alternative and much more likely hypothesis that Statius published this *epistola* separately.

4 epigrammata curione non egent et contenta sunt sua, id est mala, lingua: This *sententia* is worthy of epigram itself. A *curio* was either a type of priest or, as here, a crier or herald (more or less synonymous with *praeco*); the present passage is the earliest attested example of the latter usage (*TLL* 4.1489.43–50). The adjective *mala* probably refers to the mordant, unrestrained quality of epigrammatic language (Collesso: "mordaci et libera"). For programmatic reminders of the traditional frankness and occasional obscenity of epigram, see 1.praef. ("lascivam verborum veritatem, id est epigrammaton linguam") with Citroni ad loc., 8.praef. ("ego tamen illis non permisi tam lascive loqui quam solent").

4 in quacumque pagina visum est, epistolam faciunt: *Pagina* here, as regularly in Martial's day, does not refer to a "page" in the modern sense, since the codex format was not yet widely established (see 1.2 with Fowler 1995 for an exception), but rather to a column of text on a roll; so also at **2.6.2, 2.77.6**, and elsewhere. The point of *epistolam faciunt* is that epigrams function like epistolary prefaces, or letters in general, in that they directly address the readership (Borgo 2001: 499).

5 si tibi videtur: Like *si libet, si tibi est commodum, nisi molestum est,* and others, this polite phrase (cf. Cic. *Att.* 8.6.2, Fronto 89.22) was a more elegant and less colloquial version of *si placet* (Hofmann 1951: 134).

5 in toga saltantis . . . personam: Here, and again with the image of Decianus sitting in the audience (*inter illos sedeo*), Martial portrays his own activity using the language of stage entertainment (cf. 1.pr.); the metaphor is prepared for by the earlier references to tragedy and comedy and is varied with the imagery of gladiatorial displays in the next sentence. See further Elmore 1912.

A serious prose preface to a book of witty epigrams is as absurd as a stage character dancing in a toga. Since the toga was the preeminent symbol of the dignity of the Roman citizen (see on **2.29.4**) and since dancing, especially onstage (*personam*), was traditionally considered incompatible with that dignity (see on **2.7.5**), this is a striking paradox. Quintilian makes use of a related stage metaphor at *Inst.* 6.1.36: "nam in parvis quidem litibus has tragoedias movere tale est, quasi si personam Herculis et cothurnos aptare infantibus velis" (cf. [Longin.] *Sublim.* 30; Lucian *Hist. scrib.* 23); see also

Mart. 6.24 ("nil lascivius est Charisiano; / Saturnalibus ambulat togatus"). Martial may be drawing on a proverbial expression (Otto 1890: 274), but it is attested nowhere else.

As with *versibus* above, the MSS transmit an impossible reading (*et dein toga saltanti personam*) and the emendations of Italian humanists have won acceptance.

6 *contra retiarium ferula:* Just as a flimsy stick would be no true weapon against a *retiarius* (a gladiator armed with a net and trident), so a prose preface justifying or excusing epigrammatic practice would be a feeble defense against critics. This, too, may be a proverbial phrase (Otto 1890: 299, *OLD* s.v. *ferula*), but again there are no other extant attestations.

7–8 *quid si scias cum qua et quam longa epistola negotium fueris habiturus?* Anticipating Fowler 1995, Immisch 1911: 488 argues that our current text of Book II is based on an ancient codex edition in which the first page of Book II ended immediately after this sentence. He thus imagines a complex joke. The reader, having finished the page with a warning, will turn the leaf expecting to find a lengthy preface and instead finds a single sentence announcing that the reader will not be tired. But as Lehmann 1931 observes, this reconstruction is vitiated by the tense of *fueris habiturus:* how long a preface you *were going to have had* to deal with *if* I had not decided to heed your warning to be brief.

9 *ad primam paginam:* For the practice of considering prefaces as coming before the first *pagina,* see 8.praef. ("in ipso libelli huius limine") with Schöffel and 9.praef. ("epigramma, quod extra ordinem paginarum est"). Immisch 1911: 489 proposes that the verso of the first page of the putative codex edition contained the final two sentences of the preface along with **2.1**, and that the *prima pagina* thus began with **2.2**. A simpler explanation is that the preface itself took up a *pagina,* whether in the sense of codex leaf or papyrus column, and that **2.1** began the *prima pagina.* The preface is claiming to be so brief that when the reader comes to the first epigram he will not already be tired.

2.1

Ter centena quidem poteras epigrammata ferre,
   sed quis te ferret perlegeretque, liber?
at nunc succincti quae sint bona disce libelli.
   hoc primum est, brevior quod mihi charta perit;
deinde, quod haec una peraget librarius hora,   5
   nec tantum nugis serviet ille meis;

> tertia res haec est, quod si cui forte legeris,
>   sis licet usque malus, non odiosus eris.
> te conviva leget mixto quincunce, sed ante
>   incipiat positus quam tepuisse calix.   10
> esse tibi tanta cautus brevitate videris?
>   ei mihi, quam multis sic quoque longus eris!

To be sure, you could bear three hundred epigrams; but who would bear you, or who would read you all the way through, O book? Learn now the advantages of a compact booklet. The first is this, that I waste less paper. Second, the copyist will manage it all in just one hour and so will not devote himself exclusively to my trivialities. The third point is this: if anyone actually reads you, no matter how bad you may be, you will not be tiresome. The partygoer will read you when his five measures have been mixed, but will finish before the cup placed before him begins to grow lukewarm. Do you think you have taken sufficient precautions by means of your great brevity? Alas, how many people will find you long even so!

Themes.   The beginnings of Martial's books are without exception marked by one or both of the themes "emperor" and "book," and most books return to one or both of these themes at their ending as well (Weinreich 1928: 27; see Merli 1993 for an overall analysis of Martial's book openings). Book II illustrates the pattern perfectly: **2.praef.** and **2.1** concern the book itself, and **2.2** turns to praise of the emperor; **2.91** involves both emperor and book, **2.92** the emperor, and **2.93** the book. Indeed, any reader of Martial will be struck by the extent to which his poetry is concerned with describing, advertising, or defending itself. In Book II alone, see **2.praef.**, **2.6**, **2.8**, **2.22–23**, **2.71**, **2.77**, **2.86**, **2.91–93**, with Sullivan 1991: 56–77, Fowler 1995, Roman 2001. The present epigram is thus characteristic in its self-referentiality, but also in its (mock-) modest tone, for which see 3.1, 5.1, 6.1 (with Grewing), 10.1, 11.1 (with Kay), 12.1, 13.1, and contrast 1.1, 8.1, 9.praef. For general discussion of the ancient book see Kenyon 1951, Kleberg 1969, Cavallo 1975, and Blanck 1992.

This poem's opening and closing words are echoed in the final epigram of the eighth book of *epigrammata seria* by Henry of Huntingdon (ca. 1080–1155): "Ferre libri poteras epigrammata plura petisque. / desine! quam multis est, mihi longus erit" (Maaz 1992: 144).

Structure.   On a bipartite scheme, 1–10 outline the situation, and the final couplet offers pointed commentary. But a tripartite structure suggests itself perhaps more immediately: 1–2 (the book could have been three times as long but would have repelled readers); 3–10 (advantages of a short book); 11–12 (readers may nonetheless be bored). At the same time there is a framing, or ABA, structure: in the first couplet the poet tells his book that no one will read it if it contains as many as 300 epigrams, while in the last he observes that many readers will be bored even if it contains only a few epigrams.

The body of the poem enumerates three succinctly described advantages (*primum, deinde, tertia*) introduced by the line "at nunc succincti quae sint bona disce libelli," itself a model of simple clarity. The list is pleasingly varied in syntax and metrical structure: rather than dedicating a couplet to each of the three advantages of a short book, the poet describes the first in a single line (4), the second in an entire couplet (5–6), and the third in a couplet (7–8) that is then expanded upon with a concrete illustration in yet another couplet (9–10). This structural *tricolon crescendo* is combined with a progression in content: from writer (who wastes less paper) to copyist (who wastes less time) to reader (who will avoid boredom). In short, the protest that readers will be bored is made in a neatly turned piece that does its best to counteract tedium.

1 *ter centena:* The number is not randomly chosen, as the ideal limit for Martial is clearly 100 epigrams per book (cf. 1.118, cited on 11 below), and indeed, with the exception of the *Xenia* and *Apophoreta,* his books fluctuate around this limit, ranging from 82 poems in Book VIII to 118 in Book I.

1 *poteras . . . ferre:* Either "you could have borne" (Ker, Izaac, Norcio, Scandola) or "you could bear" (Shackleton Bailey, Barié and Schindler, Ceronetti); see KS 2.1.171–172. Examples of the former usage include Plaut. *Mil.* 911 ("bonus vates poteras esse") and of the latter **2.35.2** ("poteras lavare"), **2.43.13** ("poterat certare"). In this case, the difference in meaning would be slight: whether the book *could have* contained 300 epigrams or *could* contain them, the fact is that it does not. With *ferre* (1) and *ferret* (2) there is a play on different meanings of the verb: "to contain" (*OLD* s.v. 12b) or "to endure, bear" (*OLD* s.v. 20: cf. **2.75.1**).

2 *liber:* The technique of addressing his own verse is particularly characteristic of Martial: see 1.3, 1.70, 1.96, 3.2, 3.4–5, 4.86, 4.89, 5.10, 7.97, 10.104, 11.1, 12.2. Howell ad 5.10 traces the device back to Catullus 35 "and probably to Hellenistic poetry, if not earlier." See Citroni 1986 for detailed discussion of the technique in Horace, Ovid, and Martial; Borgo 2001 sees an especially close link with Hor. *Epist.* 1.20. A related device also favored by Martial is the personification of the book or verses: see on **2.93.2**.

3 *succincti:* Literally "having one's clothes gathered up by a belt, girdle, or sim., to allow freedom of movement" (*OLD* s.v. 1; Mart. 7.35.1, 12.24.7, 14.86.1; cf. **2.46.7**); here figuratively, "compact, concise" (*OLD* s.v. 1c).

3 *libelli:* One of the most common of Martial's designations for his own poetry; see Grewing ad 6.1. The literal sense of the diminutive is sometimes dominant (10.1.1–2: "si nimius videor . . . esse liber, legito pauca: libellus ero"), but it more often refers to the lightweight aspect of Martial's poetry, as opposed to such heavier genres as epic. In any case the term brings with it an element of mock-modesty. Prominent examples of the programmatic use of *libellus* by other authors include Catull. 1.1 ("cui dono lepidum novum libellum") and Juv. 1.86 ("nostri farrago libelli est").

4 *brevior quod mihi charta perit:* Martial begins with the most practical consideration; for the imagery, compare 6.64.23 ("miseras et perdere chartas"), 13.1.3 ("perdite Niliacas, Musae, mea damna, papyros"), Juv. 1.18 ("periturae parcere chartae"), Auson. *Epigr.* 35.1–2 ("si tineas cariemque pati te, charta, necesse est, / incipe versiculis ante perire meis"), Sidon. Apoll. *Carm.* 9.10 ("iubes . . . perire chartam").

5 *una peraget librarius hora:* Compare 4.89, where both the reader and the *librarius* tire after eighty-nine epigrams. The functions of the *librarius* were to copy out manuscripts, as here, and to sell the copies (in which case he might also be called a *bibliopola:* see 14.194 with Leary ad loc.); sometimes both functions were performed by one and the same man. Martial refers to *librarii* again at 1.2, **2.8.3**, and 4.89.8–9; see further Kleberg 1969 and McDonnell 1996. In the present case it is not clear whether (as Nauta 2002: 130 assumes) the *librarius* is Martial's own slave, in which case *tantum* emphasizes *nugis,* or a hired specialist, in which case the adverb emphasizes *meis.*

The MSS of families α and β read the present tense *peragit* (printed by Schneidewin, Lindsay, and Shackleton Bailey), while family γ reads the future *peraget* (printed by Gilbert, Heraeus, and Friedlaender). The latter seems slightly preferable in view of the universally transmitted *serviet* in 6: there would thus be a sequence from present tense (*perit*) in the first of the three advantages to future tense in the remaining two (*peraget, serviet, legeris, eris*), although precisely for this reason one might argue that *peragit* is the *lectio difficilior.*

6 *nugis serviet . . . meis:* The original meaning of *nugae* (whose etymology is unclear, and which always appears in the plural) is "that which is unprofitable or absurd" (*OLD* s.v. 1), a secondary meaning is "things not serious, frivolities" (*OLD* s.v. 3). The term is often used to refer to literary works of a light character, as opposed to, for example, epic or tragedy: see Catull. 1.4 (with Swann 1998: 53–54) and Hor. *A.P.* 322. Like Catullus, Martial applies it quite insistently to his own work: see 1.113.6, **2.86.9**, 3.55.3, 4.10.4, 4.72.3, 4.82.4, 5.80.3, 6.64.7–8, 7.11.4, 7.26.7, 7.51.1, 8.3.11, 9.praef., 10.18.4, 12.praef., 13.2.4, 14.183.2.

Seemingly the only modern translation to bring out the imagery of slavery present in the verb *serviet* is that of Barié and Schindler: "und ist nicht auf so lange Zeit der Sklave meiner poetischen Nichtigkeiten."

7 *si cui forte legeris:* How are we to interpret the dative? Ker and Shackleton Bailey take it as a true dative (if you are read *to* anyone), thus seeing a reference to the practice of having one's *lector,* usually a slave, read aloud to one (Starr 1990–1991). Others understand *cui* as a dative of agent: if you are read *by* anyone. This is somewhat more probable; Martial usually speaks of people directly reading his epigrams for themselves, and indeed in an epigram at this book's end the emperor is imagined picking up a scroll of Martial's epigrams to read it himself (cf. **2.91.4**: *detinuere oculos tuos;* admittedly, at 7.99.3–4 Martial's poems are read aloud to the emperor). For the dative of agent, compare *Sp.* 27.6 (*"huic* percussa foret tota Chimaera semel"), **2.6.12** ("totus *tibi* triduo legatur"), 7.14.5 (*"Stellae* cantata *meo"*), and perhaps **2.84.4** (reading "esse *huic* occisus"). Although KS 2.1.324–325 claim that such datives are much rarer with present-stem than with perfect passive verb forms, they actually cite quite a few examples of the former.

8 *odiosus:* The tone of the adjective ranges from extreme ("disagreeable, offensive": *OLD* s.v. 1) to mild ("tiresome, boring, annoying": *OLD* s.v. 1). Martial uses it on only one other occasion, again with reference to a literary text (8.6.1: "archetypis vetuli nihil est odiosius Aucti").

9 *te conviva leget:* For the reading of Martial's poetry at *convivia,* see **2.6.8**, 5.16.9, and especially 4.82.5–6, where the poet once again hopes that his verses will be read before the evening is too far gone. For *convivia* in general see D'Arms 1984, 1990, 1991. Nauta 2002: 93 reminds us that "the symposiast will not read the book in silence, but will recite it out loud to his drinking companions."

9 *mixto quincunce:* The noun *quincunx* means "five-twelfths," here of the liquid measure called the *sextarius.* Since one-twelfth of a *sextarius* was also called a *cyathus,* a *quincunx* is the equivalent of five *cyathi.* Martial's allusions to the number of *cyathi* drunk in one sitting or evening range from one (1.106) to five (11.36.7) to seven (3.82.29) to a hyperbolic fifty (1.27.2); compare Pl. *Per.* 771a (seven), Hor. *C.* 3.19.12 (three or nine), Plin. *N.H.* 28.64 (four). In short, the *quincunx* of the present epigram is hardly an excessive amount, approximating 227.5 milliliters and thus a large modern glass of wine; the moderate amount is part of the point. Martial's *mixto* reminds us that, at least in polite company, both Greeks and Romans drank wine mixed with water in varying proportions (Marquardt 1886: 332–333; cf. the joke at 6.89, with Grewing).

10 *incipiat positus quam tepuisse calix:* Given the range of meanings of the verb and the absence of any further specification in this context, the phrase *positus calix* may mean "the cup that has been placed before him" (Izaac, Barié and Schindler, Norcio, Ceronetti, Scandola) or "the cup he has put aside" (Ker), but the former seems more likely; compare 1.43.2 ("positum est nobis nil here praeter aprum") with Citroni, 6.94.1 ("ponuntur

... chrysendeta Calpetiano"), V. *Aen.* 1.706 ("pocula ponant"), V. *Copa* 37 ("pone merum et talos").

Heated wine was served especially in the winter, and Martial's point—surely exaggerated—is that a reader can get through Book II so quickly that his cup of heated wine will not even become tepid; see further on **2.6.12**. In 12.1 Martial proudly claims that the entire twelfth book, containing ninety-eight epigrams, can be read in less than a winter hour, itself less than a modern hour.

11–12 *esse tibi . . . videris? / ei mihi . . . eris!* The technique of posing a question and immediately supplying an answer by way of making a pointed comment at the end of an epigram appears very frequently indeed in Martial: see on **2.7.8**. For such a question followed, as here, by a correction or denial, see **2.4.6** ("lusum creditis hoc iocumque? non est."), **2.26.3–4** ("rem factam . . . credis habere? / erras."), **2.40.8** ("o stulti, febrem creditis esse? gula est."), **2.47.3** ("confidis natibus? non est pedico maritus"), **2.83.4–5** ("credis te satis esse vindicatum? / erras").

Wills 1996: 431–432 cites this couplet in his discussion of "couplet or double-line framing," but the fact that the forms of *esse* are differently inflected makes the pattern somewhat less compelling than in other examples of the phenomenon (1.32: *non amo te . . . non amo te*; 1.75: *dimidium . . . dimidium*).

11 *brevitate:* This is a virtue to which many ancient poets laid claim, heeding Callimachus' dictum μέγα βιβλίον μέγα κακόν. On several occasions Martial expresses the concern that an overly long book will bore his readers: see, among others, 1.45, 1.118, **2.6**, 4.29, 4.82, 7.85, and 8.39, with Borgo 2001. In 4.29 he makes the point that a reader may just be able to manage a whole book, but more than one book is simply too much: "obstat nostris sua turba libellis / lectoremque frequens lassat et implet opus."

12 *ei mihi:* The interjection, which occurs frequently in Plautus, Terence, Ovid, and elsewhere, but only here in Martial, adds a tone of pathos: the poet wrings his hands, worrying whether the public will like his book.

2.2

> Creta dedit magnum, maius dedit Africa nomen,
>   Scipio quod victor quodque Metellus habet;
> nobilius domito tribuit Germania Rheno,
>   et puer hoc dignus nomine, Caesar, eras.
> frater Idumaeos meruit cum patre triumphos,   5
>   quae datur ex Chattis laurea, tota tua est.

Crete gave a great name and Africa a greater one: the victorious Scipio has one, Metellus the other. Germany has granted an even nobler name with the taming of the Rhine—though you were worthy of it, Caesar, already as a boy. Your brother earned a triumph over the Idumaeans together with your father, but the laurel wreath given for the Chatti is entirely yours.

Themes. See on **2.1** for the presence of the themes "emperor" and "book" at Martial's book openings. The occasion here commemorated was one of Domitian's earliest military accomplishments. In A.D. 83 he led a campaign against the German Chatti (Jones 1992: 128–131) and in the following year celebrated a triumph for his victory over both the Chatti and the Dacians on the Danube, adding the cognomen *Germanicus* to his name. Martial's loyal flattery, with its downplaying of the objectively more significant triumph celebrated by Domitian's father, Vespasian, and brother, Titus, in A.D. 71 for the capture of Jerusalem, stands in revealing contrast to the skeptical remarks of Suetonius, who implies that the campaign against the Chatti was hardly necessary and mostly a means for Domitian to gain fame (*Dom.* 6.1); Tacitus scathingly speaks of a *falsum triumphum* over the Chatti, claiming that Domitian had resorted to buying slaves dressed up to play the role of German captives (*Agr.* 39).

This is the first of only a few epigrams in Book II (**2.91, 2.92**) that openly praise or flatter the emperor, a fact that prompts Hofmann 1983: 241 to describe the poem as "rather lost and lonely" ("etwas verloren und einsam")! In later books the flattery becomes more frequent and noticeably more extravagant; for one example among many, see 9.91.6 (*meus Iuppiter*). Following up on hints in Tacitus and Pliny, some argue that Domitian found himself increasingly in need of "reassurance about his popularity" (Sullivan 1991: 135) after A.D. 93, but Nauta 2002: 384 observes that a comparable increase in Statius' panegyric begins at a significantly later date, and that Suetonius (*Dom.* 10.5) suggests a turning point of 89 rather than 93. For accounts of the poet's relationship with the emperor, see Szelest 1974a, Coleman 1987, Citroni 1988, Merli 1993, Nauta 2002: 385–386.

Structure. There is a gradual but irresistible buildup: instead of trumpeting the addressee's identity, the first couplet lays the groundwork by citing two famous historical exempla, and only in the second couplet are we brought to the present occasion: the bestowal of the name *Germanicus* on Domitian. In the first couplet we look quickly back on the past; in the second (introduced by the comparative *nobilius,* itself marking a heightening of the panegyric tone) we are brought to the present joyous occasion, with a swift glance back on Domitian's promising youth (*puer*) and a second-person address to the emperor (*eras*). The third and final couplet continues the direct address and indulges more openly in direct flattery, even at the expense of the emperor's brother, Titus. Also notable is the concrete effect achieved by the piling up of proper names (*Creta, Africa, Scipio, Metellus, Germania, Rheno, Caesar, Idumaeos, Chattis*), the current victory being described with no fewer than three different labels (*Germania, Rheno, Chattis*), arranged in a sequence of increasing geographic specificity.

The underlying thought can easily be described as bipartite: situation (Domitian has received the name *Germanicus*) and commentary (this is even more praiseworthy than the triumphs of his father and brother because it was achieved alone). But the poem's structure does not fall so easily into two parts, as there is already some commentary in 3 (*nobilius*), while 5 adds further factual information. The absence of such a clear-cut division may be related to the epigram's very nature: panegyric requires an intricate blend of objective and subjective, of fact and praise.

1 *Creta dedit magnum, maius dedit Africa nomen:* Note the pleasing *apo koinou* structure along with the chiastic ordering of the entire first couplet: *Creta, Africa // Scipio, Metellus*. See KS 2.2.559 for *apo koinou*, which is, broadly speaking, the figure by which a word belonging to two separate clauses or phrases (in this case *nomen*) is actually found in only one of the two (generally the second, whereby a suspension of judgment is required after the first clause).

1 *Creta:* Between 69 and 65 B.C., Q. Caecilius *Metellus* (grandson of the famous Macedonicus), who had supported Verres at his trial for corruption in 70 B.C., fought in Crete as proconsul and succeeded in defeating pirates and capturing several cities. After having subdued the entire island and organized a province, he was awarded a triumph and the cognomen *Creticus* in 62.

1 *Africa:* The reference is ambiguous, bringing to mind both P. Cornelius Scipio, who defeated Hannibal at Zama in 202 B.C., and his adopted grandson P. Cornelius Scipio Aemilianus, who destroyed Carthage in 146 B.C. Both celebrated triumphs and both received the cognomen *Africanus,* although the later figure received the additional cognomen *Numantinus* in 132. But it seems likely that a Roman reader would have thought first of the elder Africanus, who acquired a semimythic status over the years that never accrued to his grandson (cf. Polybius 31–39 passim, Cic. *Rep.* 6.9ff.); furthermore, *maius* may signal an allusion to the grandfather, *Scipio Africanus maior* (see following note).

1 *magnum, maius:* Polyptoton, in this case a play with the positive and comparative degree of *magnus,* was especially appealing in references to persons with the epithet or cognomen *magnus* or *maior* (Wills 1996: 238); for Scipio Africanus *maior* see Sil. Ital. 16.33–34 ("omina ductor / magna adeo Ausonius *maiori* mole premebat") and for Pompeius Magnus see Ov. *Fast.* 1.603–606 ("*Magne,* tuum nomen rerum est mensura tuarum, / sed qui te vicit nomine *maior* erat"), *Pont.* 4.3.41 ("quid fuerat *Magno maius?*").

3 *nobilius* (sc., *nomen*): Namely, *Germanicus;* compare 14.170.1–2: "cui nomina Rhenus / vera dedit." Perhaps because *Africanus* is impossible in this meter, the epigram resorts to periphrasis for all three cognomina (Creticus, Africanus, Germanicus). There is an intensification of tone, as the sequence *magnum . . . maius . . . nobilius* marks the progression from Metellus Creticus to Scipio Africanus to Caesar Germanicus; at the same time there is an important distinction between *magnum/maius* and *nobilius,* as there is between the generic *dedit* and *tribuit;* and the climactic detail of Domitian's triumph is endowed with the added detail *domito Rheno.*

After having celebrated this triumph and adopted the cognomen Germanicus, Domitian renamed September (the month of his accession) to *Germanicus* and October (the month of his birth) to *Domitianus* (Suet. *Dom.* 13.3). Martial dutifully alludes to these innovations in 9.1 and frequently addresses Domitian as *Germanicus,* beginning with 5.2.7. Unlike the earlier renaming of Quinctilis and Sextilis to *Julius* and *Augustus* respectively, Domitian's reforms did not last.

4 *puer:* In A.D. 70, when he was eighteen or nineteen years old, Domitian accompanied Mucianus as far as Lugdunum (Lyons) when the revolt of Civilis and the Batavi was drawing to a close (Suet. *Dom.* 2.1, Jos. *Bell.* 7.85–88, Tac. *Hist.* 4.85). Like Martial, Sil. Ital. 3.608 refers to the expedition and Domitian's youthful age in flattering terms that stand in revealing contrast to Suetonius' cynical remark that Domitian undertook the expedition as a means of catching up on his brother Titus' wealth and fame.

4 *Caesar:* Following usual practice, Martial regularly refers to and addresses the current emperor, whether Titus (*Sp.*), Domitian (XIII–XIV, I–IX), Nerva (X–XI), or Trajan (XII), as *Caesar;* see Grewing ad 6.2.3 for an overview. This was originally the cognomen of a branch of the *gens Iulia* and was taken by C. Octavius (later Augustus) upon his adoption by Julius Caesar in the latter's will. Through a succession of adoptions, the subsequent emperors each bore the name, which eventually became perceived less as a family name than as a title to be passed on from one *princeps* to the next; compare Petr. *Sat.* 51.2: "admissus ergo Caesarem est"; Tac. *Hist.* 1.30: "me Galba . . . Caesarem dixit." In later European cultures, the name was taken over in exactly this sense (*czar, Kaiser*).

5 *frater . . . cum patre:* Domitian's elder brother, Titus, brought the Jewish war begun by their father, Vespasian, to a successful completion with the capture of Jerusalem in A.D. 70 and celebrated a triumph the following year; according to Suet. *Dom.* 2.1, the young Domitian was present at the celebration. Suetonius and other historians, both ancient and modern, assume that there were tensions between the two brothers, and in particular that Domitian sought to undermine the authority and prestige of his older brother (Suet. *Dom.* 2 is explicit: once their father died, Domitian "neque cessavit ex eo insidias struere fratri clam palamque"). Many modern scholars are skeptical. In any case, Martial manages his panegyric carefully: while Domitian's achievement is greater than that of his brother to the extent that he accomplished it alone (*tota tua est*), his reference to Titus' triumph (*meruit cum patre triumphos*) reminds us both that he had deserved it and that he had been in good company.

5 *Idumaeos:* Properly speaking, Idumaea was the hill country of southern Judaea, incorporated in the Roman province of Judaea since A.D. 6; see Kasher 1988. Barrett 1984 suggests that the use of the term *Idumaei* to refer to Jews was "insulting" since the name was derived from *Edom,* ancestor of an ancient enemy of the Israelites, but also notes that Martial and his Roman contemporaries would probably not have been aware of this fact.

6 *quae datur ex Chattis laurea, tota tua est:* The Chatti (again at 14.26.1) were among the most powerful of Rome's enemies in western Germany throughout the first century A.D.; they lived near the upper Weser and the Diemel in present-day Hessen, whose name might be derived from theirs. See Tac. *Germ.* 30–31 with Rives 1999 for a description that culminates with the fine *sententia* "alios ad proelium ire videas, Chattos ad bellum"; see further Thompson 1965.

The "pre-antecedent" position of the relative (*quae . . . laurea*) is common in all phases of Latin literature, both prose and verse; compare, among countless examples, Caes. *B.G.* 5.44.4 ("quae pars hostium confertissima est visa, irrumpit") and Cic. *Fam.* 3.3.2 ("quae primum navigandi nobis facultas data erit, utemur"). This may in fact have been the earliest usage, the relative having the force of an indefinite (KS 2.2.280–281, 309–311).

2.3

Sexte, nihil debes, nil debes, Sexte, fatemur.
debet enim, si quis solvere, Sexte, potest.

Sextus, you have no debts. You have no debts, Sextus, I admit it.
After all, one only has a debt, Sextus, when one can pay it back.

Themes. After the standard opening motifs of mock-modest self-reference (**2.praef.**, **2.1**) and flattery of the emperor (**2.2**), the book now offers a gentle introduction to the satiric content that will dominate. The following epigram (**2.4**) will introduce us to Martial's sexual satire. Martial's frequent allusions to the practice of lending and borrowing money include 1.75, **2.13**, **2.30**, **2.44**, 4.37, 8.9, 8.37; see Grewing ad 6.5. The prevalence and abuse of the practice are among the many features of contemporary society denounced in Juvenal's satires: see 11.46 and especially 3.171–181. The present epigram introduces with remarkable clarity one of the many facets of the phenomenon: there are those who borrow money that they are incapable of repaying. In 9.102, adopting the perspective of a borrower, Martial warns a potential creditor that he ought to lend him only as much as he is capable of repaying since "what I cannot pay back is mine" ("quod tibi non possum solvere, Phoebe, meum est").

Structure.   This is the first of Book II's many monodistichs, or epigrams consisting of a single elegiac couplet, for which see the detailed study of Lausberg 1982. Monodistichs account for 20 percent of all epigrams in *Sp.* and Books I–XII (32.27 percent of elegiac epigrams in those books), and the poet uses the form masterfully. The statistics in Scherf 2001 reveal that the proportion of two-line poems (including two-line poems not in the elegiac meter, such as **2.13** and **2.15**) varies considerably among individual books, from a low of 9.52 percent (Book IX) to a high of 28.86 percent (Book XII). The proportion is generally higher in those books dominated by satiric pieces (such as Books I, II, and III), and Laurens 1989: 286–287 offers the obvious explanation: no other type of epigram can offer the same degree of "concentration et netteté." He aptly compares two poems on the same subject: the hendecasyllabic 5.73 and the monodistich 7.3, the latter giving a memorable and lapidary form to the shared theme: "Cur non mitto meos tibi, Pontiliane, libellos? / ne mihi tu mittas, Pontiliane, tuos."

In most of Martial's monodistichs a bipartite structure readily suggests itself, each half occupying a line: in the first there is a description of a situation; in the second, commentary on it. In the present case, the first line arouses the suspicion of further complication with its insistent repetition *nihil debes/nil debes* and its double vocative *Sexte,* as also with *fatemur,* which implies the existence of a dispute or discussion. Also of structural interest in this brief poem is the threefold repetition of the vocative in two lines; for threefold vocatives in longer poems, see **2.19**, **2.28**; a fourfold repetition occurs in **2.69**. The effect is particularly striking not only because the poem has only two lines but because it opens with the vocative; see below on *Sexte* (1). The three vocatives are, moreover, intertwined with a threefold repetition of forms of the key verb *debere* (*Sexte, debes, debes, Sexte, debet, Sexte*). See Laurens 1989: 271 ("la répétition du vocatif nuance finement l'ironie") and Walter, p. 100 ("die Formulierungen dieses Epigramms haben etwas Infantiles an sich") for two very different evaluations of the technique.

Each line of the monodistich consists of a complete sentence. Other examples of this frequently found technique include, in Book II alone, **2.20**, **2.25**, **2.42**, **2.50**, **2.58**, **2.78**, **2.80**, **2.81**, **2.82**, **2.88**.

1–2: Maaz 1992: 127 observes the echo of this couplet in an epigram by the medieval poet Henry of Huntingdon (p. 170 Wright): "Petre, nihil dicis; nil dicis, Petre, fatemur; / omne malum nihil est, tu mala sola refers." The nearby **2.1** (q.v.) also served as a model for the same poet.

1 *Sexte, nihil debes, nil debes, Sexte:* The chiastic order is notable, as is the (metrically necessary) variation *nihil/nil*, again at 12.48.6. The more fully chiastic *Sexte, nihil debes, debes nil, Sexte* would also have been possible, but the actual wording, with its immediate repetition of the phrase *nihil debes* in the same sequence, is more bluntly emphatic, perhaps reflecting spoken language more directly. See Wills 1996: 181 for the "phrase-expansion" in chiastic order, also at Catull. 42.11–12 (= 19–20), 58.1–2 ("Lesbia illa, / illa Lesbia"), 66.75–76, and Ov. *Her.* 7.191 ("Anna soror, soror Anna, meae male conscia culpae").

The common praenomen *Sextus* is found also in **2.13** (again referring to a debtor), **2.44** (a moneylender!), **2.55** (he wishes to be courted as a patron), **2.87** (he is insulted for his appearance), 3.38, 4.68, 7.86, 8.17, 10.21, 10.57. Unlike such striking cases as Selius (**2.11**), Zoilus (**2.16**), or Postumus (**2.10**), there is no single personality associated with the name; "Sextus" is generally a character whom the poet teases, mocks, or ridicules. Exceptions are 5.5 and 5.38 (where the reference is to a real man, Domitian's secretary) and 3.11 (where the name occasions a play on words: *Quintus/Sextus*).

The device of opening an epigram with the vocative of the addressee's name is somewhat rare in Martial, in Book II to be found in only five out of the seventy-one epigrams having vocative addressees (**2.3**, **2.29**, **2.42**, **2.77**, **2.90**). See Citroni on 1.88.1 and Grewing on 6.25.1, who reminds us that the technique is characteristic of hymns but adds that there is no single typology in Martial.

1 *nihil debes:* Probably meant in a general sense, but the translations of Barié and Schindler and Ceronetti make Martial himself Sextus' creditor ("nichts schuldest du mir"; "non mi devi nulla").

1 *fatemur:* This use of the plural for the singular characterizes Latin prose and verse style of all periods (in verse texts the use of the plural was further encouraged by metrical considerations) and was indeed integrated into linguistic practice to such an extent that one often finds plural and singular forms juxtaposed without any apparent distinction in meaning; see **2.91.7–8** and KS 2.1.82–89 for examples. Like most other translators, I regularly render such plurals with singulars, since a literal translation would be stilted in English. Ker and Shackleton Bailey normally do so as well, yet here render "we," implying that they take the plural to be genuine (as at **2.64.9**, **2.65.1**) and thus that Martial is reporting a group opinion.

2: As often, the final *sententia* is marked by a vocative; as Howell ad 5.72.2 observes, "the vocative interrupts the flow and prepares for the final punch-word." Other examples from Book II of this frequently employed technique include **2.18.8**, **2.25.2**, **2.31.2**, **2.38.2**, **2.60.4**, **2.62.4**.

2.4

> O quam blandus es, Ammiane, matri!
> quam blanda est tibi mater, Ammiane!
> fratrem te vocat et soror vocatur.
> cur vos nomina nequiora tangunt?
> quare non iuvat hoc quod estis esse?   5
> lusum creditis hoc iocumque? non est.
> matrem, quae cupit esse se sororem,
> nec matrem iuvat esse nec sororem.

How tender you are with your mother, Ammianus! How tender your mother is with you, Ammianus! She calls you "brother" and is called "sister" in turn. Why do such naughty names excite the two of you? Why are you not happy to be what you are? You think it a joke, a game? It is not. A mother who wants to be a sister is not happy to be either mother or sister.

Themes.   The satiric commentary now becomes harsher in tone and more scandalous in content, although not yet using verbal obscenity, which is introduced only with **2.28** (*pedico* and *fututor*). Written in hendecasyllabics and placed after an initial sequence of three epigrams in elegiac couplets, the epigram also introduces us to Martial's practice of metrical variation. Scherf 2001: 68–69 observes that this poem introduces a sequence of five poems with symmetrically arranged verse lengths (4, 4, 8, 4, 4) but acknowledges that it is hard to say whether readers will detect the pattern; see on **2.9** and **2.59** for other such patterns.

Playing with the ambivalent terms of endearment *frater* and *soror* (for which see below on 3), the epigram represents a relationship between a mother and son as suspiciously intimate. Either Martial is directly insinuating that Ammianus and his mother have a sexual relationship which they are attempting to cover up by jokingly referring to each other as *frater* and *soror*, or (more likely) he is observing that their use of this language and their tender treatment of each other reveal an inappropriate kind of attraction, though he leaves open the question of consummation. The theme of mother-son incest appears nowhere else in Martial; in 12.20, an epigram containing a similar pun on *soror*, we read of a relationship between brother and sister. Watson 1983 compares Martial's epigram on a stepmother and stepson (4.16) and suggests that 1.68 might be interpreted in this light. Friedlaender compares Catull. 88–90, where Gellius is accused of incestuous relations with his mother (or perhaps stepmother) and sister. Friedlaender adds that there are no clear verbal reminiscences of these poems in Martial's epigram, but its repetition of words and phrases recalls a Catullan technique (see on 1–2), and compare Catull. 88.1–2 ("qui *cum matre atque sorore* / prurit") and especially 91.5–6 ("sed *neque* quod *matrem nec germanam esse* videbam / hanc tibi...") with verse 8 of this epigram ("*nec matrem* iuvat *esse nec sororem*").

Significantly, while the body of the epigram is addressed to both Ammianus and his mother, the harsh closing comment is aimed only at the latter. A double standard regarding Roman conjugal relations placed the burden squarely on the wife's shoulders: in Catullus' epithalamium the wife is bidden not only to be faithful to her new husband but also to give him children and to satisfy his sexual desires lest he "go elsewhere" (61.146: "ni petitum aliunde eat"; see further Williams 1999: 47–56).

Structure.   There is an overarching bipartite structure: the situation is laid out in 1–3 and the commentary comes in 4–8. The second half itself has a bipartite structure: three increasingly indignant questions (4–6) followed by a blunt reply to the last of these (*non est*) and a definitive statement (7–8) punctuated with an aphorism. Thus, a tripartite structure also suggests itself: a description of Ammianus and his mother's behavior (1–3); three questions prompted by this description, arranged in order of increasing intensity (5–6); the poet's comment on the situation (6–8).

The repetition of two closely similar verses (1–2, 7–8) one after the other is a technique much employed by Martial (1.7.4–5, 1.35.6–7, 1.41.14–15, 1.109.21–22, **2.41.3–4**, **2.68.8–9**, 3.44.10–11, 4.30.1–2, 4.46.1–2, 5.35.7–8, 6.82.10–11, 7.60.7–8, 8.54.1–2, 10.35.11–12, 10.49.4–5, 11.15.3, 11.51.4, 11.80.3, 12.15.6–7, 12.79.1–2, 12.95.1), though hardly unique to him: compare Catull. 3.3–4, 49.5–6; *FPL* 173.12, 173.13; V. *Ecl.* 4.58–59.; Ov. *Met.* 1.325–326, 3.481–482, 4.575–576. Siedschlag 1977: 123 finds no precedent in Greek epigram.

1–3: Note the swift variations in syntax in the opening lines: various forms of kinship terms (*matri, mater, fratrem, soror*), an adjective (*blandus,* *blanda*), and a verb (*vocat, vocatur*) are placed in close succession, and there are partially implicit contrasts between different cases of the personal pronoun as well (*blandus es* [*tu*] *matri; blanda est tibi mater; fratrem te vocat; soror [a te] vocatur*). The intertwined syntax characterizes the inappropriately intimate relationship between Ammianus and his mother. For the case interchange, a technique particularly characteristic of Ovid, Seneca, and Martial, see Wills 1996: 275–277.

1 *o quam blandus:* *O* is by far the most frequently occurring interjection in Martial, followed by *heu* (see on **2.18.1**); for some others, see on **2.1.12**, **2.64.9**. But we must distinguish between vocative *o* (*OLD* s.v. 1; see **2.22.1**, **2.33.4**, **2.34.6**, **2.40.8**, **2.41.1**, **2.41.23**, **2.47.2**) and, as here, exclamatory *o* (*OLD* s.v. 2, 3; see **2.44.10**, **2.65.3**), which often, as in this case, forms a part of collocations like *o quam, o quantum,* or *o quotiens.*

The adjective *blandus* can be variously translated: "charming, attractive, seductive, fawning, gentle, affectionate, sweet, soft." It appears quite frequently in Martial, with a wide range of uses, a good number of them in the realm of the erotic: compare *blanda alea* (4.14.7); *blandus somnus* (4.64.20); *blandus leo* (**2.75.2**); *blanda lascivi stagna Lucrini* (4.57.1); *blanda Circe* (10.30.8), *blanda pagina* (10.45.2); *blandae columbae* (8.32, 11.104); *blandior omnibus puellis* (the puppy Issa, 1.109.3); *blanda cura* (the attractive slave Telesphorus, 11.26.1); *blandis labellis* (of a kiss, 7.95.8); *blando amore* (8.77.6); *blandum prurit* (of sexual stimulation, 14.203.1); see also *blanditur* at **2.26.4**. For other examples of the term's association with erotically charged language, see 12.97 (*blandae voces* are likely to cause an erection), Ov. *Am.* 1.4.66, *Am.* 2.19.17–18, *Ars am.* 3.795–796 (*blandae voces*).

1 *Ammiane:* The name occurs again at **2.17**, where he is the recipient of Martial's insinuating comments about a *tonstrix,* and 4.70, where, in an interesting pendant to the present epigram, he is satirized for his less-than-tender relationship with his father.

3 *fratrem ... soror:* The terms *frater* and *soror* were powerful expressions of affection and intimacy. *Frater,* for example, was a term of endearment among male friends (see on **2.11.6**), while both *frater* and *soror* were sometimes used to designate persons whom we would call "boyfriends" and "girlfriends" (*OLD* s.v. *frater* 3b, *soror* 1d; *TLL* s.v. *frater* 6.1256.22–69: "appellatio blanda pro caro, amico, sodali, amasio"; Williams 1992: 332–349, Bannon 1997: 77–90). The phrase *nomina nequiora* in the following line suggests that the use of these terms by Ammianus and his mother bespeaks an inappropriate kind of intimacy.

4 *nomina nequiora tangunt:* The adjective *nequam* ("worthless" or, with a comparable etymology, "naughty") often has an erotic coloring (*OLD* s.v. 3), a sense in which Martial uses the word quite frequently: 1.106.6 ("sobriasque mavis / certae nequitias fututionis"), 3.69.5 ("nequam iuvenes facilesque puellae"), 3.91.4 ("insignis forma nequitiaque puer"), 9.67.1–2 ("puellam / cuius nequitias vincere nulla potest"), 11.16.7 ("nequitias nostri lususque libelli / uda, puella, leges"); compare 11.15.4 ("sit nequior omnibus libellis") with Williams 2002b. Here *nomina nequiora* builds on the tone of erotic playfulness established by *blandus/blanda* and continued with *lusum iocumque*.

For this sense of the verb *tangere* (*OLD* s.v. 8: "to touch, affect"), Friedlaender aptly compares Ov. *Met.* 10.614: "nec forma tangor, poteram tamen hac quoque tangi."

6 lusum creditis hoc iocumque? non est: The combination of *lusus* and *iocus* occurs on three other occasions in Martial (1.14.1, 1.35.13: "parcas lusibus et iocis rogamus"; 4.49.2: "qui tantum lusus illa iocosque vocat") and seems to have been a fixed phrase: see *Priap.* 44.2; Val. Max. 5.1.ext.3; Sen. *Dial.* 5.11.2, 9.17.6, *Epist.* 18.15, 95.33; Plin. *Epist.* 8.21.2. Consider also the closely related combination of *ludus* and *iocus* (Plaut. *Bacch.* 116, Ter. *Eun.* 300, Lucil. 111 Marx, Cic. *Flacc.* 12, Liv. 28.42.2). Also of relevance is the frequent use of the verb *ludere* to refer to sexual play (*TLL* 7.2.1773.81–1774.26 with Adams 1982: 162–163).

For the "rhetorical" question and subsequent reply, see on **2.7.8**.

8 nec matrem iuvat esse nec sororem: The verb may imply not only that it gives her no pleasure to be a mother or sister (*OLD* s.v. *iuvo* 5; V. *Aen.* 1.203: "et haec olim meminisse iuvabit") but that to her mind it serves no purpose (*OLD* s.v. 3; V. *Aen.* 2.776: "quid tantum insano iuvat indulgere dolori?").

2.5

Ne valeam, si non totis, Deciane, diebus
    et tecum totis noctibus esse velim.
sed duo sunt quae nos disiungunt milia passum:
    quattuor haec fiunt, cum rediturus eam.
saepe domi non es; cum sis quoque, saepe negaris: 5
    vel tantum causis vel tibi saepe vacas.
te tamen ut videam, duo milia non piget ire;
    ut te non videam, quattuor ire piget.

I'd rather die, Decianus, than not be in your company day and night.
But there are two miles between us; that makes four, there and back.

Often you are not at home; often, even if you are, they say you aren't:
often you have time only for your legal cases or for yourself. Still, it
doesn't bother me to travel two miles to see you; to travel four miles
not to see you, *that* bothers me.

Themes.   Having satirized one kind of intimate relationship, that between
Ammianus and his mother, as crossing the boundaries of the acceptable,
Martial begins the present epigram with a charming affirmation of the importance to him of another kind of relationship: male friendship (see **2.24**,
2.43, **2.55** with Kleijwegt 1998). He then proceeds to reveal a problem in
his friendship with Decianus, the man to whom the preface and thus in some
sense the entire book are dedicated. Many read the present epigram in the
context of patron-client relations, which are sometimes described openly in
terms of asymmetrical relationships (*dominus, rex:* see, e.g., **2.18**) but sometimes viewed through the lens of *amicitia* (see Saller 1989 and Nauta 2002:
1–39). Konstan 1995, 1997 offers a different perspective on the question.

The themes of friendship and proximity (or distance) are also intertwined
in 1.86, 1.108, and 5.22, the last of which stands in a close relationship with
the present epigram. Another recurring motif is Martial's complaint that his
own efforts are going unrequited or ignored. The remark that "often you
have time only for your legal cases or for yourself" introduces a characteristically delicate ambiguity: we can read this both as a sympathetic statement
to the effect that Decianus has no time for Martial because he is busy or is
taking some well-deserved time for himself and as a rather less kindly im-
putation of selfishness. Then there is the remark *saepe negaris:* Decianus'
slaves tell visitors that he is not home even when he is, and they do so presumably under instructions. How are we to react to this apparently blanket
exclusion of all visitors, even friends like Martial, who like to think they
deserve better treatment?

These gentle complaints (for harsher examples, see **2.43** and **2.44**) are
capped off by a sententious final couplet in which Martial portrays himself as
a reasonable friend who, however, has his equally reasonable limits. The
implication of the final line, smoothly flattering to both Decianus and Martial
himself, is that Martial *would* walk four miles if he knew that Decianus were
actually at home and receiving visitors.

It is just possible that a passage from Seneca's *De brevitate vitae* (2.5)
exerted some influence on the theme and language of this epigram. Seneca
criticizes those who make precisely Martial's complaint ("queruntur de
superiorum fastidio, quod ipsis adire volentibus non vacaverint") but who
do not dedicate any time to themselves ("audet quisquam de alterius superbia
queri, qui *sibi* ipse numquam *vacat?*"). In the same text, Seneca describes
running around the city in order to perform one's social duties (3.2: *officiosa*

per urbem discursatio) as one of many things that detract from one's ability to devote one's time to living fully (*vivere;* cf. **2.90**).

Structure.   Each couplet constitutes a self-contained syntactical unit that moves the thought forward: a statement of Martial's commitment to the friendship (1–2); a description of the distance between their homes (3–4); a complaint that the trip is often futile (5–6); an assertion that Martial would nonetheless undertake it if he were certain of reception (7–8). At the same time we can detect a characteristic bipartite scheme: the situation is described in the bulk of the epigram (1–6) and receives pointed commentary in the final couplet (7–8).

1 *ne valeam, si . . . :* The expression (literally, "May I not be well if . . ." or "May I become sick if . . .") is an emphatic assertion that recurs at 4.31.3 and 6.64.18. Compare the closely similar *dispeream, si . . .* (**2.69.2**) and *ne vivam, nisi . . .* (10.12.3). Such formulas of strong affirmation often have a colloquial tone; KS 2.2.413.

1 *Deciane:* See on **2.praef.** Note the positioning of the vocative in the second half of the first line of a poem in elegiac couplets, described by Laurens 1989: 267 as one of the most characteristic rhythmic techniques of Martial's epigrams. In Book II alone, see **2.7, 2.10, 2.18–19, 2.21, 2.25, 2.28, 2.38, 2.43, 2.45, 2.50, 2.53, 2.56, 2.58, 2.60, 2.63, 2.67, 2.69, 2.71–72, 2.79, 2.82, 2.88, 2.91**.

2 *tecum . . . esse:* Compare 5.20.1–2: "si *tecum* mihi, care Martialis, / securis liceat frui *diebus.*"

3 *disiungunt:* This is the reading of MS T, the sole representative of family α for this poem, and is adopted by nearly all modern editors; only Shackleton Bailey prints the majority MS reading *distinguunt*. Although both are possible, *disiungunt* seems somewhat preferable. The verb *distinguere* usually denotes separation in order to *distinguish* or *keep distinct* (Liv. 37.40.2: "partes eas [sc., exercitus] interpositis binis elephantis distinguebat"; Vell. Pat. 1.14.1; Plin. *N.H.* 4.105: "tria populorum genera . . . amnibus maxime distincta"; Plin. *Ep.* 2.17.22: "interiacens andron parietem cubiculi hortique distinguit"), whereas *disiungere* seems better suited to the more general sense of spatial separation required here (Pl. *Asin.* 665: "ne nos disiunge amantis"; Cic. *Fam.* 1.7.1: "intervallo locorum et temporum disiuncti sumus"; but see also Sall. *Jug.* 92.5: "flumine . . . quod Iugurthae Bocchique regnum disiungebat"). Neither of the two verbs occurs anywhere else in Martial.

3 *milia passum:* A "pace" (*passus*) was equivalent to 5 "feet" (*pedes*), each of which was less than a modern foot (11.65 inches). Hence, the Roman mile (1,000 paces, or 5,000 feet) was equivalent to about 4,855.5 modern feet, rather less than a modern mile. For the form *passum* (instead of *passuum*), found in a range of authors along with such other forms as *currum*, *manum*, and *exercitum*, see KS 1.1.397–398.

5 *saepe negaris:* The same complaint is later reworked in a briefer, punchier epigram (9.7; see also 5.22.9–10: "illud adhuc gravius, quod te post mille labores, / Paule, negat lasso ianitor esse domi"). Cic. *De orat.* 2.276 reports an amusing joke on this same theme. Nasica goes to visit the poet Ennius, is told by the latter's slave girl that her master is not at home, but sees through the lie. A few days later Ennius comes to visit Nasica, who calls out: "He's not in!" When Ennius exclaims, "You think I don't recognize your voice?" Nasica replies, "I believed your slave girl when she said you weren't in; you won't believe *me?*" See also Sen. *Ben.* 6.34 for the practice of ranking friends by giving differential access to one's house.

7–8: The point is marked not by a *sententia* but by another fairly common device: close but not exact repetition of a line or part of a line; see on **2.4.1–2**. The disarmingly simple parallelism between the two verses suggests straightforward, even everyday speech.

2.6

I nunc, edere me iube libellos.
lectis vix tibi paginis duabus
spectas eschatocollion, Severe,
et longas trahis oscitationes.
haec sunt, quae relegente me solebas   5
rapta exscribere, sed Vitellianis;
haec sunt, singula quae sinu ferebas
per convivia cuncta, per theatra;
haec sunt, aut meliora si qua nescis.
quid prodest mihi tam macer libellus,   10
nullo crassior ut sit umbilico,
si totus tibi triduo legatur?
numquam deliciae supiniores.
lassus tam cito deficis viator,
et cum currere debeas Bovillas,   15
interiungere quaeris ad Camenas?
i nunc, edere me iube libellos.

Go ahead now, tell me to publish my little books. When you've barely read two pages, Severus, you're already looking ahead to the last page and you draw out long yawns. These are the poems which you used to grab and write down quickly—and on Vitellian tablets at that—as I read them out. These are the poems which you used to carry with you individually in your breast-pocket to every party and to the theater. These are those poems, and perhaps even some better ones that you don't know. But what good does it do me, this book so slim that it is no fatter than a rolling-stick, if it takes you three days to read it all? No aesthete has ever been so languid. When you go on a trip, do you tire so quickly that, although you are supposed to make it as far as Bovillae, you already look to unhitch the harness at the Camenae? Go ahead now, tell me to publish my little books.

Themes.   As in the preceding epigram, Martial complains to a friend about how he is treating him—in **2.5** as a friend, here as a poet. The hendecasyllabic meter first seen in **2.4** returns, as does the theme of Martial's own poetic practice (**2.praef., 2.1**). Martial again considers the possibility that his collections (as opposed to the single epigrams: *singula,* 7) may overwhelm or bore his readers, and perhaps even teases them here: like Severus, we ourselves have now read about two pages' worth of the collection (*lectis vix tibi paginis duabus*). Are we, too, yawning? For the potential of boring readers, see further on **2.1.11** and compare 3.68.11–12 and 11.107, where Septicianus claims to have read nearly all of Martial's book but the latter slyly hints that he does not believe him.

Yet whereas in **2.praef.** the poet limits himself to a fairly bland statement of mock-modesty ("si qui in hunc librum inciderint") and in **2.1** worries that despite the book's brevity many readers will find it boring, here he takes a proactive stance, criticizing his critic first by means of the *sententia* "numquam deliciae supiniores," then with the metaphor comparing Severus to a lazy traveler (14–16), and finally by means of the sarcastic repetition of the poem's opening line. This epigram thus hints at things to come later in Book II: Martial often replies to criticism with fairly harsh attacks on his critics' own practices, especially if they happen to be poets themselves (**2.8, 2.71, 2.77**; compare also 1.91, 1.110, 3.9, 6.64).

The epigram also gives us a valuable glimpse into the mechanisms and material form of publication: first, circulation among friends and others in various private and semipublic contexts and then a more formal publication (*edere*) by means of a bookseller (*librarius;* see on **2.1.5**); compare Citroni 1988. At the same time, Martial is indulging in some self-advertisement, letting us know that his epigrams had been individually circulated and found favor at social gatherings (*per convivia cuncta, per theatra*).

Structure. The poem's most striking structural device is the verbatim repetition of the opening line at the end. Modern scholarship often associates
the technique (also found in 4.64, 4.89, 7.26, and, in varied form, 1.32, 1.67,
2.41, **2.43**, 5.73, 6.19, 7.39) above all with Martial's avowed model Catullus:
see Catull. 1, 10, 17, and for the relationship between the two poets in general, see Paukstadt 1876, Barwick 1958, Ferguson 1963, Offermann 1980,
Swann 1994 and 1998, Grewing 1996.

After an opening section describing Severus' actions that is marked by
three sentences beginning with *haec sunt* at regular intervals (5, 7, 9), the poet's
reaction is expressed in an effectively varied form: a rhetorical question (10–
12), a *sententia* (13), another rhetorical question employing a metaphor (14–
16), and finally a sarcastic imperative addressed to Severus himself (17).

1 *i nunc:* This sarcastic formula (*OLD* s.v. *eo* 10b: "introducing an ironi-
cal command which, in the face of what has just been said, is held to be
absurd or unreasonable") occurs with some frequency in Martial (*Sp.* 23.12,
1.42.6, 8.63.3, 9.2.13, 10.96.13, 11.33.3). Lease 1898 offers an overview, noting
that the formula "marks the presence, and is the product, of a stress of
emotion" (59); it is most frequently attested in Ovid, Martial, the younger
Seneca, and the declamations attributed to Quintilian.

1 *edere me iube libellos:* In 1.25 Martial plays Severus' role: "ede tuos
tandem populo, Faustine, libellos." For *libelli* see on **2.1.3**. In general, the
plural might suggest either a single book of poetry (see on **2.3.1**) or various
provisional collections (Citroni, pp. xiv–xviii); at the poem's end it clearly
refers to *this* book as a whole, as contrasted with its individual poems.

2 *paginis duabus:* In Martial's day the noun regularly refers to a column of a papyrus scroll, although it is usually translated "page"; see on
2.praef.4.

3 *eschatocollion:* Though it is not attested in any extant Greek source
(Pertsch 1911: 13; cf. *rhytium* at **2.35.2**), the word clearly refers to the end
of the papyrus roll, so called either because it was the last sheet glued on
(*OLD*) or because the roller (*umbilicus*) was glued on to it (Bridge and Lake,
Merli). It is just possible that Martial is playfully coining the term (Salemme
1976: 33–34).

3 *Severe:* The name occurs frequently in Martial (5.11, 5.80, 6.8, 7.34, 7.38,
7.49, 7.79, 8.61, 8.66, 9.86, 11.57) but does not always refer to the same man,
real or otherwise, although it is worth noting that in 5.80 Martial asks him, along
with Secundus, to read and correct his verse. As Spiegel 1891: 65 already observed, none of the various attempts to pin down the identity of the Severus of
the present epigram are compelling (Friedlaender argues that he is Silius Severus,
son of the poet Silius Italicus, mentioned in 9.86; Dau 1887: 73 claims he is the
Septimius Severus praised as a poet by Statius at *Silv.* 4.51).

5 *haec sunt:* The phrase appears three times in this epigram, each time at the beginning of its verse but with a characteristically subtle variation: in 5 it is followed by a relative clause with the relative pronoun at its beginning (*quae relegente me solebas*); in 7 it is followed once again by a relative clause but now with the relative pronoun postponed (*singula quae sinu ferebas*); in 9 it is followed by a paratactic independent clause introduced by *aut* (*aut meliora si qua nescis*). After each occurrence of the phrase is a clause whose main verb is in the second-person singular (*solebas, ferebas, nescis*): we are insistently reminded of Severus' fondness for Martial's epigrams.

5 *relegente me:* The verb "perhaps implies that Martial had to read the verse twice over at Severus' request" (Bridge and Lake; similarly Ker and Izaac). Others understand the verb in the more likely sense of "reading aloud" (cf. 4.29.9: "tu quoque de nostris releges quemcumque libellis"; 11.52.17). Nauta 2002: 93–105 carefully distinguishes between two types of recitation— "informal social exchange" and "performance for large invited audiences"— and observes that Martial never clearly represents himself as engaging in the latter type. See further on **2.20.1.**

6 *rapta:* The participle emphasizes Severus' eagerness to hear the latest Martial.

6 *sed Vitellianis:* For this use of *sed* (*OLD* s.v. 3: "[affirming and elaborating an idea] Yes and what's more") see also 1.117.7 ("scalis habito tribus sed altis"), **2.14.4, 2.41.6, 2.48.3**, 6.93.2, Juv. 5.147 ("boletos . . . sed quales Claudius edit"). *Vitelliani* are a type of writing tablet described further in 14.8–9: small, elegant, and particularly suited for love letters. The name was presumably taken from their manufacturer. Schneider 1909: 19 points out that *Vitellianis* is metrically suitable to this context, unlike *codicillis;* but the proper name is also desirable in its own right. Bridge and Lake paraphrase: "When I read my poems to you, you used to flatter me by using the most elegant note-books for scribbling down any verse which you caught and admired."

7 *singula quae sinu ferebas:* The point is that although Severus had nothing but admiration for Martial's *individual* epigrams, when too many are collected in a book he quickly tires. Collesso objects to the notion ("quod absurdum videtur"), but Martial elsewhere makes it clear that this is precisely the occupational hazard of publishing books of epigrams; see on **2.1.11**.

The noun *sinus* refers to the cavity or fold produced by the looping of a garment, especially a toga, often "as the part where a person, etc., is held as a demonstration of affection, for protection, etc." (*OLD* s.v. 2), or as a pocket to hold money and valuables (*OLD* s.v. 4). Thus, Martial's phrase underscores the value placed by Severus on Martial's epigrams, which he had carried around like money or embraced like a beloved child; compare 6.38.3 ("maternosque sinus viso genitore relinquat"); Hor. *C.* 2.18.26–27 ("pellitur paternos / in sinu ferens deos"); Flor. *Epit.* 1.22.28; Calp. Sic. *Ecl.* 5.41–42. Martial again alludes to the *sinus* when imagining his scroll being picked up and held by an affectionate reader at 3.2.6, 3.5.7, 6.60.2.

8 *per convivia cuncta, per theatra:* Both are frequently mentioned in the ancient sources as places of conversation: consider the phrase "per convivia, porticus, theatra" at 7.76.2, 8.79.4. See further Nauta 2002: 139–140, 173–179, for *convivia* as a context in which Martial's poems were read aloud; see also **2.1.9** ("te conviva leget"), 5.16.9 ("at nunc conviva est comissatorque libellus"), 7.97.11 ("te convivia, te forum sonabit").

11 *umbilico:* The noun (literally, "navel") can refer to the ornamented end of the cylinder or stick on which a papyrus roll was wound; here and elsewhere, by synecdoche, the *umbilicus* is the stick itself (see 1.66.10–11, 3.2.9, 8.66.4). Thus, at 4.89.2 the phrase *pervenire usque ad umbilicos* means "to reach the end of the book."

12 *si totus tibi triduo legatur:* This, the universal MS reading, makes perfect sense: if you need three days to read the whole book, even though one can finish it in less time than it takes for heated wine to cool down (cf. **2.1.9**). Yet there have been proposals to emend the text: Collesso supports Ramirez de Prado's emendation of *totus* to *toto* ("if you should read it in an entire three-day period"); Shackleton Bailey prints *totus* but tentatively suggests emending *totus* to *curtus* ("if you should take three days to read it, and incompletely at that"), observing that, after all, Severus had not wanted to read the whole book. Yet Martial does not actually say that Severus *refuses* to read the whole book, merely that he shows signs of boredom when undertaking the task (2–4).

13 *numquam deliciae supiniores:* Here the noun *deliciae* probably refers to "a man of exquisite taste, voluptuary" (*OLD* s.v. 6; cf. Plin. *N.H.* 22.99, Juv. 4.3–4: "aegrae solaque libidine fortes / deliciae"); otherwise, it might have an abstract sense ("fine taste"). The adjective *supinus,* literally "lying face upwards, flat on one's back," and thus the opposite of *pronus,* has metaphorical meanings that include, as here, "passive, languid" (*OLD* s.v. 5); see also 3.82.11 (*supina concubina*), 6.42.22, 12.31.1, and Quint. *Inst.* 10.2.17 ("otiosi et supini"). See **2.86.1** for another sense of *supinus.*

15 *Bovillas:* A fairly well known town on the Appian Way, about 12 miles from Rome; hence, Prop. 4.1a.33 and Ov. *Fast.* 3.667 speak of *suburbanae Bovillae.* The metaphor thus suggests a trip outside Rome but hardly an arduous journey to a distant location, just as Martial's book is hardly a lengthy tome.

16 *interiungere:* Martial uses the verb (*OLD:* "to unyoke or unharness oxen or horses for a rest") again at 3.67.7, with the object *equos* expressed.

16 *ad Camenas:* Originally spring nymphs (Serv. *Ecl.* 7.21) worshiped together with the nymph Egeria in a grove at the foot of the Caelian Hill just outside the Porta Capena, the Camenae came to be assimilated to the Greek Muses, and a false etymological connection with *carmen/canere* was detected. Here and elsewhere their name is used to refer to the location of their cult, whether the spring (which may be that of the Church of S. Gregorio Magno on the Caelian), the grove, the shrine, or the whole valley between the Caelian and the Aventine (compare the present-day Via Valle delle Camene). Since this site was located just outside the city walls, the voyage stops soon after it starts, just as Severus loses interest after reading barely two *paginae*.

2.7

Declamas belle, causas agis, Attice, belle,
  historias bellas, carmina bella facis,
componis belle mimos, epigrammata belle,
  bellus grammaticus, bellus es astrologus,
et belle cantas et saltas, Attice, belle,   5
  bellus es arte lyrae, bellus es arte pilae.
nil bene cum facias, facias tamen omnia belle,
  vis dicam quid sis? magnus es ardalio.

You declaim nicely, you plead courtroom cases nicely, Atticus; you write nice history and nice poetry; you compose mimes nicely, epigrams nicely; you are a nice literary scholar, a nice student of the stars; you both sing nicely, Atticus, and dance nicely; you are nice with the lyre, nice with the ball. Since you do nothing well but everything nicely, do you want me to say what you are? You are a great dilettante.

Themes.   After the hendecasyllabics of **2.6** we return to elegiac couplets, and the topic shifts from Martial's own poetry to a critique of someone else's activities. At the same time there is thematic continuity: **2.6** speaks of Severus' impatience and ability to become easily bored, while **2.7** implicitly criticizes Atticus for the same thing, making moreover a passing allusion to the fact that Atticus has tried his hand at Martial's own art (*epigrammata belle*). The self-referential mode will return in **2.8**.

The central motif—dilettantism taken to such an extreme that achievement in any one field is impossible—is reminiscent of an epigram from the *Palatine Anthology* (*A.P.* 11.355; see Pertsch 1911: 35). Citing some of the same accomplishments that Martial attributes to Atticus, Juvenal associates a certain type of dilettantism with the despised Greeks: "grammaticus rhetor geometres pictor aliptes / augur schoenobates medicus magus: omnia novit / Graeculus esuriens; in caelum iusseris, ibit" (3.76–78). Colton 1991: 99–101 argues that Juvenal was directly influenced by the present epigram.

The key adjective *bellus,* a diminutive of *bonus,* ranges in meaning from "pretty, handsome, charming" to "fine, excellent, smart, admirable" and, especially in the latter sense, is used ironically (*OLD*). In view of the urban and urbane world of Martial's epigrams, it comes as no surprise that he uses the term fairly often: see 1.9 with Citroni ad loc., 1.64, **2.87**, 3.37, 3.63 (with a lengthy description of the *bellus homo*), 4.31, 5.16, 5.52, 5.77, 6.44, 7.59, 7.85, 10.46, 11.34, 11.52, 12.39 (where the key term likewise occurs repeatedly). The frequent use of this and similar diminutives may be a sign of the influence of colloquial speech (Hofmann 1951: 200).

Structure.   There is a clear bipartite structure: the description of Atticus' behavior (1–6) is followed by commentary in the final couplet (7–8). This in turn is marked first by an antithesis (*bene* vs. *belle*) and then by a rhetorical question (*vis dicam quid sis?*) followed by a dismissive answer (*magnus es ardalio*) that brings home the point; see on 8 below for the technique. The epigram also exemplifies the characteristic device of *cumulatio* (creating a list, piling up attributes, or repeating a phrase several times in succession), for which see, in Book II alone, **2.11**, **2.14**, **2.27–28**, **2.33**, **2.36**, **2.43**, **2.48**, **2.89**. A memorable earlier example is Catull. 43.1–4: "Salve, nec minimo puella naso / nec bello pede nec nigris ocellis / nec longis digitis nec ore sicco / nec sane nimis elegante lingua." Laurens 1989: 279–281 suggests that the structure of an epigram attributed to Seneca may have inspired Martial in the present case: "*Semper* munditias, *semper,* Basilissa, decores, / *semper* dispositas arte decente comas / et comptos *semper* vultus unguentaque *semper* . . ." (*A.L.* 458 Riese).

Martial's list is constructed with particular care. Each of lines 1–6 cites two activities, each of them accompanied by the adjective *bellus* or the adverb *belle* (for such repetition of individual words or phrases, see Citroni ad 1.41 and Joepgen 1967: 141–160), and the presentation of Atticus' twelve spheres of achievement is marked by the following grammatical variation:

1. Verbs referring to oratory, theoretical and practical (*declamas, causas agis*)
2–3. Nouns referring to other literary genres (*historias, carmina, mimos, epigrammata*)
4. Nouns referring to two professions (*grammaticus, astrologus*)
5. Verbs referring to two leisure activities (*cantas, saltas*)
6. Nouns referring to two further leisure activities (*arte lyrae, arte pilae*)

There is a progression from one of the most respected of activities for Roman men (*declamas, causas agis*), to serious literary activity (*historias, carmina*), to less serious literary activity (*mimos, epigrammata*), to other intellectual occupations—one of them (*grammaticus*) respectable, the other (*astrologus*) potentially suspect—and finally to leisure-time activities liable to dismissal as trivial or worse (*cantas, saltas, arte lyrae, arte pilae*). There is, moreover, a pleasing variation in the use of the key term *bellus*, which occurs exactly twice in each line, once before and once after the principal caesura: the adverb *belle* (1, 3, 5) alternates with the adjective *bellus* (2, 4, 6). The whole sequence climaxes in 6 with the application of the key adjective no longer to Atticus' activities or achievements but to the man himself: *bellus es*.

The insistent but elegant listing reflects the subject matter. Atticus does a little bit of many different things and does them with a certain degree of elegance (*belle*), but the very fact that there are so many such practices precludes him, unlike Martial himself in this epigram, from doing any one thing *bene* (cf. Hutchinson 1993: 26: the poet "is luxuriating in symmetry and the very sound of the word"). Walter, p. 102 finds a deliberately monotonous quality that reflects Atticus' lifestyle.

1 *declamas belle, causas agis, Attice, belle:* The first clause refers to declamation or rhetorical exercises, whether *suasoriae* or *controversiae;* the second to actual courtroom delivery. The positioning of the vocative in the second half of the first line (see on **2.5.1**) is combined with the repetition of a key term in each half of the line also at 1.79.1 ("semper agis causas et res agis, Attale, semper") and 5.58.1 ("cras te victurum, cras dicis, Postume, semper"); see also *A.L.* 458.1 Riese (quoted above).

1 *Attice:* Given the invective tone, this would have been understood as a fictional name. It occurs in only two other epigrams: 7.32, where he is praised for his eloquence and as a descendant of Cicero's friend, and 9.99, where we learn nothing about him.

Whereas the MSS of family α read *Attice* both here and in 5, those of family γ read *Attale* in both verses and in the lemma; see on 5 for the peculiar problem in family β. As Lindsay 1903a: 20 and Heraeus 1925: 318 observe, such cases of equally possible personal names (see also 1.10, **2.18**, **2.32.5**, 6.88) are the hardest to decide. Lindsay himself tentatively favors *Atticus* because it is the reading of two families, and most modern editors have done the same. But Shackleton Bailey prints *Attale* and Walter 1995 follows him, observing that the name would suggest a man of servile origins, though it is not clear that the name *Attale* would tell us any more about the man than does *Atticus*. Citroni ad 1.79 refers to *TLL* 2.1114.65 for the name Attalus (*apud Latinos nom. serv. et cogn.*), but that entry cites the present epigram, along with Mart. 1.79 and 4.34, and nothing else.

2 *historias:* Walter 1995: 103 claims these must be anecdotes or stories rather than extensive historiographical works; but Atticus could easily have been an amateur historian.

2 *carmina:* The word (literally, "songs"; cf. *canere*) often signifies poetic texts, whether dramatic (Cic. *Sen.* 22), lyric (Hor. *Epist.* 2.2.59, 2.2.91; Stat. *Silv.* 4.pr.), elegiac (Mart. 14.189.1), or even epigrammatic (Mart. 1.4.6, **2.91.4**, 12.61.1; Tac. *Ann.* 4.34). Here, since *mimos* and *epigrammata* in the following line specify two types of "lighter" poetry, it is likely that *carmina* refers to such "heavier" genres as epic or lyric.

3 *mimos:* Improvised comic sketches originally performed on the street by clownlike figures known as *planipedes* were regularly presented at the *ludi Florales* (held annually beginning in 173 B.C.) and were given literary form by such poets as Cn. Matius and Decimus Laberius. Literary mime survives only in fragments, but it seems that its most common themes included the "rags to riches" motif, the misadventures of adulterous lovers, and trickster figures.

3 *epigrammata:* This is the first allusion in Book II to other practitioners of Martial's art; he does not yet reach the level of invective attained elsewhere (see on **2.71**). A later epigram contains a patronizing remark applicable to someone like Atticus: "facile est epigrammata belle / scribere, sed librum scribere difficile est" (7.85.3–4).

4 *grammaticus:* This term indicates much more than a "grammarian" in the modern sense, just as *grammatica* is much more than "grammar": *OLD* s.v. concisely explains it as "the study of literature and language . . . including exegesis, literary criticism, etc., as well as grammar in the modern sense." A *grammaticus,* in short, was a learned man engaged in the interpretation of texts and expert on all sorts of linguistic and literary questions, of which Cic. *De orat.* 1.187 offers an overview: "poetarum pertractatio, historiarum cognitio, verborum interpretatio, pronuntiandi sonus." He generally taught boys in the middle of their education, after the *litterator,* who taught them the rudiments of reading and writing, but before the *rhetor,* who took them to the upper levels of rhetoric. Thus, 7.64.7 mentions, in descending order, the *rhetor, grammaticus,* and *ludi magister.* See Suetonius' biographies *De grammaticis* and Kaster 1988.

4 *astrologus:* This term indicates one whose object of study comprehended what is now called "astronomy" and "astrology," that is, both the study of heavenly bodies and the attempt to interpret and predict human affairs from them. The only other occurrence of the noun in Martial is in this second sense (9.82.1: an *astrologus* predicts someone's death). The present instance constitutes an interesting problem of translation, as both "astrologer" and "astronomer" are too limited, and a clear distinction between them is anachronistic. The former is the version offered by Izaac, Norcio, Ceronetti, Scandola, and Barié and Schindler (who confusingly observe in their note that "*astrologus* ist Astronom, nicht Astrolog im engeren Sinn"); the latter, by Ker and Shackleton Bailey.

Study of the stars was always viewed with some ambivalence in Rome. In A.D. 11, for example, Augustus outlawed private consultations and those predicting death, and astrologers, like philosophers, were periodically expelled from Rome. In Juvenal's third satire the knowledge of *motus astrorum* is one of the crazes characterizing contemporary Rome that the speaker so bitterly denounces (3.41–43), and in his sixth satire *astrologi Chaldaei* are named among the various charlatans who enjoy women's favor (6.553–581). Yet Manilius' poem from the Augustan age and Firmicus Maternus' fourth-century treatise remind us that study of the stars came with a long and complex tradition and was taken quite seriously; see Cramer 1954, Barton 1994, Bakhouche 2002. Friedlaender explains the connection between *grammaticus* and *astrologus* in the present passage: among the many bodies of knowledge that *grammatici* needed to master in order to explicate literary texts was *astrologia*.

5 cantas et saltas: These accomplishments, too, were viewed with ambivalence by traditionalist Romans. Cicero scathingly alludes to Catiline's young male followers' expertise as nude dancers (*Cat.* 2.23), and the term *saltator* could be used as an insult (Cic. *Mur.* 13, *Red. Sen.* 13, *Pis.* 18). Horace's Bore boasts of his accomplishments as poet, dancer, and singer in terms that were intended to impress Horace but that had the opposite effect (Hor. *Sat.* 1.9.23–25). Nepos (pr., *Epam.* 1.2) observes that skill in singing, dancing, and playing musical instruments was in general viewed as suspect and un-Roman by traditionalists, and the elder Seneca complains that the effete youth of his day have an unbecoming interest in singing and dancing (*Contr.* 1.pr.8: "cantandi saltandique obscena studia effeminatos tenent"). On the other hand, a certain amount of musical education was clearly acceptable, and Quintilian makes an obvious point: "cantatur et saltatur per omnes gentes aliquo modo" (*Inst.* 2.17.10). See Marquardt 1886: 118–119 and Weeber 1995: 353–355.

5 Attice: The MSS of family β read *Attice* here but *Attale* in 1 and in the lemma. For other self-contradictory readings and some possible explanations, see on **2.18.8**.

6 arte lyrae ... arte pilae: Praise of Atticus' skill at the lyre, coming after an allusion to his abilities at dancing and singing, constitutes yet another ambivalent type of flattery. For ball games along with other forms of exercise and entertainment, compare 7.32.7–10, 10.86.2, 14.45–48 with Leary ad loc., Petr. *Sat.* 27, and see Blümner 1911: 439ff., Harris 1972: 75–111.

The line is an example of a pure isocolic pentameter, its two halves being identical in both meter and word shape. Compare 3.26.2 ("aurea solus habes, murrina solus habes") and (with slight deviations) 4.5.8 ("plaudere nec Cano, plaudere nec Glaphyro"), 11.73.2 ("constituisque horam constituisque locum"); and see Siedschlag 1977: 111.

7 *nil bene cum facias, facias tamen omnia belle:* There is probably an etymological play in the contrast *bene/belle* (also at 10.46.1–2); Priscian (GLK 2.30.22) observes the relationship between the two. Grewing 1998a cites the line as an example of etymological play in framing position: compare 4.67.8 (*equiti/equo*), 13.11.1 (*mulio/mulis*), 14.135.2 (*teget/togas*).

8 *vis dicam quid sis?* Martial was fond of the technique of posing a question—often *vis?*—and immediately supplying its answer at the end of an epigram. See Siedschlag 1977: 26, Laurens 1989: 261–262, and, in Book II alone, **2.1**, **2.10** ("vis dare . . . ? / hoc tibi habe . . ."), **2.11**, **2.16** ("vis fieri sanus? stragula sume mea."), **2.17**, **2.26**, **2.28–29**, **2.39** ("vis dare quae meruit munera? mitte togam."), **2.40**, **2.45**, **2.56**, **2.72** ("vis hoc me credere? credo."), **2.83**. The technique is rare in Greek epigram and only occasionally present in earlier Latin epigram: compare Catull. 85.2 ("quare id faciam fortasse requiris? nescio.") and Calvus apud Sen. *Contr.* 7.4.77 ("quid credas hunc sibi velle? virum.").

8 *magnus es ardalio:* The noun *ardalio,* referring to a busybody or dabbler and here functioning as an insult (Opelt 1965: 113), is rarely attested: compare 4.78.9–10 ("deformius, Afer, / omnino nihil est ardalione sene"), *CIL* 4.4765 ("Aephebe, ardalio es"), and Phaedr. 2.5 ("ardalionum quaedam Romae natio . . . / multa agendo nil agens"). Laurens 1989: 279–281 points to the effective contrast between the preceding instances of the diminutive *bellus* and *magnus* and describes the pairing of *magnus* and *ardalio* itself as "une alliance aussi plaisante que juste."

2.8

Si qua videbuntur chartis tibi, lector, in istis
    sive obscura nimis sive Latina parum,
non meus est error: nocuit librarius illis
    dum properat versus adnumerare tibi.
quod si non illum sed me peccasse putabis,   5
    tunc ego te credam cordis habere nihil.
"ista tamen mala sunt." quasi nos manifesta negemus!
    haec mala sunt, sed tu non meliora facis.

Reader, if it seems to you that something in these pages has too
much obscurity or too little Latinity, I am not the one at fault: the
copyist damaged them while he was hastening to count out the verses
for you. If you think that the mistake is not his but mine, *I* will think
that you are brainless. "Still, they're bad," you say. As if I were denying the obvious! They *are* bad, but you write no better.

Themes.   The opening line signals a return to Martial's self-referential mode
(for which see also **2.1**, **2.6**, **2.23**, **2.71**, **2.77**, **2.86**, **2.91**, **2.93**) and introduces the technique of directly addressing the reader, for which see on *lec-
tor* (1). The poet offers an apology for any potential obscurities, stylistic
infelicities, or even grammatical errors, attributing them to a hasty copyist.
The technique of blaming others continues into the following couplet, with
its assertion that the reader who finds fault not with the copyist's errors but
with the epigrams themselves is an idiot, while the final couplet exemplifies
Martial's practice of reporting others' criticism only to strike back with a
counterattack: compare 1.91, 1.110 ("scribere me quereris epigrammata longa.
/ ipse nihil scribis: tu breviora facis."), **2.77.8** ("sed tu, Cosconi, disticha longa
facis"), 3.9, 3.83, 6.64, 6.65 with Citroni 1968. Here the technique is especially interesting, as it amounts to an attack on the reader, or at least a certain kind of reader; compare 1.40, where Martial insults a reader who reacts
bitterly to his praise of Decianus in 1.39. The assumption that Martial's readers might be ill-disposed or even positively hostile is especially characteristic of his earlier books (Citroni 1988).

Structure.   The epigram has a tripartite structure: any obscure or ungram-
matical language is due to a copyist's error (1–4); if the reader finds fault
with Martial himself rather than the copyist, he is a fool (5–6); the epigrams
may be bad, but the reader has not written anything better himself (7–8).
Beginning with 3, the epigram is marked by clear syntactic structures occupying half-lines or entire lines and straightforward, even prosaic vocabulary. Might this clarity itself be an illustration of the poet's point, that he is
not guilty of writing anything *nimis obscurum* or *parum Latinum?*

1 lector: A direct address to the reader in the form of a vocative *lector*
is a characteristic technique of this poet (1.1, 1.113, 4.55, 5.16, 7.12, 9.praef.,
10.2, 11.16, 11.108; see also 1.2, 1.40), who is markedly concerned with his
reception. The device seems to be Ovidian in inspiration and is rarely found
elsewhere: apart from twelve instances in Martial and seven in Ovid, a search
of the PHI disk brings up only two in Phaedrus and three in Apuleius. For
general discussion of the technique of addressing the reader see Citroni 1995,
and for Martial's relationship to his reader see Spisak 1998b.

1 chartis... in istis: In addition to the more common *hic* (e.g., **2.6.5**), Martial sometimes uses the demonstrative *iste* to refer to "this" book, that is, the one before us (**2.93.1**, 4.49.10, 8.1.3, 11.2.8; cf. 1.40.1, 1.70.17–18, 7.72.16). See Citroni ad 1.26.6 for Martial's use of *iste* for *hic* in general.

2 Latina parum: References to the Latin language may imply "correct Latin," as here and at Ov. *Tr.* 3.1.17 ("si qua videbuntur casu non dicta latine") and Plin. *Epist.* 5.5.3 ("tres libros ... subtiles et diligentes et Latinos"), or else "plain Latin" (i.e., blunt or obscene language), as at 11.20.2 ("qui tristis verba Latina legis"). There is a pleasing antithesis between *obscura* **nimis** and *Latina* **parum**; Watson and Watson observe that the two phrases complement each other, since the concept of *Latinitas* often includes the idea of clarity (cf. Cic. *De orat.* 3.49).

3 librarius: See on **2.1.5**. Szelest 1986: 2565 assumes that this *librarius* is Martial's slave, but in fact his status is hardly certain (Garrido-Hory 1981: 79). We hear rather frequently of copyists' errors (Marquardt 1886: 807); at 7.11.1 and 7.17.6 Martial alludes to copies corrected by the author's own hand.

4 adnumerare: The verb simultaneously suggests the image of the *librarius* copying out line after line ("to enumerate, run through, count," *OLD* s.v. 2; cf. 11.41.8: "te satis est nobis adnumerare pecus") and hints at the financial aspect of the transaction ("to pay out," *OLD* s.v. 1), since copyists were paid on the basis of the number of lines copied (cf. Turner 1987: 1). Watson and Watson point to the contrast between the verb's connotations of precision and the sloppiness of the actual transaction.

5 quod si: *Quod si* (literally, "with respect to which, if ...") usually has an adversative force: "but if." Compare **2.24.7** ("quod si deus ore sereno / adnuerit ...") and see *OLD* s.v. *quod* 1, Galán Vioque ad 7.38.3.

6 cordis habere nihil: The heart being viewed as the center not only of character and emotions but also of intelligence (cf. *OLD* s.v. *cor*), the phrase *cor habere,* quite differently from English "have a heart," signifies "to have good sense, to be intelligent." Compare 3.26.4 ("et cor solus habes, solus et ingenium"), 3.27.4 ("et mihi cor non est et tibi, Galle, pudor"), 6.64.16, 7.78.4 ("habes nec cor, Papyle, nec genium"), 14.219.

7 ista tamen mala sunt: The practice of anticipating an opponent's objection by imagining his words was common in ancient oratory and was known as *praeceptio, anticipatio,* or πρόληψις (cf. Quint. *Inst.* 4.1.49; Lausberg 1973: no. 855). Martial uses the technique often, usually with an explicit marker such as *inquis, dicis, dices,* or *respondes* (see on **2.21.2**) but sometimes, as here and at **2.24.6, 2.27.3–4**, with no clear marker. In such cases, ancient writers relied on rhetorical devices like *tamen* here, rather than punctuation, to mark shifts in voice. See Burnikel 1980 for discussion of the problem in conjunction with the practice of reading aloud.

7 *quasi nos manifesta negemus:* Observe the similar argument and language at 14.1.7–8: "'sunt apinae tricaeque et si quid vilius istis.' / quis nescit? vel quis tam manifesta negat?" The technique is reminiscent of what Quintilian calls *confessionis simulatio,* which he identifies as an occasionally effective means of wittily answering an attack (*Inst.* 6.3.81). Compare **2.28.5** ("ex istis nihil es fateor"), **2.58.2** ("sunt haec trita quidem"), **2.69.6** ("verum est").

8 *haec mala sunt:* Compare Martial's memorable formulation of his opinion of his own work: "Sunt bona, sunt quaedam mediocria, sunt mala plura / quae legis hic: aliter non fit, Avite, liber" (1.16; cf. 7.81); he describes his poetry as *malus* again at **2.praef.** ("sua, id est mala, lingua"), 7.81, 7.90. Some have seen a double entendre with *malus* in the sense "abusive," as famously at Hor. *Sat.* 2.1.82–83 and perhaps also Mart. 9.89 (Henriksén ad loc.).

8 *tu non meliora facis:* The retort has received two different interpretations, of which the more likely is this: "You do not write better (poems than mine)" and thus have no right to criticize me (Collesso, Ker, Izaac, Norcio, Ceronetti, Shackleton Bailey, Scandola, Watson and Watson). A similar argument appears in 1.91 ("Cum tua non edas, carpis mea carmina, Laeli. / carpere vel noli nostra vel ede tua.") and 1.110 ("Scribere me quereris, Velox, epigrammata longa. / ipse nihil scribis: tu breviora facis"), parallels which suggest that the unnamed reader, like Laelius and Velox, has probably not written any epigrams himself. Friedlaender proposes another interpretation: "You do not make (my poems) better (by criticizing them)." Despite Housman's harsh dismissal ("not merely wrong but obviously and perversely wrong," 1907: 234), Hutchinson 1993: 24 n. 43 accepts Friedlaender's interpretation, and Barié and Schindler's translation follows suit ("Ja, das hier ist schlecht, doch du machst es nicht besser"), though they cite the alternative interpretation in a note.

2.9

Scripsi, rescripsit nil Naevia: non dabit ergo.
sed, puto, quod scripsi legerat: ergo dabit.

I wrote; Naevia wrote back nothing: she won't be putting out, then.
But I think she read what I wrote. She *will* put out, then.

Themes.   In this, the book's second monodistich (the first is **2.3**), the focus remains on Martial as writer (*scripsi*)—now not, as in **2.8**, of epigrams but of private letters. With characteristic efficiency the poet sketches a situation in which a man has written a woman, has had no reply, and draws two opposed conclusions from the fact in rapid succession. Some commentators have wondered what might have been contained in Martial's letter. Barié and Schindler ask whether it contained some generous offer on the poet's part, but this would be rather out of character for Martial's *persona* in his relations with women and would deprive the poem of the zing (*sal* and *fel* in Pliny's terms) characteristic of his epigrams. Shackleton Bailey asks in his Loeb edition, "Did the letter contain some sort of blackmail?" La Penna 2000: 87 sees an allusion to the persuasive quality of Martial's writing: Naevia will not be able to resist his seductive style.

More fruitful is the approach taken by Collesso and Izaac: the content of the letter is irrelevant, and what the epigram invites us to consider instead is why Martial should reach the conclusion that he will in the end get what he wants from Naevia. The fact that she sent no reply at first discourages him, but on second thought the fact that she has *not said no* gives him hope. Indeed, the weight of the second line lies on Martial's assumption that Naevia has actually read the letter: "sed, puto, quod scripsi legerat." She might have simply seen the sender's name and refused to read further (cf. Ov. *Ars am.* 1.469: "si non accipiet scriptum inlectumque remittet").

Scherf 2001: 68–69 observes that this poem introduces a sequence of five poems with symmetrically arranged verse lengths (2, 4, 10, 4, 2); see on **2.4** and **2.59** for other such patterns.

Structure. The first part of each line, ending with a diaeresis, refers to the actions of writing and reading ("scripsi, rescripsit nil Naevia"; "sed, puto, quod scripsi legerat"), while the remainder of each line contains Martial's two contradictory conclusions as to whether or not Naevia will yield: *non dabit ergo / ergo dabit*. See Laurens 1989: 260 for an appreciation of "ce monologue naturel et vif où l'humoriste s'est plu à ménager d'ironiques effets de miroirs." He aptly compares 9.10 ("Nubere vis Prisco: non miror, Paula; sapisti. / ducere te non vult Priscus: et ille sapit.") and, for the reinforcement of the parallelism between the two lines effected by linguistic means (*non dabit ergo / ergo dabit*), **2.3**, **2.25**, **2.38**, and others (p. 297).

1 *scripsi:* For letters between actual or potential lovers, sometimes on Vitellian tablets (see on **2.6.6**), see also 14.6 and 14.8. The practice is a central feature of the world depicted in Roman elegiac poetry (Ov. *Am.* 1.11.1–8, 2.2.5–6, 2.19.41, *Ars am.* 1.383, 3.469–470; Prop. 4.3) and lies behind Ovid's literary experiment, the *Heroides*. See further Peter 1901: 188–194. Note the double alliteration in ***scripsi, rescripsit nil Naevia***.

1 *Naevia:* The name appears again in 1.68 and 1.106 (where she is Rufus' unfaithful partner), **2.26** (where she manipulates Bithynicus into courting her), and 3.13 (where she mistreats her cook). It is interesting that Martial uses the name only in the first three books and then never again; compare Selius (**2.11**) and Postumus (**2.10**). For Martial's female addressees, see on **2.25.1**.

1 *non dabit:* The verb *dare* is capable of a double meaning, referring to the bestowal of sexual favors (*OLD* s.v. 4d), as in Italian slang *darla* or English "put out." It can refer to the activity of either partner in a penetrative sexual encounter: see, for example, Suet. *Jul.* 49.3 (Cicero's scathing remark to Caesar regarding the latter's relationship with Nicomedes: "notum est et quid ille tibi et quid illi tute dederis"), where it is used to refer to both partners. In Book II alone, see **2.25**, **2.49**, and **2.56**.

2 *puto . . . ergo:* The shortening of the final -*o* of each of these words is an example of "correption," a phenomenon with a long history (see KS 1.112–113) and, thanks to the metrical flexibility it affords, occurring frequently indeed in Latin verse, especially with first-person singular verb forms. In Book II alone, see **2.10.2** (*laudo*), **2.14.18** (*rogo*), **2.18.1** (*capto*), **2.21.2** (*malo*), **2.25.2** (*rogo*), **2.28.6** (*nescio*), **2.30.6** (*peto* twice), **2.33.1–3** (*basio* three times), **2.36.2, 4** (*nolo*), **2.37.3** (the noun *pedico*), **2.41.2** (*puto*), **2.55.3** (*colo*), **2.56.4** (*ergo*), **2.57.8** (*octo*), **2.59.1** (*cenatio*), **2.63.4** (*amo*), **2.67.4** (*puto*), **2.71.6** (*malo*), **2.75.1** (*leo*), **2.79.2** (*rogo, ceno*), **2.80.2** (*rogo*), **2.86.2** (*lego*), **2.90.4** (*nemo*).

2.10

Basia dimidio quod das mihi, Postume, labro,
    laudo: licet demas hinc quoque dimidium.
vis dare maius adhuc et inenarrabile munus?
    hoc tibi habe totum, Postume, dimidium.

You give me kisses with half your lips, Postumus: splendid! In fact, you can take away half of that. Would you like to give me an even greater gift, one that defies description? Keep the whole half to yourself, Postumus.

Themes.   As in the preceding epigram, the poet sets up a situation in which he is personally involved (*mihi*) in order to satirize someone else. With this, the first of several epigrams in Book II concerning Postumus and his repulsive kisses, is initiated what Barwick and others after him have referred to as the "Postumus cycle" (**2.10**, **2.12**, **2.21–23**). Also worth considering is the possibility of a sequential reading: moving from **2.10** through to **2.15** we encounter Postumus, Selius, Postumus, Sextus, Selius, and Hormus (a variant on Postumus); that is, the pattern is ABACBA'. At the same time there is a pleasing metrical variety: elegiac couplets (**2.10**), choliambics (**2.11**), elegiac couplets (**2.12**), two-line hendecasyllabics (**2.13**), elegiac couplets (**2.14**), two-line hendecasyllabics (**2.15**), or ABACAC.

This introductory poem makes clear one thing in a distinctly lighthearted way: that the poet wishes at all costs to avoid Postumus' kisses. There is as yet no hint as to the cause of the poet's distaste: it might simply be that Postumus suffers from bad breath (thus Izaac on **2.21**: "il craint d'être asphyxié par son haleine"; cf. 3.17, 3.28), but an experienced reader of Martial, and perhaps any Roman reader, will guess at the possibility that Postumus has befouled his mouth by means of oral sex, whether fellatio or cunnilinctus (see Williams 1999: 197–203 for the frequent overlaps between the two practices; Barié and Schindler ad loc., Holzberg 2002: 98, and Lorenz 2002: 120 n. 35 assume that Postumus is specifically a *fellator*). Similarly, referring to Mart. 11.98, Housman 1907: 257 claims that "when a Roman reader's eye fell upon a poem written in scazons and having the word *basiator* in the first line, he knew what was coming." For the association between oral sex and the "dirty mouth" (*os impurum*), see, among many others, **2.50**, **2.61**, **2.70**, 3.75, 6.50, 9.63, 14.70, with Richlin 1992: 26–30, Obermayer 1998: 214–231, and note Martial's characteristically lapidary formulation in 11.95: "Whenever you encounter fellators' kisses, imagine that you are lowering your head into a bathtub" ("Incideris quotiens in basia fellatorum, / in solium puta te mergere, Flacce, caput").

"Kissing with half one's lips" is a peculiar formulation (does it refer to giving a light touch of the lips?), but regardless of exactly what kind of kiss is at stake, the point is that Postumus greets Martial only perfunctorily (to change the metaphor, half-heartedly), presumably out of a sense of social superiority (cf. Sen. *Dial.* 4.24.1: "ille me parum humane salutavit; ille osculo meo non adhaesit"). The poet then turns the tables, here and elsewhere exposing Postumus himself as one who is truly worthy of being kept at a distance; a similar technique is found in **2.15**.

The poem's imagery seems characteristically Roman, as there may be a hint at a mathematical puzzle: if you halve a whole and then subtract half of that half (cf. *OLD* s.v. *demo* 4b), what are you left with? For the centrality of arithmetic in the education of the young Roman, see Hor. *A.P.* 325–330, where manipulation of fractions is likewise at stake. Interestingly enough, the mathematical element is missing in an otherwise similar epigram by Nikarkhos ("If you kiss me, you hate me. And if you hate me, you kiss me. But if you don't hate me, my friend, don't kiss me": *A.P.* 11.252).

Structure.   The situation is, as often, concisely sketched in the first verse, and the rest of the poem is taken up with the poet's reaction. At the same time there is a notable progression from an introductory statement of fact (*quod das*) to a comment (*laudo*) to an indirect request (*licet demas*) to a rhetorical question (*vis dare?*) leading up to the punch line in the form of a direct imperative (*habe*).

The repetition of the vocative *Postume* in the second half of the first and final lines respectively is a fairly common device in Martial's elegiac epigrams (in Book II alone see **2.18–19**, **2.43**, **2.60**, **2.67**, **2.71–72**) but rarely found elsewhere; in Catullus, for example, we find it only in the hendecasyllabic poem 13. The technique often functions by way of emphasizing a bipartite structure (Laurens 1989: 270).

1 *basia . . . quod das:* A frequent opening technique in Martial is to begin with a *quod*-clause that brings to our attention the person or activity to be commented upon; see Citroni ad 1.8.1 and, in Book II alone, **2.11**, **2.15**, **2.26**, **2.50**, **2.62**, **2.68**, **2.86**, **2.89**. For the practice of greeting friends or acquaintances with a kiss ("social kissing"), see also 7.95, 11.95, 11.98 (with Kay ad loc.), 12.26, 12.59. The practice seems to have come to Rome from eastern courts during the Augustan period; under Tiberius it was apparently usual only among the nobility (Plin. *N.H.* 26.3), but by Martial's day it had become widespread.

The collocution *basia dare* reappears in two other poems on Postumus (**2.21.1**, **2.22.3–4**) and frequently elsewhere in Martial (6.34.1, 6.50.6, 8.46.6, 9.93.7, 11.6.14, 11.23.10, 11.26.3); otherwise, it is attested only at Catull. 5.7. It substitutes for the metrically intractable *osculare* or *basiare* (Schneider 1909: 31); other periphrases include *oscula dare* (11.23.13, 13.18.2), *basia carpere* (4.22.7, 5.46.1), *basia terere* (11.22.2), *basia imprimere* (10.42.5).

1 *dimidio . . . labro:* In the singular, *labrum* literally refers to a single lip, but Martial's peculiar phrase, attested here and in **2.22** but nowhere else in extant Latin literature, surely means "half of your lips" rather than "half of a lip": at **2.22.3** *dimidio labro* is opposed to *labro utroque*. Izaac, Barié and Schindler, and Scandola render it literally ("la moitié d'une lèvre"; "mit halber Lippe"; "a mezzo labbro"); Ceronetti translates "con mezza bocca" here but, inconsistently, "con mezzo labro" at **2.22.3**.

1 *Postume:* See on **2.23.1–2** for the possibility that there was a real man lying behind the object of the kiss poems. Otherwise, the name appears in various contexts (**2.67**, **2.72**, 4.26, 4.40, 5.52, 5.58, 6.19) and, unlike Selius (**2.11**) or Zoilus (**2.16**), is not associated with a single dominant image. The name never appears after Book VI, as if, in the interest of variety, Martial decided not to recycle it (cf. on *Naevia* at **2.9.1**).

2 *laudo:* Appearing at the beginning of the second line, this verb comes as a surprise, since one would hardly expect such a reaction to Postumus' cool greeting. For parenthetical or exclamatory *laudo,* apparently a colloquial usage, see also 3.69.3, Plaut. *Curc.* 670, Cic. *S. Rosc.* 137, with *OLD* s.v. 2. For the correption of the final vowel, see on **2.9.2.**

3-4 *vis dare... munus? / hoc tibi habe:* For the "rhetorical" question followed by an answer which brings home the point, see on **2.7.8.** The adjective *inenarrabile* is rather drastic (cf. Vell. 2.99.2: "mira quadam et incredibili atque inenarrabili pietate").

For the phrase *tibi habe,* a fairly direct expression of rejection (*TLL* 6.2429.21–48), compare **2.48.8,** 8.37.3, 10.51.16, 13.53.2; Plaut. *Bacch.* 1143; Cic. *Verr.* 2.4.18, 2.4.151 ("tibi habe sane istam laudationem"); Sen. *Ben.* 6.23.8 ("nolo. sibi habeat."); Juv. 3.187–188, 5.118.

4 *totum, Postume, dimidium:* The positioning of the vocative immediately after the principal caesura of the final line is typical; see **2.18.8, 2.19.4, 2.24.8, 2.35.2, 2.36.6, 2.42.2, 2.43.16, 2.46.10, 2.50.2, 2.58.2, 2.67.4, 2.71.6, 2.72.8, 2.78.2, 2.81.2, 2.84.4, 2.87.2.**

The phrase *totum dimidium* is slightly paradoxical. For even more obvious paradoxes at the end of epigrams, see on **2.12.4.** A similar play on *dimidium* and *totum* is found in 1.75: "Dimidium donare Lino quam credere totum / qui mavult, mavult perdere dimidium."

2.11

Quod fronte Selium nubila vides, Rufe,
quod ambulator porticum terit seram,
lugubre quiddam quod tacet piger vultus,
quod paene terram nasus indecens tangit,
quod dextra pectus pulsat et comam vellit: 5
non ille amici fata luget aut fratris,
uterque natus vivit et precor vivat,
salva est et uxor sarcinaeque servique,
nihil colonus vilicusque decoxit.
maeroris igitur causa quae? domi cenat.   10

You see Selius' face clouded over, Rufus; he walks around the portico late in the day; his sluggish expression hints at a silent grief; he almost touches ugly nose to ground; he beats his breast with his

right hand and tears at his hair. Yet he is not mourning the death of
a friend or brother; each of his two sons is alive, and I pray they
may continue to live; his wife, his possessions, his slaves are all safe
and sound; neither his tenant farmer nor his overseer has wasted
his resources away. So what is the reason for his mourning? He's
having dinner at home.

Themes.   Another memorable character is introduced, as is a theme of some
importance to Book II and Martial's epigrams in general: the hunt for dinner
invitations. Barwick 1958: 300–301 speaks of a "cycle" of epigrams on Selius
(**2.11**, **2.14**, **2.27**; mentioned at **2.69.6**) introduced by the present epigram,
observing that **2.11** and **2.14** offer a variation on more or less the same theme
but in different meters, and detecting a pattern in the arrangement: in **2.11**
Selius has been unsuccessful in his quest; in **2.14** it remains unclear whether
he is successful or not; in **2.27** he has succeeded.

The dinner, or *cena,* and the various types of social (mis)behavior associated with it constitute a central theme of Martial's epigrams: in Book II alone,
see **2.14**, **2.18–19**, **2.27**, **2.37**, **2.40**, **2.53**, **2.57**, **2.59**, **2.69**, **2.79**. While the
subject matter was clearly taken from everyday life (see Marquardt 1886: 289–
331, D'Arms 1990), Martial had literary precedents to drawn upon as well; some
examples among many include Catull. 13, 44, 47, Hor. *Sat.* 2.8. This epigram
introduces us to the problem neatly described by Sullivan 1991: 160 as "the
undignified scrounging for dinner invitations": see **2.14**, **2.27**, **2.53**, **2.69**, **2.79**,
5.44, 5.50, 9.10, 9.14, 9.19, 9.35, 11.77, 12.82, and see Damon 1997: 148–158
for the figure of the "parasite" in Martial. At Juv. 1.132–134 we find a description of characters like Selius, though they are pitied rather than ridiculed.

Modern scholarship on the phenomenon described here sometimes uses
the term *captatio cenae* ("dinner hunting"), a handy phrase inspired by language such as Martial's *cenam captare* in **2.18** and 7.20, and men like Selius
are variously called *cenipetae* ("dinner seekers": Szelest 1986: 2585 and Prinz
1911: 37–39, who adds the Greek equivalent τρεχέδειπνος, "dinner runner")
or *laudiceni* ("dinner praisers": Szelest 1986: 2585). The noun *cenipeta* is not
actually attested in any surviving classical text, but this may be an accident of
survival, as the presumably late-antique or medieval lemma to **2.37** in E reads
Ad Caecilianum cenipetam (L *Ad Celipetam*). For *laudiceni,* on the other hand,
we have the explicit testimony of Pliny the Younger (*Epist.* 2.14.5).

This epigram is characteristic not only in its subject matter but also in its
tone (satiric but not savage) and structure (building up a scenario, posing a
question, and offering an unexpected, sharply pointed answer, or *aprosdoke-*
ton), and it has been singled out for praise by various critics over the centuries (Pontanus, *De sermone* III.xviii [1499]), Van Stockum 1884: 77, Laurens
1989: 317, Sullivan 1991: 242).

This is the first appearance of the scazon, or choliambic, meter in Book II; see also **2.17**, **2.57**, **2.65**, **2.74**. The meter was traditionally associated with an aggressively satirical tone, most famously in the case of the archaic Greek poet Hipponax. In this case Salemme 1976: 54 sees the meter as expressing an "ironia canzonatoria."

Structure. A description of Selius' distraught behavior (1–5) is followed by the affirmation that none of the expected causes is at stake (6–9) and a final question-and-answer line culminating in a two-word point (10); Salemme 1976: 67–68 thus speaks of a "triple rhythm." Each element in the description of Selius in 1–5 (Laurens 1989: 317 calls them "savamment graduées") occupies a single line and takes the form of a *quod*-clause; each rejected explanation in 6–9 similarly takes up a whole verse. For the vivid accumulative technique, see on **2.7**, and for sequences of subordinate clauses compare **2.53**, **2.57**, **2.62**, **2.89**, with Siedschlag 1977: 41, who points out that the technique is barely attested in Greek epigram, and Laurens 1989: 325.

The positioning of the conjunction *quod* is noteworthy. In 1–2 it begins the lines; in the central verse, 3, it is found in the middle of the verse, after the caesura; in 4–5 it is once again at the beginning. Verses 6–9 display a different but equally chiastic structure. Verse 6 begins emphatically with *non,* thus signaling that various explanations are being rejected; 7–8 are phrased affirmatively; 9 returns to a negative formulation, beginning emphatically with *nihil.* Thus, each half of the poem's first part is given a chiastic structure, and the entire epigram has the structure ABACDCE. At the same time the epigram is framed by two lively devices: deictic *vides* and the question-and-answer format.

A tripartite structure is also provided by the "*quod-non-sed* structure" (Siedschlag 1977: 65–68) found here and elsewhere in Martial's epigrams: see *Sp.* 17, 1.28, **2.15**, **2.26**, 3.62, 4.80, 7.31, 9.62, 12.89, 14.88. In the present case *sed* is implied: *quod vides . . . non luget . . . (sed) domi cenat.* The medieval poet Godfrey of Winchester imitates the technique in some of his epigrams (Maaz 1992: 64).

1 *quod:* See on **2.10.1** for this opening technique.

1 *fronte . . . nubila:* In this poetic expression, the metaphorical use of *nubila* is perhaps Ovidian in inspiration: compare 6.10.5 ("nulla nubilus ira"), Ov. *Met.* 5.512 ("toto nubila vultu"). As the *variorum* commentary observes, *nubila* in this sense is the opposite of *serena* (cf. **2.24.7**, *ore sereno*), the metaphor in both cases being that of the sky's appearance.

1 *Selium:* He appears again only in **2.14**, **2.27**, and **2.69**, and most likely represents a "type" rather than a real man hidden behind a pseudonym. See on **2.16.1** for the comparable case of Zoilus.

1 *vides:* For the technique of opening an epigram with a deictic verb of seeing, compare **2.29.1** (*vides*), **2.57.1** (*videtis*), and **2.74.4** (*cernis*), with Grewing ad 6.38.1 ("aspicis ut . . . ?").

1 *Rufe:* Rufus is the most frequently occurring personal name in all of Martial (33 occurrences) after Caesar (126 occurrences!); it is followed by Flaccus (31 occurrences). Since Rufus is a cognomen, it could refer to any number of different men, fictional or real; Martial often distinguishes among the latter by specifying their nomina (e.g., Camonius Rufus, Canius Rufus, Julius Rufus, Safronius Rufus; see Nauta 2002: 41–47). Friedlaender tentatively identifies the man addressed in this epigram, and perhaps also in **2.29**, 4.13, and 4.82, with Martial's friend Canius Rufus, a poet and historian from Cadiz (1.61, 1.69, 3.20, 7.69, 10.48), but since the current epigram gives us no direct information about its addressee, the identification is hardly compelling.

Indeed, as in several others out of the seventy-one epigrams in Book II having a vocative addressee (**2.17**, **2.29**, **2.31**, **2.74**, **2.84**, and probably **2.48**), the addressee here has no obvious relationship to the epigram's subject. The vocative serves primarily to create an atmosphere of lively discussion: we overhear Martial pointing out Selius' absurd behavior to his friend Rufus, who himself remains in the shadows. Nauta 2002: 46 suggests that such "isolated vocatives" will generally have referred to real persons to whom the poem was dedicated "as a mark of homage," but it is worth emphasizing that, given the plurality of men named Rufus and the lack of specificity in this and other examples, such homage would have been a private matter.

2 *ambulator porticum terit seram:* It was a common habit to take strolls through the porticoes of the Campus Martius in the late afternoon and early evening, after the day's business was done but before dinner: see also **2.14.16** (*serum carpit iter*) and 3.20.2 (*porticum terit*). These porticoes, and the adjoining temples and shops, as well as the *thermae,* where one might bathe before the evening meal, were thus sought out by those interested in snagging a dinner invitation. Some claim that the *porticus* of this verse is specifically the "Portico of Europa," to which Martial alludes in conjunction with Selius at **2.14.3** (Collesso, Norcio, Merli), but a first-time reader of this epigram will probably not be led to think of any particular portico.

Martial is fond of using *tero,* as here, with a spatial direct object (*OLD* s.v. 5b, "to tread or traverse [ground] repeatedly"): compare **2.29.1** (*subsellia prima*), 3.20.10 (*porticum*), 10.10.2 (*limina mille*), 10.28.4 (*medium iter*), 11.13.1 (*Flaminiam*), 12.18.3 (*collem*), 12.29.1 (*limina*), 14.51.2 (*lintea*).

The phrase *porticum . . . seram* is unusual, probably poetic in tone, as *serus* ("occurring at a late hour") normally modifies actions, events, and conditions (cf. **2.14.16**: *serum carpat iter;* Liv. 28.15.3: *sera pugna*) rather than, as here and at 6.89.1 ("cum peteret seram media iam nocte matellam"), a static object or place. Manuscripts of family β read *sera* rather than *seram,* and Lindsay comments in his apparatus that this is just possibly correct; if so, *sera* would stand for *sera hora;* compare Ov. *Her.* 19.14 (*serior hora*) and Italian *sera.*

3 *piger vultus:* Like *fronte nubila,* this is a striking phrase in that *piger* ("lazy") does not usually describe faces or facial expressions. The *variorum* commentary explains the image: a sad man looks slow and lazy ("quia maestus pigro similis et lento").

Although many modern editors print *voltus,* the shift from *vo* to *vu* in *volnus, volt, servos,* etc. > *vulnus, vult, servus,* etc., was more or less complete by Martial's day (LHS 1.49). It is thus almost certain that Martial himself wrote *vultus,* etc., and consequently, like Shackleton Bailey, I print the forms in *vu* (see, e.g., **2.29.6**). Lindsay 1904: 32–33 suggests, by contrast, that Martial himself may not have been consistent and argues for flexibility based on the MS readings.

4 *indecens:* Like most translators, I have taken this as an attributive adjective modifying *nasus* ("his ugly nose almost touches the ground"). For this sense of the adjective, compare 5.37.12: "cui comparatus indecens erat pavo." A parallel suggests itself between *nasus indecens* and *piger vultus* (3), and the passing insult of physical appearance is characteristic of Martial (cf. **2.35, 2.87**; Damon 1997: 155 sees a different kind of insult: "his nose— none too clean"). But some translators have taken *indecens* to be adverbial, modifying *tangit* ("his nose almost touches the ground, disgracefully": Izaac, Ceronetti); compare 5.14.7 ("oculoque ludos spectat indecens uno"). In this case there would be no insult of Selius' physical appearance but rather a criticism of his indecent behavior.

5 *pectus pulsat:* Note the expressive alliteration, coincidentally reproducible in English: "beats his breast." The phrase *pectus pulsare* is common throughout Latin literature, and in Martial describes a hypocrite at 5.37.19 (with an extended alliteration: "pectusque pulsans pariter et comam vellens").

6 *non ille amici fata luget aut fratris:* It is interesting to observe that the first possible cause of Selius' distraught appearance proposed by the speaker is the loss of a male friend or of a brother. These two relationships played a central role in Roman male social relations, and the discourses of friendship and brotherly love often overlap: see, for example, Cic. *Att.* 1.5.8 ("te a me fraterne amari"), Ov. *Tr.* 1.3.65 ("quos . . . ego dilexi fraterno more sodales"), Domitius Marsus (*FLP* 300–302), *A.L.* 428 Riese, Mart. 7.24, 9.pr.; Williams 1992: 331–367, Bannon 1997.

7 *vivit et precor vivat:* A fervently expressed wish; see Wills 1996: 307 for discussion of the phenomenon ("verb-shift"). Examples, often with a verb like *precor* or *rogo,* include V. *Aen.* 12.828 ("*occidit, occideritque* sinas cum nomine Troia"), Ov. *Pont.* 1.9.5–6 ("nec quicquam ad nostras *pervenit* acerbius aures, / ut sumus in Ponto, *perveniatque precor*"), *Pont.* 2.6.15

("idque *facis faciasque precor*"), *Pont*. 3.1.90 ("quod *facis* ut *facias* teque imitere rogo").

8 *salva est et uxor sarcinaeque servique:* It is striking, but not surprising in a Roman context, that Martial groups Selius' wife along with his slaves and possessions rather than with his sons. For the division of one's possessions into human and nonhuman, as well as for the alliteration (*salva . . . sarcinaeque servique*) and the use of the adjective *salva,* we might compare a phrase from Cato's prayer for the *suovetaurilia* preserved in his treatise *De agricultura* (141): "pastores pecoraque salva servassis." It may be that Martial is drawing on some ancient, solemn formulations.

The primary meaning of *sarcina* is "a bundle of things tied together so as to be conveniently carried by a man or animal" (*OLD* s.v.; cf. *sarcio,* "mend, repair"); compare 8.75.14. In the plural, *sarcinae* can refer to any movable goods or belongings (**2.68.4**, 12.32.2, 12.32.25). Bridge and Lake describe Martial's use of the noun to mean "property" as colloquial, but [Quint.] *Decl.* 12.13 ("iacent relictae sine herede sarcinae") suggests otherwise.

Garrido-Hory 1981: 91–92 observes that the term *servus,* as opposed to *puer* or *minister,* is often found in the context of enumerations of property.

9 *colonus vilicusque:* The former is a freeborn tenant farmer, the latter, a slave in charge of the other slaves of a country estate, accountable either to the master himself or to his *procurator* (see Colum. 11.1 with Marquardt 1886: 139). Martial's remark reveals an awareness of the potential risk involved with these two types of dependents. Elsewhere, in more humorous vein, he imagines a potential advantage: among the pleasures of life in an Italian town is the possibility of having sexual relations with the wife of one's *vilicus* or *colonus* (4.66.11). The *vilicus* and *colonus* are again cited together at 7.31.9; see also Colum. 1.7.6 ("cum omne genus agri tolerabilius sit sub liberis colonis quam sub vilicis servis habere") and Sen. *Epist.* 123.2 (*vilicus, atriensis, colonus*).

9 *decoxit:* The verb literally means "to boil down, melt down, melt away," and is here, as elsewhere, most likely used transitively in a figurative sense to refer to squandering money or property, taking objects like *patrimonium* or *pecuniam* (*OLD* s.v. 4, *TLL* 5.1.205.12–35). Ker and Shackleton Bailey translate "default," a meaning the verb can have when intransitive (*OLD* s.v. 5); if that is the sense here, *nihil* is not the direct object of *decoxit* but rather an adverb.

10 *maeroris igitur causa quae?* For the closing technique of posing a "rhetorical" question and immediately supplying its answer, see on **2.7.8**. *Maeror* is a fairly strong word. This is the only occurrence of the noun in Martial, while the verb *maereo* occurs twice (9.5.5: "virilitatis damna maeret ereptae"; 14.217.2: "captas non sibi maeret aves"). Martial uses the adjective *maestus* to describe a mother mourning the death of a child (**2.41.19**), himself upon a friend's death (6.85.11), and the sufferings of the mythological figure Io (**2.14.8**). Illustrative examples of the intensity of *maeror* in other authors include Lucr. 5.175 ("in tenebris vita ac maerore iacebat"), Cic. *Att.* 3.17.1 ("sane sum in meo infinito maerore sollicitus"), Sen. *Herc. F.* 705 (in Hades, "cuncta maerore horrida"), Tac. *Ann.* 12.26 ("nemo . . . fuit quem non Britannici fortuna maerore adficeret"). There is thus a comic effect when *maeror* is used to describe Selius' feelings at not having received a dinner invitation.

10 domi cenat: Presumably alone, because no one else has invited him to dinner. In the group-oriented, status-conscious world of Martial's Rome, dining alone at home could be taken as a sign that one has received no invitations, and perhaps for a good reason; thus, a mere allusion to *domi cenare* could suffice to make a point. Not only does the phrase appear on several other occasions in Martial (**2.14.2**, **2.79.2** [where *ceno domi* likewise constitutes the epigram's sharp point], 3.50.10, 5.47.1, 5.50.1, 6.94.2 with Grewing, 11.24.15, 12.19.2; contrast *cenare foris* at **2.53.3**, **2.69.1**, 9.10.1), but the poet uses and indeed perhaps coins the noun *domicenium:* see 5.78.1 ("si tristi domicenio laboras") and 12.77.6 (where Martial jokingly represents *domicenium* as the punishment inflicted by Jupiter on a man for having farted in his temple). See further Braund 1996, and consider the etymology reported by Plutarch (*Mor.* 726e: *cena* was derived from κοινωνία), as well as the saying of Epicurus repeated by Seneca (*Epist.* 19.10): to eat without friends is to live the life of a lion or a wolf.

2.12

Esse quid hoc dicam, quod olent tua basia murram
   quodque tibi est numquam non alienus odor?
hoc mihi suspectum est, quod oles bene, Postume, semper.
   Postume, non bene olet qui bene semper olet.

What am I to make of the fact that your kisses smell of myrrh, and that you never have an odor that doesn't come from somewhere else? It strikes me as suspicious that you always smell good, Postumus. Postumus, whoever smells good all the time does not smell good.

Themes.   After an interlude on Selius in choliambics (**2.11**) we return to the elegiac meter and theme of **2.10**—Postumus' repulsive kisses—and further detail is added: Postumus attempts to cover up his bad breath with myrrh. Martial sees through the trick and delivers a damning and characteristically paradoxical *sententia* to the effect that one who always smells of perfume must be trying to cover something up. Closely comparable is an epigram on Fescennia's attempt to cover up her winy breath by sucking on lozenges (1.87). For other allusions to unpleasant mouth and body odors, see 4.4.12, 6.93, 11.30, 13.18 (from eating leeks), and for attempts to cover them up, 3.63.4, 5.4 (Myrtale eats laurel leaves to cover up the smell of wine), 7.41, 13.101.2.

Walter 1995: 108 proposes that there is a pun in *bene olere,* but the equivalence "smell good" = "have a good reputation" seems to be characteristic only of German (*in gutem Geruch stehen*) and not of Latin. Walter also detects an allusion to bad breath as a sign of *cinaedi* or *pathici,* but there is no compelling evidence for such a belief in antiquity. If there is any hint at sexual practices in this epigram, cunnilinctus and/or fellatio are at stake, and neither of these practices was necessarily associated with *cinaedi;* see on **2.10**.

Structure.   The epigram readily lends itself to a bipartite analysis: the situation is sketched in the first couplet, and commentary is provided in the second. The fact that the first couplet takes the form of a question subtly links the poem's two halves, as it creates the expectation of a reply. Observe also the sequence *olent* (1), *odor* (2), *oles* (3), *olet . . . olet* (4), and see Laurens 1989: 275 for the epigram's careful buildup to its sententious point. Salemme 1976: 57 is unimpressed, including the technique found in this epigram among those which quickly become tiresome ("molto presto stancano").

1 *esse quid hoc dicam:* For the technique of opening with a question and then answering it, compare 1.praef. epigr., **2.65**, 4.7, 5.10 ("esse quid hoc dicam?"), 5.44, 5.55, 9.66, 10.10, 10.65, 12.91, 14.215; Catull. 28, 89; Ov. *Am.* 1.2.1 ("esse quid hoc dicam?"); *Priap.* 44.1; Siedschlag 1977: 22–23. It seems to have been imitated by the medieval poet Godfrey of Winchester (Maaz 1992: 63). Detecting a specific echo of Ov. *Am.* 1.2.1, Siedschlag 1977: 116–117 observes that allusions found in the first verse of Martial's epigrams are often to phrases found in the first verse of the earlier text: compare 1.15.1 (Ov. *Trist.* 1.5.1), 1.70.1 (Ov. *Trist.* 3.7.1), 1.108.1 (Ov. *Trist.* 1.10.1), 8.23.1 (*A.L.* 431 Riese).

1 *murram:* The aromatic resin of the bush *Commiphora myrrha* was frequently used in perfumes, cosmetics, and medicines (Theophr. *Hist. pl.* 9.4.2–9, Plin. *N.H.* 12.35; Miller 1969).

2 *numquam non alienus odor:* A rhetorically colored equivalent of *semper alienus odor* or *numquam tuus odor*. Martial uses the same litotes in the phrase *non alienus eques* (5.19.10, 14.122.2); compare Cic. *Verr.* 4.80 ("non alienam mihi laudem appeto").

3–4 *Postume . . . Postume:* The close repetition of the vocative leading into a paradoxical *sententia* has a jabbing effect; compare 1.79.3–4. The vocative serves not merely to specify the victim's name, but in 3 underscores the significant word *semper* and in 4 introduces the closing pronouncement (Laurens 1989: 271).

4 *non bene olet qui bene semper olet:* A striking example of several characteristic ending techniques at once: the delivery of the point in the form of a *sententia,* the use of paradox, the repetition of a key word (*bene*), and homoeoteleuton (*olet . . . olet*). For other examples of a final *sententia* see **2.18** ("qui rex est regem . . . non habeat"), **2.20** ("quod emas possis iure vocare tuum"), **2.32** ("sit liber, dominus qui volet esse meus"), **2.44** ("quanto durius [est negare] antequam rogeris"), among many others; in Greek epigram, see *A.P.* 5.72, 11.18, 11.31, 11.47, 12.12 (Pertsch 1911: 41–42). For the final paradox, compare 1.72 ("calvus cum fueris, eris comatus"), 1.90 ("hic ubi vir non est, ut sit adulterium"), **2.80** ("ne moriare mori"), 3.34 ("non es et es Chione"), 3.39 ("quam bene lusca videt"), and others. For the repetition of a key word, often in paradoxical formulations, compare *Sp.* 9.4 ("quantus erat taurus, cui pila taurus erat"), 1.46 ("si properas, dic mihi ne properem"), **2.18** ("qui rex est regem . . . non habeat"), 3.90 ("vult, non vult dare . . . nec dicere possum, / quod vult et non vult, quid sibi Galla velit"), 5.83 ("velle tuum nolo, Dindyme, nolle volo"), 6.11 ("ut ameris, ama," with Grewing ad loc.), 7.73 ("quisquis ubique habitat, Maxime, nusquam habitat"), and others. For homoeoteleuton that establishes a parallelism or antithesis, compare *Sp.* 2.12 (*populi/domini*), 1.31.8 (*tonsum/virum*), 3.26.2 (*solus habes/solus habes*), 9.21.4 (*amat/arat*), with Pertsch 1911: 54.

Martial's well-turned phrase reappears at 6.55.5 ("malo quam bene olere nil olere") and was later quoted, but falsely attributed to Petronius, by Jerome (*Epist.* 130.19). It is hard to say whether Auson. *Epigr.* 125.2 ("nec male olere mihi nec bene olere placet") is directly inspired by Martial, since Martial seems to be drawing on a proverbial saying: see Plaut. *Most.* 273 ("mulier recte olet, ubi nihil olet"), Cic. *Att.* 2.1.1 ("ut mulieres ideo bene olere, quia nihil olebant, videbantur"), and compare Sen. *Epist.* 108.16 ("optimus odor in corpore est nullus"). Salanitro 1998–1999 suggests that Martial's phrase derives from a Menippean satire of Varro. If, as the passages from Plautus and Cicero suggest, the phrase was particularly connected with women, the insult takes on a particular point.

2.13

Et iudex petit et petit patronus.
solvas censeo, Sexte, creditori.

Both the judge and your lawyer are asking for money. It is my rec-
ommendation, Sextus, that you pay back your creditor!

Themes.   Returning to hendecasyllabics (**2.4**, **2.6**) and to the two-line format (**2.3**, **2.9**), the poet broaches yet another recurring topic in his social
satire: the vicissitudes associated with moneylending, for which see on **2.3**.
Sextus has been brought before court for nonpayment of debt (Friedlaender
suggests that Sextus has initiated the proceedings himself) and has hired a
patronus to defend him. Now not only is the *patronus* asking for his fee,
but the judge is demanding a bribe, and Martial's wry advice is presumably
prompted by the consideration that the cost of paying off both judge and
lawyer would exceed the debt itself.

Structure.   Martial's two-line epigrams are most often elegiac monodistichs
(see on **2.3**); there is only one other two-line hendecasyllabic poem in Book
II (**2.15**). The epigram falls naturally into two halves, the situation being
sketched in the first verse and commentary provided in the second. Here the
dryly humorous effect is heightened by the asyndeton abruptly introducing
the poet's response in the second line.

  1: Note the chiastic order *iudex petit . . . petit patronus* adorned by the
symmetrically positioned *et . . . et*.
  Although in the context of criminal law the function of *iudices* combined
those of modern jurors and judges, the present epigram alludes to a civil
procedure, in which the *iudex* was usually a single individual appointed
(normally by both parties involved, after having been approved by the responsible magistrate) to conduct the hearing. In Martial's day *patroni* might
legitimately accept a small fee or honorarium (3.38.6 with Walter 1995), but
iudices obviously not. Bribery of jurors or judges was a much lamented risk
(see Petr. *Sat.* 14.2: "ergo iudicium nihil est nisi publica merces, / atque eques
in causa qui sedet empta probat"; and Dio 54.18.3) and could provoke excesses of moralizing outrage, as in the case of the trial of P. Clodius Pulcher
in 61 B.C. (Cic. *Att.* 1.16.5, 1.18.3, *Mil.* 87, Dio 37.45–46, Val. Max. 9.1.7,
Sen. *Epist.* 97.2).

1 *petit:* Martial often uses this verb with money as its implicit or explicit object: see 1.76.5 ("quid petis a Phoebo? nummos habet arca Minervae"), **2.30.6** ("quod peto da, Gai: non peto consilium"), **2.44.5** ("ne quid forte petam timet cavetque"), 3.61, 4.76.1, 10.15.3 ("mutua cum peterem sestertia quinque"), 10.70.13–14 ("centumque petuntur / quadrantes").

1 *patronus:* An important item in the Roman language of social relations, *patronus* (derived from *pater*) denotes various roles in which a man might exert influence, protection, or authority over another, such as a *libertus* (5.34, 5.70, 6.28–29, 9.73, 10.34) or, as here, a defendant in a legal action. In the latter case, *patronus* is thus the equivalent of *causidicus* (see 1.97.2 with Citroni ad loc., **2.27.2**, 7.72.14). Although Martial has much to say about *clientela* (see on **2.18**), he never uses the term *patronus* to refer to a "patron" of a "client" (*pace* the *OLD* entry, 5.34 refers to the former masters of a dead slave girl), nor indeed does any other classical literary writer; *amicus* (e.g., **2.32.7**) is generally preferred to the blunt *patronus*. (See White 1978: 79, who discusses the one apparent exception at Hor. *Epist.* 1.7, and Saller 1982: 10, who observes that inscriptions of the classical period do use the term in this sense.)

2 *censeo:* The verb suggests a response to a deliberative question previously posed by Sextus: "Should I pay, or go through with the trial?" (Walter 1995: 101).

2 *Sexte:* See on **2.3.1**.

2 *creditori:* This fairly prosaic word brings home the point with emphasis. Of the numerous occurrences cited in *OLD* and *TLL,* nearly all are found in prose texts, and those few verse passages using the word are all satiric in nature: Hor. *Sat.* 2.3.65, Bibac. fr. 2, Publ. Syrus. Q 33 ("qui debet, limen creditoris non amat"), Mart. 9.3.2, Juv. 7.108, 11.10. The writer of the inscription *CLE* 1001.4 uses the term to refer to Death, and the effect is presumably quite blunt: "in requiem excessi; quod quaeritis, id repetitum / apstulit iniustus creditor ante diem."

2.14

Nil intemptatum Selius, nil linquit inausum,
    cenandum quotiens iam videt esse domi.
currit ad Europen et te, Pauline, tuosque
    laudat Achilleos, sed sine fine, pedes.
si nihil Europe fecit, tunc Saepta petuntur,   5
    si quid Phillyrides praestet et Aesonides.

hinc quoque deceptus Memphitica templa frequentat,
    adsidet et cathedris, maesta iuvenca, tuis.
inde petit centum pendentia tecta columnis,
    illinc Pompei dona nemusque duplex.   10
nec Fortunati spernit nec balnea Fausti,
    nec Grylli tenebras Aeoliamque Lupi:
nam thermis iterumque iterumque iterumque lavatur.
    omnia cum fecit, sed renuente deo,
lotus ad Europes tepidae buxeta recurrit,   15
    si quis ibi serum carpat amicus iter.
per te perque tuam, vector lascive, puellam,
    ad cenam Selium tu, rogo, taure, voca.

Selius leaves nothing untried, nothing unventured, whenever he sees himself compelled to have dinner at home. He runs to Europa and praises you, Paulinus, and your swift Achillean feet, quite interminably at that. If Europa brings him nothing, he then heads for the Saepta to see if perhaps Chiron and Jason will give him something. Frustrated here too, he then spends time at the Egyptian temple, sitting by your ladies' chairs, O sorrowful heifer. From there he goes to the roof supported by a hundred columns, and from there to Pompey's gift and the double grove. Nor does he overlook the baths of Fortunatus or Faustus, nor the shadows of Gryllus and Lupus' cave of the winds; not to mention the public baths, where he washes himself again and again and again. Finally, when he has tried everything but the god still denies him, he runs back, well washed, to the boxwood trees of the sun-warmed Europa, to see if perchance a friend of his is taking a late walk there. I beg you, O wanton girl-bearing bull—I invoke both you and your girl—please invite Selius to dinner yourself.

Themes. We return to third-person commentary and to the figure introduced in **2.11**: Selius, the hunter for dinner invitations. Here his desperate search is given a memorably concrete form as we see him trotting from one meeting place to the next in a poem notable for its combination of gentle satire and lively scenery. Comparable is 12.82, in which Menogenes frequents the *thermae* and *balnea* in order to pester people for an invitation and likewise uses the flattering image *Achilleas comas* (cf. *Achilleos pedes*, 4); see also Statius' representation of his own acquisition of a dinner invitation in *Silvae* 4.6 (Damon 1997: 169).

The technique of anchoring the satire in topography finds a noteworthy precedent in Catull. 55, where the poet recounts his search for a friend through the streets of Rome. In Mart. 5.44 the invitation-seeker Dento is said to have visited the public baths, theaters, and toilets (*thermis, theatris, conclavibus*). Epigrams 3.20 and 11.1 list many of the same places mentioned in the present epigram: the *porticus Argonautarum,* the *buxeta* of Europa, and the *thermae* of Titus and Agrippa in the former; the Porticoes of Pompey, Europa, and the Argonauts as gathering places in the latter. See also 1.70, **2.17**, **2.57**, 3.47, 5.52, 7.73, and 10.51.

Nearly all of the sites mentioned here are located in the Campus Martius, the large area enclosed by the loop of the Tiber between the Theater of Marcellus in the south and the Mausoleum of Augustus in the north. In Martial's day this area was filled with temples, theaters, porticoes, and baths, and thus was a part of the city where one could go to see and be seen, to run into friends or acquaintances. See Sullivan 1991: 151–153, Prior 1996, and Sposi 1997, and, for Martial's topography of Rome overall, Lugli 1961, Castagnoli 1993, Darwall-Smith 1996, Scheithauer 2000: 136–153.

Structure. Lines 1–16 present a detailed description of Selius' behavior; the final couplet, the poet's commentary. But the epigram's artistry is more complex than this. One might, for example, detect a chiastic structure: an outer frame is established by 1–2 (the poet's summary description) and 17–18 (his sarcastic response); within this 3–4 and 15–16 further frame the narrative of Selius' search, which begins and ends with Europa (as Laurens 1989: 234 puts it, "le retour au point de départ produit un effet de boucle ironique"); the central verses 5–13 list the various stops on his route in an easy progression marked by clear connectives (*si nihil Europe fecit; hinc quoque deceptus; inde petit; nec . . . spernit*), and 14 summarizes his failure.

The core of the epigram exemplifies a technique especially characteristic of this poet: a list or sequence of clauses or sentences is used to achieve a cumulative effect; see on **2.7**. Here this is joined to a threefold pattern: statement, accumulation, conclusion (Siedschlag 1977: 43: "Aussage, Häufung, Schlußeffekt"). Compare *Sp.* 3, *Sp.* 21, **2.1**, **2.27**, 4.39, 4.42, 8.46, 8.59, 8.70, 11.5. Siedschlag can find no Latin predecessors for this structure, and in Greek epigram only *A.P.* 11.74 (Nicarchus) and 11.239 (Lucillius).

1–2: The opening couplet, as so often, succinctly sets the scene and establishes the tone. The first line, alluding to Selius' persistent attempts in hyperbolic language (*nil intemptatum, nil inausum*), stands in bathetic contrast to the second: it is all for the sake of an invitation to dinner. The first line has, moreover, a distinctly poetic tone, with its *apo koinou* structure (see on **2.2.1**) and two apparent echoes of earlier poets: for *nil intemptatum* compare Hor. *A.P.* 285 ("nil intemptatum nostri liquere poetae," likewise opening a hexameter) and for *nil linquit inausum* compare V. *Aen.*

7.308 (*nil linquere inausum*, likewise a hexameter clausula). The effect can be described as comic-heroic (Laurens 1989: 228).

3 *ad Europen:* Martial elsewhere refers to a depiction of the rape of Europa by Jupiter in the form of a bull that adorns a public space, probably a portico, planted with boxwood trees (3.20.12, 7.32.11, 11.1.10). In 3.20 and 11.1, as here, it is identified as a meeting place, along with the Porticoes of Pompey and the Argonauts, the former housing another depiction of Europa (Plin. *N.H.* 35.114). Since it is mentioned only by Martial, much about this structure is uncertain: whether the depiction of Europa was a wall painting (Friedlaender) or a sculpture group (Sullivan 1991: 152); whether it was housed in a portico or some other structure with a garden; and where precisely it was located. Some identify the structure with the *porticus Vipsania* (also called the *porticus Pollae*) built by Agrippa's sister Vipsania Polla, but most imagine an independent *porticus Europae* (Platner 1929, Richardson 1992: s.v.). It was clearly located in the Campus Martius, but more specificity regarding the location must elude us: M. R. Russo in Steinby 1993–2000: s.v. *porticus Europae* lists seven different possibilities.

3–4 *te, Pauline, tuosque / laudat Achilleos . . . pedes:* The name *Paulinus* occurs again in 3.78. *Pace* Friedlaender, that epigram does not suggest that he was a well-known runner, nor does the present epigram support Friedlaender's view, taken up by Barié and Schindler, that Paulinus was renowned as a fast runner. The hyperbole *Achilleos pedes* is Selius' rather than Martial's, and Paulinus was probably just exercising (Sullivan 1991: 152): at 7.32.11–12 a structure adorned with a depiction of Europa and the bull is described as a place where one might run for sport. Prior 1996: 129–130 sees 3.78 as hinting that Palinurus is incontinent and *Achilleos pedes* in the present epigram as alluding to his "mad dash for the facilities," but 3.78 is playing on words more than anything else. Damon 1997: 157 suggests that Paulinus is "walking quickly in an attempt to shed Selius."

For Achilles as exemplar of manly strength and beauty (cf. Serv. *Ecl.* 3.79: "virum fortem plerumque Achillem vocamus") but also of towering wrath, see Otto 1890: 3, Sonny 1896: 53, Sutphen 1901: 126, Szelinski 1903: 472. Other mythological exempla include **2.41.14** (Hecuba and Andromache), **2.43.14** (Ganymede), **2.64.3** (Peleus, Priam, and Nestor), and **2.75.10** (the she-wolf); see Weinreich 1928: 31–32, Szelest 1974b.

For the coordinated pronominal pairings *te . . . tuosque Achilleos pedes* and *te . . . tuam puellam* (17), compare Catull. 15.1 (*me ac meos amores*), Catull. 30.9 (*te ac tua dicta omnia*), V. *Aen.* 4.27 (*te aut tua iura*) with Wills 1996: 268.

4 *sed sine fine:* For this use of *sed*, see on **2.6.6**.

5 *Saepta:* Originally, this was a fenced-in space (also called the *ovile,* or "sheepfold") used for popular elections in the area just east of the Pantheon and the Baths of Agrippa and west of the Temple of Isis and Serapis. Julius Caesar began a monumental rebuilding of the structure in marble, and the work was completed by Agrippa, who dedicated it to Caesar's memory as the Saepta Iulia in 26 B.C. (see Steinby 1993–2000: s.v.). The structure outlived its original purpose when Tiberius transferred elections from the people to the Senate; thereupon, it came to be used for spectacles and shows, gladiatorial fights, mock naval battles, and the like. After the Colosseum took over most of these functions in A.D. 80, the Saepta became a public space for strolling and shopping (**2.57**, 9.59, 10.80).

6–10: Note the moderately learned patro- and matronymics *Aesonides* and *Phillyrides,* together with the elevated periphrases *Memphitica templa* (7), *maesta iuvenca* (8), *centum pendentia tecta columnis* (9), *Pompei dona nemusque duplex* (10).

6 *Phillyrides:* Chiron, the centaur son of the Oceanid Philyra and teacher of, among others, the young Achilles; the matronymic is here spelled with a double consonant for metrical reasons. The elder Pliny (*N.H.* 36.29) confirms that there was a sculptural group of Chiron and Achilles located in the Saepta.

6 *Aesonides:* Jason, son of Aeson, hero of the Argonaut cycle of myth. As with the *porticus Europae* (see on 3 above), there is some disagreement among scholars about precisely where this monument (probably a painting depicting Jason) was. Most likely Martial is referring to the *porticus Argonautarum* that he mentions elsewhere (3.20, 11.1). Platner 1929: s.v. places the structure near, or even surrounding, the later Temple of Hadrian and suggests that it was identical with the "stoa of Poseidon" mentioned by Cassius Dio and the *porticus Agrippiana* to which a scholiast on Juv. 6.154 refers. More recently, Richardson 1992: 340 and M. P. Guidobaldi in Steinby 1993–2000: s.v. identify the *porticus Argonautarum* as the colonnade that ran along the western side of the Saepta, mirroring the *porticus Meleagri* on its eastern side. Part of this colonnade is still intact, but as its outer wall is interrupted at regular intervals by large niches, presumably for sculpture, this probably represents a later rebuilding of an earlier structure that had been more suitable for a mural.

7 *Memphitica templa:* A poetic periphrasis (Zingerle 1877: 34 compares Ov. *Ars* 1.77: "linigerae Memphitica templa iuvencae") for what is variously referred to as the "Temple of Isis and Serapis," the "Iseum and Serapeum," or the "Temple of Isis Campensis." The principal temple in Rome dedicated to the popular Egyptian goddess Isis, it directly adjoined the Saepta Julia (Juv. 6.528–529) near the present site of the Church of S. Maria sopra Minerva.

Tibullus (1.3.27–30) and Ovid (*Ars am.* 1.77, *Am.* 2.13.7) associate it with women and particularly prostitutes; see also Catull. 10.26, Juv. 9.22, and Mart. 10.48.1). For the possibility that Martial's phrase refers specifically to Domitian's rebuilding of the temple, see Darwall-Smith 1996: 139, 145.

8 *cathedris . . . tuis:* These are armchairs or easy chairs especially used by women; compare *femineae cathedrae* at 3.63.7, 12.38.1. The noun reminds us that the Temple of Isis and Serapis was especially frequented by women (see Heyob 1975), and hints that Selius seeks invitations from both sexes. Tibull. 1.3.29–30 likewise alludes to the fact that worshippers of Isis normally remained seated, an unusual practice in ancient cult (Watson and Watson; Stambaugh 1978). For the homoeoteleuton *cathedris . . . tuis* (here of the most common type, a noun and its adjective) marking the end of each of the two halves of the pentameter, see on **2.12.4**.

8 *maesta iuvenca:* A humorously pretentious way (compare the periphrases *Niliaca iuvenca* at 8.82.2 and *Pharia iuvenca* at 10.48.1) of referring to Isis, who was often identified with Io, the mythic figure first transformed into a heifer in order to avoid Hera's detection of her affair with Zeus, and then compelled to wander all the way to Egypt. Io's sufferings, alluded to with the adjective *maesta*, are memorably evoked in Aeschylus' *Prometheus Bound* and Ovid's *Metamorphoses* (1.568–747). The adjective may simultaneously make reference to the famous mourning of Isis upon the death of her husband Osiris (Watson and Watson).

9 *centum pendentia tecta columnis:* The Hecatostylon, a portico with a hundred columns located between the Portico of Pompey and the Baths of Agrippa (3.19.1, 5.13.5, 12.30.3). The elevated periphrasis is perhaps inspired by V. *Aen.* 7.170: "tectum augustum, ingens, centum sublime columnis" (Wagner 1880: 13).

10 *Pompei dona nemusque duplex:* Yet another elevated periphrasis (Friedlaender observes that Martial elsewhere uses the more prosaic *munera* for *dona*), referring to the portico built in 55 B.C. to the east of the Theater of Pompey in order to offer shelter for spectators in case of rain and to provide space for stage machinery (Vitr. 5.9.1; Mart. 5.10.5, 11.1, 11.21, 14.29, 14.166). Martial again cites the portico in conjunction with the Temple of Isis as a good place to meet women in 11.47. *Nemus duplex* refers to the double groves of plane trees planted in the space enclosed by the portico (11.47.3 and Prop. 2.32.11–12).

11–12: Note the *apo koinou* structure of the first line (*balnea* modifies both *Fortunati* and *Fausti;* cf. on **2.2.1**) and the variation achieved by switching from *nec* to *-que* at the end of this list. The reference is to four privately owned bathing establishments of a kind found all over the ancient city and usually known by their builder's or owner's name: compare the *Stephani balnea* in 11.52 and 14.60 and the *balnea Phoebi* at Juv. 7.233, and see Weber

1996: 101–117. In Constantine's day there were at least 856 such facilities in Rome, many of them occupying the ground floor of *insulae* (Sullivan 1991: 153; cf. Plin. *N.H.* 36.121). For the centrality of *balnea* in Roman life, see *CIL* 6.15258.5–8 = *CLE* 1499.1–2: "Balnea, vina, Venus corrumpunt corpora nostra, / set vitam faciunt b(alnea), v(ina), V(enus)." Allusions to bathhouses, both single-sex and mixed, as the site of various kinds of social interaction pervade Martial's epigrams: see *Sp.* 2.7, 1.23, **2.40**, **2.52**, **2.70**, **2.78**, 3.7, 3.36, 3.51, 3.72, 5.44, 6.42–43, 6.53, 6.81, 7.34–35, 7.76, 7.82, 8.42, 9.19, 9.33, 9.75, 10.70, 11.22, 11.47, 11.51–52, 11.59, 11.63, 11.75, 12.19, 12.50, 12.70, 12.82–83. See Nielsen 1990, Yegül 1992, Weber 1996, Fagan 1999 for general discussion, and Fagan 1999: 12–39 for Martial in particular.

At 1.59.3 Martial again names the Baths of Gryllus and Lupus together and refers to the former as *tenebrosa*. Gryllus' establishment was thus unpleasantly dark, and the phrase *Aeoliam Lupi* almost certainly signifies that Lupus' baths were as drafty as the cave of Aeolus, king of the winds (cf. *Aeolia antra,* Ov. *Met.* 1.262), and not, as Freidlaender suggests, that they housed a painting depicting Aeolus. As for the other two establishments, the name *Faustus* appears also at 11.64.1, but surely he is not the same man. The name *Fortunatus* occurs only here in Martial. E. Rodríguez Almeida identifies the four baths named here with the *balnea quattuor* to which Martial refers at 5.70.4, arguing that they constituted a cluster of small baths in the southwestern Campus Martius (Steinby 1993–2000: s.v. *balnea quattuor*). As *nec . . . spernit* in 11 implies and the remarks in 12 make explicit, these baths will not have been particularly desirable (Watson and Watson: "Becoming increasingly desperate, Selius visits unappealing private baths which, it is implied, the more discriminating would shun").

13 *nam thermis:* A linguistic distinction was sometimes (but hardly always: Weber 1996: 71–79, Fagan 1999: 14–19) made between privately owned bathhouses (*balnea*) and public facilities, or *thermae*, of which there were three in Martial's day: those of Agrippa, Nero, and Titus. Here the topographical references suggest that the *thermae* are the Baths of Agrippa and Nero (see next note); if so, *nam* marks a shift of topic from *balnea* to *thermae* (see *OLD* s.v. 4, "in transitions to a new subject").

13 *iterumque iterumque iterumque:* A challenging textual problem. The reading printed here (and also by Gilbert, Lindsay, Izaac, Ceronetti, and Watson and Watson) is that of MS family β; manuscript G reads *thermis iterum cunctis iterumque,* accepted by Collesso but no one since. Schneidewin in his second edition accepts Heinsius' emendation *ternis iterum thermis iterumque,* and Gilbert's subsequent revision to *thermis iterum ternis iterumque* has been accepted by many (Ker, Giarratano, Norcio, Barié and Schindler, Shackleton Bailey). The "three baths" would be those of Agrippa, Nero, and Titus (cf. 10.51.12: *triplices thermae*).

Yet an explicit reference to *all three* public baths seems inappropriate here: while the Baths of Agrippa and Nero were located in the Campus Martius in close proximity to the other monuments mentioned here, the Baths of Titus were far away, on the slope of the Mons Oppius. Such a lengthy side trip seems unlikely; the *thermae* mentioned here will probably have been understood to be those of Agrippa and Nero (so also Prior 1996: 138). For other allusions to only one or two of the three *thermae*, see *Sp.* 2.7 (Titus), 3.20.15 (Titus and Agrippa), 3.36.6 (Titus and Agrippa), 12.83.5 (Nero).

The reading *iterumque iterumque iterumque* thus seems more likely. The triplication is, to be sure, unparalleled (a search of the PHI disk turns up only this phrase) but is certainly within the realm of the acceptable, particularly if one considers the poetic phrase *iterumque iterumque* (V. *Aen.* 2.770, 3.436; Ov. *Ars am.* 2.127, *Met.* 11.619; *Cons. ad Liv.* 219); indeed, Wagner 1880: 15 considers Martial's *iterumque iterumque iterumque* a Virgilian borrowing. An interesting parallel is *Priap.* 77.8–10: "ergo qui prius *usque et usque et usque* / furum scindere podices solebam, / per noctes aliquot diesque cesso." In both cases, the diction vividly reflects a repeated action, and here it might also humorously suggest a threefold ritual ablution (Hor. *Sat.* 2.1.7–8, *Epist.* 1.1.37; V. *Ecl.* 8.73; Tib. 1.2.56).

14 renuente deo: The phrase occurs only here and at Tib. 1.5.20 and Ov. *Met.* 8.325. For the meaning of *renuo* (literally, "to throw the head backward in denial," a gesture still alive in contemporary Greece) and its frequent association with divine disapproval, see Apul. *Met.* 6.7 ("nec renuit Iovis caerulum supercilium"), 9.1 ("Fortuna renuente"); Mart. **2.46.10** ("quid renuis?"); and contrast Mart. **2.24.7–8** ("si deus ore sereno / *adnuerit*"). Other references in Martial to the gods granting a man success or failure, riches or poverty, include 1.99, 1.103, **2.24.1**, 4.21. As usual, the singular *deus* refers nonspecifically to divinity, and need not imply any particular deity, much less a monotheistic belief system.

15 Europes tepidae buxeta: A pleasing example of transferred epithet. The boxwood trees themselves would have been warmed by the sun (cf. 3.20.12: "an delicatae sole rursus Europae / inter tepentes post meridiem buxos"), but here the adjective is applied to the image of Europa. Apparently as the result of a scribe's "retransferral" of the epithet, MSS of family β read the metrically impossible *Europes tepida buxeta*. Though most translators render *tepidae* as "sun-warmed," and the parallel with 3.20.12 points in this direction, the anonymous reader for Oxford University Press suggests an alternative worth considering: the end of the day has come (cf. *serum iter* in the following line) and the trees are beginning to cool down (cf. *OLD* s.v. *tepesco* 1b).

16 serum carpat ... iter: For the poetic *serum iter*, see on **2.11.2** (*porticum seram*). The phrase *carpere iter* is common enough, both in prose and in verse (Hor. *C.* 2.17.12, Ov. *Ep.* 17.34, Ov. *Tr.* 1.10.4, Sen. *N.Q.* 7.8.2; cf. *carpe viam* at V. *Aen.* 6.629). The related phrase *spatia carpere* is found in another of Martial's epigrams describing Rome's leisure spaces, again mostly in the Campus Martius (3.20).

17 *vector lascive:* A witty phrase. The noun *vector* ("bearer, carrier") occurs only here in Martial and elsewhere appears to have a loftily poetic tone (Sen. *Her. F.* 9: "per undas vector Europae nitet"; Sen. *Her. O.* 1907: "stelligeri vector Olympi . . . Atlas"; V. Fl. 1.425: "vectorem pavidae . . . dum quaereret Helles"; Stat. *Theb.* 9.858: "feri vectorem fulminis albus / cum supra respexit olor"). The adjective *lascivus* ("naughty, wanton") is a favorite of Martial's, occurring thirty-nine times; the juxtaposition with *vector* is especially effective.

18 *ad cenam Selium tu, rogo, taure, voca:* What exactly is Martial asking Jupiter to do? According to Friedlaender (followed by Ker, Pertsch 1911: 52, and Merli), Martial's wish is that Selius be thrown to a bull in the arena; compare 1.43.13: "tu ponaris cui Charidemus apro." Yet, as Izaac observes, there is an important difference between wild boars and bulls in that the latter do not devour their victims, which is surely the implication of *ad cenam voca*. Ker, Izaac, and Joepgen 1967: 79–80 thus follow Rader: Martial is sarcastically using the image of a dinner invitation in order to express the wish that Jupiter remove Selius from the world, that is, bring about his death. But this seems an unnecessarily violent interpretation of Martial's witty phrase. Shackleton Bailey, following Hirst 1950, understands a somewhat gentler point: "Give him grass to eat—or perhaps nothing at all." Another possibility is that Martial is simply hoping that Selius will finally obtain his goal of being invited to dinner—*any* dinner—so that he will stop pestering others. Similarly Watson and Watson: "There being no humans left in the Portico, the bull is asked to invite Selius, to put him out of his misery."

For parenthetical *rogo* with a named addressee, see **2.25.2, 2.80.2,** 3.44.9, 3.52.3, 3.73.3, 3.95.3, 5.44.1, 5.82.3, 6.17.2, 7.86.3, 9.25.3, 10.15.2, 10.21.2, 10.41.3, 10.66.1, 12.63.6; with no specific addressee and thus having an exclamatory function, see on **2.80.1**. The frequency of both types is symptomatic of the chatty, discursive nature of Martial's epigrams. For the shortening of the final vowel in *rogo*, see on **2.9.2**.

2.15

Quod nulli calicem tuum propinas
humane facis, Horme, non superbe.

By never passing your cup to anyone as a toast, you're acting humanely, Hormus, not arrogantly.

Themes.   Reverting to second-person address and to the two-line hendecasyllabic form of **2.13** after a lengthy epigram in elegiac couplets, the poet also returns to, but varies, the theme of the Postumus poems (**2.10**, **2.12**). Like Postumus' half-kiss, Hormus' action might be interpreted as arrogant but is actually considerate in view of the implicit accusation of bad breath or oral uncleanness. Again the specific cause of this problem is not adumbrated, but an experienced reader of Martial or of Roman invective in general will suspect a predilection for oral sexual practices. The image of drinking from a common cup appears elsewhere in conjunction with an even more directly sexual implication: in 12.91, Magulla shares both a bed and a male prostitute with her husband, but refuses to drink out of the same cup, no doubt because she knows what her husband does.

As often, the scenario sketched in the present epigram is approached from a different perspective by Juvenal, who imagines a dinner guest dismayed that his host will not offer him the courtesy of a toast: "quando propinat / Virro tibi, sumitve tuis contacta libellis / pocula?" (Juv. 5.127–129). Colton 1991: 197–198 argues for a direct relationship between the two texts.

Structure.   The epigram is a model of simplicity, consisting of a single sentence and easily falling into two parts, each of which occupies a line. The first consists of a straightforward *quod*-clause with indirect object, direct object, and verb; the second presents the main clause of the sentence, itself divided into two parts separated by the vocative *Horme*. The epigram offers a variation on the *quod-non-sed* structure (see on **2.11**): *quod propinas—humane facis—non superbe* is essentially equivalent to *quod propinas—non superbe facis—sed humane;* similarly in 11.77 (*quod consumit—cenaturit—non cacaturit*).

1 *propinas:* The technical term denoting the practice of proposing a toast in someone's honor, tasting the wine in one's own cup, and then passing it to the person honored so that he or she may take a drink (1.68, 3.82, 6.44, 8.6, 10.49, 12.74; Plaut. *Stich.* 710; Cic. *Tusc.* 1.40.96; V. *Aen.* 1.737–738; Sen. *De ira* 2.33.4). Here and at 3.82.31 and 6.44.6, the prefix is *pro-;* elsewhere (3.82.25, 8.6.13, 10.49.3, 12.74.9), it is *prō-*.

2 *humane facis . . . non superbe:* The epigram's point is based on an antithesis between *humane* and *superbe facere,* between respecting one's fellows and acting as if one were above them; the two opposed adjectives frame the verse. For the contrast between *humanitas* and *superbia* see Phaedr. 3.16.1–2 ("*humanitati* qui se non accommodat / plerumque poenas oppetit *superbiae*"); Sen. *Epist.* 88.30 ("*humanitas* vetat *superbum* esse adversus socios, vetat amarum"), 116.5; Plin. *Paneg.* 3.4. The phrase *humane facere* occurs again at 12.55.11–13, where kissing and oral sex also play a role ("humane tamen hoc facit, sed unum, / gratis quae dare basium recusat, / gratis lingere nec recusat, Aegle"), and at Cic. *Phil.* 13.36, *Att.* 12.44.

2 Horme: This is the only occurrence of the name in Martial. Stein (*RE* s.v.) describes him as "an arrogant freedman." Friedlaender sees an allusion to a freedman of Vespasian's who became a leader in the Flavian faction in A.D. 69 and was subsequently rewarded with equestrian status (Tac. *Hist.* 3.12, 27, 28, 4.39); he adds that if so, the epigram will be one of Martial's oldest poems. But there is no hint that the addressee of this epigram is a freedman, and even if there is a reminiscence of the historical figure, we need not conclude that the poem was composed during or shortly after Vespasian's reign.

2.16

Zoilus aegrotat: faciunt hanc stragula febrem.
   si fuerit sanus, coccina quid facient?
quid torus a Nilo, quid Sidone tinctus olenti?
   ostendit stultas quid nisi morbus opes?
quid tibi cum medicis? dimitte Machaonas omnis.   5
   vis fieri sanus? stragula sume mea.

Zoilus is sick. His blankets are causing this fever. If he regains his health, what use will his scarlet bedclothes be? What use will his Egyptian bed furnishings be, or those dyed with strong-smelling Sidonian purple? What else besides sickness displays foolish riches? Why are you bothering with doctors? Dismiss all of your Machaons. Do you want to recover? Take my blankets, please.

Themes. This is our introduction to another memorable character, the wealthy former slave Zoilus, a flashy parvenu of a kind most famously embodied by Petronius' Trimalchio. The poem's first two words describe a situation with particular concentration (Zoilus is ill) and are followed by a paradoxical explanation (his blankets are causing the fever), which causes us to expect more, and which may raise the suspicion that the illness is feigned; compare **2.26**, **2.40**, 9.85, 11.86. Indeed, we are quickly given to understand that Zoilus is faking illness in order to display his wealth; in 5.79

he is said to change his clothing eleven times during the course of a banquet. The slyly aggressive final line invites a double reading: (*a*) if Zoilus
really wants to recover, he ought to exchange his luxurious bedding for
Martial's simpler blankets, since out of shame at the thought of putting these
on display, Zoilus will miraculously recover; (*b*) if Zoilus really wants to
become healthy both physically and morally (see below on *sanus,* 2), he
need only adopt the poet's own simpler lifestyle.

For illness and medical themes in Martial, see Peyer and Remund 1928.
For Martial's protests or boasts of poverty, which we must always relativize
(Allen et al. 1969–1970, Saller 1983; less skeptical is Tennant 2000), see **2.43**,
2.85, **2.90.3** (*pauper*), 4.77 ("numquam divitias deos rogavi / contentus modicis
meoque laetus"), 5.13.1–2 ("sum, fateor, semperque fui, Callistrate, pauper /
sed non obscurus nec male notus eques"), 7.46 (he is among the *pauperes*),
7.48 (he contrasts himself with *lauti*), 12.57 (*pauper*), and others.

Structure. In the opening line we encounter both a simple statement of
the situation (*Zoilus aegrotat*) and a comment on it (*faciunt hanc stragula
febrem*). A series of rhetorical questions follows, each governed by *quid*
placed in various positions. The final couplet (5–6) begins with the last of
these, which unlike its predecessors is addressed to Zoilus himself (*quid
tibi cum medicis?*), and displays a strictly parallel structure: each line contains a challenging question occupying the half-line up to the principal caesura (*quid tibi cum medicis? ~ vis fieri sanus?*), followed by a blunt response
with an imperative (*dimitte Machaonas omnis ~ stragula sume mea*). With
the final image of the *stragula* we detect a ring-composition: the poem begins with an announcement in the third person that Zoilus is ill (*aegrotat*)
because of his blankets (*stragula*), and ends with a second-person challenge
to Zoilus himself. If he wants to be healthy (*sanus,* which also echoes *sanus*
in 2, the second line of its own couplet), he ought to take Martial's blankets
(*stragula*). The technique of describing a person in the third person (1–4)
and then shifting (often fairly abruptly) to a second-person address is found
also in **2.30**, **2.44**, **2.65–66**.

1 *Zoilus aegrotat*: This two-word sentence, lacking any syntactic connection with what follows, creates a particularly striking opening effect.
Compare 1.74 (*moechus erat*), **2.59** (*mica vocor*), 4.48 (*percidi gaudes*).

Along with Selius (see on **2.11**) and Postumus (see on **2.10**), Zoilus is
one of the most memorable characters in Book II, appearing again in **2.19**,
2.42, **2.58**, **2.81**. Unlike those figures, he is the subject of another cluster, or
"cycle," of epigrams in a later book (XI) and comes with a fairly consistent
set of characteristics throughout Martial's corpus: he is ostentatiously wealthy
(**2.16**, 3.82, 5.79, 11.37, 11.54) but stingy with his dinner guests (**2.19**); he

has the *os impurum* (**2.42**, 3.82, 6.91, 11.30, 11.85); he was born a slave, and was a runaway (*fugitivus*) at that (3.29, 11.12, 11.37, 11.54). Elsewhere (**2.58**, **2.81**, 4.77, 11.92, 12.54), he is the butt of various other jokes, some of them unusually harsh. The name recalls that of a fourth-century B.C. Cynic philosopher known for his sharp attacks on Homer, Plato, and others (Ael. *V.H.* 11.10).

Unlike Friedlaender, Barwick 1958 (similarly, Grewing ad 6.91.2) believes that, as in the case of Selius (see on **2.11.1**, **2.69.6**), these allusions to Zoilus refer to a real man whom Martial's contemporaries would probably have been able to identify, particularly in view of the striking description in 12.54 (*crine ruber, niger ore, brevis pede, lumine laesus*). But 12.54 was published at least fifteen years after Zoilus' first appearance in Book II, and the description offered there of an ugly man could be just as generic as is the invective in this and other epigrams from Book II.

1 stragula: The noun refers to bedclothes—the bottom and perhaps also the top "sheet" on a Roman bed (14.147 with Leary ad loc.)—but also to other kinds of coverings, such as saddle coverings (14.86.1) or even a shroud (Petr. *Sat.* 42.6). See further *RE* s.v. *stragulum* and, for Roman bedding, Marquardt 1886: 724 and Blümner 1911: 116.

2 si fuerit sanus, coccina quid facient? Both here and in 6 below *sanus* has a double sense, referring to both physical and moral health (cf. 6.84 with Grewing, 12.47; *OLD* s.v. 1, 3), as also does *morbus* (4). Scarlet (*coccina*) is a sign of a luxurious lifestyle, as is the purple mentioned in the following line; compare **2.39.1**, **2.43.8**, **2.57.2**; Plin. *N.H.* 21.45-46, Suet. *Nero* 30.3.

3 quid torus a Nilo, quid Sidone tinctus olenti? The diction is poetic: note the synecdoche *Nilo* (for *Aegypto*) and the metonymy *Sidone olenti* (see below).

The exact meaning of *torus* here is unclear, although it obviously has to do with Zoilus' bed and its furnishings. Ker, Izaac, and Ceronetti take it to refer to a mattress, Barié and Schindler to a cushion, Shackleton Bailey to an underblanket; Scandola translates "giaciglio" and Norcio "letto." Friedlaender explains, "Bettpfühle und Kopfkissen aus Antinoopolis in Aegypten," adding that *torus* might also refer to bedcovers. Antinoopolis, however, did not yet exist in Martial's day. Watson and Watson propose the most convincing solution: Martial is referring to "a *torus* with embroidered coverlets of the type known as 'Alexandrina' or 'polymita'." See 14.150 and, for the use of *torus* to refer to coverlets, Prop. 1.14.20. Presumably inspired by **2.81**, Barié and Schindler suggest that *stragulum* and *torus* might create associations with a burial shroud and bier.

Sidone olenti is a poetic metonymy for the expensive purple dye obtained from *murex* shellfish, the most desirable of which came from the area of Tyre and Sidon, and which had a characteristic odor; compare 1.39.32

(*olidae vestes murice*), 4.4.6, 9.62, and see in general Reinhold 1970. The metonymy recurs at 11.1.2; Friedlaender compares *Tyros* for Tyrian purple at **2.29.3** (but see my note ad loc.) and 6.11.7. Here the metonymy may be encouraged by the metrical intractability of *purpura;* compare also *murice* (8.48.5) and *ostro* (12.38.3), likewise in dactylic contexts (Schneider 1909: 49). For purple bedclothes, see 14.147.

4 ostendit stultas quid nisi morbus opes? A *sententia* in the form of a "rhetorical" question. For the double meaning of *morbus,* see *OLD* s.v. 1 ("disease, illness, sickness, infirmity") and 3a ("weakness, failing, vice"), and compare Williams 1999: 180–181.

5 Machaonas: Son of the healing god Asclepius, Machaon appears as a physician in the *Iliad.* See on **2.14.3–4** for Martial's use of mythological *exempla,* here in the form of a metonymy (*Machaonas* = *medicos*). Note the Greek ending -*as;* the Latin -*ēs* would not fit the metrical context (Schneider 1909: 52 n. 1; cf. **2.64.1**, *rhetora*).

6 vis fieri sanus? This construction echoes the phrasing and metrical shape of *si fuerit sanus* (2), for which see above. The *variorum* commentary explains the double meaning: "sapies et valebis" (you will be wise and healthy). For such final questions, often with the verb *vis,* see on **2.7.8**; for *vis fieri,* compare **2.53.1** ("vis fieri liber?") and 6.50.5 ("vis fieri dives, Bithynice?").

6 stragula sume mea: My translation raises the possibility of a double meaning: both "take my blankets and use them yourself" and "take my blankets away from me so that I may have better and more expensive ones" (cf. **2.85**). It is also worth noting that *sumere* could be used to describe the taking of medical remedies (*OLD* s.v. 3a; cf. Mart. 14.56).

2.17

    Tonstrix Suburae faucibus sedet primis,
    cruenta pendent qua flagella tortorum
    Argique Letum multus obsidet sutor.
    sed ista tonstrix, Ammiane, non tondet,
    non tondet, inquam. quid igitur facit? radit.   5

A woman barber sits right at the entrance to the Subura, where the bloody whips of the torturers hang and where many a shoemaker occupies the Argiletum. But this barber does not cut hair, Ammianus: she does not cut hair, I say. What does she do, then? She fleeces.

Themes.   We return to the choliambic meter (see on **2.11**) but are introduced to a new topic. The implication of the final words is not only that this
woman charges too much, but that the services she offers go beyond those
of a barber: in short, that she is a prostitute (see on 5 below). For barbers,
usually male, who shaved beards and trimmed hair and who are sometimes
the object of satire, see on **2.48.2**. For prostitutes with a fixed place of business, see 1.34 (*Submemmi fornice*), 6.66 ("quales in media sedent Subura"),
11.45 (*cella*), 11.61 (a *fornix* in the Subura).

There is a comparable joke, with the sex roles reversed, in 4.28. Here
Chloe has given all her possessions to Lupercus, and the speaker comments,
"vae glabraria, vae tibi misella: / nudam te statuet tuus Lupercus"—that is,
he will "strip" her both of her clothes and of her possessions.

Structure.   A single sentence describing the *tonstrix* at work (1–3) is followed by an additional detail that complicates the picture (*sed*, 4). The
paradoxical remark that, although a barber (*tonstrix*), she does not actually cut hair (*tondet*) is reinforced by the repetition *non tondet, inquam,*
and shades into a riddle: *quid igitur facit?* There is a progression from the
three-line opening sentence to a shorter sentence ending with the deictic
repetition (4–5), to an even shorter rhetorical question (5), to a one-word
sentence that brings the point home; but at the same time each line, a unit
in itself, introduces an increasing degree of specificity in content.

For the introductory technique of anchoring the action in a specific place,
compare 1.12, 3.19, 3.47, 4.18, 7.80, 9.40, 9.59, 9.61, 10.79, 11.82; see **2.72**
for an introduction that anchors the action in a specific time. There are Greek
predecessors, but Martial's descriptions tend to be longer (Siedschlag 1977:
35 n. 1).

1 *Suburae faucibus sedet primis:* The Subura was a famous district
of Rome, more or less coextensive with the valley between the southern
end of the Viminal and the western slope of the Esquiline Hills. Various
sources describe it as noisy, busy, crowded—in short, quintessentially urban (see Juv. 3.5, where the speaker prefers even Prochyta, a small island
off Misenum, to the Subura). Most revealing among Martial's many allusions
to the Subura are 12.18, where the *clamosa Subura,* along with the Aventine
and Caelian, is a feature of the busy city life, and 12.21, where both the
media Subura and the Capitoline function as emblems of Rome. The district was also known for its brothels: see 6.66.2 (quoted below, on *sedet*),
11.61, 11.78 (a prostitute is, significantly, called *Suburana magistra*), and
Priap. 40.1 with Stumpp 1998: 166–169. Martial's phrase *faucibus primis,*
attested only here and perhaps an ad hoc designation (cf. *prima Subura* at
12.2.9), would seem to refer to the southern opening of the valley, that is,

the area just behind the later Forum Transitorium (Richardson 1992: s.v. *Argiletum*).

As Shackleton Bailey notes, the verb *sedet* contributes to the implicit portrayal of the woman as a prostitute: compare 6.66.2 ("famae non nimium bonae puellam, / quales in media sedent Subura") with *OLD* s.v. *sedere* 1c.

2 *cruenta pendent qua flagella tortorum:* There is some disagreement as to the precise meaning of this phrase. Collesso vaguely explains: "hoc est, locus ubi rei puniebantur." Friedlaender and Barié and Schindler suggest that Martial is referring to the shops of those who made whips that could be used in torture; in this case, the adjective *cruenta* is proleptic. Platner 1929: s.v. "Subura" suggests that the *primae fauces Suburae* lay near the *Praefectura Urbana,* where torture was carried out. Sen. *Epist.* 51.4 ("quemadmodum inter tortores habitare nolim, sic ne inter popinas quidem") implies that certain areas of Rome were known for *tortores* just as others were known for their taverns, and perhaps the part of the Subura where this *tonstrix* works was one of the former.

3 *Argique Letum:* *Argiletum* (originally probably *Argilletum*) was the name of the zone connecting the Subura with the area of the imperial fora; it was also applied, as here, to the main street of this zone. This was one of the city's major thoroughfares, constituting a principal approach to the forum area; a stretch of ancient roadway still runs alongside the Curia. To judge by Martial's allusions, the Argiletum was a center of trade, containing booksellers' and cobblers' shops, and perhaps also brothels (1.2, 1.3, 1.117). The name is most likely derived from *argilla,* referring to the clay that was dug nearby (cf. *Lauretum, Aesculetum, Quercetum;* Jordan 1878: 1.1.181). This etymology is cited by ancient commentators along with an alternative, mythic derivation: that a certain Argus, variously identified, was killed nearby (Varro *L.L.* 5.157, Serv. ad *Aen.* 8.345, Mart. Cap. 3.273). The insertion of *-que* into the midst of *Argiletum,* a device that gave the poet metrical flexibility, obviously depends on the latter etymology (*Argi letum,* "death of Argus"). The same division of the word is found at 1.117.9 ("Argi nempe soles subire Letum") but nowhere else in extant Latin.

4 *ista tonstrix, Ammiane, non tondet:* For paradoxical formulations toward the end of epigrams, see on **2.12.4**. For the parenthetical vocative leading into the final point, see on **2.3.2** and **2.18.8**. The name *Ammianus* has already appeared at **2.4.1**, and Friedlaender suggests that since the name there refers to a man whose relationship with his mother is suspiciously intimate, here Martial may be implying that he has visited the *tonstrix* himself, and not for a shave. But it is not clear that a Roman readership would have been inclined to make any connection between incest and a visit to a prostitute.

4–5 *non tondet, / non tondet, inquam:* The use of *inquam* to mark a gemination is a technique probably influenced by the rhetorical tradition (cf. Cic. *Verr.* 5.162: "crux, crux, inquam"; Cic. *Font.* 3: "nemo, nemo, inquam"). Wills 1996: 65–66 cites several instances from poetry (Lucil. 110–111; Ov. *Met.* 13.284; [V.] *Catal.* 9.55; Sil. 2.302–303, 11.570; Mart. 6.64.7–8: "felicis carpere nugas, / has, inquam, nugas").

5 *quid igitur facit?* For the question leading up to the conclusion, see on **2.7.8**. Combined with the earlier paradoxical statement *ista tonstrix non tondet,* the question has the effect of a riddle. For comparable mental puzzles at the end of epigrams, see **2.28.5** ("ex istis nihil es fateor, Sextille: quid ergo es?") and 3.88.2 ("dicite, dissimiles sunt magis an similes?"), and for the riddle format in general, see **2.33** and 13.11 with Leary.

5 *radit:* For the execution of the final point by means of a single word see, in Book II alone, **2.33.4** (*fellat*), **2.49.2** (*volo*), **2.56.4** (*dare*), and **2.73.1** (again *fellat*); Rodón Binué 1987: 292–293. In the present case, translators and commentators agree that there is a double meaning in *radit,* but what is it? Almost certainly there is a pun on a financial second meaning (thus already Collesso): this barber doesn't shave, she strips her customers of all they've got (cf. Pers. 3.49: "damnosa canicula quantum raderet"). The pun is reproducible by English "fleece" (Bridge and Lake, Shackleton Bailey). Prompted by the hint of prostitution already made in the first line, some have looked for sexual double meaning in *radit:* the *variorum* commentary proposes that the verb may suggest *glubit,* famously used in Catull. 58 to evoke the peeling back of the foreskin and likewise the climactic final word in a poem imagining a woman in action at street corners and in alleys ("in quadriviis et angiportis") (similarly, Plass 1985: 202, LaPenna 2000: 94 n. 19). Yet "peeling" or "stripping" (*glubere*) and "shaving" (*radit*) are hardly the same thing. Housman 1931b: 82 thus argues that there is no sexual double meaning in *radit.*

2.18

Capto tuam, pudet heu, sed capto, Maxime, cenam,
    tu captas aliam: iam sumus ergo pares.
mane salutatum venio, tu diceris ipse
    ante salutatum: iam sumus ergo pares.
sum comes ipse tuus tumidique anteambulo regis,   5
    tu comes alterius: iam sumus ergo pares.
esse sat est servum, iam nolo vicarius esse.
    qui rex est regem, Maxime, non habeat.

I'm ashamed to admit it, Maximus, but alas, it's true: I'm angling for
a dinner invitation from you. But you're angling for someone else's.
We're equal, then. I come to greet you at your morning reception;
but I'm told that you have already gone out to greet someone else.
We're equal, then. I accompany you on your rounds, walking in
front of you as footman to a puffed-up lord; but you accompany
someone else. We're equal, then. It is enough to be a slave; I don't
want to be a slave's slave. A lord, Maximus, ought not to have a
lord.

Themes.   The object of Selius' desire, the *cena* (**2.11**, **2.14**), appears in
this epigram's opening couplet, now as a way of offering ironic commentary on Martial's own involvement in the network of patron-client relationships characterizing Roman society from its earliest beginnings and
conventionally known as *clientela*. A higher-status man (the "patron") took
one or more lower-status men under his protection and offered them such
services as advocacy in legal disputes, dinners, gifts, and the monetary contribution known as the *sportula;* in exchange the "client" was expected to
attend on his "patron," being present at morning *salutationes* (3), accompanying him in public (5), voting for him if he should be a candidate for of-
fice, and otherwise offering him the services of a dependent. The institution
provides the subject matter for a great number of Martial's epigrams—see,
for example, 1.80, 1.112, **2.32**, **2.53** (with which the present epigram perhaps forms a pair), **2.68**, 3.7, 3.14, 3.30, 3.36–37, 3.46, 4.26, 4.40, 6.88, 9.7,
9.85, 9.100, 10.10, 10.18, 10.47, 10.56, 10.82, 10.96, 12.13, 12.36, 12.40—
but, not surprisingly, is absent from Greek epigram (Prinz 1911: 79). As here,
Martial's epigrams on the theme often voice complaints from the perspective of the client, and in Juvenal the debasing situations in which a client
might often find himself provide the fuel for characteristically vitriolic comment (1.95–117, 1.132–146, 3.119–125; 5 passim; 9 passim with Braund 1988:
130–177). Modern discussions of *clientela* include White 1972, 1975, 1978;
Saller 1982; Garrido-Hory 1985b; Wallace-Hadrill 1989; Damon 1997 (especially 158–171); Nauta 2002 (especially 37–90).

    Many scholars take Martial's comments in the present epigram quite
seriously, praising the poet for being able to rise above his personal situation and look at the system's defects with a cold eye. Thus, Laurens 1989:
246–249 cites this epigram, along with **2.32**, **2.53**, and **2.68**, as illustrations
of how Martial's "analyse la plus cohérente concerne la dégradation du lien
de clientèle," and Sullivan 1991: 126 claims that "Martial can show flashes of
self-awareness within the fetters of patronage." Similarly, Damon 1997: 151–
152 suggests that epigrams like this "have a strong flavor of social criticism
about them: something is rotten in the (people of the) state of Denmark,

and the poet is going to point it out for all to see; perhaps they will be shamed or shocked into improving themselves." But if one approaches Martial from a perspective like that of Anderson 1982, these epigrams come across less as issuing sweeping criticism aimed at stimulating social change, and more as offering ironic commentary aimed principally at amusing and entertaining readers.

In the present epigram Martial is addressing a problem that was inherent in the system, although scholarly discussion tends not to emphasize the point. When he complains that "a lord ought not to have a lord" (cf. the closely similar remark at **2.32.7–8**), he runs up against the very nature of *clientela*. The system depended on a flexible hierarchical network according to which many or even most patrons did indeed have patrons of their own: consider Juvenal's revealing phrase *dominus et domini rex* (5.137) and see Mart. 10.10, 12.29, and Juv. 10.95–126 for allusions to knights and senators playing the role of *cliens*.

Structure.   The poem has a classic bipartite scheme: verses 1–6 lay out the situation, and the final couplet (7–8) offers the poet's reaction. The first part of the poem (1–6) itself has an ABA structure: in the first and third couplets (1–2, 5–6) the hexameter portrays Martial's own activity and the first half of the pentameter describes that of Maximus, beginning with a contrastive *tu* and then echoing the language of the preceding hexameter (*captas* and *capto, comes* and *comes*). The intervening couplet (3–4) spreads a description of Maximus' activity over both the hexameter and pentameter (*tu diceris isse / ante salutatum*), but there is still a linguistic echo between the two parts (*mane salutatum* and *ante salutatum,* in the same position). These three couplets are capped off by the final distich (7–8), which consists of two syntactically independent but closely similar formulations of the fundamental thought, each occupying a line: the first an ironic reflection on the poet's own situation, the second a *sententia* with universal scope, the first using the metaphor of slavery, the second that of kingship. Seen this way, the epigram displays an ABAC structure.

For the repetition of contrasts that structures this poem, compare 1.76, **2.32**, **2.33**, **2.43**, **2.89**, 3.38, 3.60, 6.11, 9.2, 9.92, 10.10, and others (Joepgen 1967: 157–158, Siedschlag 1977: 44, Laurens 1989: 318–322). Many of these poems offer commentary on *clientela* (Siedschlag 1977: 53–54), and such a technique is indeed well adapted to the theme, especially when approached from the perspective of the client, who will be particularly sensitive to the contrast between *patronus* and *cliens*.

1 *capto:* When we read this opening word, and above all when we discover at the line's end that its object is *cenam,* we see Martial placing himself in a position for which he often mocks others (e.g., Selius in **2.11**, **2.14**). Compare the self-mockery of 11.24.14–15: "sic fit / cum cenare domi poeta non vult." The impact of this surprising opening is heightened by the parenthetical *pudet heu*—he ought indeed to be ashamed!—followed by the repetition of the striking verb *capto,* which regularly has a negative tone when describing social relations: see 6.63.1–2, 8.38.3, 9.88.1, 11.55.3, 12.10.1, 12.82.3, and, for *cenam captare,* 7.20.1–3 with Galán Vioque, Petr. *Sat.* 7.20.2–3, 3.3, 5.5 (Fletcher 1983: 408). For *captatores* in general see Tracy 1980.

Of metrical interest is the variation *captŏ . . . captō.* For the shortening, or "correption," of final *-ō* to *-ŏ* in the first instance of the word, see on **2.9.2**, and for the repetition of two different metrical forms of the same word in close proximity, compare 1.36.1 (*tibī/tibĭ*) and **2.36.2, 4** (*nōlō/nōlŏ*) with Hopkinson 1982 (Latin examples mostly from Ovid).

1 *heu:* After *o* (see on **2.4.1**), *heu* is the most frequently occurring of interjections in Martial (twelve examples, including the present case).

1 *Maxime:* Friedlaender distinguishes between a fictional Maximus (**2.53**, 3.18) and a real one (1.7, 1.69, 5.70, 7.73, 10.77), asserting that the man addressed in the present epigram cannot be the latter. Prinz 1911: 22–23 n. 2 is rightly skeptical, as this poem does not attack the man harshly enough to require the use of a pseudonym. See on 8 below for the possibility that this poem was originally addressed not to Maximus at all, but rather to Postumus.

1 *cenam:* Over the course of these few epigrams we see how the *cena,* or banquet, can localize various kinds of social critique: of those who desperately seek invitations (Selius in **2.11, 2.14**); of those involved in the depressing necessities created by the *clientela* system (Martial and Maximus in the present epigram); of stingy rich men (Zoilus in **2.19**). Indeed, a reference to a dinner is a favorite opening technique in Martial: in Book II alone, the noun *cena* or the verb *cenare* appears in the first line of **2.19, 2.27, 2.69,** and **2.72.**

2 *iam sumus ergo pares:* For the use of a recurring line or half-line as a refrain, compare 1.77 (*et tamen pallet*), **2.33** (*cur non basio te, Philaeni?*), 7.10 (*Ole, quid ad te?*), 9.97 (*rumpitur invidia*), 11.47 (*ne futuat*), 11.94 (*verpe poeta, sapis*) with Siedschlag 1977: 45 (who finds no parallels in Greek epigram) and Laurens 1989: 330. Prinz 1911: 87 speaks of "metrical games" ("metrische Spielereien"), but the phrase is perhaps too dismissive, and the phenomenon is not merely metrical.

Along with Norcio and Scandola, I take *iam* and *ergo* together in the sense "therefore"; for the collocation, see *TLL* 7.1.129.37–54: *vi conclusiva, i.q. tum ergo, sim.* Shackleton Bailey takes *iam* and *ergo* separately ("so we are even thus far").

3 *mane salutatum venio:* For the *salutatio,* or morning reception, held by patrons, often represented from the client's perspective as a disagreeable duty, see 1.55.6, 1.70, 1.108, 3.36, 3.58, 4.8, 4.26, 4.78.3, 5.22, 6.88 (with Grewing), 7.39, 8.44, 9.92 (a slave should be grateful that, unlike his master, he does not have to perform this ritual), 9.100, 12.26, 12.68 ("matutine cliens, urbis mihi causa relictae"). Juvenal's Umbricius alludes to the *salutatio* as one of the many unpleasant features of life in the city that he is happily abandoning (3.127–128; cf. 5.19–23). See also V. *Geo.* 2.461 (with *mane salutantum* at the beginning of a hexameter); Sen. *Dial.* 9.12.6, 10.14.3, *Epist.* 4.10, 68.10; Plin. *Epist.* 3.12.

5 comes: Martial refers quite frequently to the practice of escorting one's patron on the street while wearing the toga: **2.57.5**, **2.74.1**, 3.7.2, 3.46.1, 6.48.1, 10.74.3. Compare also Juvenal 7.141–143 ("an tibi servi / octo, decem *comites,* an post te sella, *togati /ante pedes*"), 10.44–46.

5 tumidique anteambulo regis: The noun *anteambulo* (again at 3.7.2, 10.74.3) is derogatory in tone, as is *servus* below. Strictly speaking, the term may have designated those slaves who walked in front of their masters on the streets just as *pedisequi* followed them (Marquardt 1886: 148 with n. 2), or it may have more generally referred to anyone, such as a freeborn client, who accompanied a more powerful man (Mau, *RE* s.v. *anteambulo*). The only other text apart from Martial in which the noun appears (Suet. *Vesp.* 2.2: "per contumeliam anteambulonem fratris appellat") offers no information on the point, but it certainly illustrates the pejorative tone the word could assume.

The use of the term *rex* to refer to one's patron (*OLD* s.v. 8) is attested as far back as Plautus (*St.* 455) and Terence (*Ph.* 338); in Martial see also **2.68.9**, 3.7, 4.40.9, 5.19.3, 5.22, 10.96.3, (and see White 1978: 81, Fraenkel 1960: 182–183). The term bore a heavy ideological burden at Rome ever since the expulsion of the last king, Tarquinius Superbus, in 510 B.C. (see Opelt 1965: 129–131) but was not always necessarily negative in tone: Martial himself uses the figure of the Parthian king as an illustration of living freely (**2.53.10**).

The phrase *tumidi regis* occurs again at 5.19.13 ("tumidique vocant haec munera reges"). For this use of *tumidus* in the sense "swollen with pride and/or ostentation," see 5.8.6 ("et iactat tumido superbus ore"), 8.3.15, 10.87.9, 10.104.16.

7 esse sat est servum: Epigrams **2.32** and **2.68** similarly end with *sententiae* comparing the patron-client relationship to that between master and slave and underscoring the fact that a patron in turn may be someone else's client; see also 10.56.1: "totis, Galle, iubes tibi me *servire* diebus." See on **2.32.8** for the use of *dominus* ("master") to refer to one's patron. Martial's representation of himself as a slave is obviously hyperbolic—a rhetorical indulgence allowed only to those who were not actually slaves— and the self-pitying nature of the remark is reminiscent of his recurring complaints of poverty. Still, the phrase offers a fruitful insight into the dynamics of masculine society at Rome. Because of its hierarchical structure, a man would necessarily assume a subordinate position in certain contexts, especially with respect to his *patronus.*

Martial was hardly the first to use the imagery of slavery with regard to patron-client relations: see Sen. *De brev. vit.* 2.1 ("sunt quos ingratus superiorum cultus *voluntaria servitute* consumat"). Indeed, the turning around of the language of slavery such that free Roman men could be described as "slaves" (e.g., to their own appetites and desires or to more powerful men) was especially characteristic of Stoic argumentation. See further on **2.53.1** and compare Hor. *Sat.* 2.7, Sen. *Epist.* 47, together with the discussion of "servile" social relations in Fitzgerald 2000: 71–77.

7 *iam nolo:* For *iam* in a logical sense, see *TLL* 7.1.120.72–124.11 and compare **2.25.2** ("iam rogo"): it is enough to be a slave; therefore, I don't want to be a slave's slave as well (Scandola). Alternatively, *iam* with verbs like *nequeo* and *nolo* may have the sense "no longer, no more" (*TLL* 7.1.101.6–28). Damon 1997: 151 thus argues that "the dissatisfaction of this speaker is such that he breaks off with his patron," but the present tenses of the epigram (*capto, venio, sum,* and indeed *sumus*) seem to contradict Damon's thesis that Martial speaks "from the vantage point of after-the-fact" (152).

7 *vicarius:* The noun, occurring only here in Martial, refers to various kinds of substitutes or deputies, including, as here, "a slave's slave"—an especially degrading image for the position of the *cliens.* Strictly speaking, slaves could legally own no property and thus no slaves; yet they could be allowed to have a sum of money that they were free to administer as they saw fit (the so-called *peculium;* see D. 15.1.5.4 and *RE* s.v.). With this they might purchase objects, including other slaves, or even eventually their own freedom, but as long as they remained slaves, the ownership both of the *peculium* and of anything puchased with it ultimately lay in the hands of their masters.

8 *qui rex est regem, Maxime, non habeat:* For similarly forthright descriptions of the kind of patron Martial seeks, see also **2.32.8** ("sit liber, dominus qui volet esse meus") and 5.22.14 ("rex, nisi dormieris, non potes esse meus"). For *non* instead of *ne* with jussive and optative subjunctives, found in poetic texts of all periods and in late prose, see KS 2.1.192.

This line illustrates a number of characteristic structural features. For the use of a final *sententia,* here of the type that Quintilian (*Inst.* 8.5.5) calls *apagoreutikê,* see on **2.12.4** and Barwick 1959: 40. For the repetition in the last line of a vocative also found in the first line, see on **2.10**; for its positioning immediately after the principal caesura, see on **2.10.4**. For the technique of repeating a word, often with a shift in form, in the final line of an epigram (*rex, regem*), see on **2.12.4**.

8 *Maxime:* Although MSS of family γ transmit the epigram with the lemma *Ad Maximum* and with *Maxime* in 1, here they read not *Maxime* but *Postume*. This family's archetype thus seems to have presented a blatantly self-contradictory text, but this did not disturb scribes enough to attempt correction; see **2.7.5**, **2.16.3**, **2.23.5**, **2.43.1**, and **2.44.2** for other examples of clearly impossible readings. The most satisfying explanation of this case (Lindsay 1903a: 33) is that the addressee of the poem was always Maximus, and that the scribe of the archetype of γ mistakenly wrote *Postume* for *Maxime* in 8, an error attributable to the more frequent appearance of the name Postumus in Book II (**2.10**, **2.12**, **2.21–23**, **2.67**, **2.72**) than of Maximus (only here and **2.53**). Granting this possibility, Lehmann 1931: 12 proposes a less convincing explanation as an alternative: the variants might stem from the poet himself in connection with a second edition of Book II (see Introduction, section 1). Lehmann conjectures that in the first edition, this epigram was addressed to Postumus, but for the second edition Martial decided to change the addressee's name to Maximus (similarly in 1.10 and **2.7**) because the poem no longer fit into the context of the other Postumus poems in the revised Book II. In a similar vein, Barwick 1958: 300 and Burnikel 1980: 89 go so far as to propose that the entire cycle on Postumus' kisses (**2.10**, **2.12**, **2.21**, **2.22**, **2.23**) constituted a new addition to the second edition, while the present epigram, originally addressed to Postumus, was an older piece that Martial decided to keep in its place (but why?) while renaming the figure to Maximus.

2.19

Felicem fieri credis me, Zoile, cena?
  felicem cena, Zoile, deinde tua?
debet Aricino conviva recumbere clivo,
  quem tua felicem, Zoile, cena facit.

Do you think I'm made happy by a dinner, Zoilus? *Your* dinner, of all things, Zoilus? Whoever is made happy, Zoilus, by your dinner ought to settle down to eat with the beggars on the Arician slope.

Themes.   As in the preceding epigram, the *cena* appears in the epigram's opening line, providing the focus for satiric commentary on yet another kind of behavior. The character Zoilus, already introduced as a man who will feign illness in order to display his wealth, and later revealed to be an ex-slave (see on **2.16.1**), is now the butt of a different but related insult. Al-though rich, he is such a stingy host that his dinners would satisfy only a beggar (*pace* Barwick 1958: 302–303, who understands Martial to be repre-senting Zoilus' tasteless display as repulsive).

For other remarks on bad hosting, see 1.23, 1.43 with Citroni ad loc., 7.79, 8.22; *A.P.* 11.96, 325, 377, 387, 413 (Pertsch 1911: 19). Particularly relevant is 3.82, where Zoilus appears once again as a host who reserves all the luxuries for himself. Juv. 11.129–131 denigrates a snobbish dinner guest in terms that could easily apply to Martial's own persona in the present epigram ("ergo superbum / convivam caveo, qui me sibi comparat et res / despicit exiguas"), and the same satire insistently praises a decently modest meal over extrava-gant banquets, such as that given by Martial himself in **2.37** (q.v.).

Damon 1997: 150–151 observes that the speaker in this epigram is "the untrustworthy friend himself (and proud of it)," and sees a deeper criticism of the whole system: "This speaker, who vents his annoyance at the trivial-ity of the services for which he is expected to show gratitude, is in much the same position as the guest of Horace's Calabrian host who offers unwanted pears (*Epist.* 1.7.14–21). Like the Calabrian host, Zoilus thinks that a trivial *beneficium* (a meager dinner; a gift of pears that will otherwise be fed to the pigs) ought to produce real obligation in a *cliens*."

Structure.   The epigram falls neatly into two halves: the first couplet de-scribes Zoilus' attitude, the second presents Martial's sarcastic reaction. The first couplet in turn consists of two incredulous questions, each occupying a line, each introduced with the key word *felicem,* and each with an emphatic vocative in the second half of the line. Striking, too, is the fact that the combination *felicem . . . cena* is repeated three times in this four-line epigram, as is the vocative *Zoile*. Out of the seventy-one epigrams in Book II having a vocative addressee, a threefold repetition appears only here, in **2.3**, and in **2.28**; for a fourfold repetition, see **2.69**. See Laurens 1989: 270–271, 277–278, for a reading of the epigram that treats the rep-etitions of *Zoile* and *felicem . . . cena* as an important element in "la syntaxe de l'ironie": the vocative is neutral in the first verse, sarcastic in the sec-ond, brutal in the fourth.

1 *credis?* For leading questions like *putas?* and *credis?* see 1.72, **2.26** ("iam te rem factam credis habere?"), 6.56, 7.63, 8.37, 9.14, 9.41. Siedschlag 1977: 20 cites Catull. 37, 104, V. *Catal.* 13, and Sen. *Epigr.* 6 as Latin prede-cessors but finds no Greek parallels.

3 *Aricino conviva recumbere clivo:* The reference is to the town of Aricia (modern Ariccia), on the Appian Way about 16 miles from Rome. From the present epigram, as well as 12.32.10, Pers. 6.56, and Juv. 4.117, it is clear that a nearby slope, the *clivus Aricinus,* was well known as a place where beggars gathered because carriages traveling the road at this point had to slow down considerably (Courtney ad Juv. 4.116).

The verb *recumbere* (literally, "to recline") refers to the usual posture at Roman dinner parties: reclining on a couch on the left elbow, the right arm free to reach for food (Marquardt 1886: 300). There may also be a play on the literal sense of "lying down," that is, on the ground as the beggars do (Collesso).

2.20

Carmina Paulus emit, recitat sua carmina Paulus.
　　nam quod emas possis iure vocare tuum.

Paulus buys poems; Paulus gives readings from his poems. After all, what you buy you can rightfully call your own.

Themes.   With the characteristic punch of a monodistich, the epigram re-turns to the theme of poetry (**2.1**, **2.6**, **2.7.2–3**, **2.8**) but introduces a new topic: plagiarism. Given the conditions of publication, and the absence of anything comparable to a copyright, this was a constant threat. Epigram 1.29 is very similar, though directly involving the poet himself. There, having heard that Fidentinus is reciting Martial's poems as his own, Martial urges him either to acknowledge their true authorship or else to pay him, where-upon the poems would then be his: "si dici tua vis, hoc eme, ne mea sint." See also 1.38, 1.52–53, 1.63, 1.72, 7.77, 10.3, 10.100, 10.102, 11.94, 12.63; Plin. *Epist.* 2.10. In 1.66 Martial consoles himself by observing that one who attempts to plagiarize a well-known author risks being caught; he ends with a memorable warning: "Whoever recites someone else's work and seeks fame needs to buy not a book but silence" ("aliena quisquis reci-tat et petit famam, / non emere librum, sed silentium debet," 13–14). In 12.47 he reminds us of the other side of the coin: that poets might sell their work to others. The theme is not characteristic of Greek epigram (Prinz 1911: 79).

Structure.   As is often the case with monodistichs (see on **2.3**), the first line describes a situation and the second comments on it; here the transition is marked by the causal *nam.* After an effectively compressed opening (cf. **2.16.1**, "Zoilus aegrotat"), we learn that Paulus has bought some poems and that he is reciting his poetry. In itself, the phrase *sua carmina* does not necessarily refer to the poems that he has bought (so too Joepgen 1967: 85; though see below), but the second line clearly identifies the two, thereby simultaneously filling out the picture and offering ironic commentary. Holzberg 2002: 87 cites this epigram as a good example of the applicability of Lessing's bipartite model; in this case the *Aufschluss* consists of commentary on the material provided in the *Erwartung*.

1 Paulus: The name appears with some frequency in Martial: in 5.28 and perhaps 7.72 referring to a real man, and in the present epigram and eight others to various fictional characters. Interestingly, another poem playing with the sense of the possessive adjective (6.12, quoted on 2 below) is addressed to a Paulus, although the reading is not entirely certain.

1 recitat sua carmina: Martial frequently refers to the practice of recitation, whether to a small group of friends (as at Hor. *Sat.* 1.4.73) or to a broader public (according to Sen. *Contr.* 4.praef.2, a practice formalized for the first time by C. Asinius Pollio at some point after 38 B.C.): see 1.63 with Citroni, **2.27.2**, **2.71.2**, **2.88**, and compare Petr. *Sat.* 90, 115; Sen. *Epist.* 95.2; Juv. 1.1ff., 3.9ff.; Hutchinson 1993: 146–148; Binder 1995; Nauta 2002: 93–105.

Most translators take the possessive adjective to be attributive; Ker and Walter, p. 84 understand it to be predicative ("Paulus recites the poetry as his"). The difference in meaning is slight: if *sua* is predicative, the point that Paulus is passing off as his the poetry he has bought is made already in the first line; if it is attributive, we learn this in the second verse. For *carmina*, see on **2.7.2**; here the genre is left unspecified.

2 quod emas possis iure vocare tuum: Like most translators, I construe *iure* with *possis,* understanding it in its broad sense ("rightly, justly"; cf. 8.58.2: "possim te Sagarim *iure vocare meo*"), and I take the second-person verbs *emas* and *possis* to be indefinite. Walter, p. 84 understands the phrase quite differently, taking *iure* with *emas* and the second-person forms as referring to Paulus: "*You* believe that what you have purchased in a juridically unobjectionable way you can also call your property in an ideal sense" ("*Du* meinst, du könntest das, was du juristisch einwandfrei gekauft hast, auch im ideellen Sinn als dein Eigentum bezeichnen").

The text printed above is the reading of R, the sole representative of family α for this epigram; the MSS of family β omit the line; the reading of family γ is *possis dicere iure tuum.* Lindsay 1903a: 15 suggests that the variants may be traceable to Martial himself. But if we assume scribal error, it is more likely that Martial wrote *possis iure vocare tuum.* A scribe's eye could have skipped from *iure* to *vocare* by *saut du même au même,* causing the omission of *iure,* and a subsequent scribe, confronted with the incomplete *possis iure tuum,* could then have supplied *dicere.* Shackleton Bailey observes that family γ shows similar signs of scribal supplement at 1.76.3, 3.27.1, 9.100.5, 10.15.8, and possibly 5.42.7.

2 *tuum:* This simple word at the poem's end brings home the point and addresses a problem of definition; compare the question regarding the sense of *debere* implied by **2.3**.

Play with possessives characterizes several of Martial's epigrams on plagiarism: see 1.29.4 with Citroni, 1.38, 1.52–53, 10.100. For emphatic possessives in other contexts, see **2.58**, 6.12 with Grewing ("Iurat capillos esse, quos emit, suos / Fabulla: numquid, Paule, <numquid> peierat?"), and 14.46.2 with Leary, as well as Joepgen 1967: 85–86.

2.21

Basia das aliis, aliis das, Postume, dextram.
dicis "utrum mavis? elige." malo manum.

To some you give kisses and to others, Postumus, your right hand.
You say, "Which do you prefer? The choice is yours." I prefer the
hand.

Themes.   We return to invective on Postumus and his repulsive kisses (**2.10**, **2.12**; cf. Hormus in **2.15**) with an epigram that initiates a three-poem cluster. The point is the same as in **2.10**—Martial would prefer not to kiss Postumus—but made even more bluntly. Walter 1995: 109 suggests that Martial is resisting "the fashion of greeting with a kiss" ("der Mode des Begrüßungskusses"), but this seems unlikely. Although in 11.98 Martial expresses impatience with *basiatores,* the problem is their insistence rather than the practice itself; just as in **2.67** Martial is hardly rejecting the practice of greeting people with the formula "Quid agis?" Nor would it be in line with Martial's persona to reject a practice simply because it is fashionable.

Structure.   Rather than displaying the bipartite structure frequently characterizing monodistichs, the epigram's three sentences correspond to its tripartite structure: Postumus' practice; his offer to Martial; the latter's response. At the same time we observe the decreasing length and complexity of the three sentences, culminating as they do in a two-word point.

1: The chiastic structure *das aliis, aliis das* is itself positioned between the two opposed objects *basia* and *dextram,* but a perfect ABCCBA structure is compromised by the inserted vocative *Postume.* For the phrase *basia das* and for the practice of kissing as social greeting, see on **2.10.1.**

1 *dextram:* For the handclasp as alternative to the kiss, see Suet. *Dom.* 12: when his father's concubine Caenis offered him a kiss in greeting, the young Domitian extended his hand instead, a sign of his being *minime civilis animi.*

2 *dicis "utrum mavis?"* The technique of anticipating or imagining an interlocutor's response or comment with a verb of saying (*dicis, inquis, ais, respondes*) is found frequently enough in Martial: in Book II alone, see **2.32.6, 2.60.3, 2.63.4, 2.65.2, 2.67.1, 2.69.6, 2.93.1.** For the omission of an explicit verb of saying, see on **2.8.7.**

2 *malo manum:* For the shortening of the final vowel in *malo,* see on **2.9.2** (again with this verb at **2.71.6**). The dry alliterative formulation functions simultaneously as a direct response addressed to Postumus and as a general statement of preference addressed to the readership.

2.22

Quid mihi vobiscum est, o Phoebe novemque sorores?
  ecce nocet vati Musa iocosa suo.
dimidio nobis dare Postumus ante solebat
  basia, nunc labro coepit utroque dare.

Why do I have anything to do with you, Phoebus and the nine sisters? Behold, the playful Muse is harming her bard. Postumus used to kiss me with only half his lips, but now he has begun to kiss me with both.

Themes. The cluster of Postumus poems continues, the meter remaining the same but the length increasing. An attentive reader may observe that this epigram concludes a chiastic sequence: **2.19–22** are all in elegiac couplets, the first and last consisting of two couplets each, the central two consisting of a single couplet each.

Here the invective is given an amusing twist with the ironically self-pitying statement of Ovidian inspiration at the poem's beginning: Martial is suffering because of his success, insofar as Postumus, described in **2.10** as greeting him with an aloof half-kiss, now plants full kisses on the renowned poet. Recalling the opening of *Trist.* 2 ("Quid mihi vobiscum est, infelix cura, libelli, / ingenio perii qui miser ipse meo?"), these lines jokingly draw a parallel between Ovid's punishment by Augustus and Martial's by Postumus (Holzberg 2002: 98–99). Martial's reference in this epigram to his achieved fame, as also in 1.1, is sometimes taken as a sign that these epigrams were composed for a second edition of Books I and II (see Introduction, section 1; Dau 1887: 77, Barwick 1958: 300, Citroni ad 1.1).

In 3–4 we encounter a direct cross-reference back to **2.10.1**: "basia dimidio quod das mihi, Postume, labro." This is a sign of deliberate ordering on the poet's part: regardless of when the epigrams were actually composed (for all we know, they may have been written more or less contemporaneously), the present epigram has been positioned so as to be read after **2.10** within the framework of the published book we have before us. For examples of back-reference to a specific epigram *as text,* as opposed to back-references to subjects treated earlier (for which see **2.23** and on **2.69.6**), see 3.11, where *distichon* refers back to 3.8, and 6.65, where *hoc longum est* refers to the immediately preceding 6.64.

Structure.   There is a clear and amusing contrast between the first couplet, which loftily and portentously announces Martial's suffering in Ovidian terms, and the second, which bathetically describes its cause in down-to-earth detail, naming Postumus in the first line and describing his horrific deed in the second. The shift in tone reminds us of the distance between Martial's and Ovid's situations. Each couplet in turn has a back-and-forth movement. In the first, a questioning apostrophe to Apollo and the Muses is followed by a statement explaining the source of the poet's distress (*ecce*). In the second, Postumus' previous behavior (*ante*) is contrasted with the disturbing recent development (*nunc*).

1 *quid mihi vobiscum est:* Echoing Ov. *Trist.* 2.1: "quid mihi vobiscum est, infelix cura, libelli?" For the technique of opening with strongly worded questions of this type (*quid tibi/mihi cum . . . ?*), compare 3.81 ("quid cum femineo tibi barathro?"), 9.68 ("quid tibi nobiscum est, ludi scelerate magister?"), 14.56 ("quid mecum est tibi?"), along with Tib. 1.6.3, *Priap.* 17, and Siedschlag 1977: 21.
1 *o Phoebe novemque sorores:* This elevated phrase contributes to the lofty tone of the first couplet. For the periphrasis for the Muses, often associated with Apollo, compare 5.6.18 ("dominum novem sororum"), 12.3.4 ("novem dominas"), 1.70.15 ("nec propior quam Phoebus amet doctaeque sorores"), 1.76.3–5 ("sorores"), 9.42.3 ("doctaeque sorores"), 1.76.3 and 4.31.5 ("sorores"); Ov. *Trist.* 2.14 ("doctas . . . sorores"), 5.12.45 ("sorores"). Apos-

trophe, or direct address, to a deity is surprisingly rare in Martial (1.31.1, 4.40.10, 6.10.9, 6.38.9, 11.60.9).

2 ecce nocet vati Musa iocosa suo: Both the concept and the wording are clearly inspired by Ovid's exile poetry: cf. *Trist.* 2.13 ("si saperem, doctas odissem iure sorores, / numina cultori perniciosa meo"), 2.354, 2.411 ("nec nocet auctori"), 3.2.5 ("Musa iocosa mea"), 3.7.9 ("ad Musas, quamvis nocuere"), 3.14.6 ("artifici quae nocuere suo"), 5.12.45 ("pace novem vestra liceat dixisse sorores"), *Pont.* 4.13.41 ("nocuerunt carmina quondam").

3–4 dare ... basia: For this phrase, also found in the immediately preceding epigram (**2.21.1**), see on **2.10.1**. Among extant texts, it is found only in Martial and Catullus.

3–4 dimidio ... labro: For the meaning of the phrase, see on **2.10.1**; for the *apo koinou* structure, see on **2.2.1**.

2.23

Non dicam, licet usque me rogetis,
qui sit Postumus in meo libello,
non dicam: quid enim mihi necesse est
has offendere basiationes
quae se tam bene vindicare possunt?   5

As much as you might ask me, I won't say who the Postumus of my
book is. I won't! After all, why should I offend those kisses of his
when they can avenge themselves so well?

Themes.   The cluster of poems on Postumus comes to an end with a shift in meter from elegiacs to hendecasyllabics, made all the more noticeable by the fact that this is the only epigram between **2.18** and **2.32** not in elegiac couplets. As in **2.22**, the theme of Postumus' kisses is combined with that of Martial's poetry and its implicitly wide readership (why else would Postumus seek to avenge himself?). Burnikel 1980: 91 cites **2.22** and **2.23** as an example of juxtaposed poems in which the second constitutes a reaction or reply to the first, but the present epigram is rather a response to the whole series on Postumus than specifically to the preceding poem.

Structure.   The poem falls into two parts: Martial emphatically refuses to reveal Postumus' identity (1–3, a statement framed by the emphatic repeti-

tion *non dicam*) and then explains why. The shift between the two halves
is marked not only by the second occurrence of the phrase *non dicam* but
also by a transition from emphatic statement to rhetorical question, as well
as the explanatory *enim*.

1 *licet usque:* The collocation *licet usque* + subjunctive, to be distinguished from *licet* with a verb and the preposition *usque,* occurs several times
in Martial (**2.1.8**, 5.60.1, 6.51.3, 11.52.17, 14.55.1, 14.130.1) but rarely elsewhere: compare Ov. *Her.* 1.83 ("increpet usque licet"); *Priap.* 45.5 ("iuras te
licet usque torqueasque"), 64.5 ("furetur licet usque, non videbo").

1 *rogetis:* This may be understood simultaneously as being addressed
to us readers, who hold the papyrus, codex, or book in our hands, and to an
imagined group of friends or acquaintances (cf. the first-person plurals in
1.14, **2.64**, and **2.65**), although admittedly Martial's direct addresses to his
readers are usually in the singular (1.1–2, 1.40, **2.8**, 4.55, 5.16, 6.88, 7.12,
10.2, 11.16).

2 *qui sit Postumus in meo libello:* This forces the ever lurking question regarding the identity of the objects of Martial's invective. Given the
poet's stated policy of not attacking real people by name (1.praef.; 10.33.10:
"parcere personis, dicere de vitiis"), "Postumus" will be a pseudonym. But
did a real man—now unknown to us but potentially known to some of
Martial's original readership—lie behind this figure? Or is he a creation of
the poet, perhaps a pastiche of real persons known to him, the implication
that there is a real man behind the name being part of a literary game? See
the Introduction, section 3.2.

3 *non dicam:* For the teasing refusal to name names, compare 1.96.14
("quaeris quis hic sit? excidit mihi nomen"), 11.8.13–14 ("scire cupis nomen?
si propter basia, dicam. / iurasti. nimium scire, Sabine, cupis"), *A.P.* 11.325.
At 5.60.6–7 the motif recurs in the context of invective: by refusing to name
one of his critics, Martial denies him fame.

4 *basiationes:* Perhaps a Catullan touch, as this humorously elevated
abstract noun is attested only at 7.95.17 and Catull. 7.1, just as *fututio* is likewise found only in Catullus (32.8), Martial (1.106.6), and possibly a poem
from the *Anthologia Latina* (460.7 Riese, as supplemented by L. Müller: "nil
est deprensa mel<ius fututione>").

5 *quae se tam bene vindicare possunt:* Note the humorous exaggeration: the mere possibility of a kiss from Postumus keeps Martial from
revealing his identity. An epigram on Zoilus likewise blends the themes
of the poet's relationship to a character, revenge, and oral impurity (3.82).
The *variorum* commentary cites an interesting parallel from Plautus
(*Asin.* 902–903): "nam si domum / redierit hodie, osculando ego ulciscar
potissimum."

2.24

Si det iniqua tibi tristem fortuna reatum,
  squalidus haerebo pallidiorque reo:
si iubeat patria damnatum excedere terra,
  per freta, per scopulos exulis ibo comes.
dat tibi divitias: ecquid sunt ista duorum?   5
  das partem? multum est? Candide, das aliquid?
mecum eris ergo miser: quod si deus ore sereno
  adnuerit, felix, Candide, solus eris.

If an unjust Fortune should cause you to be accused of a grim crime, I will stand by you, disheveled and even more pallid than you, though you would be the one on trial. If she should decree that you be condemned to abandon your homeland, I will go with you over the sea and among the rocky islets as a companion in exile. Instead, she grants you wealth. Doesn't that belong to two? Won't you give me a share? Is it too much to ask? Candidus, won't you give me anything? Well, then: you'll share your misery with me, but if the god smiles beneficently on you, Candidus, you will be alone in your good fortune.

Themes. After the three preceding Postumus poems, the tone becomes more serious with this epigram's opening imagery of condemnation and exile, along with its fervent expression of commitment to a friend. Here, as again in **2.44**, we find combined two common themes: a complaint regarding friends who fail to live up to the ideals of *amicitia*, especially that of sharing (see **2.6** and **2.43**), and a request for financial help which, when refused, is met with reproach (see **2.30**). For the image of a rich friend or patron who selfishly keeps his riches or food to himself, see also 1.99 with Citroni ad loc., 1.103, **2.30**, **2.46**, 3.12, 3.60, 3.82, 4.40, 4.67, 5.19 (where this is represented as a general problem of the times), 5.25, 5.42, 6.11, 7.53, 7.92, 8.14, 8.33, 9.2, 9.22, 9.46, 10.15, 10.19 (note the revealing phrase *sterilis amicus*, implying that one might normally expect some kind of "harvest" from him), 12.13, 12.53. The theme is not characteristic of Greek epigram (Prinz 1911: 79).

The present epigram offers an interesting twist on the theme of the "fair-weather friend," enunciated among others in a passage from Ovid's *Tristia* that clearly lies behind this epigram: "donec eris sospes, multos numerabis amicos, / tempora si fuerint nubila, *solus eris*" (1.9.5–6). See also Juv. 1.135–146 and 4.11–33, the latter passage ending with a consolatory curse comparable to Martial's final remark here: in the end, it is the selfish rich man who will suffer. See Maaz 2001 for discussion of this epigram, **2.43**, 3.26, and 3.46 in conjunction with epigrams on the theme of friendship by the eleventh-century poet Godfrey of Winchester.

It is emblematic of Martial's satirical tendency that there is not a single epigram in Book II and only a few elsewhere (e.g., 1.93, 9.52, 10.13, 10.44, 10.47) that praise without reservation a friend in particular or friendship in general. See further Spisak 1998a; Kleijwegt 1998; and, for Roman ideals of masculine friendship in general, Cic. *Amic.*, Pizzolato 1993, Konstan 1997, Peachin 2001.

Structure.   The first two couplets, each of them a conditional sentence beginning with *si,* constitute a strong assertion of Martial's commitment to Candidus: if things go badly for him, Martial will stand by him. Each line consists of an entire clause, whose subjects alternate between *fortuna* (1, 3) and Martial himself (2, 4). In the third and fourth couplets, introduced with an aversative asyndeton, Candidus himself becomes the principal subject (*das, das, eris, eris*) as we learn that things are going well for him. A quick series of pointed questions (5–6) asks whether he will share his good fortune with his friend, and the final couplet, in a shift marked by *ergo,* begins with a negative reply and ends (*quod si*) with Martial's barbed commentary.

Due to the absence of quotation marks in ancient editions, we cannot be entirely certain as to who is saying what. Indeed, the epigram's structure has been understood in various ways: as a dialogue between Candidus and Martial; as consisting almost entirely of Martial's words, with only *multum est* being Candidus' reply; or as being entirely Martial's words. Ker, Izaac, and Norcio, for example, place 1–4 in the present epigram within quotation marks, thus taking them to be the words of Candidus, who makes sweeping promises to his friend Martial; the second half of the epigram, in Martial's voice, reveals the hollowness of the promises. Read this way, the epigram anticipates **2.43**, where once again Candidus speaks quite grandly of friendship as sharing but is at once revealed to be a fraud. I have, however, tentatively followed Lindsay in placing nothing in quotation marks. This produces a more insistent tone: Martial makes stirring promises to Candidus and then observes that the latter does not reciprocate. For a second, independent problem of punctuation see on 6 (*multum est*).

1 *si det iniqua tibi tristem fortuna reatum:* Note the elevated tone of this opening line, with its personification of *fortuna,* imagined as actively shaping the circumstances of someone's life (cf. **2.91.5**: "quod fortuna vetat"), and its use of the technical term *reatum* (according to Quint. *Inst.* 8.3.34, first used by Messalla Corvinus). For *Fortuna* see 4.40, 4.51 (*dea caeca*), 6.79; for the imagery of "the god(s)" granting a man success, failure, riches, poverty, etc., see on **2.14.14** (*renuente deo*). Martial nowhere else uses the phrase *iniqua fortuna,* but compare *saeva fortuna* at 4.18.7.

2 *squalidus haerebo pallidiorque reo:* For the stereotype of the *squalidus reus,* or unkempt defendant, compare **2.36.3** (*barba reorum*) and **2.74.3** (*tonsus reus*), Ov. *Met.* 15.38, Val. Max. 6.5.2, Quint. *Inst.* 6.1.30, Tac. *Hist.* 2.60, Juv. 15.134–135, Gell. 3.4.1, Marquardt 1886: 582–583. For the attribution of a fearful pallor to defendants, compare 1.49.35 (*pallidus reus*), Hor. *Epist.* 1.1.61, Pers. 5.80, Stat. *Silv.* 4.4.41, Juv. 10.82.

3 *patria damnatum excedere terra:* This poetic phrase (cf. Val. Flacc. 2.297: "patria liceat decedere terra"; for *patria terra* instead of the more prosaic *patria,* see Lucr. 2.642; Sil. Ital. 12.304; Stat. *Theb.* 11.698, *Silv.* 3.5.13; Gell. 15.20.10) describes a harsh reality, famously suffered by Cicero, Ovid, and Seneca. By Martial's day, exile as formal punishment usually took the form of a sentence of *deportatio* (often to remote islands) or the milder *relegatio;* see Grasmück 1978.

4 *per freta:* The elevated tone continues. The plural of *fretum* is a common poeticism for "the deep" (*OLD* s.v.); the phrase *per freta* recurs at 8.50.16, 10.36.4, 12.98.4.

4 *per scopulos:* Literally referring to projecting rocks in the sea or on the coast, *scopuli* is a vivid way of referring to rocky islands serving as places of exile: Tac. *Hist.* 1.2 ("plenum exiliis mare, infecti caedibus scopuli"), Juv. 13.246–247 ("maris Aegaei rupem scopulosque frequentes / exulibus magnis").

4 *exulis ibo comes:* A strong statement of friendly solidarity; see 7.44 and 7.45 for high praise of an Ovidius for having accompanied his friend Caesonius Maximus in exile, and compare Ov. *Pont.* 2.3, 2.10.21–42; Sen. *Epist.* 9.10; Petr. *Sat.* 94.2. The phrase *exulis comes* may have been a technical term: cf. 6.83.8 ("esse quod et comiti contigit et reduci") with Grewing, 7.44.5 ("aequora per Scyllae magnus comes exulis isti"), 12.25.6 ("exilio comitem quaeris"), Cic. *Att.* 9.10.2, Liv. 6.3.4, Vell. Pat. 2.100.5.

5 *ecquid:* Especially used to introduce impatient questions to which an affirmative answer is expected (*OLD* s.v.); compare 7.35.7, 10.103.3.

6 *das partem:* Many translators (Ker, Bridge and Lake, Izaac, Ceronetti, Scandola, Shackleton Bailey) render *partem* as "half" (so too *OLD* s.v. 4b), but is Martial requesting precisely 50 percent of Candidus' windfall? Friedlaender cites 3.86.1 ("ne legeres partem lascivi, casta, libelli"), but there the noun refers to the second part, not literally half, of Book III, consisting of epigrams 69–100.

6 *multum est:* Ker, Shackleton Bailey, and Barié and Schindler, following a suggestion of Schneidewin, place a period rather than a question mark after these words and surround them with quotation marks. The phrase would thus be Candidus' objection to Martial's request: "That is a lot to ask!" For the possibility of introducing a quotation without marking it with *dicis, vel sim.,* see on **2.8.7**. If so, Martial asks *das partem?* Candidus replies in the negative (*multum est*), and Martial repeats the question with a slight variation (*das aliquid?*). I have, however, followed Lindsay, Izaac, and Norcio in printing 5–6 as a continuous sequence of insistent questions on Martial's part.

6 Candide: The (fictional) name appears only five times in Martial and is scattered through various books. It consistently designates someone who is the object of Martial's satire or invective: he is selfish (**2.24**, **2.43**, 3.26); he fails to live up to ideals of *amicitia* (**2.24**, **2.43**, 3.46); he is a cuckold (3.26, 12.38). Thus, the name (literally, "bright, radiant, clear") has more than a touch of irony, especially in the present epigram: see *OLD* s.v. *candidus* 8 ("good-natured") for the association of this adjective with ideals of friendship, and see further on **2.71.1**. Maaz 1992: 80 observes that this is one of six names attested only in Martial and Godfrey of Winchester; the others are Aper, Caecilianus (see on **2.37.11**), Didymus, Postumianus, and Probus.

7 quod si: See on **2.8.5**.

7–8 deus ore sereno / adnuerit: Another lofty phrase; the adjective's basic reference is to a cloudless sky. For the *os serenum* of Jupiter or the emperor, see 5.6.9, 7.12.1, 9.24.3; for divine nods of permission or refusal, see **2.14.14** (*renuente deo*) and 9.42.7 (*adnuatque Caesar*), and compare V. *Geo.* 1.40 ("audacibus adnue coeptis"), Ov. *Met.* 7.178, Sil. 3.115, Stat. *Silv.* 3.2.40.

8 felix ... solus eris: In a group-oriented culture like that of ancient Rome, the statement that Candidus will be alone in his good fortune amounts simultaneously to a paradox and a curse (cf. the image of dining alone at home at **2.11.10**): by keeping his riches to himself, Candidus will be creating for himself another kind of exile. More explicit curses appear at the end of other epigrams: see 1.99, **2.34** ("perpetuam di te faciant Philerotis amicam"), **2.66** ("hoc salamandra notet vel saeva novacula nudet"), 4.24 ("uxori fiat amica meae"), 4.51 ("di reddant sellam, Caeciliane, tibi"), 4.77 ("pendentem volo Zoilum videre"), 6.86, 7.24. Epigram 10.5 as a whole constitutes a protracted curse.

2.25

Das numquam, semper promittis, Galla, roganti.
 si semper fallis, iam rogo, Galla, nega.

You never give but always promise, Galla, when asked. If you always deceive, Galla, well then, please say no!

Themes.   This is the second in a series of poems in elegiac couplets (**2.24–32**) arranged symmetrically: the second and next-to-last epigrams of the block (the present epigram and **2.31**) are monodistichs, while the rest consist of two or more couplets each. Like an earlier monodistich addressed to a woman (**2.9**), the poem plays with the sexual meaning of the verb *dare,* here bringing in other verbs forming part of the traditional erotic lexicon (*promittere, rogare, fallere, negare;* see Pichon 1902: s.vv.). Martial is sexually interested in Galla but is rebuffed (for the figure of the woman in charge, especially in a sexual context, see **2.47**, 6.6, 6.22, 8.12, 10.41, 11.7). His response comes in the form of a paradoxical, manipulative request by means of which he not only hopes to attain his objective but strikes the pose of the clever underdog who has the last word.

The argumentative ploy is characteristic of this poet. In 4.76, for example, Martial has asked for 12,000 sesterces but has received 6,000; now he understands that if he really wants 12,000, he should ask for 24,000 (see also 11.68, 12.12). Siedschlag 1977: 84 finds the technique in no other epigrammatist, although *A.P.* 11.15 approximates it. In any case, the word and thought games of this epigram seem to have pleased Martial. Galla, *dare, rogare,* and *negare* all appear together again in 3.54, another monodistich with sexual overtones: "Cum dare non possim quod poscis, Galla, rogantem, / multo simplicius, Galla, negare potes" (Since I cannot give what you demand of the one who asks you, Galla, you can much more simply say no, Galla). Epigram 4.38 reads rather like a revision of the present epigram: "Galla, nega: satiatur amor nisi gaudia torquent: / sed noli nimium, Galla, negare diu" (Galla, say no. Love is satiated unless pleasures torment. But, Galla, do not say no for too long!). Consider also 12.71: "Nil non, Lygde, mihi negas roganti: / at quondam mihi, Lygde, nil negabas" (There is nothing, Lygdus, that you don't deny me when I ask; but there was a time, Lygdus, when you denied me nothing"). Martial further plays with *negare* and *rogare,* although referring not to sexual but to financial favors, at **2.44.11–12** ("durum est negare cum rogaris, / quanto durius, antequam rogeris") and 6.20.4 ("iam rogo, Phoebe, nega"; note the close similarity to the present epigram's ending); see further 7.43 for a play on *rogare, praestare,* and *negare.*

The humor resembles what Freud calls the *skeptischer Witz,* a type of tendentious humor ultimately aimed not at any single individual or an institution but rather at the uncertainty of human knowledge itself. The joke he cites as an example (Freud 1992: 130 = 1960: 115) regards two Galician Jews on a train. One asks the other where he is going, and when the second replies, "Krakow," the first bursts out: "What a liar! When you tell me you're going to Krakow, you actually want me to believe you're going to Lemberg. But I know that you are in fact going to Krakow. So why lie?"

Structure. As often in monodistichs, the first verse neatly describes the situation and the second offers a reaction. For the repetition of the vocative in the first and last lines of an epigram, see on **2.10**; in a monodistich, as here and in **2.38**, **2.42**, **2.50**, and **2.58**, the effect is somewhat different. Barwick 1959: 35 argues that the technique emphasizes the distinction between the epigram's two halves, but one could just as well see it as bringing the two parts into a tighter relationship.

1 *das numquam, semper promittis:* For *dare* see on **2.9.1**; for its juxtaposition with *promittere* (in a nonsexual sense), cf. 10.17.1: "si donare vocas *promittere nec dare*, Gai." Note the simple but effective chiastic structure, which underscores the contrast between Galla's words and deeds, and ultimately the conflict between Martial's and Galla's desires. Laurens 1989: 297 observes the chiastic ordering ("un chassé croisé sémantique") of *promittis, Galla, roganti / rogo, Galla, nega.*

1 *Galla:* Out of seventy-one epigrams with a vocative addressee in Book II, only six are addressed to women—the present epigram, **2.33** (Philaenis), **2.34** (Galla), **2.41** (Maximina), **2.50** (Lesbia), **2.66** (Lalage)—and all of them are negative in tone. In **2.34** Galla is the object of a much harsher reproach: she has spent all of her dowry on a male slave and sexual partner, preferring to let her three children starve to death. Common to the two allusions to Galla in Book II is thus that she is a woman who does what she wants in her sexual relations with men. The name occurs in fourteen other epigrams, almost always referring to a woman who is depicted negatively in the context of sexual relations or marriage (3.51, 3.54, 3.90, 4.38, 4.58, 7.18, 7.58, 9.4, 9.37, 9.78, 10.75, 10.95, 11.19); only at 5.84 is there no such connection. An epigram attributed to Seneca imagines a sexual liaison between the speaker and a married woman named Galla (*A.L.* 450 Riese).

Pace Barié and Schindler, there is no compelling reason to identify Martial's Galla as a prostitute. Indeed, here and elsewhere (cf. **2.9**), the game of courtship and the woman's ability to hold out or simply refuse suggest that characters like Galla and Naevia are neither slaves nor prostitutes, and in 3.33 Martial explicitly declares a preference for freeborn women over slaves and freedwomen. We are thus reminded of the mistresses populating the poetry of Catullus and the elegiac poets.

2 *iam rogo, Galla, nega:* The phrase may be of Ovidian inspiration (*Am.* 19–20: "tu quoque, quae nostros rapuisti nuper ocellos, / saepe time simulans, *saepe rogata nega*"). The formulation is not as strikingly oxymoronic as others (e.g., 3.34.2: "non es et es Chione"), but the tension created by the juxtaposition of the first-person *rogo* (for the shortened final vowel, see on **2.9.2**) and the imperative *nega* approaches paradox and reflects Galla's contradictory behavior itself (Lausberg 1982: 306–307). For the technique of ending with a paradox, see on **2.12.4**.

For the use of *negare* to refer to the denial of sexual favors, see also 1.106.7, 4.7.1 ("cur, here quod dederas, hodie, puer Hylle, negasti?"), 4.12 ("hoc saltem pudeat, Thai, negare nihil"), 4.71 ("nulla puella negat"; cf. 4.81), 11.49, 11.104, 12.75, 12.79, with Pichon 1902: s.v.

2.26

Quod querulum spirat, quod acerbum Naevia tussit,
    inque tuos mittit sputa subinde sinus,
iam te rem factam, Bithynice, credis habere?
    erras. blanditur Naevia, non moritur.

Because Naevia breathes laboriously, because her cough is severe and she is constantly hurling spit into your bosom, do you think you're set, Bithynicus? You're wrong. Naevia is teasing, not dying.

Themes.   The satiric focus continues to rest on a woman in this, the first epigram in Book II to allude to the frequently satirized phenomenon of legacy hunting, or *captatio*. Naevia is either feigning or exaggerating her illness— the epigram leaves the point open—in order to manipulate Bithynicus, who is perhaps her lover (see on 2 below), into thinking that she is near death; in hopes of an inheritance, he will do whatever she asks of him. A passage from Seneca implies that figures like Naevia were a real feature of the Roman urban landscape, though it is hard to know how widespread the phenomenon was (*De brev. vit.* 7.7: "ille ad irritandam avaritiam captantium simulatus aeger"); see on *tussit* below. For the practice of courting the friendship or intimacy of wealthy people, especially the old and childless, in hopes of making it into their wills, see 1.10 with Citroni ad loc., 1.49.34 (*imperia viduarum*), **2.32.6**, **2.76**, 3.76, 4.5, 4.56, 6.33, 6.62 (with Grewing), 6.63, 8.27, 8.38, 9.8, 9.48, 9.80, 9.88, 9.100, 11.44 ("orbus es et locuples et Bruto consule natus: / esse tibi veras credis amicitias?"), 11.83, 11.87, 12.10, 12.90; Hor. *Epist.* 1.1.77ff.; Ov. *Ars am.* 2.271–272, 332; Sen. *Ben.* 4.20, 6.38; Plin. *Epist.* 2.20.4. The theme is central to the Roman satiric tradition (Hor. *Sat.* 2.5, Petron. *Sat.* 117, Pers. 5.73; cf. Hopkins 1983: 238–247), and indeed Juvenal cites *captatio* in his opening programmatic satire as one of the key factors that leads him to write satire (1.37–39). It is characteristic of Martial's *persona,* and of its distance from that of Juvenal (see on **2.19**, **2.37**, **2.43**, and **2.44**), that he himself acts as a *captator* on a number of occasions: see 5.39, 9.48, 10.8 (he would marry an old woman if she were yet older!), 11.67, 12.40, 12.73.

Here we see how those courted by *captatores* might try to take advantage of the situation. In 11.55 Martial suggests another possible countermeasure: if you suspect that you are the object of *captatio,* pretend that you are going to have a child!

Structure. The first three lines, consisting of a single sentence in the form of a question, introduce the subject, while Martial's dry commentary in the final line, introduced with the single-word sentence *erras* in asyndeton, brings the point home. For the technique of building up the scenario by means of initial *quod*-clauses (here three, varied by the omission of the conjunction in the third clause), compare **2.11**. For the underlying *quod-non-sed* structure (*quod spirat . . . blanditur . . . non moritur* being a variation on *quod spirat . . . non moritur . . . sed blanditur*), see on **2.11**.

1 quod: See on **2.10.1** for this opening technique.

1 querulum spirat: Watson and Watson point to the double sense in the adjective *querulum,* here used adverbially: it refers both to Naevia's wheezing breath and to her (faked) lamentation of her imminent death. They compare the similar ambiguity at Sen. *Thy.* 766-767: "illa (sc., viscera) flammatus latex / querente aeno iactat."

1 Naevia: For the name, see on **2.9.1**.

1 tussit: In 1.10 we read of a man who courts an implicitly rich but explicitly ugly woman because she is ill, and again the focus is on her cough: "quid ergo in illa petitur et placet? tussit" (4). See also 5.39.6 ("mentitur tua quod subinde tussis") and Hor. *Sat.* 2.5.106–107 ("si quis / forte coheredum senior male tussiet").

2 inque tuos mittit sputa subinde sinus: Note the expressive alliteration of *s.* For *sinus* see on **2.6.7**; its frequent function as a sign of affection or intimacy makes the image particularly repulsive. The detail that Bithynicus allows Naevia to do this emphasizes his abject submission (*variorum* commentary); we might also see *sinus* as hinting that the two are lovers (cf. Pichon 1902: 264). Collesso prints the Italian humanist emendation of *tuos* to *suos,* explaining that Naevia is (or wishes to seem) so weak that she cannot spit any farther than her own lap.

The phrase *mittit sputa,* attested in no other surviving Latin text, is a periphrasis for the direct *sputat* or *spuit,* neither of which occurs in Martial. The imagery is humorously forceful: in the sense "to discharge, let fly (a missile)" (*OLD* s.v. 7), *mittere* usually takes such objects as *telum* (Caes. *B.C.*

1.45.6), *hastam* (Enn. *Ann.* 364), *sagittas* (Ov. *Ars am.* 2.195), *lapides* (Petr. *Sat.* 90.1), or *fulmina* (Hor. *C.* 1.12.59, Ov. *Trist.* 2.33, Mart. 6.83.3); cf. 1.3.8: "ibis ab excusso missus in astra sago."

3 *iam te rem factam, Bithynice, credis habere?* For the question-and-answer format leading up to the final point, see on **2.7.8**. For the phrase *rem factam habere,* see also 1.27.4 ("tu factam tibi rem statim putasti") and 6.61.1 ("rem factam Pompullus habet") and cf. **2.27.4** ("facta est iam tibi cena"). The name Bithynicus occurs again in 6.50, 9.8, and 12.78: in every case he is a friend to whom Martial gives ironic advice, and in 9.8 he is a duped *captator* (Watson and Watson).

4 *blanditur:* The verb denotes "to flatter; to coax, urge with or persuade by blandishments" (*OLD* 1); see on **2.4.1** for its possible erotic undertone (already perhaps established with *sinus* in 2). The paradoxical representation of spitting and coughing as *blanditiae* is worth noting: for someone interested in Naevia's money, this is a turn-on!

2.27

Laudantem Selium cenae cum retia tendit
   accipe, sive legas sive patronus agas:
"effecte! graviter! cito! nequiter! euge! beate!
   hoc volui!" facta est iam tibi cena, tace.

Hear how Selius sings your praises as he casts his net for dinner, whether you are reciting your work or pleading cases at court. "How consummate! How grand! How quick-witted! How wicked! Bravo! Splendid! Just what I was looking for!" You've got your dinner now, so be quiet.

Themes. We return to the theme of the *cena,* last seen in **2.19**, and to the character of Selius (**2.11**, **2.14**). Although there have been different interpretations of who says what in this epigram, and although the precise meaning of Selius' exclamations of praise has been understood in various ways (see below), the central idea is clear: eternally in search of a dinner invitation, Selius obtains his goal after luxuriantly flattering a potential host, much like Menogenes in 12.82. Compare also 6.48, where Pomponius' guests vociferously praise his recitations and Martial observes that it is not Pomponius himself but rather his dinner that is eloquent. The practice is alluded to, among others, by Petr. *Sat.* 40.1, Sen. *Epist.* 122.12 ("cenarum bonarum assectator, quas improbitate linguae merebatur"), Plin. *Epist.* 2.14, Juv. 3.86–107 (Umbricius attributes it to the Greeks); see further Grewing ad 6.48.

Structure. The first line sets out the situation with admirable concision, naming the central actor and identifying his behavior (*laudantem Selium*) and goal (*cenae*); further specificity is provided in the second line. There follows a dramatically effective direct quote with an accumulation of exclamations in asyndeton (see on **2.7** for the technique of *cumulatio,* and for the asyndeton cf. 3.58, 7.78, 7.97, 12.8, 12.49), all of them except for the climactic *hoc volui* consisting of a single word. The final sentence with its cut-and-dry parataxis reveals that Selius has been successful and ends on a note of blunt dismissal: *tace.*

1 *Selium:* See on **2.11.1**.

1 *cenae cum retia tendit:* The metaphor of casting a net appears again at **2.40.3, 2.47.1**, and 3.58.26. Earlier examples include Hor. *Epod.* 2.33; Prop. 2.32.20; Ov. *Am.* 1.8.69, *Ars am.* 1.45, *Met.* 8.331; cf. Otto 1890: 299, Sutphen 1901: 367, Szelinski 1904: 317. With the image of casting a net we might compare the use of the verb *captare* to refer to the phenomenon of "hunting" for dinner invitations, legacies, patronage, and the like (cf. on **2.11, 2.18, 2.26**). For *cenae* in the opening line, see on **2.18.1**.

2 *accipe:* The verb has received two distinct interpretations: either "take him along with you," that is, bring him along as a praise machine (Ker, Shackleton Bailey, Izaac, Ceronetti, Scandola), or "listen to him, hear him" (Collesso, Barié and Schindler, Norcio, Siedschlag 1977: 13, Walter 1995: 111). The latter is endorsed by *TLL* 1.306.45–308.32, where this passage is cited along with other instances of the imperative *accipe* or *accipite* (e.g., Plaut. *Amph.* 1101: "haec quae dicam accipe"; Mart. 12.praef.: "accipe ergo rationem"; Juv. 7.36: "accipe nunc artes"). This sense indeed seems more likely in the present context, given what immediately follows: *accipe* introduces the quotation and has a deictic function comparable to that of *vides* at **2.11.1, 2.29.1**.

2 *legas:* For the widespread practice of reciting one's works, whether to a small group of friends or to a broader public, see on **2.20.1**.

3 *graviter:* Translations vary rather significantly, from "weighty" and "impressive" (Ker, Damon 1997) to "a hit!" (Shackleton Bailey) to "che dottrina" (Norcio).

3 *cito:* Literally "quickly," a term of praise taken from the language of rhetorical criticism: cf. 7.34.4 ("dicam, sed cito"); Hor. *A.P.* 335; Sen. *Epist.* 9.2, 71.32; Heraeus 1925: 333 n. 2. Both here and at 5.25.2 (*sta*), Schneidewin emends to *st,* an interjection found in a verse quoted at Cic. *De orat.* 2.257: "st, tacete, quid hoc clamoris?" Friedlaender suggests that *cito* is equivalent to Italian *zitto,* that is, a call for silence, presumably addressed to critics in the audience. Neither suggestion has won acceptance.

3 *nequiter:* For the semantic range of *nequitia,* see on **2.4.4**. This is the only occurrence of the adverb in Martial; translations range from "a hard hit!" (Ker) to "cunning" (Shackleton Bailey; cf. Norcio's "che sagacia") to "malin" (Izaac) and "wie raffiniert" (Barié and Schindler). Walter unconvincingly suggests that *nequiter* is directed at critics of the speaker.

3 *euge:* This is the only occurrence of this Greek interjection in Martial; cf. *sophos* at 1.3.7, 1.49.37, 1.66.4, 1.76.10, 3.46.8, 6.48.1. For the use of Greek words or phrases in Martial, see on **2.43.1**.

4 *hoc volui:* This expression of satisfaction appears again at 6.60.4: "hoc volo: nunc nobis carmina nostra placent." Collesso, Heraeus, Ker, and Izaac take these to be the words not of Selius but rather of the man whom he is praising, and punctuate accordingly; Heraeus observes that all the other exclamations in the *cumulatio* are one-word adverbs. Nonetheless, it seems somewhat preferable to take *hoc volui* as the final and culminating element in Selius' string of laudatory exclamations.

4 *facta est iam tibi cena, tace:* Some editors (Heraeus, Lindsay, Shackleton Bailey) print these words—but not the epigram's first two lines—in quotation marks, thus implying that they are spoken by the unnamed addressee, who, having been the recipient of Selius' flattery, gives him his reward. I have followed others in not printing quotation marks, thus attributing the sentence to the narrative voice: having first spoken of Selius in the third person, the narrator now addresses him directly in the second person. For the shift from third to second person, cf. **2.16**, **2.44**, **2.65**.

2.28

Rideto multum qui te, Sextille, cinaedum
    dixerit et digitum porrigito medium.
sed nec pedico es nec tu, Sextille, fututor,
    calda Vetustinae nec tibi bucca placet.
ex istis nihil es, fateor, Sextille. quid ergo es?   5
    nescio, sed tu scis res superesse duas.

Laugh heartily at whoever calls you a *cinaedus*, Sextillus, and show him your middle finger. And yet you are not one to fuck either asses or cunts, Sextillus, nor do the warm cheeks of Vetustina give you pleasure. I admit it, Sextillus: you are none of these. So what, then, are you? I don't know, but *you* know that two things are left.

Themes. We are brought back with a bang to the realm of the sexual. While previous epigrams dealing with sexual topics in Book II have been euphemistic (**2.9**, **2.25**) or insinuating (**2.4**, **2.17**), with this epigram we are introduced to Martial's use of primary obscenities (*pedico, fututor*); at the same time we are given a clear glimpse into the conceptual mechanisms of sexual classification shared by poet and Roman readers. Martial defends Sextillus on the charge of being a *cinaedus* (see below on the meaning), then puzzles his way through other possible identities: if he is not a *cinaedus,* but also not an acceptably masculine *pedico, fututor,* or *irrumator,* what is he? The implied answer, that he is either *fellator* or *cunnilingus* or both, is hardly flattering and indeed probably constitutes a harsher insult than the original *cinaedus.* Thus, an epigram which begins by defending Sextillus' masculine sexual identity ends by delivering him a devastating blow. For the sexual hierarchy and the invective against *cunnilingi* and/or *fellatores* compare 1.77 with Citroni, **2.84**, 4.43, 6.56, 11.45, 12.35 with Obermayer 1998: 241–245, and Williams 1999: 201–203. For the three acceptably masculine sexual roles to which Martial alludes (*pedico, fututor, irrumator*), see Williams 1999: 163–172, and note that these are precisely the three roles which Martial portrays himself as playing (e.g., 1.46, 1.58, 3.96, 4.17, 9.67, 11.21, 11.58, 11.104), as does the hypermasculine figure of Priapus in the *Carmina Priapea.* Manuscript L transmits the poem with the lemma *De Sextillo fallace* rather than, for example, *De Sextillo fellatore* or *cunnilingo.* The writer of this title interprets Sextillus in light of the stereotype of the man who tries to conceal his sexual practices; cf. 1.96 with Citroni, 9.27, 9.47.

Structure. The epigram has a pleasingly tight structure, based on a cool process of elimination, couplet by couplet: you are not a *cinaedus* (1–2); you are not a *pedico, fututor,* or *irrumator* (3–4); therefore, you must be a *fellator* or *cunnilingus* (5–6). The sequence is thus that of a syllogism: premise 1, premise 2, conclusion. Also noteworthy is the presence of the vocative *Sextille* in the first line of each of the three couplets, always in the same metrical position; in **2.3** and **2.19** the vocative also occurs three times, but it is distributed differently and placed in varying metrical positions.

1 *Sextille:* This is the only occurrence in Martial of the name, a teasing diminutive of the common name *Sextus,* which usually refers to a man who is the object of negative commentary or invective; see on **2.3.1**.

1 *cinaedum:* See Williams 1999: 175–178 for this untranslatable noun. It originally referred to an effeminate Eastern dancer but was also used as an insult referring to an effeminate man who most likely, though not necessarily always, played the receptive role in anal intercourse. No attempts at translation (Ker: "———"; Izaac: "inverti"; Norcio: "sodomita"; Barié and Schindler: "schwul"; Shackleton Bailey: "queen") have been successful, either because they are insufficiently precise or because they rely on categories alien to Roman ideas regarding sexuality. Ceronetti's "culatto," specifically suggesting as it does the receptive role in anal intercourse, comes close.

2 *digitum porrigito medium:* The so-called *digitus impudicus* (6.70.5 with Grewing) or *digitus infamis* (Pers. 2.33): the middle finger displayed as a token of insulting aggression or jocular dismissal (see *Priap.* 56.1, Juv. 10.52–53, Suet. *Cal.* 56.2, SHA *Elag.* 10.7, Isid. *Orig.* 11.1.71) but also in defense against the evil eye (Pers. 2.33). The visual significance of the gesture is particularly appropriate here: the actual or symbolic display of the erect phallus not only has an aggressive and apotropaic significance (Fehling 1974 discusses the practice among certain primates) but is also a reminder of masculine potency. Martial encourages Sextillus not only to deny the charge of being a *cinaedus* but effectively to reply in kind. For Roman gestures in general see Sittl 1890 (101–102 for the *digitus impudicus*), Aldrete 1999.

3–4 *Sed nec . . . nec . . . nec:* A key logical transition. Granted that you are not a *cinaedus,* one might believe that you play one or more of the three acceptably masculine roles (*pedico, fututor, irrumator*), but you do not. For the syntax, cf. 12.97.8–9 ("sed nec vocibus excitata blandis / molli pollice nec rogata surgit") with Friedlaender.

3 *pedico . . . fututor:* Quintessentially Roman in their physical specificity, these obscenities denote a man who plays the insertive role in, respectively, anal and vaginal intercourse, the former regardless of the gender of the partner; see Adams 1982: 122–124, Williams 1999: 166–172. They are not equivalent to "homosexual" and "heterosexual," being narrower in denotation (a man who practices cunnilinctus, for example, is not a *fututor* but would certainly be liable to being called a "heterosexual"). Translations such as "sodomite" and "fornicator" (Shackleton Bailey; the former again at **2.47.3**) are unsatisfactory for similar reasons (unlike *pedico,* e.g., "sodomite" can refer to a man who plays the receptive role in anal intercourse or who practices fellatio) and in any case introduce a moralizing and slightly archaic tone not present in the Latin. Ceronetti ("non sei cultore di culo né di fica") and Obermayer 1998: 244 ("doch du bist kein Arschficker und kein Fotzenficker") more accurately render Martial's rude specificity.

4: In contrast to the blunt obscenity of the preceding line, this is a colorful but roundabout way of saying that Sextillus is not an *irrumator* (the word is here metrically impossible); that is, he is not one who orally penetrates others.

Originally designating the lower part of the cheeks, especially when puffed out (cf. 14.63.1: "ebria nos madidis rumpit tibicina buccis"), *bucca* came to refer to the mouth as a whole, a meaning that survives in Romance derivatives (*bocca, boca, bouche*). It seems to have been fairly low in tone, in verse extant only among satiric writers (Citroni ad 1.41.13), and is again associated with sexual practices at 3.75.5 ("coepisti puras opibus corrumpere buccas") and 11.61.2 ("Summemmianis inquinatior buccis"), as at Pompon. *Com.* 150 and Var. *Men.* 282. But this is hardly always the case: cf. 12.24.5 ("quidquid in buccam tibi venerit") and Cic. *Att.* 1.12.4 ("si rem nullam habebis, quod in buccam venerit scribito").

The name *Vetustina* appears only here in Martial; as with *Vetustilla* in 3.93, it may suggest a repulsive old woman. In Hor. *Epod.* 8 it is claimed that an ugly old woman will have to resort to fellatio; we may be dealing with a stereotype. Barié and Schindler identify Vetustina as a prostitute, but, as in the case of Galla in **2.25**, there is no clear justification for this.

5 *ex istis nihil es, fateor:* For the granting of an interlocutor's argument, see on **2.8.7**.

5 *quid ergo es?* For a rhetorical question followed by an answer that brings home the point, see on **2.7.8**. Citroni (ad 1.10.4: "quid ergo in illa petitur et placet? tussit.") observes that *ergo* in an interrogative phrase often serves to prepare the way for an unexpected conclusion: cf. **2.56.4** ("quid solet ergo? dare."), 3.46.11, 4.71.5, 4.87.4, 5.32.2, 6.14.2, 6.94.4, 10.74.12.

For the final monosyllable, see on **2.84.3**. Here, as again at **2.66.3** (*ulta est*), the rhythmical effect is rather different thanks to the aphaeresis (*ergo [e]s, ulta [e]st*); see Marina Sáez 1998: 155–156.

6 *nescio, sed tu scis res superesse duas:* There is a touch of the riddle here (see on **2.17.5**) and possibly an intertextual relationship with Catull. 85.2 ("nescio, sed fieri sentio et excrucior"; note the opening two words with correption of the final vowel in *nescio,* for which see on **2.9.2**), from a poem that itself opens with a paradoxical, riddling phrase ("odi et amo").

In view of the contrast between the sexual identities that were earlier explicitly or indirectly named and those passed over in silence here at the end, Obermayer 1998: 244–245 sees a hint at the representation of fellatio and cunnilinctus as "the unspeakable," for which compare the Greek euphemism *arretopoiein* at Artemid. 1.79. Obermayer adds that the speaker not only does not wish to name the unspeakable acts but would rather not even know them, but this places too much weight on *nescio,* which is after all different from *scire nolo.*

2.29

Rufe, vides illum subsellia prima terentem,
    cuius et hinc lucet sardonychata manus,
quaeque Tyron totiens epotavere lacernae,
    et toga non tactas vincere iussa nives,
cuius olet toto pinguis coma Marcelliano   5
    et splendent vulso bracchia trita pilo,
non hesterna sedet lunata lingula planta,
    coccina non laesum pingit aluta pedem,
et numerosa linunt stellantem splenia frontem?
    ignoras quid sit? splenia tolle, leges.   10

Rufus, do you see that man spending all his time in the front rows
of the theater; whose hand gleams with its sardonyx ring even at
this distance, as does his cloak, which has soaked up Tyrian purple
many times over, and his toga made to outdo untouched snow;
whose pomaded hair fills the Theater of Marcellus with its aroma;
whose depilated arms gleam in their smoothness; whose shoe with
its crescent buckle has only the latest strap; whose foot is decorated
by a soft piece of scarlet leather that leaves it uninjured; whose
forehead is bespangled with any number of patches? Do you not
realize what is going on? Take off the patches and you'll read.

Themes. We move from the exposure of a man's sexual tastes to the revelation of a man's humble origins. With its cumulative portrait reminiscent of
the descriptions of Selius' behavior in **2.11** and **2.14**, the poem builds up a
description of a man ostentatiously living the life of one wealthy enough to
achieve equestrian status, and of patrician descent at that. Only in the final
line does the point come: this man was previously (perhaps even still is) a
slave. We might compare **2.57** in terms of both content and structure. There,
a man who lives a life of ostentatious luxury—the portrait is again built up
cumulatively over the course of a single sentence, one relative clause following another—is revealed to be in such financial difficulty that he must
pawn a ring in order to pay for dinner.

The invective against parvenus, in particular against slaves or ex-slaves
who try to disguise their origins, is exploited at greater and more vicious
length in later epigrams on Zoilus, for whom see on **2.16.1**. See also 6.17
with Grewing, and 5.35 (Euclides, dressed in expensive scarlet clothing, is
revealed to be a slave when a key falls out of his pocket). An anonymous

epigram of the *Palatine Anthology* (*A.P.* 11.260) exposes the attempts of a former slave—who, as in Martial, remains unnamed—to pass himself off as a member of the Council (*bouleutes*). Juvenal's satires are characteristically even more bitter on the point: see especially 1.99–116 and 3.34–40. In general, Roman criticism of such men is based on the notion that they are pretending to be something they are not (Malnati 1988, Walter 1998: 235) and on a prejudice against freedmen and their children (cf. Hor. *Epist.* 1.20.20, *Sat.* 1.6.6: "libertino patre natum"). See further **2.32.4**, Treggiari 1969, Garrido-Hory 1985a, Eck and Heinrichs 1993, Rosen 1995.

Structure.   Almost the entire epigram is taken up with the description of the unnamed man and his flashy behavior in phrases themselves notable for their hyperbole (see on 2). Only in the last line do we find, simultaneously, commentary and the point. The accumulation of detail is notable and characteristic—cf. **2.7**, **2.14**, **2.27–28**, **2.33**, **2.36**, **2.43**, **2.48**, **2.89**—as is the structure of the sequence. After the remark to the effect that he occupies the front rows reserved for *equites* (1) comes an ABAB movement from clothing (ring, cloak, toga in 2–4, with a vivid contrast between the intense purple of the cloak and the bright white of the toga) to self-care (perfume and depilation in 5–6) to clothing (shoes, 7–8) to self-care (beauty-patches, 9).

1 *Rufe:* See on **2.11.1**. For the vocative of the addressee as the first word of the epigram, see on **2.3.1**.

1 *vides illum:* For the opening verb of seeing, see on **2.11.1**. Siedschlag 1977: 35 observes that it is often associated with the exposure of a hypocrite or pretender: see 1.24, **2.74**, 4.53, 5.51, 6.74. As here, the verb is sometimes given increased focus by means of a demonstrative pronoun (for which see 5.51.1, 5.61.1, 6.74.1, 9.14.1, 12.38.1), frequently in the context of a rhetorical question: see 1.24.1 ("aspicis . . . illum?") with Citroni, **2.57.1** ("hic quem videtis"), 4.53.1 ("hunc quem saepe vides"), 8.59.1 ("aspicis hunc?"), along with *A.L.* 461 Riese, attributed to Seneca ("hic quem cernis"). The technique is probably connected with the origins of epigram (Pascucci 1957, Siedschlag 1977: 7–10, Laurens 1989: 261, Sullivan 1991: 221) and is hardly unique to Martial: see Catull. 4.1 ("Phaselus ille quem videtis, hospites") together with V. *Catal.* 10.1 ("Sabinus ille quem videtis, hospites").

Since other instances of opening *aspicis* (1.24, 4.74, 6.38, 8.30, 8.59) and *cernis* (**2.74.4**) are normally printed as questions, I have departed from the practice of nearly all modern editions and have printed the protracted opening sentence of the present epigram as a question (so too Salanitro 1991), but the possibility that it is a statement of course remains. A similar ambiguity is found in the famous opening of the Horatian Soracte ode (Hor. *C.* 1.9.1–2: "vides ut alta stet nive candidum / Soracte . . .").

1 *subsellia prima:* The man displays himself in the midst of a theater audience; 5 specifically locates the scene in the Theater of Marcellus in Rome. The *lex Roscia theatralis* of 67 B.C. designated the first fourteen rows of seats (*subsellia*) in theaters for the knights, or *equites* (and not, as Izaac and Shackleton Bailey claim, for senators): see Cic. *Mur.* 40, Liv. *Epit.* 99, Hor. *Epod.* 4.15 with Porph., Juv. 3.159, Dio 36.42.1, Plut. *Cic.* 13, and compare Mart. 5.8.2–3: "quo subsellia certiora fiunt / et puros eques ordines recepit"; Martial again refers to the law in 5.14, 5.23, 5.25, 5.27, 5.35, 5.38, 5.41. The *orchestra* was designated for the senators (Vitr. 5.6.2); for the resulting tripartite division, see Petr. *Sat.* 126.7 ("usque ab orchestra quattuordecim transilit et in extrema plebe quaerit quod diligat") with Lilja 1985.

1 *terentem:* See on **2.11.2** (*porticum terit seram*).

2 *et hinc lucet:* This is the first of a series of vivid, often hyperbolic images for the unnamed man's ostentatious display. His ring shines like a beacon (2), his cloak has repeatedly soaked up Tyrian purple (3), his toga is as white as freshly fallen snow (4), his unguent fills the Theater of Marcellus with its fragrance (5), his arms are plucked so clean of their hairs that they gleam (6), the strap on his shoes is brand-new, not even from yesterday (7), the bright scarlet leather of his shoe is so soft that it leaves his foot uninjured (8), and his forehead is bespangled with beauty-patches (9). Many of these details are also found in Ovid's portrait of a dandy whom women might find attractive but who may be less interested in the women themselves than in their money and clothes: "nec coma vos fallat liquido nitidissima *nardo* / nec brevis in rugas *lingula* pressa suas / nec *toga* decipiat filo tenuissima, nec si / *anulus* in digitis alter et alter erit. / forsitan ex horum numero cultissimus ille / fur sit et uratur vestis amore tuae" (*Ars am.* 3.443–448). Martial's depiction of the simple life in Bilbilis includes the detail "lunata nusquam pellis et nusquam toga / olidaeque vestes murice" (1.49.31–32), a telling contrast with the man depicted here.

The detail *et hinc* probably implies that Martial and Rufus are sitting among the last of the fourteen rows reserved for *equites* and are thus fairly distant from the *subsellia prima* (Watson and Watson; Allen et al. 1969–1970 argue that Martial had received the knighthood under Nero). Alternatively, *et hinc* might make the point that Martial is *not* sitting in the first fourteen rows. While Martial later boasts that he is eligible to sit in the knights' seats (3.95.9–10), it could be that Martial was made an *eques* only after composing the present epigram, or else that in this regard he adopts various and sometimes contradictory personae, regardless of the facts of his biography (see on **2.92.3** for his on-again, off-again wife and, in general, Watson and Watson, pp. 5–7)

2 *sardonychata manus:* For sardonyx as an emblem of wealth or luxury, see 4.28.4, 4.61.6, 5.11.1, 9.59.19, 10.87.14, 11.27.10, 11.37.2; Pers. 1.16; D. 48.20.6. Martial's other allusions to expensive rings include **2.57.8**,

5.61.5–6, 11.59, and 14.123. Juvenal also cites a sardonyx ring as a sign of luxury, placing it on the hand of an effeminate nouveau riche (1.26–29, 7.144); see also Plin. *N.H.* 37.86–89, Marshall 1907.

3 *Tyron totiens epotavere:* *Tyron* is a metonymy for *purpuram;* compare *Sidone* at **2.16.3**. With the image of the cloak "drinking up" the purple dye compare 14.154.1: "ebria Sidoniae cum sim de sanguine conchae." The adverb *totiens* suggests expensive fabrics that have been dyed two or more times; compare Ovid's description of the practice at *Med. fac.* 9 ("vellera saepe eadem Tyrio medicantur aeno") and Pliny's reference to *purpuras Tyrias dibaphasque* (*N.H.* 21.45). For brightly colored and especially purple clothing on men as a token of extravagance, see **2.43.7**, **2.46.3–4**, **2.57.2**, 5.23; Sen. *N.H.* 7.31.2 ("colores meretricios matronis quidem non induendos viri sumimus"), *Epist.* 114.21; and compare Zoilus' purple and scarlet bedclothes in **2.16**.

4 *toga:* Clothing in general, and the toga in particular, play an important role in Martial's epigrams. The noun *toga* occurs fifty-six times and *togula* eight times; the adjectives *togatus* and *togatulus,* thirteen and two times respectively. The toga had a profound symbolic importance in Roman culture, being among the most visible of emblems of the Roman citizen that set him apart from others. Consider Virgil's ringing line "Romanos rerum dominos gentemque togatam," cited by Martial at 14.124.1, and see in general Marquardt 1886: 552–564, Potthoff 1992: 196–201, Lindsay 1998, Stone 2001.

Bright new togas of fine wool frequently function in Martial as a token of wealth and well-being, just as dirty old togas signify poverty: see **2.43.3–6**, **2.44.1**, **2.46**, **2.53.6**, **2.58**, **2.85**, 3.36.9, 8.28, 9.49.1–2, 10.11.5–6, 10.73, 11.56.5–6, 12.36.2, 12.72.4, 13.48.1, 14.135.2.

4 *non tactas vincere iussa nives:* For proverbial phrases of the type "as white as snow," see Otto 1890: 244, Sonny 1896: 71, Sutphen 1901: 253–254, Weyman 1904: 392. The comparison of the man's toga to *untouched* snow contributes to the atmosphere of hyperbolic description; the image appears again at 5.37.6 (*nives primas*), 7.33.2 (*candidior prima nive*), and 8.28.15 (*primis nivibus*) and may be Ovidian in inspiration (*Pont.* 2.5.38: "nive non calcata"; Zingerle 1877: 29). Heraeus 1925: 334 notes that the formulation *non tactas* is used instead of *intactas* for metrical reasons, but note also the parallelism with *non hesterna lingula* (7) and *non laesum pedem* (8).

The participle *iussa* suggests that the togas have been whitened by a fuller (Watson and Watson). For the process, notoriously involving the use of urine as bleaching substance, see Non. Marcell. 34, Isid. *Orig.* 11.1.138; Forbes 1955–1958: 4.81; Brown 1994.

5–6: By means of the allusion to excessive perfume and depilation, the man's lifestyle is explicitly marked as effeminate (see Herter 1959, Williams 1999: 129–132). To be sure, perfume and depilation in themselves were not necessarily markers of excessive effeminacy: in 14.59 *opobalsama* are said to be acceptably masculine (though Juv. 2.40–42 suggests that this was controversial; see Miller 1969: 101ff.); in 13.127 *unguentum* and *vina* are jokingly described as items that you should not leave to your heirs but rather enjoy yourself; Sen. *Epist.* 114.14 observes that a moderate depilation of the underarms was acceptable, though depilating the legs was going too far. Indeed, it was the use of too much (or the wrong kind of) perfume or excessive depilation, especially of the arms, legs, chest, or pubic region, that laid a man open to a charge of effeminacy: see **2.36**, **2.62**, 3.63.3–6 (the *bellus homo* "balsama qui semper, cinnama semper olet . . . / qui movet in varios bracchia vulsa modos"), 3.74, 5.41, 5.61 (with Howell), 6.56 (with Grewing), 9.27, 10.65, 12.38.

5 olet . . . pinguis coma: For the use of perfumed unguent in hair, especially at banquets, see also 5.64 and 11.39.11, Ov. *Ars am.* 3.443; Tracy 1976: 61. For the characteristic smell of this and other cosmetics, see 3.55; Lilja 1972: 86–87. The adjective *pinguis* (*OLD* s.v. 2: "rich in fat, fatty, greasy") can be used to describe cheese (V. *Ecl.* 1.34), meat (Cels. 4.9.3), and hair-unguent (Mart. 11.15.6, 11.98.6). Referring to the man's hair, it is hardly flattering; the adjective *madidus* is more usual (see Mart. 14.50.2, Ov. *Met.* 3.55, *Her.* 14.30; *OLD* s.v. *madeo* 2d).

5 Marcelliano: The second stone theater built at Rome after that of Pompey (for which see on **2.14.10**), the Theater of Marcellus was dedicated in 13 B.C. Martial refers to it here and at 10.51.11 (*sed nec Marcelli Pompeianumque*); the latter passage reminds us that it was just as much a landmark of Rome as was the Theater of Pompey, the imperial fora, and the Temple of Jupiter Optimus Maximus on the Capitoline. Here it is cited as a large public space (capable of holding about 13,000 spectators, it was slightly larger than Pompey's theater), and even today it is one of the principal monuments of the city.

The reading *Marcelliano* is handed down by all MSS except for G (*Marcellino*) and E (*Marcelliniano;* Lindsay suggests that this represents the conflation of an original *Marcelliano* and an interlinear variant *Marcellino*). If the reading is correct, there is a synizesis, such that the word scans as *Marcelljano;* compare 6.61.3 (*Usipjorum*) and 6.94.1 (*Calpetjano*). Some scholars have been disturbed by the synizesis: Collesso proposes the fairly desperate measure (adopted by Forcellini s.v.) of emending to *Marceliano* and taking the reference to be to a well-known but otherwise unattested perfume-maker named Marcelius. Shackleton Bailey, following Heraeus and Salmasius, emends to *Marcellano* here (as do also Watson and Watson), and *Usiporum* and *Calpetano* in the remaining two cases. But the form *Marcellanum* is nowhere else attested; Suet. *Vesp.* 19.1 speaks of the *theatrum Marcellianum,* as does *CIL* 6.33838a (although, tantalizingly, the carver of the inscription first wrote

MARCELLANO and then inserted an ɪ after the second ʟ). Even more significantly, synizeses like *Marcelljanus, Usipjorum,* and *Calpetjano* are well attested elsewhere: consider *insidjantes* (Enn. *Ann.* 424), *vindemjator* (Hor. *Sat.* 1.7.30), *fluvjorum* (V. *Geo.* 1.482); examples of proper names include *Nasidjeni* (Hor. *Sat.* 2.8.1, 75, 84), *Serviljo* (Hor. *Sat.* 2.8.21), *Lavinjaque* (V. *Aen.* 1.2), and *Antjum* (Ov. *Met.* 15.718); see further KS 1.148.

Regardless of its spelling, the word must consist of four long syllables, resulting in a spondaic line (in Book II cf. **2.38.1, 2.61.3**). Such lines are quite rare in Martial (15 out of a total of 3,308 hexameters, 12 of them being proper names); see Marina Sáez 1998: 50–51. That the final two spondees should be formed by a single word (*Marcelliano*) is also a rarity in Latin poetry in general after Catullus, being found in 3.12 percent of Catullus' hexameters, 0.5 percent of Lucretius,' 0.16 percent of Virgil's, 0.5 percent of Propertius,' 0.11 percent of Ovid's, 0.20 percent of Lucan's, 0.03 percent of Statius,' never in Tibullus or the *Priapea,* and 0.42 percent of Martial's hexameters (Marina Sáez 1998: 138–139, 158–162).

6 *vulso bracchia trita pilo:* For men who depilate—their arms in particular—see on **2.36, 2.62.1**. For the spelling *vulso,* see on **2.11.3**.

7 *non hesterna sedet lunata lingula planta:* The *lingula* was a flap on the shoe, not to be confused with *ligula,* a type of spoon sometimes (incorrectly, according to 14.120) also called *lingula.* Barié and Schindler take the phrase *non hesterna* to mean that it was of the latest fashion; Ker, Bridge and Lake, Shackleton Bailey, and *OLD* s.v. *hesternus* take it to mean "brand-new" (i.e., not even 24 hours old). The latter seems more in keeping with this epigram's series of hyperbolic images for this man's ostentatious fashion (see on 2 above).

Literally denoting the sole of the foot, *planta* can be used synecdochically to refer to the foot as a whole, here (via a further metonymy) to a shoe. The adjective *lunata* denotes the crescent worn on the shoes of patricians (Stat. *Silv.* 5.2.28, Juv. 7.192 with schol., Isid. *Orig.* 19.34.4), probably not of senators in general (*pace* Barié and Schindler, Merli, and *OLD* s.v. *lunatus*); see Citroni ad 1.49.31 (*lunata pellis*) for the conflicting allusions to this ornament.

8 *coccina non laesum pingit aluta pedem:* An *aluta* is a piece of soft leather, here (and at Ov. *Ars am.* 3.271, Mart. 12.29.9, Juv. 7.192) used to make a shoe. For the association of scarlet-dyed items with luxury, see on **2.16.2**. For *pingere* in the sense of "embellish, decorate," referring to colored things, compare **2.46.1**, 9.76.4 ("gaudebatque suas pingere barba genas"), and see *OLD* s.v. 3c.

9 *numerosa linunt stellantem splenia frontem:* *Splenia* were patches or plasters, sometimes used for aesthetic purposes (8.33.22, 10.22.1; cf. Plin. *Epist.* 6.2.2), here to hide the marks of the branding iron; see further on 11 below. Bridge and Lake take *stellantem* to imply that the patches "were in the shape of a star," but the word more likely suggests that the forehead is dotted with patches as the sky is dotted with stars. As Watson and Watson observe, the implication is that his face "carries the traces of repeated punishments," or else that "he bears a single inscription so large that several patches are needed to cover it" (cf. Petr. *Sat.* 103).

Note the accumulative effect achieved by the first three words: the patches are numerous (*numerosa*); they cover or coat his forehead (*linunt*, "smear, plaster, coat," sometimes used to refer to the sealing off of a wine jar, as at Hor. *C.* 1.20.3, Juv. 9.58), which is thereby bespangled (*stellantem*).

10 *ignoras quid sit?* For the sequence of rhetorical question followed by answer, which in turn usually constitutes the point, see on **2.7.8**. The question has been understood in two ways: "Do you not know what it [the reason] is?" (Ker, Izaac, Ceronetti) or "Do you not know who/what he is?" (Norcio, Shackleton Bailey, Barié and Schindler, Watson and Watson; some Italian humanists emended *quid* to *qui,* for which cf. **2.23.2**). The former seems more likely: see *OLD* s.v. *quis* 8 ("*quid est?* What is the matter? What's up? What is the meaning of this?") with Varr. *R.R.* 3.5.18 ("cum . . . scire vellemus, quid esset"), *Rhet. Her.* 4.68 ("dubitanti Graccho, quid esset . . ."), Cic. *Cat.* 1.20 ("quid est? ecquid attendis?").

10 *leges:* The use of the verb *legere* (rather than, e.g., *videre*) implies that there are letters branded or tattooed onto this man's forehead. This is the key to understanding the entire epigram, as such a mark would constitute a shaming sign of the man's origins as a slave. For the Roman practice—also attested among Greeks—of branding or tattooing slaves on the forehead as punishment for attempts to escape or other misdeeds, especially stealing, see Petr. *Sat.* 69, 103.2, Quint. *Inst.* 7.4.17, Sen. *Dial.* 5.3.6 (*inscriptiones frontis*), Juv. 14.21ff., Auson. *Epigr.* 15.3, Boeth. *De cons.* 1.4.19, with *RE* s.v. στιγματίας (Hug), Marquardt 1886: 184, Blümner 1911: 294, Jones 1987. Slaves so branded could be called *inscripti* (8.75.9, Plin. *N.H.* 18.21, Macrob. *Sat.* 1.11.19), *notati* (3.21.1), or, with cruel irony, *litterati* (Plaut. *Cas.* 401, Apul. *Met.* 9.12). What precisely was branded or tattooed on the foreheads of these unfortunate slaves? Cic. *Rosc. Amerin.* 57 (*litteram illam*) suggests a single letter, presumably F for *fugitivus,* but other sources envision more than one letter (Petr. *Sat.* 105.2, Val. Max. 6.8, Scribon. Larg. 231; cf. the phrase *trium litterarum homo* at Plaut. *Aul.* 325). Barié and Schindler suggest FHE (*fugitivus hic est*); Hug suggests FVG (*itivus*) for runaways, FVR for thieves. The present epigram offers no hint as to what exactly was branded or tattooed on the man's forehead, but the mere suggestion not only that he is (or was) a slave but also that he was once punished for a misdeed is damning enough.

There are occasional allusions to attempts by freedmen to conceal such marks, which were designed to be indelible (Petr. *Sat.* 45, Macrob. *Sat.* 1.11.19): Athen. 6.225 speaks of an attempt to cover them up with one's hair, and Mart. 6.64.26 and 10.56.6 (reading *servorum*) point to the existence of doctors who tried to remove the marks (cf. Plin. *N.H.* 30.30, Scribon. Larg. 231). The present epigram seems to contain the only reference to the use of *splenia* for this purpose.

2.30

Mutua viginti sestertia forte rogabam,
   quae vel donanti non grave munus erat.
quippe rogabatur fidusque vetusque sodalis
   et cuius laxas arca flagellat opes.
is mihi "dives eris si causas egeris" inquit.   5
   quod peto da, Gai: non peto consilium.

Once I happened to ask for a loan of twenty thousand sesterces, which would not have been so burdensome a favor even as a gift. After all, the person I asked was an old and faithful friend, and one whose money chest whips up ample wealth. His response to me was this: "You'll be a rich man if you plead court cases." Give me what I'm asking for, Gaius: I'm not asking for advice!

Themes.   In an epigram that, like its predecessor, makes use of the imagery of wealth, Martial returns to the technique of sketching a scenario in which he is personally involved, as also in the next three epigrams (**2.31–33**). We return to the theme of **2.24** (see also **2.43–44**): Martial's requests for money, whether in the form of a loan or a gift, are refused and he expresses disappointment at the disregard for ideals of friendship on the part of wealthy friends. Martial frequently portrays himself as the one who seeks and only sometimes obtains a loan: see **2.44**, 6.5 (where he cheekily admits that he doesn't expect to pay it back), 6.10 (where he even asks the emperor!), 6.20, 6.30, 9.100, 10.15 (similar in content to the present epigram), 11.76, 12.25.

Another recurrent theme touched upon in the present epigram is the contrast between Martial's chosen profession and a more remunerative career in law: cf. 1.17 (where Titus, like Gaius, urges the poet to plead court

cases), 1.76 (though see Citroni ad loc.), **2.90**, 5.16, and 12.68, with Van
Stockum 1884: 25, Sullivan 1991: 2–3. In 8.17, uniquely, Martial adopts the
persona of one who has engaged to plead someone's case in court for 2,000
sesterces.

Structure.   Most of the epigram is taken up with the description of the situation, each line constituting a syntactic unit and each adding some important detail. As in **2.29**, the final line is both commentary and point. For the
shift from third-person narrative to second-person address in the final line,
see on **2.16**.

   1 *viginti sestertia:* Not 20 sesterces but 20,000; see *OLD* s.v. *sestertius*
3b for the ellipsis of *milia* with cardinal or distributive numerals. This is a
solid amount of money, though hardly astronomical. We may contextualize
the figure by surveying other sums that Martial mentions: he had borrowed
10,000 from Paetus (11.76); Sextus had borrowed 7,000 from Secundus,
4,000 from Phoebus, and 11,000 from Philetus (**2.44**); Martial himself elsewhere asks for loans ranging from 5,000 (10.14.3) to 100,000 (6.20.1); 20,000
is a lot to pay (*pretium grave*) for a deaf slave (11.38); 100,000 for a slave
boy is *luxuria;* Milichus has "only" 100,000 to his name and spends it all
on Leda (**2.63**); 400,000 (the amount required to be an *eques*) is an absurdly high price for a small hatchet (14.35 with Leary ad loc.). See further
Ramirez Sabada 1987.
   2 *non grave munus:* For *grave* in an economic sense, compare 11.38
(*pretium grave*), Cic. *Flac.* 59 (*gravi faenore*), Liv. 23.32.9 (*gravi tributo*),
Suet. *Nero* 10.1 (*graviora vectigalia*). It likewise modifies *munus* at Cic. *Verr.*
2.5.81, Stat. *Theb.* 3.706, Gell. 12.1.5.
   3 *fidusque vetusque sodalis:* This is the reading of family β; families
α and γ read *felixque vetusque sodalis,* while MS T offers *verusque vetusque
sodalis.* This last reading has been universally discounted as a scribal error
(no doubt introduced under the influence of the juxtaposed *vetus*), but the
decision between *fidusque* and *felixque* is not as easy: Lindsay 1903a: 24
includes this passage among 106 cases of ancient variants in Martial between
which the choice is "extremely uncertain" (cf. **2.40.2**, **2.46.10**, **2.61.1**). Yet
nearly all modern editors print *felixque,* with the exception of Shackleton
Bailey, whose arguments for *fidusque* are worth considering. Not only is
the phrase *veteri fidoque sodali* found again at **2.43.15** and 5.19.9, but *felix*
would anticipate the content of 4 in a slightly awkward way: *fidusque vetusque
sodalis / et cuius* . . . (he is an old, faithful friend, and rich to boot) is tighter
and more effective than the redundant *felixque vetusque sodalis / et cuius*
. . . (he is a successful old friend, and rich). Moreover, the attribute *fidus*
naturally attaches itself to friends and clients: see Cic. *Off.* 2.30 ("familiaritates

habere fidas amantium nos amicorum"), Nep. *Reg.* 3.3 ("neque eo magis fida inter eos amicitia manere potuisset"), Sall. *Cat.* 19.5 ("Cn. Pompei veteres fidosque clientes"), and Ov. *Pont.* 2.4.33–34 ("constantique fide veterem tutare sodalem / qua licet et quantum non onerosus ero").

Regardless of whether we read *fidus* or *felix,* the collocation *vetus sodalis* is especially characteristic of Martial. Phrases like *vetus amicus* are amply attested in other authors (e.g., Plaut. *Truc.* 173, Ov. *Tr.* 3.5.10, Juv. 3.1), but a search of the PHI disk for *vetus sodalis* yields only one passage from Ovid (*Pont.* 2.4.33) and nine from Martial, including the present instance, **2.43.15** (*veteri fidoque sodali*), and **2.44.4** (*veterem meum sodalem*).

The use of *-que . . . -que* is generally poetic in tone and often joins elements of a complementary pair (*OLD* s.v. 3); cf. **2.41.7**, **2.48.1**, **2.57.6**.

4 laxas arca flagellat opes: The application of the adjective *laxus* to riches is unusual but must be related to the sense "spacious, wide, ample, roomy" (*OLD* s.v. 1; Catull. 95.8: *laxas tunicas;* Manil. 5.599: *laxum per aethera;* Colum. 7.12.10: *laxa rura*). The verb *flagellare* ("to whip") here probably means "to keep (prices, money) in a state of constant progress" (*OLD* s.v.); cf. 5.13.6 ("et libertinas arca flagellat opes"), 9.59.2 ("Roma suas aurea vexat opes"), Plin. *N.H.* 32.164 ("annonam flagellare"). This is the understanding of Friedlaender, Shackleton Bailey ("the coffer would contain records of money lent at interest as well as coin and other valuables"), and Howell ad 5.13.6 ("the idea is that the money does not rest quietly in the cash-box, but is kept on the move, pushed to its fastest speed to get the greatest return"). Ker, Bridge and Lake, and Merli, by contrast, follow Collesso in understanding *flagellat* to mean "keep in check, keep from being dispersed" (cf. 3.41.2: "ex opibus tantis quas gravis arca premit"). Merli adds that this detail would sharpen the point: Gaius is so attached to money that he refuses to let it circulate even in the form of loans.

6 *quod peto da, Gai: non peto consilium:* Pertsch 1911: 53 quotes a traditional French tale in which an old beggar on the road to Madrid is asked by a traveler whether he is not ashamed to be begging when he could work. With his "Castilian pride," the beggar replies: "Sir, I'm asking you for money, not advice" ("Monsieur, c'est de l'argent et non des conseils que je vous demande"). Pertsch is confident that the tale was directly inspired by the present epigram, but the joke is of a type that spontaneously arises. Indeed, the *variorum* commentary aptly compares a remark from a letter of Seneca (*Epist.* 45.2). Lucilius has complained that there are too few books in Syracuse, and Seneca remarks that quality is more important than quantity, but imagines his friend's retort: "I would rather you gave me less advice and more books" ("vellem <non> magis consilium mihi quam libros dares").

The name *Gaius* is so common in Latin that it may be "used for any chance person, like Tom, Dick, and Harry" (*OLD* s.v. c). Martial uses the name in this sense at 5.14.5 ("post Gaiumque Luciumque consedit") and only on two other occasions: in 10.17 he is a man who never follows up on his promise to give gifts; in 9.92 the name refers to a typical freeman.

Out of the seventy-one epigrams in Book II having a vocative addressee, only five (not counting monodistichs) first present the vocative in the poem's last line: the present epigram, **2.37**, **2.46**, **2.65**, **2.84**. See Grewing ad 6.19.9.

2.31

Saepe ego Chrestinam futui. det quam bene quaeris?
supra quod fieri nil, Mariane, potest.

I have often fucked Chrestina. How good is she, you ask? It doesn't go any higher, Marianus.

Themes.   The monodistich returns us to the blunt sexual language of **2.28**, beginning with a crude macho boast reminiscent of graffiti (see below on 1) and quickly culminating with the point that nothing surpasses sex with Chrestina. Commentators have long suspected a double meaning, and indeed the simple affirmation that a sexual encounter with Chrestina is the ultimate lacks the sharp point or clever twist characteristic of Martial's epigrams, especially those on sexual matters. The double meaning has been identified by most readers as residing in *supra,* which suggests that she performs fellatio (see on 2 below). Earlier explanations are less convincing. Collesso suggests that intercourse with Chrestina is so splendid that her partner will keep at it to the point of being incapable of anything further ("ut qui eam faciat a coitu nequeat abstinere, quin defatigatus sit, effeto prorsus et enervato corpore"). The *variorum* commentary offers a strikingly different interpretation: an encounter with Chrestina is so *unpleasant* that one could not bear to repeat it ("ut *supra,* id est, *ultra* vel *iterum* eam non sustineas facere").

For the combination of wordplay and allusion to fellatio, Pertsch 1911: 47–48 compares the exposure of a fellator in *A.P.* 11.223 (εἰ βινεῖ Φαβορῖνος ἀπιστεῖς. μηκέτ' ἀπίστει. / αὐτός μοι βινεῖν εἶπ' ἰδίωι στόματι), where ἰδίωι στόματι can be taken with εἶπε or βινεῖν, just as *supra quod* can be taken both spatially and figuratively.

Structure.   For the monodistich format, see on **2.3**. Here we find a quick tripartite structure corresponding to the three sentences: (*a*) Martial has had numerous sexual encounters with Chrestina; (*b*) his interlocutor wants to know how good it was; (*c*) Martial gives an emphatic reply punctuated by the vocative *Mariane* and laden with double meaning. At the same time there is a contrast between the two brutally simple sentences in 1 and the more complex structure of 2.

1 *saepe ego Chrestinam futui:* This blunt opening sentence recalls some of the first-person graffiti scratched on the walls of Pompeii, Rome, Ostia, and elsewhere: compare *CIL* 4.2175 (*hic ego puellas multas futui*), 4.2145, and Catull. 97.9 ("hic futuit multas et se facit esse venustum").

With *futui* we have the second direct obscenity in Book II, after *pedico* and *fututor* in **2.28**. Manuscripts of family α replace the verb with *tetigi*, which, unlike the usual euphemism *subegi*, is metrically equivalent; for *tangere* compare 1.73.1: "qui tangere vellet / uxorem" with Citroni ad loc. Further examples of apparently deliberate scribal emendation in MSS of this family, all of which show careful concern for meter, include 1.34.10 (*futui > subigi*), 1.73.4 (*fututorum > salitorum*), 1.77.6 (*cunnum Charinus lingit > lingua nefas Charinus*), 1.90.6 (*fututor > adulter*), 1.90.7 (*cunnos > turpes* [!]), 3.87.1 (*fututam > salitam*), 6.67.2 (*futui > subigi*), 7.18 (*cunnus > monstrum* [!], *fututor > salitor*). In short, family α seems to derive from an archetype that offered a partially cleaned-up version of Martial. Lindsay 1903a: 9 describes it as *in usum elegantiorum:* it tended to remove and replace "words more fit for the 'graffiti' of Pompeii than for a Roman gentleman's library" so as to produce "a form that would be less offensive to refined readers." While the tendency of this MS family to euphemize is undeniable, Lindsay's "Roman gentleman" sounds more like an English gentleman of 1903 than anything else; Roman readers of all backgrounds knew what they were getting into when they picked up a book of epigrams (see 1.praef., **2.praef.**). Nor does the archetype of family α seem to have consistently emended objectionable language away: obscenities remain, in Book II alone, at **2.33.4** (*fellat*), **2.34.3** (*cunno*), and **2.45.1** (*mentula*). Housman 1925: 202 sees the origins of the emendations in this family in a "monkish horror of woman," but *cunnus* remains not only at **2.34.3** but also at 3.81.4 and 3.93.27.

Recalling Greek χρηστός, Chrestina's name is particularly ironic: she is "useful" and "good" indeed. The name occurs only here in Martial, but compare *Chrestillus* in 11.90 and *Chrestus* in 7.55, 9.27.

1 *det quam bene quaeris?* For *det*, see on **2.9.1**. The device of asking—and often beginning an epigram with—a question whose function is to stimulate an answer appears frequently in Martial; see Sullivan 1991: 221 and Siedschlag 1977: 23. Sometimes it is Martial himself who poses the question (cf. **2.65**), but more often, as here, the poet reports someone else's question using such formulas as *quaeris, requiris,* or *inquis:* compare **2.38.1** ("quid mihi reddat ager quaeris, Line, Nomentanus?"), **2.78.1** ("aestivo serves ubi piscem tempore, quaeris?"), **2.93.1** ("'primus ubi est' inquis"), and many others. Siedschlag cites Latin predecessors beginning with Catullus (Catull. 7; Prop. 1.22, 2.1, 2.31, 3.13; Ov. *Pont.* 3.5; *Priap.* 9, 37; *FPL* 133.5); in comparable Greek epigrams, a verb corresponding to *quaeris, requiris,* or *inquis* is almost never to be found. The one exception (*A.P.* 11.214, ζητεῖς) happens to be by Lucillius, one of Martial's principal models.

2 supra quod fieri nil, Mariane, potest: The phrase literally means "Above which nothing can happen"—that is, "nothing surpasses it" (cf. *OLD* s.v. *supra*² 6)—but plays on the spatial sense of *supra* ("it gets no higher," cf. *OLD* s.v. *supra*² 2), thus hinting at fellatio (Friedlaender). Joepgen 1967: 87 and Siedschlag 1977: 86–87 explain the wordplay more closely: *supra* has both the transferred sense of "greater than, more valuable than," and the literal sense of "higher up"; one cannot go any higher spatially because her mouth is already being put to use. We might add that since fellatio is sometimes implied to be a particularly exquisite pleasure (9.40, 9.67, 12.65), one truly cannot surpass Chrestina's services.

For spatial imagery in conjunction with fellatio, compare 11.46.5–6 ("quid miseros frustra cunnos culosque lacessis? / *summa petas:* illic mentula vivit anus") with Kay ad loc.; *Priap.* 74 ("per medios ibit pueros mediasque puellas / mentula, barbatis non nisi *summa petet";* cf. *Priap.* 13, 22); Auson. *Cent. nupt.* 104–105 ("occupat os faciemque, pedem pede fervidus urget. / perfidus *alta petens* ramum, qui veste latebat . . ."). For the mouth as *summum* as opposed to the genitals, which are *medium,* see also 11.61.5 ("mediumque mavult basiare quam summum").

The name *Marianus* appears also in 5.61 (a cuckold) and 6.63 (the object of *captatio*). Here the name serves as a prop, by way of creating the impression of a lively macho discussion between two friends.

2.32

Lis mihi cum Balbo est, tu Balbum offendere non vis,
    Pontice: cum Licino est, hic quoque magnus homo est.
vexat saepe meum Patrobas confinis agellum,
    contra libertum Caesaris ire times.
abnegat et retinet nostrum Laronia servum,   5
    respondes "orba est, dives, anus, vidua."

non bene, crede mihi, servo servitur amico:
  sit liber, dominus qui volet esse meus.

I am involved in a lawsuit with Balbus; Balbus you do not wish to
offend, Ponticus. Likewise with Licinus—he too is a great man. My
neighbor Patrobas keeps damaging my field; you are afraid to take
action against Caesar's freedman. Laronia issues denials and holds
on to my slave; you say: "She is childless, rich, old, unmarried." Trust
me: it is not good to be a slave to an enslaved friend. Whoever wants
to be my lord should be free.

Themes.   Returning to the intertwined themes of friendship, *clientela,* and
disappointment at others' behavior in these respects (last touched upon in **2.30**),
Martial asks Ponticus to fulfill one of the traditional duties of a patron with
regard to his client—protection in legal cases—and expresses disappointment
that Ponticus will not come to his assistance because he fears offending Martial's
opponents, who exercise various types of power over him. This leads Martial
to describe Ponticus as servile and to observe that this is not the kind of *dominus* (i.e., patron) he wants. The epigram thus stands in a close relationship to
2.18, where Martial again applies the language of slavery to his patron and
likewise concludes with a protest: "qui rex est regem, Maxime, non habeat."

  This epigram is given a particularly concrete quality by the series of
names. Friedlaender finds resonances in every one of them, arguing that they
nearly all suggest freedmen. If so, the nasty point made with the remark
that Patrobas is *libertus Caesaris* actually applies to the whole poem: Ponticus,
although Martial's *dominus,* is acting like a *servus* in his fear of offending
people who once really were slaves. Less convincing is Friedlaender's suggestion, in view of his interpretation of the names *Patrobas* and *Laronia* (see
below), that this poem was an early composition, perhaps composed soon
after Nero's death in A.D. 68.

Structure.   This epigram offers a fine illustration of the characteristic technique of accumulation, in this case both of names and of sentence pairs
expressing oppositions: see on **2.11** and **2.18**. The first line introduces the
situation by means of a simply worded example; the second line names the
addressee and continues by presenting another example of the problem and
maintaining the syntax: *cum Licino est* (sc., *lis mihi*). The second and third
couplets add further illustrations, each presenting Martial's problem in its
first line and Ponticus' justification for inactivity in its second line. The final
couplet offers pointed commentary in the form of a *sententia* in each line,
the first marked by the emphatic parenthesis *crede mihi.*

1 *lis mihi cum Balbo est:* For other allusions to lawsuits in Martial, see **2.90.10** ("sit sine lite dies"), 10.47.5 (where he represents them as an unpleasant aspect of living in Rome), along with *Sp*.20.3, **2.64.7**, 3.46.9, 5.20.6, 7.65.1, 10.87.4, 12.68.3, 12.72.3; in general, see Kelly 1966. The name *Balbus* occurs only here in Martial. The fact that Ponticus does not wish to offend him may suggest that he is a man of some importance or else simply that Ponticus is in some way indebted to him.

2 *Pontice:* The (fictional) name appears also in **2.82**, 3.60, 4.85, 5.63, 9.19, 9.41. In a quirky but provocative discussion, Tanner 1986: 2671 considers the "tone, content and aim which appear to be associated with a particular metre": elegiacs have an "outer apodeictic layer" and an "inner protreptic layer." Here the outer layer is "Ponticus, you are afraid to defend me against rich men. My *patronus* must be a *dominus,* not a *servus*"; the inner layer is "Plead the case of justice for others, not of your own self-interest!" Putting together all of the epigrams on Ponticus, Tanner arrives at the following portrait: "Ponticus is cruel, vain, mean and self-centred, deceiving his guests and also getting the cheapest sexual satisfaction by masturbating, while using his wealth and legal skill for his own benefits alone." But, as Citroni 1988 reminds us, it is doubtful whether such widely separated uses of a single fictitious name can be interpreted as referring to a uniform character.

2 *Licino:* The name occurs in Martial only here and at 8.3.6, where it refers to Augustus' freedman of the same name (Juv. 1.09, 14.306); it is to be distinguished from various *Licinii,* such as L. Licinius Sura in 1.49, 6.64, 7.47.

3 *vexat saepe meum Patrobas confinis agellum:* The verb has been interpreted variously. Ker and Ceronetti see a reference to trespassing, Shackleton Bailey somewhat opaquely translates "harasses," while Norcio renders "altera i confini del mio campo." Cato, *Orat.* 177 ("cum Hannibal terram Italiam laceraret atque vexaret") and other passages (*OLD* s.v. 3) suggest "damage."

The name *Patrobas,* together with his status as *libertus Caesaris,* might recall Patrobios, a freedman of Nero's (Van Stockum 1884: 59–60, Friedlaender). Instead of *Patrobas,* however, family β reads *Protas,* a possibility that Shackleton Bailey considers worth taking into consideration.

4 *libertum Caesaris:* *Liberti Caesaris,* slaves of the imperial household who had been freed, existed in great numbers, at times exercising an influence that provoked outbursts of resentment, especially among satirists: see Sen. *Apocol.* with Weaver 1972, Brockmeyer 1979: 178–180. An earlier illustration of the influence wielded by freedmen of the powerful is provided by the case of Sulla's Chrysogonus (Cic. *S. Rosc.*).

5 *abnegat et retinet nostrum Laronia servum:* Laronia is presumably denying that Martial had ever lent her his slave (cf. 8.52); for the term *servus,* see on **2.11.8**. Among many indications of the importance of slaves in Martial's world, see **2.43.13–14**, **2.48.5–6**, **2.90.9**, 7.80, 8.13, 8.52, 11.108,

12.18, 12.66 (for their prices, see on **2.63.1**), with Garrido-Hory 1981 and 1984, Sullivan 1991: 162–166. General treatments of Roman slavery include Bradley 1987 and 1994.

The name *Laronia* is found only here and in Juvenal 2, where it refers to a woman who makes an outspoken attack on hypocritical *cinaedi*. Colton 1991: 73 suggests that Juvenal borrowed the name from Martial, while Friedlaender proposes that both poets used the name because it recalled a well-known person, perhaps from Nero's day. Lieben (*RE* s.v. Laronius) likewise speculates that there was a real woman named Laronia who was wealthy and childless but argues that the character of the present epigram is not that woman but rather a fictional person! MSS of family β read *Letoria, Laetoria* (cf. 6.45), and *Lectoria* instead of *Laronia*. Lehmann 1931: 12 suggests that the variant *Laetoria* may go back to Martial himself; see on **2.18.8** for the possibility of author variants.

6 orba est, dives, anus, vidua: See on **2.26** for the theme of *captatio,* or legacy hunting, sometimes (as here) with rich, old, childless women.

7 non bene, crede mihi, servo servitur amico: For the imagery of freedom and slavery, most likely inspired by philosophical commonplaces, in this and the following line, compare **2.18.7** and see on **2.53.1**. For the use of *amicus* to refer to one's patron, compare 6.50.1–2 ("cum coleret puros pauper Telesinus amicos, / errabat gelida sordidus in togula") and see on **2.13.1, 2.55**.

For this use of *non bene* ("one does not serve well" = "it is not good to serve"), see *TLL* 2.2.118.72ff. (*bene*) and compare 8.241.58ff. (*male*).

The parenthesis *crede mihi* underscores the *sententia,* as also at 1.15.11–12, 4.49.1–2, 5.52.7–8, 6.27.9–10, 9.99.9–10. The phrase has a colloquial tone; compare Hofmann 1951: 126, Citroni ad 1.3.4.

8 sit liber, dominus qui volet esse meus: For the use of *dominus* to refer to one's patron, see *TLL* 5.1.1924.59–63 and compare on **2.68.2** for the juxtaposition of *dominus* with *rex*. There is more than a touch of paradox here, as it normally goes without saying that a *dominus* is *liber;* for paradoxical endings, see on **2.12.4** and compare **2.44, 2.80**. For Martial's upfront descriptions of the kind of patron he wishes to have, see on **2.18.8**.

2.33

Cur non basio te, Philaeni? calva es.
cur non basio te, Philaeni? rufa es.
cur non basio te, Philaeni? lusca es.
haec qui basiat, o Philaeni, fellat.

Why don't I kiss you, Philaenis? You're bald. Why don't I kiss you, Philaenis? You're red-headed. Why don't I kiss you, Philaenis? You're one-eyed. Whoever kisses all that, Philaenis, sucks.

Themes.   After the intervening epigram dedicated to patron-client relations, we return to the sexual thematic and obscene language of **2.31** and before that **2.28**, combined with the invective mode and focus on kissing that characterized the Postumus poems; after a long sequence in elegiac couplets (**2.24–32**), we again have a poem in hendecasyllabics. An insult of Philaenis' physical appearance is joined to a characteristically macho assertion on the part of the persona that he does not perform fellatio; being on the other end of such a transaction, of course, is nothing but a pleasure (cf. **2.31**, 3.96, 4.17, 9.40, 9.67, 11.49, 12.65). Plass 1985: 198 observes the riddle (see on **2.17.5**) underlying Martial's joke: "What is bald, red, and one-eyed?"

A further effect of this epigram is to deter *anyone else* from kissing Philaenis. Mockery of physical deformities or ugliness is stock in trade in Martial's epigrams and was an important element of ancient humor (see on **2.35**), as was invective aimed at unattractive women: in Martial, see 3.8 (Thais is *lusca,* but the man who loves her lacks both eyes!), 3.32, 3.42, 3.72, 3.93, 4.62, 5.29, 6.23 (with Grewing ad loc.), 6.93, 7.18, 7.75 ("vis futui gratis, cum sis deformis anusque"), 8.60, 8.79, 9.37, 10.90, 11.21, 11.97, 11.99–102, 12.6, 12.22–23; Opelt 1965: 26–28; Sullivan 1991: 197–207; Richlin 1992 passim. For the related tradition of invective against old women, see on **2.34.3**.

Structure.   A bipartite structure can be detected (1–3 lay out a description of Philaenis, while 4 constitutes the punch line), but the structure that more immediately impresses itself on the reader is more complex. A threefold repetition of the bipartite line *cur non basio te, Philaeni?* X *es* is followed by the punch line, which breaks the question-and-answer pattern but still falls into two halves distinguished by the pause after the vocative *Philaeni;* the sharp point is then driven home by the final word *fellat.* Laurens 1989: 328–330 speaks of a "vertical axis" here and in 1.39, 1.65, 1.77, 6.26, 7.43, 12.16. For the use of repetitions or refrains see on **2.18.2**; the technique again appears in obscene contexts in 1.77 (*et tamen pallet*) and 11.47 (*ne futuat*). For the accumulation of sentence pairs, see on **2.18**.

1 *basio:* Here and in each of the following two metrically identical lines, the final vowel of the verb is shortened; see on **2.9.2**.

1 *Philaeni:* This is the first appearance of a name that appears fairly frequently in Martial, almost always referring to a woman whose sexual tastes or practices are held up for criticism. In 7.67 and 7.70 the name is applied to a hypermasculine *tribas;* in 9.40 she has vowed to fellate her husband, Diodorus, if he returns home from a trip. A book with the title περὶ σχημάτων συνουσίας, evidently a type of sex manual, had been circulating under the name of Philaenis since at least the third century B.C.; see *RE* s.v. *Philainis,* Vessey 1976, Burzachini 1977, Herrero Inguelmo and Montero Cartelle 1990, Parker 1992.

Although there is no one single character associated with the name in Martial (e.g., she is dead in 9.29 but quite alive in 10.22 and 12.22), nonetheless the similarities among the present epigram and 4.65, 10.22, and 12.22 (she is *lusca* and Martial does not wish to kiss her), as in the cases of Galla (**2.25.1**), Phoebus (**2.35.2**), Cordus (**2.57.4**), Ponticus (**2.82.1**), and Cosconius (**2.77.1**), contradict Shackleton Bailey's assertion that "as a rule" no identities are maintained across book boundaries.

1 calva: At 14.27.2 Martial implies that some women might pluck their gray hairs to such an extent that they approached baldness (cf. Ov. *Ars am.* 2.66, Tib. 1.8.45, Prop. 3.25.13, Macr. *Sat.* 2.5.7). Female baldness is cited by Seneca (*Epist.* 95) as a symptom of a shocking masculinity among women who are described in terms closely reminiscent of Martial's *tribades* (including, interestingly, one named Philaenis in 7.67 and 7.70): they engage in sport; eat, drink, and vomit to excess; and are sexually dominant, penetrating both males and females. See further Williams 1999: 214–215.

3 lusca: Philaenis is once again ridiculed as one-eyed in 4.65; for other jokes at the expense of *lusci,* see 3.8, 3.11, 3.39, 4.65, 6.78 (with Grewing), 8.9, 8.59, 11.73.6, and 12.22. The loss of the use of one eye afflicted enough Romans to be a frequent subject of comment (Cic. *De orat.* 2.246), and *lusce* or *unocule* could be used as terms of abuse void of their literal sense (Plaut. *Curc.* 392, 505; Pers. 1.128).

In a discussion of Martial's *lusci,* Watson 1982 observes that the only physical feature this poet mocks more frequently is baldness (N.B.), adding that such jokes are rarely to be found in earlier literary sources, being "a stock example of the lowest type of humor" (71). Yet since the objects of his attacks are not real people, Martial has "transfer[red] a type of joke normally associated with scurrility to the genre of epigram and a higher realm of wit" (72).

4 fellat: For the execution of the point by means of a single word, see on **2.17.5**. The effect in this case is particularly noteworthy thanks to the harsh obscenity of the verb. Manuscript T, a member of family α, which often emends obscenities away (see on **2.31.1**), omits the entire final verse.

2.34

Cum placeat Phileros tota tibi dote redemptus,
   tres pateris natos, Galla, perire fame.
praestatur cano tanta indulgentia cunno
   quem nec casta potest iam decuisse Venus.
perpetuam di te faciant Philerotis amicam,   5
   o mater, qua nec Pontia deterior.

So taken with Phileros that you have bought him using your entire
dowry, you are allowing your three sons to starve to death, Galla.
To such an extent do you indulge your ancient cunt, though not
even a decent Venus would befit it now. May the gods make you
forever Phileros' girlfriend; as a mother you are worse even than
Pontia.

Themes.   As in the preceding poem, invective is directed at a woman, sexual
imagery is predominant, and a Greek name beginning *Phil-* appears in the
first line (see Introduction, section 3.4, for the sequence of Greek names in
2.33–36). For sexual relations between women and their male slaves, for
which the women are usually called to task (or, if married, their husbands
tweaked as cuckolds), see 1.81, 6.2, 6.39, 6.67, 7.14, 7.35, 10.91, 12.49, 12.58.
In Martial, as indeed throughout the Roman textual tradition, this distinctly
negative view stands in clear contrast with the easygoing acceptance of relations between men and their slaves of either sex (Williams 1999: 30–38,
51–52). Whereas Galla is the target of demeaning physical invective and is
compared to a murderous mother, Milichus, who has spent all his fortune
on the prostitute Leda, is teased for his self-indulgence (*luxuria;* **2.63**). The
difference lies, of course, in the fact that Galla has abandoned her responsibility to her children (the reference to starvation may well be humorous
exaggeration; LaPenna 2000: 99) in order to indulge her sexual desires.

Structure.   The opening couplet lays out the situation and names names,
and the remainder of the epigram constitutes Martial's nasty commentary. At
the same time a tripartite structure suggests itself, each couplet consisting of
an independent sentence: the situation (1–2); the remark that Galla is too
old to be indulging her sexual desires (3–4); a double assault on Galla in the
form of the wish that she may always be with Phileros (5) and the declara-
tion that she is worse than Pontia (6), the two halves of the point being signaled by the juxtaposition *amicam, / o mater.*

1 *Phileros:* This Greek name is found in Martial only here and in 10.43, where he has buried seven wives. It is a clear example of a *redender Name,* or significant name ("lover of Eros"): compare *Glyptus* (**2.45.1**), *Plecusa* (**2.66.4**), *Fidentinus* the plagiarist (1.29, 1.38, 1.53, 1.72), *Velox* the critic of long epigrams (1.110), *Theodorus* the wretched poet (5.73, 11.93). See Friedlaender, p. 21, for a list of examples and Giegengack 1969 for general discussion of the phenomenon in Martial.

1 *tota tibi dote redemptus:* Note the strongly alliterative quality of the phrase, with its repeated *t-* and *d-* sounds. Some have taken these words to mean that Galla has bought Phileros' freedom (Ker, Norcio, Ceronetti, Scandola). But the more straightforward way of understanding the words is that she, like Milichus in **2.63**, has purchased him from a slave dealer in order to enjoy him at home (Izaac, Shackleton Bailey, Barié and Schindler); in other words, he remains a slave. Martial's emphasis is unflinchingly on Galla's satisfaction of her sexual desires (3–4); why would she pay to set Phileros free when she could just as easily pay to have him in her possession?

2 *Galla:* See on **2.25**.1 for the name.

3 *cano . . . cunno:* *Cunnus* is the basic obscenity for the female genitalia, a *vox propria* and no metaphor (Adams 1982: 80–81); as such, it represents the third occurrence of undisguised obscenity in Book II after **2.28** and **2.31**. For the invective against old women, compare 1.64, **2.41**, 3.76, 4.20, 5.45, 7.75 ("vis futui gratis cum sis deformis anusque"), 10.39, 10.67, 10.90, and see Richlin 1992: 109–116.

4 *quem nec casta potest iam decuisse Venus:* The phrase *casta Venus* appears again at 6.45.2 and 10.33.4. The adjective is hard to translate into English, as it is not the same as "abstinent," one of the most common meanings of the English derivative "chaste." A woman praised as *casta* is one who engages in sexual relations only with her husband; see 1.13.3 and 1.62.1, where it describes married women. Martial's nasty implication is that not even Galla's husband will be attracted to her aging body or perhaps also that she is so ugly that no man will marry her.

For the use of the perfect infinitive with present meaning, see KS 2.1.133–135. Schneider 1909: 15 sees metrical factors at work, but *decere* is perfectly amenable to being used in dactylic verse.

5 *di te faciant:* For the closing curse, whether in the second or the third person, see on **2.24.8**; for the form "may the gods . . ." see 4.51.6 ("di reddant sellam . . . tibi") and 7.67.16 ("di mentem tibi dent tuam"). But what precisely is the content of this curse? Most likely it is a dismissive insult of Phileros as ugly or disgraceful: simply being his girlfriend is enough of a curse. Such seems to be the implication of the *variorum* commentary: "ut quam diutissime vivas misere cum Philerote tuo." Barié and Schindler offer an improbable explanation: Phileros may soon die and Galla follow him, thereafter to be his *perpetua amica*. They add that in 10.43 a man named Phileros has buried seven wives, but a first-time reader of Book II will not have this knowledge.

5 amicam: When used in relation to a man, *amica* is an unequivocal euphemism for his sexual partner ("girlfriend"): see 1.71.3, **2.62.3**, 3.69.6, 4.29.5, 9.2.1, 11.27.2, 11.100.1, 14.9.1, 14.156.1.

6 Pontia: A renowned poisoner and murderer of her own children in Nero's day; compare 4.43.5, 6.75.3 with Grewing. Juv. 6.638–642 cites Pontia by way of showing that the dangers he describes are found in real life and not only in myth. The MSS of family β read *Pontica*, that is, Medea as mythic paradigm of the murderous mother.

2.35

Cum sint crura tibi similent quae cornua lunae,
    in rhytio poteras, Phoebe, lavare pedes.

Since your legs have the form of the crescent moon, Phoebus, you could wash your feet in a drinking horn.

Themes.   In another epigram opening with a *cum-* clause, satiric commentary is now directed at a man. We leave the realm of the sexual, but the focus on Phoebus' physical appearance recalls the description of Philaenis in **2.33**. The insult of Phoebus' bowleggedness is straightforward enough; some spice may be added by the play between *cornua lunae* ("the horns of the moon," i.e., the crescent moon) and *rhytio* ("drinking horn") and perhaps also by a contrast between the moon and the name *Phoebus* ("Shining"), an epithet of Apollo, who was associated with the sun (*variorum* commentary). Walter 1995: 78 detects a further contrast between Apollo's divine beauty and Phoebus' all-too-human ugliness.

For jokes at the expense of others' appearance, see, among others, 1.19 (Aelia's four teeth) with Walter 1995: 78, **2.33**, **2.41**, **2.87**, 3.89.2 ("faciem durum, Phoebe, cacantis habes"), 10.83.11 ("calvo turpius est nihil comato"), 12.54.1 ("crine ruber, niger ore, brevis pede, lumine laesus"). Such jokes were a traditional element in ancient humor (Cic. *De orat.* 2.239, 266).

Structure.   The monodistich (see on **2.3**) has the nature of a sharp remark made in the course of a conversation or witty exchange; as usual, the first line offers a piece of information and the second line comments on it. Laurens 1989: 293–294 observes that here and in other similar monodistichs, monotony is avoided by the syntactical subordination of the first line, in this case by means of *cum sint.*

1 *similent:* Modern editors are divided between the two possible orthographies of this verb: *similent* (Heraeus, Lindsay, Izaac, Giarratano) and *simulent* (Schneidewin, Gilbert, Shackleton Bailey).

1 *cornua lunae:* Probably an Ovidian touch, since the phrase occurs several times in the earlier poet, likewise at the end of a hexameter (*Am.* 2.1.23; *Met.* 3.682, 8.11, 10.479, 12.264; Zingerle 1877: 22). It is also found at Lucan 3.595 and Stat. *Ach.* 1.644.

2 *rhytio:* Although the diminutive is nowhere else attested in Greek or Latin (cf. *eschatocollion,* **2.6.3**), an entry in an ancient bilingual word list tells us that it refers to a silver drinking vessel (*CGL* 3.324.52), and we can infer its shape from the present joke.

2 *poteras:* For the use of the imperfect indicative to express potential (*poteras* = *possis* or *posses*), see on **2.1.1**.

2 *Phoebe:* The name occurs sixteen times in Martial, and a few thematic clusters adhere to it. Most relevantly to the present epigram, he is again mocked for his unattractive appearance in 3.89 and 6.57; otherwise, he is associated with moneylending at **2.24.8** (where he is a creditor), 6.20, 9.92, 9.102 (where he is a potential creditor) and envied for his considerable genital endowment in 1.58 and 9.63. Certain coherent identities associated with the name thus span book divisions; see on **2.33.1**.

2.36

Flectere te nolim, sed nec turbare capillos;
    splendida sit nolo, sordida nolo cutis;
nec tibi mitrarum nec sit tibi barba reorum:
    nolo virum nimium, Pannyche, nolo parum.
nunc sunt crura pilis et sunt tibi pectora saetis   5
    horrida, sed mens est, Pannyche, vulsa tibi.

I wouldn't want you to curl your hair, but neither would I want you to muss it up. I don't want your skin to be shiny, nor do I want it filthy. Don't wear the beard of a man who uses hairnets, nor that of a defendant. I want neither too much of a man, Pannychus, nor too little. As it is, your legs are shaggy with hairs and your chest with bristles, but your mind, Pannychus, is plucked.

Themes.   After the previous monodistich mocking Phoebus for his unattractive legs, the focus continues to be placed on a man's appearance, now in a longer and more complex poem announcing a generalized ideal. The ancient theme of the golden mean (Siedschlag 1977: 59–62 compares in particular the Greek *mesotes*-epigram, in which each of two opposed extremes is rejected [*A.P.* 5.20, 37, 42; 10.102; 12.200]; see also Citroni ad 1.57) is here rephrased in terms of Roman discourses on masculinity. Artificially curling one's hair, taking too much care of one's skin, and shaving one's beard entirely or even plucking it out are signs of effeminacy, yet the other extreme (unkempt hair, filthy skin, bristly untrimmed beard) is equally undesirable, constituting an excess of manliness. Pannychus thus represents the worst of both worlds: physically too manly (*virum nimium*), mentally he is without substance (*mens vulsa*), and thus too little of a man (*virum parum*). An implication is that women and effeminate men are prone to a lack of intellectual rigor.

For the thematization of depilation among males and for hairiness as emblem of masculinity, see also **2.29.6**, **2.62**, 3.63, 3.74, 5.41, 5.61 (with Howell), 6.56 (with Grewing), 7.58, 9.27, 9.47, 10.65, 12.38; *A.P.* 11.190, 11.368; Williams 1999: 127–132. In a passage that may well have inspired the present epigram, Seneca compares two stylistic extremes to depilatory practices in a passage culminating with a *sententia* worthy of Martial: those who depilate their legs are overly attentive, while those who do not even depilate their underarms are insufficiently concerned with their appearance (*Epist.* 114.14: "tam hunc dicam peccare quam illum: alter se plus iusto colit, alter plus iusto neglegit; ille et crura, hic ne alas quidem vellit").

Citroni ad 1.57, Obermayer 1998: 56–57, and LaPenna 2000: 109 take Pannychus to be an actual or potential sexual partner of the poet. Yet Martial nowhere hints at Pannychus' sexual activities, ending instead with a reference to his *mens,* nor does *nolo virum nimium* necessarily constitute an announcement of the narrator's sexual tastes. To be sure, *velle* and *nolle* are often used in this way (1.57.2: "nolo nimis facilem difficilemque nimis"; 1.115.4: "quandam volo nocte nigriorem"; 9.32.1: "hanc volo quae . . ."), but not always (cf. 1.8.5–6: "nolo virum facili redimit qui sanguine famam; / hunc volo, qui . . ."). Obermayer's conclusion that the poet here expresses a preference for hairy, bearded sexual partners does not seem justified by the text.

Structure.   Siedschlag 1977: 126 cites the present epigram as an illustration of Martial's mastery of epigrammatic technique. The first two couplets lay out Martial's ideals, and the final couplet, introduced with the contrastive *nunc sunt,* tells us how Pannychus really is. The opening line also introduces the physical imagery that will be continued throughout the balanced antitheses structuring the remainder of the poem. Each of the subsequent three lines offers a new pair of contrasts—skin (*splendida cutis* vs. *sordida,* 2), beard (*mitrarum barba* vs. *reorum,* 3), overall manliness (*virum nimium* vs. *parum,* 4)—while the final antithetical pair (*crura et pectora horrida* vs. *mens vulsa*) is spread out over the entire final couplet (5–6) with an enjambment (*horrida*). Also of interest is the ABCB pattern in the distribution of the emphatic verb *nolo* over the first four lines: once in 1, twice in 2, absent from 3, twice in 4.

1 *flectere:* Martial's advice echoes Ovid's at *Ars am.* 1.505–506: "sed tibi nec ferro placeat torquere capillos, / nec tua mordaci pumice crura teras." Curling the hair with a *calamistrum* (curling-tongs) could always lay a man open to insult: see Pl. *Asin.* 627 ("cinaede calamistrate"), Cic. *Red. Sen.* 13 ("in lustris et helluationibus huius calamistrati saltatoris"), along with the disparaging description of the *bellus homo* at Mart. 3.63.3–4: "bellus homo est, flexos qui digerit ordine crines, / balsama qui semper, cinnama semper olet." See also 5.61, where an effeminate adulterer is described as *crispulus,* along with the contrast Martial draws between himself and the effeminate Charmenion at 10.65.6–9: "tu flexa nitidus coma vagaris, / Hispanis ego contumax capillis; / levis dropace tu cotidiano, / hirsutis ego cruribus genisque."

1 *turbare capillos:* Zingerle 1877: 22 reasonably detects Ovidian influence: the combination of *turbare* with *capillos* is attested only at Tibull. 1.3.91 ("longos turbata capillos") and five times in Ovid (*Am.* 3.2.75, 3.14.33; *Ars am.* 2.169; *Met.* 4.474, 8.859).

2 *nōlō ... nōlŏ:* See on **2.18.1** (*captŏ/captō*) and, for the correption, **2.9.2**. In 4 below, only the correpted form *nōlŏ* appears.

3 *nec tibi mitrarum nec sit tibi barba reorum:* The *mitra* was an Eastern headdress worn by women and effeminate men (for the latter, consider Cicero's allusion to Clodius at Cic. *Har.* 44 and Iarbas' view of Aeneas at V. *Aen.* 4.215–217). Friedlaender and Shackleton Bailey detect an allusion to the *galli,* or castrated priests of the Asian mother goddess; alternatively, Friedlaender notes, the phrase may suggest Greek dandies who pluck their beards (but this is based on a reading of the text of Cic. *Rab. Post.* 27 that is no longer accepted). In any case, the beard of men wearing the *mitra* would be nonexistent, whether plucked out or simply not growing, while that of a *reus* would be excessively long and unkempt (see on the following line). Martial is thus suggesting a mean between the extremes that in fact corresponds to the normative practice of his day: regularly shaving or trimming the beard but not extirpating it (Blümner 1911: 267–271). In the thematically related passage quoted above, Ovid urges: "sit trita barba resecta manu" (*Ars am.* 1.518).

Mitrarum requires further explanation. Friedlaender takes it to be a metonymy for men who wear the *mitra,* just as *abolla* and *toga* can refer to those who wear them (Juv. 3.115 and Mart. 10.18.4 respectively); Hofmann 1951: 202 compares the use of *frigus* for "cold places" at 4.64.14, and Heraeus points to *lacernae* at 5.8.12. But Housman 1907: 233 is troubled by the juxtaposition of this metonymy with the literal *barba reorum:* "If Martial wrote this [*mitrarum*] instead of writing 'nec *mitratorum* nec sit tibi barba reorum,' he must have had some motive which has not yet been discovered." His emendation of *tibi mitrarum* to *mitratorum,* lacking any manuscript support, has been taken up only by Shackleton Bailey and seems unnecessary. Poets' "motives" cannot always be cleanly explained, and in any case it is not clear why Martial could *not* have combined a metonymy (*mitrarum*) with a direct reference (*reorum*). The structure of the line avoids the admittedly jarring juxtaposition *mitrarum barba.*

Although it does not actually occur anywhere else in extant Latin texts, the phrase *barba reorum* is often used in modern scholarship as a handy way of referring to desperate defendants' practice of letting their beards grow so as to put on the appearance of mourning. Compare **2.74.3** (*tonsum reum*) and see further on **2.24.2** (*squalidus reus*).

4: The culmination of Martial's exposition of his ideal type is carefully structured: the first half ends at the caesura with *nimium,* balanced at the end of the second half by the contrasting *parum.* It is in this line, moreover, that the addressee and soon-to-be target is identified, his name located between the line's two halves.

4 *Pannyche:* The name appears again in 6.39 (a slave who has fathered a child on Cinna's wife), 6.67 (a man whose wife has sex with her eunuchs), 9.47 (a hairy *pathicus* who professes austerity), and 12.72 (a former courtroom pleader in the city who now leads the life of a farmer). There is clearly no single personality behind the name—indeed, two epigrams within a single book (6.39, 6.67) present mutually exclusive images. Pointing to 9.47, Obermayer 1998: 119–120 takes Pannychus to be an example of the type *cinaedus latens,* but one who reads through Martial's corpus successively will have no hint of this when reading the present epigram, as Obermayer himself acknowledges (79 n. 269). Nor is a reader of Book IX likely to recall a passing epigram from Book II.

5–6 *nunc sunt crura pilis et sunt tibi pectora saetis / horrida:* Note the accumulation of the vocabulary of hairiness and compare 6.56.1 ("quod tibi crura rigent saetis et pectora villis"), V. *Aen.* 8.266 ("villosaque saetis / pectora"), Juv. 2.11–12 ("hispida membra quidem et durae per bracchia saetae

/ promittunt atrocem animum"). *Crura* may refer either to the entire legs or to the shins in particular (see *OLD* s.v.). *Pili* are hairs in general, while *saetae* are, strictly speaking, the hairs of an animal (Isid. *Orig.* 12.1.26) and thus when attributed to human beings are "a mark of roughness or lack of culture" (*OLD* s.v.).

6 mens ... vulsa: The phrase is an example of catachresis, or especially bold metaphor; compare the technique of ending with a paradox (**2.12.4, 2.37.11**).

2.37

Quidquid ponitur hinc et inde verris,
mammas suminis imbricemque porci
communemque duobus attagenam,
mullum dimidium lupumque totum
muraenaeque latus femurque pulli   5
stillantemque alica sua palumbum.
haec cum condita sunt madente mappa,
traduntur puero domum ferenda;
nos accumbimus, otiosa turba.
ullus si pudor est, repone cenam!   10
cras te, Caeciliane, non vocavi.

Whatever is set down on the table you sweep up from this side and that: the teats of a sow's udder and a pork roast, a game bird for two, half of a mullet and a whole bass, a side of lamprey and a chicken thigh, a wood pigeon dripping in its sauce. Once you've hidden all this in a sodden napkin, it is handed over to a slave to be taken back home; meanwhile, we sit there, an idle crowd. If you have any sense of shame, put the dinner back! I didn't invite you to dinner tomorrow, Caecilianus.

Themes.   We return to the *cena,* last the focus in **2.27;** for the centrality of dinner parties in Martial's world, see on **2.11.** Since a guest might pack up and take home a small amount of food without raising eyebrows (Petr. *Sat.* 60.7; Marquardt 1886: 313–314), the problem with Caecilianus is one of degree, a point made by the accumulative effect of 2–6. Thus, Caecilianus takes home food "as unofficial *apophoreta*" (Leary ad 13.44). Thieving dinner guests are again satirized in 3.23, 7.20, and 8.59. Greek epigrams on the theme include *A.P.* 11.11, 11.20, and 11.205, the latter two by Martial's influential predecessor Lucillius (see Burnikel 1980: 18–21 for a comparative discussion), but the sharply formulated point of the present epigram is characteristic of Martial.

Only with the last word (*vocavi*) do we learn that Martial himself is the host. In view of the impressive list of delicacies that has preceded (for which cf. Hor. *Sat.* 2.4), the poem thus also takes on the function of self-advertisement for the persona: he can give a decent dinner party. Noticeably more modest menus chez Martial are found in 5.78 and 11.52, the latter explicitly excluding sow's udder. See André 1981 for an overview of Roman foods, Gowers 1993: 245–267 for Martial's invitation poems, and Lindsay 1998 for a general discussion of food in Martial. Juv. 11 praises modest meals over extravagant banquets like the one described in the present epigram (cf. Juv. 11.37, where the *mullus* is contrasted with a much cheaper fish, the *gobius*). See on **2.19**, **2.26**, **2.43.13–14**, and **2.44** for comparable contrasts between the personae of the two poets.

Structure.   The bulk of the epigram describes a dinner guest's misbehavior and the other guests' passive response (1–9); the final two verses present the poet's own reaction, culminating with the memorable phrase *cras te non vocavi*. The accumulative technique (for which see on **2.7**) is here put to particularly effective use, as one delectable food item is named after another, consistently connected by *-que;* there is not a single *et* or an asyndeton.

The food items themselves are arranged in a satisfying pattern—pork, fowl, fish, fowl (ABCB)—with the following syntactic variations, line by line:

> *mammas suminis imbricemque porci* (2): two items, each accusative + genitive
> *communemque duobus attagenam* (3): one item occupying the entire line
> *mullum dimidium lupumque totum* (4): two items, each noun + adjective, contrasted by *dimidium* and *totum*
> *muraenaeque latus femurque pulli* (5): two items, each designated with a body part (*latus, femur*), arranged chiastically (genitive + accusative, accusative + genitive)
> *stillantemque alica sua palumbum* (6): as in 3, one item occupies the entire line, with the name of a fowl coming at the end of the line.

1 *quidquid ponitur:*   The verb is often used of setting out food or drink before a guest at a meal: see on **2.1.10**.

1 *hinc et inde:* The expression is particularly characteristic of Martial (again at 1.117.11, 3.82.6, 5.51.3, 9.90.2, 10.83.6) and is not otherwise attested before the first century A.D.

2: For the delicacy *sumen* (sow's udder), see 13.44; Plaut. *Curc.* 323, *Pseud.* 166; Pers. 1.53; Plin. *N.H.* 11.211. Since the noun literally refers to the udder as a whole, *mammas* may be pleonastic, achieving syntactic balance within the line: *mammas suminis imbricemque porci* (Barié and Schindler, Norcio, Ceronetti, Scandola). Alternatively, *mammas* may refer specifically to the nipples (Ker, Izaac, and Shackleton Bailey). Walter suggests the unlikely possibility that *suminis* is a synecdoche for "sow."

The noun *imbrex* signifies a semicylindrical tile placed over the joints between roof tiles; here, uniquely, it is used to refer to a cut of meat, obviously based on a similarity in form. Most thus translate "fillet" or "cutlet," but Ceronetti and Scandola, following a suggestion of Collesso, suggest that the phrase refers to pig's ears.

3 *attagenam:* A game bird resembling the partridge; also *attagen, -genis* (13.61.2).

4 *mullum dimidium lupumque totum:* Two prized types of fish, probably the red mullet and the bass respectively, both amply attested. Martial cites them together again at **2.40.4** and 11.49.9, the *mullus* at **2.43.11**, 3.45.5, 10.31.3, 13.79 (see Leary ad loc.), 13.89.

If, with Bridge and Lake and others, we take the point of *dimidium* to be that the fish is half eaten, there is a particularly sharp insinuation of gluttony. On the other hand, the *mullus* may simply have been served in two halves, as opposed to a whole *lupus*.

5 *muraenae:* For lamprey as a delicacy, see 13.80 with Leary.

5 *femurque pulli:* *Femur* refers literally to the thigh, and Izaac, Ceronetti, Norcio, and Scandola translate accordingly. Others (Ker, Shackleton Bailey, Barié and Schindler) take *femur* to refer by synecdoche to the whole leg. Ker and Shackleton Bailey render *pulli* with the generic "fowl," while others translate specifically "chicken," the meaning of the Romance derivatives of the noun. The latter is somewhat more likely, since when *pullus* refers to the young of other types of bird, the species is normally identified: *columbae pulli* at Plaut. *Asin.* 209; *pullus hirundinis* at Juv. 10.231; *cygni pullus* at Apul. *Pl.* 1.1.

6 *stillantemque alica sua palumbum:* Other references to this prized game bird include 13.67 (where it is said to have an antiaphrodisiac effect), Hor. *Sat.* 2.8.91, Cat. *Agr.* 90. Normally *alica* (or *halica*) refers to a type of porridge or gruel made from emmer groats that was among the traditional gifts given at the Saturnalia (12.81, 13.6, 13.9; *OLD* s.v. 1), and Friedlaender and *TLL* s.v. (1.1557.2) understand the word in this sense here. But the imagery of dripping (*stillantem*) causes others to suspect that *(h)alica* here refers to what is usually called *(h)al(l)ec*, a type of fish sauce (see *OLD* s.v. *alica* 2 and *hallec*). Collesso suggests a compromise solution: that the reference is to a grain-based sauce.

7 *cum condita sunt:* See on *traduntur puero* (8) for the passive.

7 *madente mappa:* Guests sometimes brought their own napkins to dinner parties (12.29); they might be given as gifts at the Saturnalia (5.18.1, 7.72.2; Stat. *Silv.* 4.9.25) and were sometimes the object of theft (8.59.8; Catull. 12). For the phrase *madente mappa*, evoking both its greasiness and the fact that it is dripping because of all that is tucked away inside, compare 7.20.8: "buccis placentae sordidam linit mappam."

8 *traduntur puero:* This may be equivalent to *tradis puero* (cf. 3.23.1: "omnia cum retro pueris obsonia tradas"), just as *condita sunt* (7) may stand for *condidisti:* the passive verbs would express (mock-) polite indirection. Taken literally, on the other hand, the passives would add a further satiric touch: Caecilianus does not even bother to wrap the food up and give it to the slave boy himself but leaves the job to someone else, presumably another slave. For the practice of bringing along a slave or slaves to social events in the evening, see 8.75, 12.87.

The basic meaning of *puer* is "boy," that is, a young male whether pre- or postpubescent (in 7.14 we read of a 20-year-old *puer*), but frequently it refers, as here, to a slave (Garrido-Hory 1981: 99–103). It is the single most frequently occurring of all nouns in Martial, followed by *dominus* (Siedschlag 1979): a small but telling reminder of the extent to which slavery permeates the world of these epigrams (cf. on **2.32.5**). By contrast, the five most frequently occurring nouns in the broad sample of Latin prose and poetry analyzed by Delatte et al. 1981 are, in descending order, *res, animus, rex, deus,* and *pars; puer* is found much lower on their list.

9 *nos accumbimus, otiosa turba:* At 1.43.11 ("tantum spectavimus omnes") we read of a group of dinner guests sitting idly by as the host eats up the wild boar placed before them. Walter 1995: 115 brings out the implications of *otiosa:* on the one hand, we have nothing to do because all the food is gone; on the other hand, eating is hard work (cf. *A.P.* 11.11 with Prinz 1911: 59–60). The phrase *otiosa turba* occurs again at 11.1.10, where it refers to crowds of leisurely Romans in the Campus Martius, but nowhere else in extant Latin.

10 *ullus si pudor est:* For the use of this and similar phrases in order to prod someone to action, compare Plaut. *Stich.* 322 ("si in te pudor adsit, non me appelles"), V. *Ecl.* 7.44, Ov. *Am.* 3.2.24, Stat. *Theb.* 10.710, Juv. 3.153–154.

11 *cras te, Caeciliane, non vocavi:* Note the paradoxical effect created by the combination of *cras* with a perfect-tense verb; Burnikel 1980: 20

aptly speaks of a syntactical oxymoron, while Collesso observes, "soloecismus est, sed argutissimus." For Martial's paradoxical endings, see on **2.12.4**. The MSS of family α smooth out the paradox and remove the oxymoronic effect, reading *cras te . . . non vocabo.*

Caecilianus is one of the most common of men's names in Martial, no doubt partly because of its convenient metrical shape: it fits easily into dactylic verse, and indeed, apart from the present hendecasyllabic epigram, the name appears exclusively in elegiac couplets. Unlike such names as *Selius* (**2.11.1**) or *Zoilus* (**2.16.1**), it is not linked to a single, easily identifiable character; like *Sextus* (**2.3.1**), the name is consistently attached to the object of various kinds of invective or satiric commentary (in **2.71** he is tweaked as a poetaster, and in **2.78** he is the owner or manager of an unpleasantly cold bathhouse). In a later poem that reworks the themes of the present epigram (8.67) the name again designates a disagreeable guest at Martial's dinner party and there is once again a final joke involving the time of the invitation ("mane veni potius; nam cur te quinta moretur? / ut iantes, sero, Caeciliane, venis."). Maaz 1992: 80 observes that *Caecilianus* is one of six names attested only in Martial and the medieval poet Godfrey of Winchester; the others are Aper, Candidus (see on **2.24.6**), Didymus, Postumianus, and Probus. See further on **2.78.2**.

For the first appearance of the vocative of the addressee in the epigram's final line, see on **2.30.6**. Here the technique generates a certain tension, as the offender's name is only revealed at the end.

2.38

Quid mihi reddat ager quaeris, Line, Nomentanus?
    hoc mihi reddit ager: te, Line, non video.

You ask what my estate at Nomentum produces for me, Linus? It produces this: that I don't see you, Linus.

Themes.   In this, the first of two juxtaposed monodistichs offering ironic commentary on two different stereotypes, one male (the annoying acquaintance in the present case) and one female (the adulteress in **2.39**), the motif of "nearness" found in **2.5** is inverted: just as the poet would like to spend as much time as possible with Decianus, he is happy to keep Linus at a safe distance.

A harsher monodistich from a later book likewise combines the phrase *reddit ager* with a repetition of the noun *ager* in both lines: since Phileros has buried his seventh wife in his *ager*, his estate has yielded more to him than it has to anyone else (10.43.2: "plus nulli, Phileros, quam tibi reddit ager").

Structure. The monodistich, as usual, falls naturally into two parts, each occupying a line; Laurens 1989: 292–293 notes the particularly vivid effect achieved by the question-and-answer format. Also of note is the contrast between the first line, which consists of an entire sentence, and the second, which is divided at the principal caesura into two independent sentences. The technique is found quite rarely in Martial's monodistichs: in Book II, only **2.76** comes close, and among the collections of monodistichs in Books XIII and XIV, only 13.76, 13.98, and 14.133 display the structure; cf. 13.53. More frequently, a first verse containing an entire sentence is followed by a verse that is divided into two syntactic units, but not at the principal caesura: see on **2.39**.

For the device of posing (and, as here, opening with) a question that leads directly to the point, see on **2.31.1**. Here Linus' question at first seems unremarkable, but the poet's reuse of his wording (*quid mihi reddat ager ~ hoc mihi reddit ager*) raises the possibility that it had perhaps not been entirely innocuous: it might also have been a challenge.

1 *ager... Nomentanus:* Martial's epigrams are full of allusions, sometimes quite enthusiastic, to an estate at Nomentum, about 20 kilometers northeast of Rome (many scholars identify this with the modern town Mentana, but Sullivan 1991: 4 n. 8 favors the modern Casali, located above the Via Nomentana). Sullivan 1991: 27 provides a useful summary of Martial's allusions to his property: he "criticis[es] its lack of firewood (13.15), the second-rate quality of its wine (13.42; cf. Plin. *NH* 14.34) and its pomegranates (13.42). . . . It was small (9.18.2), but it provided him with a great deal of pleasure. . . . It was not a self-sufficient holding; its produce had to be supplemented by market-shopping (7.31; 10.58.9; 10.94), but it had some poultry, which served as gifts (9.54.12). Its rusticity, with the pines, holm-oaks and laurel grove, and the primitive altars built by his bailiff to celebrate his birthday and similar occasions, is described nostalgically after its sale in 97 to Marrius (10.92)." Various well-known personages had owned estates in the area, including Atticus (Nepos *Att.* 14), Remmius Palaemon (Plin. *N.H.* 14.49), and Seneca (Colum. 3.3.3, Plin. *N.H.* 14.51; compare Sen. *Epist.* 104.1, 110.1).

How did Martial come to possess this property? With near unanimity scholars describe it as "probably a gift from Seneca himself or his heirs"

(Sullivan 1991: 4 with n. 8). This idea seems to have originated in a suggestion made by Friedlaender in his 1870 *Dissertatio de personis quibusdam a Martiale commemoratis* and has long since become dogma. Only Van Stockum 1884: 35–36 and Kleijwegt 1998 express serious doubts about the theory, for which indeed there is no direct evidence.

For the spondaic line and the four-syllable ending *Nomentanus,* see on **2.29.5**.

1 Line: Apart from 9.86, where it refers to the mythological figure killed by Heracles with his own lyre, and 12.49, where he is a slave in charge of a troop of *concubini,* the name serves as a more or less generic butt for insults, with a noticeable tendency toward the sexual and the financial: see 1.75, **2.54** (his wife suspects he likes to be anally penetrated; q.v. for Scherf's unconvincing suggestion that this and the present epigram form a thematic pair), 4.66, 7.10, 7.95, 11.25.

2 te, Line, non video: When Martial replies that the farm's yield (*quid reddat ager*) is not a certain amount of grapes, grain, or olives but the fact that he does not see Linus, the latter is effectively identified as a *fructus* (cf. Ter. *Ph.* 680: "fructum quem Lemni uxori' reddunt praedia"). For the repetition of the vocative *Line* in the first and second lines, see on **2.25**; for the vocative in the second half of the final pentameter, see on **2.18.8**.

2.39

Coccina famosae donas et ianthina moechae.
vis dare quae meruit munera? mitte togam.

You are giving the notorious adulteress scarlet and violet clothes as gifts. Do you want to give her what she has earned? Send her a toga.

Themes. The second of two juxtaposed satiric monodistichs makes a swipe at a favorite target, the adulterous woman; compare 1.34, 1.62, 1.68, 1.74, 1.81, **2.34**, **2.47**, **2.49**, **2.56**, **2.60**, 3.26, 3.85 (cf. **2.83**), 3.92, 5.61, 5.75, 6.6, 6.22, 6.31, 6.39, 6.45, 6.90, 7.10, 8.31, 9.2, 10.14, 10.95, 11.7, 11.11, 12.38, 12.93, and see below on 1 for the meaning of *moecha*. The joke of the present epigram is based on the traditional practice of compelling women condemned for adultery to exchange the characteristic garb of matrons, the *stola,* for the toga worn by prostitutes (cf. Hor. *Sat.* 1.2.62

with Porph. and ps.-Acro; Ov. *Fast.* 4.134; Mart. 6.24 with Grewing, 6.64.5; Juv. 2.70; D. 47.10.15.15; Marquardt 1886: 44 n. 1). The same practice allows Martial to use the image of a prostitute in a *stola* as a metaphor for an incongruity (1.35.9–10; cf. Afran. fr. 133: "meretrix cum veste longa") and lends a nasty point to Cicero's sarcastic remark that the young Antony put on the *toga virilis* only to turn it into a woman's toga (Cic. *Phil.* 2.44–45). See also 10.52, where a eunuch wearing a toga is called a *damnata moecha*. If the note provided by Porphyrio and pseudo-Acro on Hor. *Sat.* 1.2.62 is correct ("prostare solebant cum togis pullis, ut discernerentur a matronis"), the toga in question will have been drab in color, and Martial's epigram will thus also be playing off the visual contrast between this woman's brightly colored gifts hitherto (*coccina, ianthina*) and what she really deserves (*toga*).

Structure.   Once again we see the effective simplicity of which the monodistich form is capable. The first line sets out a situation and the second line responds to it, employing the characteristic technique of question and answer, for which see on **2.7.8** (*vis?*), **2.31.1**. As in **2.38**, the second verse is divided into two syntactically independent units, but here the division does not coincide with the principal caesura. For this more frequent structure, see also **2.9**, **2.45**, **2.79**.

   1 *coccina* . . . *ianthina:* These neuter plural forms (cf. *coccina nostra* at **2.43.8** and *tua candida* at **2.46.5**) of Greek adjectives refer to articles of clothing dyed scarlet and violet respectively, both colors being signs of luxury (cf. **2.16.2**).
   1 *famosae* . . . *moechae:* The same phrase occurs in the same metrical position at **2.47.1** but nowhere else in extant Latin literature. The Greek borrowing *moecha* is more or less equivalent to *adultera,* designating a freeborn married woman who has sexual relations with someone other than her husband. It is colloquial in tone; Grewing ad 6.2.5 observes that juridical texts always use *adultera,* never *moecha.* Martial himself uses *adultera* only twice (6.7.5, 9.2.3) but *moecha* frequently indeed, usually in a dismissive or insulting way: in Book II alone see **2.47.1**, **2.49.2**, and compare Catull. 42 (*moecha putida*), Opelt 1965: 200, 205. For the use of the adjective *famosus* to suggest sexual notoriety, see Cic. *De orat.* 2.277, Hor. *Sat.* 1.4.3–5, Juv. 2.70, Suet. *Tib.* 28 with *OLD* s.v. *fama* 6a.
   2: Note the alliterative sequence *meruit munera mitte.* The verb *meruit* alludes to a common term for a female prostitute: *meretrix,* literally "a woman who earns a living" with her body. Compare the phrase *corpore quaestum facere* at Val. Max. 6.1.10 and *CIL* 1².593, as well as the term *puer meritorius,* designating a boy prostitute at Cic. *Phil.* 2.105, Serv. *Ecl.* 8.29.

2.40

Uri Tongilius male dicitur hemitritaeo.
  novi hominis fraudes: esurit atque sitit.
subdola tenduntur crassis nunc retia turdis,
  hamus et in mullum mittitur atque lupum.
Caecuba saccentur quaeque annus coxit Opimi,   5
  condantur parco fusca Falerna vitro.
omnes Tongilium medici iussere lavari:
  o stulti, febrem creditis esse? gula est.

They say Tongilius is being burned up by a bad semitertian fever. I know the man's deceitful ways: he is hungry and thirsty. The treacherous nets are now being spread for the fat thrushes, the hook is being lowered for the mullet and bass. Let the Caecuban wine be strained, along with the one ripened in Opimius' year; let the dark Falernian be stored in small glass bottles. Tongilius' doctors have all ordered him to bathe. You fools! Do you really believe it's a fever? It's his appetite.

Themes.   The tone of blunt satire is sustained as the poet takes aim at yet another recurring target. Although the poem has no fewer than three interpretive cruces (see on 1, 3–4, 5–6), its central image is clear: Tongilius is pretending to be seriously ill in order to snag dinner invitations, or at least gifts of food and wine. For the theme of feigned illness, see on **2.16** and **2.26**. There is a close similarity in subject matter to 11.86, where Parthenopaeus feigns a bad cough for the sake of the delicious cough drops, and the punch line reads: "non est haec tussis, Parthenopaee, gula est" (6). Friedlaender, followed by Prinz 1911: 79, claims that the men who will be inviting Tongilius to dinner are interested in having a place in his will and thus understands the epigram, like **2.16** and **2.26**, to be touching on the theme of legacy hunting.

Celsus remarks that food given at the right time was the best remedy for fever (3.4: "optimum vero medicamentum eius est opportune cibus datus"). But there seems to have been no consensus among physicians as to when the right time was. Asclepiades recommends following a harsh three-day regime with food on the fourth day, but Celsus himself argues for a flexible approach depending on the patient's strength and other factors (3.4.7).

Structure.   The first line describes the situation and the second line immediately offers commentary, bluntly exposing the illness as a fake (*fraudes*);

in **2.26** and 11.86 it is only at the epigram's end that the cat is let out of the bag. Thus, the point is already delivered in the first couplet, and the epigram ends not with a sharp and unexpected turn but with a rephrasing of the final words of the opening couplet (*esurit atque sitit ~ gula est*). The ring-composition effect is reinforced by the repetition of Tongilius' name in the same metrical position in the first line of the first and last couplet respectively (*uri Tongilius ~ omnes Tongilium*).

See Siedschlag 1977: 35 for Martial's practice of introducing an epigram by citing rumors or otherwise referring to what people are saying (cf. 1.29: *fama refert;* **2.72**: *narratur;* 3.9; 3.87; 5.77; 7.88), and see Greenwood 1998a for overall discussion of Martial's vocabulary of rumor. Other introductory techniques include anchoring the event in a specific time (**2.72**) or place (**2.17**).

1 *uri Tongilius male dicitur hemitritaeo:* The name *Tongilius* is found only here in Martial (cf. *Tongilianus* in 3.52 and 12.88) and is rare overall: Schulze 1904: 455 is able to cite only the present epigram, Juv. 7.129–134 (where, interestingly, he is also associated with the baths; Colton 1991: 311 argues that Juvenal has borrowed the name from Martial), and *CIL* 6.12863, 36438, 27547. To this should be added Cic. *Cat.* 2.4 (one of Catiline's unsavory associates).

Does *male* modify *dicitur* ("it is said falsely" that he is burning with a fever: Collesso, Ker, Izaac, Norcio, Ceronetti) or *uri* (it is said that he is "burning badly" with a fever: Shackleton Bailey, Barié and Schindler, Scandola)? Taking *male* with *uri* has the advantage of postponing the revelation that the illness is feigned until the next line; this corresponds to Martial's frequent practice of first setting out a situation clearly and concisely and *then* making his ironic comment or revealing the truth. The adverb *male* is, moreover, often used to intensify words having an unpleasant sense (*OLD* s.v. 10; cf. Hor. *Sat.* 2.5.107: "si quis . . . male tussiet") and was easily associated with illness; compare 8.25.2 (*aegrum me male*) and consider the phrases *male esse* and *male valere* (*TLL* 8.237.7–40). Yet taking *male* with *dicitur* is hardly impossible: see *TLL* 8.240.34–76 (*i.q. falso; praecipue de hominum opinionibus, dictis vel probandis vel refutandis*) with Plaut. *Curc.* 513 ("male dictum"), Plaut. *Stich.* 118, Cic. *Tusc.* 1.93, D. 9.2.11.pr. (Ulpian); compare also **2.32.7** ("non bene servitur"). In short, the syntactic function of *male* may be deliberately ambivalent.

The *hemitritaeus* is a serious type of fever described by Celsus (3.3.2): it is a tertian (i.e., it recurs on the third day, counting inclusively) but is accompanied by paroxysms for nearly 36 out of the 48-hour cycle and never truly disappears in the period of remission. Martial uses it as an image for serious illness again at 4.80.3 and 12.90.2.

2 *novi hominis fraudes:* This is the reading of families α and β; family γ offers *novi hominis mores*. All modern editors since Schneidewin have printed *fraudes*, even though a change from an original *mores* to *fraudes* (the latter perhaps having its origin in an interlinear gloss on the former) seems easier to explain than the other way around. Indeed, Lindsay 1903a: 24 includes this line in a list of 106 examples of ancient variants between which "the choice is often extremely uncertain"; see also **2.30.3**, **2.46.10**, **2.61.1**.

3–4: Another interpretive crux. Is the language metaphorical (the victims of Tongilius' fraud are portrayed as birds and fish caught with nets and hooks) or literal (sumptuous meals are being prepared for Tongilius)? Following Collesso, Shackleton Bailey argues for the literal reading. Yet the metaphor of "hooking fish" is found in closely similar contexts at 6.63.5–6 ("'munera magna tamen misit.' sed misit in hamo; / et piscatorem piscis amare potest?") and 5.18.7–8 ("imitantur hamos dona: namque quis nescit / avidum vorata decipi scarum musca?"), and the metaphorical use of *retia* recurs at **2.27.1** ("cenae cum retia tendit") and **2.47.1** ("subdola famosae moneo fuge retia moechae"). For "hooks" and "nets" see also Hor. *Epist.* 1.7.74, Ov. *Ars am.* 3.425–426, Sen. *Ben.* 4.20.3 ("captator est et hamum iacit"), Juv. 12.123, Plin. *Epist.* 9.30.2, Suet. *Aug.* 25.4, *TLL* 6.3.2523.30–77, Otto 1890: 299. While the immediate context (5–6 in particular) may suggest a literal understanding of Martial's phrase, the metaphorical sense of "hooks" and "nets" surely also comes into play in this couplet, especially in view of the adjective *subdola*, also at **2.47.1**.

5–6 *saccentur . . . condantur:* As against all other modern editors, who print the subjunctives *saccentur* and *condantur,* Shackleton Bailey prints the indicatives *saccantur* (not found in any MS) and *conduntur* (T). The emendation has the advantage of creating a protracted series of indicative verbs (*esurit, sitit, tenduntur, mittitur, saccantur, conduntur, iussere*); otherwise, the sequence is interrupted by an ironic exclamation with jussive subjunctives.

The verb *saccare* refers to the pouring of wine through a porous bag (*saccus*) designed to filter out sediment and to make the flavor milder; see Marquardt 1886: 324.

5–6 *Caecuba . . . quaeque annus coxit Opimi, / . . . fusca Falerna:* Martial here cites three types of highly valued wines. The *Caecubum* took its name from a district in southern Latium; compare 12.17, Hor. *Sat.* 2.8.15, Plin. *N.H.* 3.60. The *Falernum* was named after the *ager Falernus,* a territory between Latium and Campania that was home to famous vineyards at the foot of the *mons Massicus;* compare 3.76, 9.73, 9.90, 9.93 (*immortale Falernum:* again in 11.36), 11.26, 12.17; Catull. 27.1; Cic. *Brut.* 287; Hor. *C.* 1.20.10; Tibull. 2.1.27; Petr. *Sat.* 55.3. The *Opimianum* derived its name from L. Opimius, consul in 121 B.C., a year whose wines were proverbially fine; compare 1.26.7,

3.26.3, 3.82.24, 9.87.1, 10.49.2, 13.113; Cic. *Brut.* 287; Vell. Pat. 2.7.5; Petr. *Sat.* 34.6; Plin. *N.H.* 14.55, 94. Pliny reports that wines from the year still existed in his day, nearly two hundred years later, and that although they could no longer be drunk on their own, they could be used in small amounts to flavor other wines. It has also been suggested that rather than literally referring to the vintage of 121 B.C., *Opimianum* may be a metonymy for wine of superior quality (Citroni ad 1.26.7). For the central role of wine in "the good life," see 8.77 and 11.26, and for an overview of different types of wine in Martial and contemporary poets in general see LaPenna 1999 and Mart. 13.106–125 with Leary. For wines of poor quality, see on **2.53.4**.

6 *parco . . . vitro:* "In small glasses, because it was so precious" (Bridge and Lake); or ironically representing the supposedly sick man's modest request (*variorum*); or because it is being dispensed like medicine (anonymous reader for Oxford University Press).

7 *medici iussere lavari:* Martial's references to this profession are usually disparaging: 1.30, 1.47, **2.16.5**, 11.74. For bathing as part of a medical cure, see Jackson 1988: 48–50, Fagan 1999: 85–103.

8 *o stulti:* For this common insult, see Opelt 1965: index s.v.

8 *gula est:* The noun literally denotes the throat and may be used metonymically to refer to the appetite for food, often, as here, with a disparaging reference to gluttony: see 1.20.3, 5.50.6, 5.70.5, 7.49.2, 11.86.6; Cic. *Att.* 13.31.4; Sall. *Jug.* 89.7; Sen. *Epist.* 89.22; Juv. 1.140, 5.94. It is in this sense that the adjective *gulosus* is usually used: see 3.22.5, 7.20.1–2, 8.23.1, 9.9.4, 10.59.5, 11.61.13, 12.41.1, 12.64.2, 13.71.1.

2.41

"Ride si sapis, o puella, ride,"
Paelignus, puto, dixerat poeta.
sed non dixerat omnibus puellis.
verum ut dixerit omnibus puellis,
non dixit tibi: tu puella non es,   5
et tres sunt tibi, Maximina, dentes,
sed plane piceique buxeique.
quare si speculo mihique credis,
debes non aliter timere risum
quam ventum Spanius manumque Priscus,   10
quam cretata timet Fabulla nimbum,

cerussata timet Sabella solem.
vultus indue tu magis severos
quam coniunx Priami nurusque maior.
mimos ridiculi Philistionis   15
et convivia nequiora vita
et quidquid lepida procacitate
laxat perspicuo labella risu.
te maestae decet adsidere matri
lugentique virum piumve fratrem,   20
et tantum tragicis vacare Musis.
at tu iudicium secuta nostrum
plora si sapis, o puella, plora.

"Laugh, girl; if you're clever, laugh!"—so, I believe, the Paelignian poet once said. But he didn't say it to every girl; or even if he did say it to every girl, he didn't say it to you. You're not a girl and you've got three teeth, Maximina, the color of pitch and boxwood at that. So if you trust your mirror and me, you ought to fear laughter as much as Spanius fears the wind and Priscus the touch of a hand, as much as Fabulla with all her makeup fears a rain cloud, or Sabella with her white lead fears the sun. Adopt a facial expression grimmer than that of Priam's wife or the eldest of his daughters-in-law. Avoid the mime plays of the comic Philistion and naughtier parties and whatever with delightful wantonness causes the lips to relax in a broad smile. Instead, you should sit with a grieving mother or with one mourning her husband or faithful brother; you should dedicate all your time to the tragic Muses. So then, take my advice: weep, girl; if you're clever, weep!

Themes. We return to the hendecasyllabic meter of **2.37** and the mode shifts from the ironic commentary of the preceding epigram to direct invective. Citing, interpreting, and then reinterpreting an alleged quotation from Ovid, the epigram offers harsh commentary on Maximina, no longer in the bloom of youth and with such hideous teeth that not only should she avoid smiling, but she should in fact try to weep. For mockery of physical shortcomings in Martial, see on **2.33**; for invective against old women, see on **2.34.3**; for bad teeth, see on 6 below. As Friedlaender observes, Catullus' invective against Egnatius, who smiles even in the company of a mother mourning her only son (39.4–5: "si ad pii rogum fili / lugetur, orba cum flet unicum mater"), probably influenced Martial's attack on Maximina.

One MS (T) presents the text of the epigram in the following sequence: 9, 10, 12, 11, 6, 7, 13–23. By omitting 1–5 and 8, this version entirely excises the Ovidian allusion and Martial's comments on it, and yet what remains is successful enough as a self-contained invective poem.

Structure.   There is a lively sequence. After citing the Ovidian verse and identifying it as such, the epigram makes an interpretive comment (3); modulates into self-correction or allowance of an alternative (4), at the same time zeroing in on a second-person addressee (5). The invective now begins (*tu puella non es*), and the target is named in 6 (see Laurens 1989: 273–274 for the "cruel ease" of the extended repetition of *puella* and *dicere* over the first five lines). The next sentence (*quare*) expands on the basic point—in view of her hideous teeth, Maximina ought to avoid laughter—presenting by means of a characteristic *cumulatio* a list of paradigms, both negative (9–12) and positive (13–14), taken from real life (10–12) and myth (14). The tragic scenes that Maximina ought to conjure up or imitate so as to avoid smiling (13–14) are then contrasted with the pleasant environments that she ought to avoid (15–17). Verses 19–21 return to the grim scenarios, and the concluding verses 22–23 represent the culmination and conclusion (*at tu*), repeating but varying the opening line and thus establishing a ring-composition. For the repetition, here with variation, of the opening verse at the poem's end, see Siedschlag 1977: 121–124. The technique is particularly characteristic of Catullus (16, 36, 52, 57) and Martial (**2.6**, 4.64, 4.89, 7.26); see further Wills 1996: 96–102.

1–2: The explicit identification of a quotation as such is a fairly rare technique in Latin literature and seems particularly characteristic of Martial; see Conte 1986: 59–60, Williams forthcoming. Epigram 9.70 is directly comparable: it begins with an identified citation of Cicero ("Dixerat 'o mores! o tempora!' Tullius olim"), modulates into invective against Caecilianus, and ends by rephrasing the quotation to the detriment of the addressee ("non nostri faciunt tibi quod *tua tempora* sordent, / sed faciunt *mores*, Caeciliane, *tui*"). Other examples are found in 8.55 (Virgil), 10.64 (Lucan), 11.20 (Augustus), and 11.90 (Lucilius), all of them epigrams concerned with Martial's poetic practice. Elsewhere, see Pers. 6.9, Auson. *Epigr.* 77.8 and (clearly inspired by the present epigram) *Ecl.* 1.1 ("'Cui dono lepidum novum libellum?' / Veronensis ait poeta quondam"), Apoll. Sidon. 3.1–4. Noteworthy among Greek predecessors for the technique is *A.P.* 9.572, whose author, Lucillius, was one of Martial's most important models (Burnikel 1980).

The line *ride si sapis, o puella, ride* is nowhere to be found in our text of Ovid. Since Martial's epigram is in hendecasyllabics and none of Ovid's extant works is in that meter, scholars of Martial have assumed that the poet is paraphrasing. But paraphrasing what? At least since Zingerle 1877: 5–6 (who gives a list of earlier speculations), scholars have usually pointed to two lines from the third book of the *Ars amatoria:* "quis credat? discunt etiam ridere puellae" (3.281) and "spectantem specta, ridenti mollia ride" (3.513). Cristante 1990 points instead to 3.279–280 ("si niger aut ingens aut non erit ordine natus / dens tibi, ridendo maxima damna feres"); 3.288 ("cum risu laeta est altera, flere putes"), where unattractive laughter is juxtaposed to weeping, ought also to be considered. For further discussion of the different senses in which these Ovidian passages might serve as "models" both for Martial's purported citation and for the epigram as a whole, see Williams forthcoming.

Another possibility, less likely but not entirely to be discounted, is that Ovid actually published a poem in hendecasyllabics, probably an epigram, that included the line *ride si sapis, o puella, ride.* This is in fact the assumption of Sullivan 1991: 225, along with most editors of Ovid and of Latin fragments: the line is listed among *incertae sedis versus* or *fragmenta* in Lenz's 1932 Teubner edition and Owen's 1933 OCT edition of Ovid (fr. 11 and fr. 13 respectively), as well as in *FPL* (Ovid fr. 6). Seemingly alone among modern editors of Ovid or of Latin fragments, *FLP* 310 identifies the line as *falsum.*

The ABA imperative structure of *ride si sapis, o puella, ride* is found in various contexts and languages; compare Cic. *Fam.* 14.2.4: "valete, mea desideria, valete"; Sen. *Dial.* 5.23.8: "fruere, mi Pollio, fruere"; and the English "burn, baby, burn" (Wills 1996: 92). For the formulaic and usually parenthetic phrase *si sapis* see also 4.54.3, 8.27.3, 8.77.3, 10.72.12, 13.5.2.; [Tib.] 3.8.2.

2 *Paelignus ... poeta:* The Paeligni were a people of central Italy, whose cities included Corfinium, Superaequum, and Ovid's birthplace, Sulmo; compare 1.61.6 ("Nasone Paeligni sonant") with Citroni. The periphrasis may itself be Ovidian in inspiration (*Am.* 2.1.1: "Paelignis natus aquosis"; 3.15.3: "Paeligni ruris alumnus").

2 *puto:* Parenthetical *puto* ("I believe; unless I am mistaken": see *OLD* s.v. 8 and Hofmann 1951: 106–107) is very common in Martial (Siedschlag 1979 lists forty occurrences), as is the shortening of the final vowel in such first-person verb forms (see on **2.9.2**). If the Ovidian quotation is self-evidently inexact, there is an especially ironic ambivalence in the phrase (Zingerle 1877: 5–6, Cristante 1990: 183–184).

3–4: See on **2.4.** for the juxtaposition of two identical or nearly identical verses, a frequent technique in Martial, but hardly unique to him.

3 *dixerat:* Martial displays a tendency to use the pluperfect where one might have expected a perfect or imperfect; see 1.107.3 with Friedlaender ad loc. and, in Book II alone, **2.63.1**, **2.83.2**. KS 2.140–141 consider this a "popular" usage, especially common with *fueram* and *habueram.*

4 *ut dixerit:* For this use of *ut* + subjunctive ("even if, supposing that"), marking a concession for argument's sake, see *OLD* s.v. 35.

5 *tu puella non es:* For this sense of *puella,* standing in implicit or explicit contast with *vetula* or other terms designating old women and almost always having a sexual charge, see 1.64, 3.76, 5.45, 8.79, 9.66. In 14.56 the addressee, who owns false teeth, is contrasted with *puellae.*

6–7 *tres sunt tibi . . . dentes, / sed plane piceique buxeique:* In 1.19 and 3.93 we read of women with four teeth; 8.57 speaks of a man with three. Other references to toothlessness, bad teeth, and artificial teeth include 1.72, 5.43, 6.74 (with Grewing), 7.13, 8.57 (with Schöffel), 9.37, 12.23, 14.56 (with Leary); Plaut. *Most.* 275; Caecil. 268 Ribb.; Hor. *C.* 2.8.3, 4.13.10ff., *Epod.* 8.3. The importance of teeth in men's and women's appearance is emphasized at Ov. *Ars am.* 1.515 and 3.197, respectively. The adjectives *picei* and *buxei* most likely refer to the unattractive color of Maximina's teeth (cf. 5.43: "Thais habet nigros, niveos Laecania dentes"; Ov. *Ars am.* 3.279–280: *niger dens;* Hor. *Epod.* 8.3: *dens ater*) rather than, as Leary ad 14.56.2 suggests, false teeth made of pine and boxwood; in 1.72 Martial speaks of false teeth made of horn and ivory. For dental care in ancient Rome in general, see Leary ad 14.22 and Jackson 1988: 118–121.

For the usage of *sed,* see on **2.6.6**. For *-que . . . -que,* see on **2.30.3**; its use to link the last two words in a hendecasyllabic verse (cf. 1.109.7, **2.48.1– 2**, 4.28.2, 4.46.11) had been common since Catullus: see Catull. 15.19, 32.11, 57.2; *Priap.* 23.3, 26.8, 37.12, 57.4, 61.8; Stat. *Silv.* 4.9.26; Siedschlag 1977: 41 n. 4.

6 *Maximina:* This is the only occurrence of the name in Martial.

8 *si speculo mihique credis:* The juxtaposition of mirrors and unattractive women seems particularly Ovidian: see *Met.* 15.232 ("flet quoque, ut in speculo rugas adspexit aniles"), *Am.* 1.14.36 ("quid speculum maesta ponis, inepta, manu?"), *Am.* 2.17.9 ("scilicet a speculi sumuntur imagine fastus"), *Med. fac.* 47 ("tempus erit, quo vos speculum vidisse pigebit"), *Trist.* 3.7.38 ("et speculum mendax esse querere tuum"). The specific language of "believing the mirror" is found in extant Latin only in the present epigram and in a characteristic Ovidian apostrophe to Pasiphae, who looks into the mirror hoping to see a cow (*Ars am.* 1.307: *"crede tamen speculo,* quod te negat esse iuvencam").

Consider also, though, Catullus' scornful remark on an ugly woman who appears *not* to have consulted her mirror (41.7–8: "nec rogare / qualis sit solet aes imaginosum"; *aes imaginosum* is a nineteenth-century conjecture that has been accepted by nearly all modern editors) and Cicero's brilliant adaptation of the imagery to the case of Clodius, who had dressed himself up as a woman in order to gain access to Caesar's wife (*Orat. fr.* 14.25: "sed, credo, postquam speculum tibi adlatum est, longe te a pulchris abesse sensisti").

10–12: In view of Martial's declared practice of not attacking real people by name, Spanius, Priscus, Fabulla, and Sabella will be fictional names. The context suggests that *Spanius* (only here in Martial) was a bald man who, like the Marinus satirized in 10.83, tries to make up for his loss by combing his few remaining hairs over his head (cf. σπάνιος, "scarce, scanty"). *Priscus* will be a dandy worried that any contact might ruin the effect of his carefully arranged clothing (cf. 3.63.10: "pallia vicini qui refugit cubiti"); the name also appears at 1.112, 9.5, 12.92. *Fabulla* overindulges in a facial powder based on chalk (*creta:* cf. 7.13 with Galán Vioque) and thus fears the catastrophic effect of rainfall; compare the following epigram attributed to Seneca: "Cum cretam sumit, faciem Sertoria sumit. / perdidit <ut> cretam, perdidit et faciem" (436 Riese). The name *Fabulla* appears again in conjunction with chalk powder at 8.33.17, and otherwise in 1.64, 4.81, 6.12, and 8.79. *Sabella* uses a product based on lead (*cerussa:* cf. 1.72.6, 7.25.2, 10.22.2; Pl. *Most.* 258; Ov. *Med. fac.* 73), which would presumably melt when exposed to too much heat. The name, which does not reappear in Martial, may make ironic reference to the Sabelli, a group of Italian peoples said to descend from the Sabini and praised for their austerity and in particular for their wives' chastity (1.62.1 with Citroni). In his poetic treatise on women's makeup, Ovid describes the Sabine women of old as being uninterested in their own appearance (*Med. fac.* 11–12: "forsitan antiquae Tatio sub rege Sabinae / maluerint, quam se, rura paterna coli").

11 *nimbum:* Translators render "shower" or "rain shower," but the noun can also signify "rain cloud" (*OLD* s.v. 1). This would give a particularly fine point: Fabulla is so concerned for her makeup that even the sight of a cloud worries her.

13 *vultus indue tu magis severos:* The phrase *vultus induere* is common enough but seems to have been favored by Seneca. See *Dial.* 11.5.5: "indue dissimilem animo tuo vultum"; *Ben.* 2.2.2: "induit sibi animi sui vultum"; *Med.* 751: "veni pessimos induta vultus"; and *A.L.* 409.1 Riese: "Corduba, solve comas et tristes indue vultus."

14 *coniunx Priami nurusque maior:* Note the ironically elevated tone of these periphrases for Hecuba and Andromache respectively: Martial generally uses *coniunx* with positive, and *uxor* with negative, undertones (Hoyo Calleja 1987: 114).

Thanks to their appearance in memorable scenes from the *Iliad* and various tragedies, Hecuba and Andromache function as figures for women in grief, having lost Hector—son and husband respectively—and other loved ones. Hecuba is also cited as a prototype of an old, sexually undesirable woman in 3.32 and is *contrasted* with her daughter-in-law Andromache at 3.76.4: "cum possis Hecaben, non potes Andromachen." As in the present epigram, however, Andromache is paradigmatic for the antierotic, along with Ajax' captive woman Tecmessa, at Ov. *Ars am.* 3.109–112, 3.517–522, and

Rem. am. 383–386. For Martial's use of mythic prototypes in general, see on **2.14.3–4.**

15 *mimos ridiculi Philistionis:* As its name suggests, mime was known for its imitation of daily life on the stage; this passage reminds us that it was characterized by ribald humor. Philistion was a Greek poet from Asia Minor whose floruit Jerome assigns to A.D. 5 and who is celebrated, surely with exaggeration, by Cassiod. *Var.* 4.51 as the inventor of the literary mime. Martial's remark is the earliest existing reference to this poet and suggests that his plays were still being staged toward the end of the first century A.D.

16 *convivia nequiora:* For the use of this adjective in contexts of erotic playfulness, see on **2.4.4.** Here it suggests a world of carefree partying; compare 4.14.9: "et ludit tropa nequiore talo."

19–20: The epithet *pium* refers to a quintessentially Roman virtue, most famously attributed by Virgil to Aeneas and consisting in dutiful devotion, especially to the gods, to Rome, and to one's parents or other family members (see Val. Max. 5.4.1: "de pietate erga parentes et fratres et patriam"). For the particular association of *pietas* with brothers, see 1.36.3 with Citroni ad loc., 12.44.3–4; Ov. *Trist.* 4.5.30; Sen. *Dial.* 11.5.3; *A.L.* 428 Riese (attributed to Seneca).

As opposed to the interpretation of Martial's phrase implied by my own and other modern translations, Collesso suggests the following: Maximina ought to sit in the audience at a performance of tragedies on such subjects as Hecuba (*matri*), Andromache (*lugenti virum*), and Electra (*lugenti fratrem*). This sense of *adsidere* is not otherwise attested.

22–23: The contrast between the opening line and Martial's reformulation in 23 is underscored by the words framing the line (*at . . . nostrum*), which set up a joking poetic *agon:* Don't listen to Ovid, listen to me. The final line makes a further contribution to the invective. Instead of smiling, Maximina should weep—so as to avoid horrifying men but also in reaction to her own ugliness.

2.42

Zoile, quid solium subluto podice perdis?
spurcius ut fiat, Zoile, merge caput.

Zoilus, why are you ruining the bathtub by washing your anus? To make it even dirtier, Zoilus, stick your head in.

Themes.   After the lengthy and fairly complex poem on Maximina, we find a blunt monodistich that brings us back to Zoilus (**2.16**, **2.19**) but maintains the invective tone. The point is brutally clear: Zoilus' mouth is filthier even than his anus, and as with the epigrams on Postumus' unwanted kisses (see on **2.10**), there is a suggestion that Zoilus has befouled his mouth by sexual practices. If, as Obermayer 1998: 220 observes, there is the added insinuation that his anus too has played a role in sexual practices, we once again find the *fellator* being portrayed as even more repugnant than the *pathicus;* see on **2.28**. Barwick 1958 speaks of a "sub-cycle" consisting of **2.42**, **2.58**, and **2.61**, but it is hard to see what unites these three as against the other epigrams on Zoilus.

For the theme of water, body parts, and pollution, see also **2.50**, **2.70**, 6.81 (if Charidemus washes his head in the public bath, he dirties the water even more than if he washes his genitals), and 11.95 (kissing *fellatores* is comparable to immersing one's head in a cesspool), with Obermayer 1998: 220–222.

Structure.   As often, the punchy monodistich falls cleanly into two parts that are brought into a closer relationship by the repetition of the vocative *Zoile,* for which see on **2.25**. The first line makes an accusation and the second offers a wry suggestion for improvement. Variety is achieved by syntax: an opening rhetorical question is followed asyndetically by a new sentence that itself falls into two halves separated by the vocative.

1 *quid:* Shackleton Bailey emends this, the universal MS reading, to *quod* and punctuates as follows: "Zoile, quod solium subluto podice perdis, / spurcius ut fiat, Zoile, merge caput." He describes *quid . . . perdis?* as "a foolish question" (Shackleton Bailey 1978), but it is hard to see how this is any more foolish than many other rhetorical questions found in Martial's epigrams. See Siedschlag 1977: 20 for Martial's common practice of posing *quid*-questions at the beginning of an epigram so as to express amazement, surprise, or anger: 1.11, 1.22, **2.82** ("abscisa servom quid figis lingua?"), 4.41, 4.50, 5.53, 9.93, 10.90, 10.100, 11.89, 11.96, 12.96, 14.49, 14.74, 14.131. Shackleton Bailey's version presents, moreover, a clumsy sequence of three clauses (*quod perdis . . . ut fiat . . . merge*). He cites 12.89 as a parallel, but that epigram is structured around two clauses in a much smoother sequence (*quod alligas . . . non dolent;* compare **2.50:** *quod fellas et potas . . . nil peccas*).

1 *solium:* Based on the root present in *sedere,* this word (also at **2.70.1**) designates a small bathtub placed in a *caldarium,* designed such that an individual might sit in it (Fest. 386.9–11 L; Vitr. 9.praef.10, Cels. 1.3.4, Suet. *Aug.* 82.2).

1 *subluto podice:* The verb specifically denotes "bathing the under parts of the body" (*OLD* s.v. 1): see Mart. 6.81.2 ("inguina sic toto subluis in solio"), Colum. 6.32.1 ("bis die subluitur aqua calida"). The noun *podex* is a blunt but not obscene term for the anus, used by Juvenal, who avoids such obscenities as *mentula, cunnus,* or *futuere,* and later by medical writers (Adams 1982: 112). The obscene term is *culus,* for which see on **2.51.2**.

2 *spurcius:* Compare Lucil. 398 Marx (*spurcus ore*), likewise with a hint at oral sexual practices, and for *spurcus* as an insult in general, see Opelt 1965: 156–157.

2 *caput:* For the metonymic transfer from *os* to *caput* in conjunction with sexual practices, see **2.61.3**, **2.70.5**, 3.81.5, 6.26.1 with Grewing, 6.81.2 ("et caput ecce lavas: inguina malo laves"), 14.74.2; *Priap.* 22.2 ("haec cunnum, caput hic, praebeat ille nates"); Sen. *Ben.* 4.31.4; Juv. 6.49, 301; Suet. *Jul.* 22.2, *Tib.* 45.

2.43

"Κοινὰ φίλων." haec sunt, haec sunt tua, Candide, κοινά,   1
    quae tu magniloquus nocte dieque sonas?
te Lacedaemonio velat toga lota Galaeso
    vel quam seposito de grege Parma dedit:
at me, quae passa est furias et cornua tauri,   5
    noluerit dici quam pila prima suam.
misit Agenoreas Cadmi tibi terra lacernas:
    non vendes nummis coccina nostra tribus.
tu Libycos Indis suspendis dentibus orbis:
    fulcitur testa fagina mensa mihi.   10
immodici tibi flava tegunt chrysendeta mulli:
    concolor in nostra, cammare, lance rubes.
grex tuus Iliaco poterat certare cinaedo:
    at mihi succurrit pro Ganymede manus.
ex opibus tantis veteri fidoque sodali   15
    das nihil et dicis, Candide, "κοινὰ φίλων"?

"Friends share." Is this what you mean, Candidus, by the "sharing" that you talk so grandly about day and night? You are swathed in a toga that was rinsed in the river of Spartan Tarentum or produced in Parma from the wool of a select flock; but I am covered with a toga that not even the first rag doll subjected to the wrath and horns of a bull in the arena would want to call its own. The land of Cadmus has sent you Tyrian mantles; my scarlet clothes you won't be able to sell for three sesterces. Your tabletops of Libyan citrus-wood rest on legs of Indian ivory; my beech-wood table is propped up on fragments of pottery. Oversized mullet fish cover your gold-inlaid plates; a simple lobster lies on my crockery of the same color. Your flock of slave boys could vie with the Trojan *cinaedus;* instead of Ganymede, it is my own hand that helps me out. Out of such great wealth you give your old and faithful friend nothing, Candidus, and yet you say, "Friends share"?

Themes.   In a noticeable shift from the crude invective of the preceding epigram, this poem begins with a Greek quotation invoking a lofty ideal of friendship. The specific preoccupation of this epigram, as well as the narrator's own involvement, becomes clear only with the fifth verse and the contrast it effects by means of *at me.* Whereas Candidus loudly pays tribute to the ideal of sharing among friends, in reality he keeps his considerable wealth to himself and allows those whom he calls his friends—such as Martial—to continue their lives of (relative) poverty. The technique of offering a series of concrete examples is characteristic, as are the examples themselves: clothing, dining tables and the food served on them, and slaves, especially as potential sexual partners. In 6.11 the unequal distribution of food and clothing is cited as contributing to a general breakdown in contemporary friendships and/or client-patron relationships (for the overlap, see on **2.5**). See also 3.37, 3.60, 4.40, 4.61, 5.42, 6.59 with Grewing, 7.92, 9.2, 10.11, 10.15, 10.29, 12.13, 12.36, 12.53; Juv. 1.92–93 ("simplexne furor sestertia centum / perdere et horrenti tunicam non reddere servo?"), 3.132–136.

See on **2.24** for Martial's recurring meditations on friendship and his frequent complaints that others fail to live up to the ideals of sharing that he observes. For Martial's complaints of poverty, see on **2.16**. In 6.82 the poor quality of Martial's clothing is again the central theme; see also **2.58, 2.85**. In **2.37**, by contrast, Martial depicts himself as hosting a fairly elaborate banquet that includes among its delicacies the mullet fish which he here portrays himself as unable to afford!

Structure.   Two structural features are particularly noteworthy. The first of these is the accumulation of contrasts between Candidus and Martial (cf. **2.18**), highlighted by a nearly continuous string of personal pronouns and possessive adjectives (*tua,* 1; *tu,* 2; *te,* 3; *me,* 5; *tibi,* 7; *nostra,* 8; *tu,* 9; *mihi,* 10; *tibi,* 11; *nostra,* 12; *tuus,* 13; *mihi,* 14). After an initial contrast in which each person is given a couplet (3–4 for Candidus, 5–6 for Martial), the subsequent contrasting depictions each occupy a line (7–14).

Second, the poem begins and ends with the same words (κοινὰ φίλων), a technique Martial uses elsewhere, sometimes with slight variation, to frame monodistichs: 1.32 (*non amo te ~ non amo te*) with Citroni ad loc., 1.67 (*liber homo es ~ liber homo est*), 1.75 (*dimidium ~ dimidium*), **2.88** (*nil recitas ~ nil recites*), 8.74 (*oplomachus ~ oplomachus*), 12.88 (*Tongilianus habet ~ Tongilianus habet*); couplets forming part of larger poems: 1.79.1–2 (*semper agis ~ semper agis*), 3.91.11–12 (*suppositam ~ supposita est*), 4.83.5–6 (*sollicitus ~ sollicitus*), 5.79.1–2 (*undecies ~ undecies*), 7.51.13–14 (*ille leget ~ ille leget*); or, more rarely, entire poems: 3.63 (*Cotile, bellus homo es ~ Cotile, bellus homo*). See Siedschlag 1977: 123–124, Laurens 1989: 299–305, Maaz 1992: 92–94, and Wills 1996: 431 n. 76, with examples from other poets.

1–2: The opening sentence may be printed either as a statement or a question (cf. on **2.29.1**). The emphatic repetition *haec sunt, haec sunt* suggests rather the latter (cf. **2.65.4**: "illa, illa dives mortua est Secundilla?"), but certainty is not possible.

For the name *Candidus,* see on **2.24.6**. Manuscripts of family β read the feminine *Candida* here, but *Candide* in 16. For such self-contradictory readings, compare **2.7.1** and **2.18.8**.

1 κοινὰ φίλων: This is a proverbial saying that seems to have arisen in Pythagorean circles; the wording is usually κοινὰ τὰ (τῶν) φίλων (Diog. Laert. 8.10, Zenob. 4.79, Plat. *Laws* 739C, Arist. *E.N.* 9.8.2, Menander fr. 9 Kock), but Martial's version omits the article, probably for metrical reasons. Lindsay prints κοινὰ φίλων *haec sunt,* presumably because it strains Greek syntax to take the phrase without the article as an independent sentence; yet at the epigram's end it clearly has this function.

The use of a Greek proverb (as in 1.27 and 5.38) creates an urbanely conversational tone, as knowledge of Greek was generally assumed among educated Romans in Martial's day: see 14.58 (a *rusticus* will not understand the Greek word *aphronitrum*) with Leary ad loc. Following a generally accepted reconstruction of Martial's own practice (Weinreich 1928: 161–162), most modern editors print entire Greek phrases in the Greek alphabet but transliterate single words; compare *eschatocollion* at **2.6.3**, *euge* at **2.27.3**.

The proverb, whose usual Latin version was *amicorum esse communia omnia* (Ter. *Ad.* 802, Cic. *Off.* 1.16.51; Otto 1890: 20), continued to be popular well into the medieval period; an epigram by Godfrey of Winchester specifically echoes this and other poems on Candidus (*Epigr.* 156, with Maaz 2001: 300).

3–6: For the toga as emblem of well-being (when new and shiny or of fine wool) or of poverty (when raggedy and old), see on **2.29.4**. For the fine wool products of Tarentum—the *Galaesus* was the nearby river in which the wool would have been rinsed (cf. 5.37.2), here called *Lacedaemonius* because Tarentum was a Spartan colony—and Apulia in general, see **2.46.6**, 4.28, 5.37, 8.28, 12.63, 13.125, 14.155, along with Varr. *L.L.* 9.28, *R.R.* 2.praef.6; Colum. 7.2; Strab. 6.281, 283; Plin. *N.H.* 3.16, 8.73, 190; 29.9; Pallad. 2.13. The wool of *Parma* and of the Po Valley in general is awarded second prize at 14.155; see also 5.13 and Colum. 7.2.3.

The *pila* was a dummy figure thrown into the arena to provoke the bull: see *Sp.* 9.4, 10.86, 14.52.2 with Leary ad loc.; the first one thrown (*prima*) would be the worst gored. Like Scandola and Shackleton Bailey, I take the "antecedent" of the relative clause *quae passa est* to be the following *pila,* and the second relative clause *quam pila prima noluerit dici suam* in turn to modify the implied *toga.* The syntax is admittedly slightly contorted, and other translators see a more straightforward structure: both relative clauses (*quae passa est* and *noluerit dici quam*) refer to the understood *toga* ("a toga covers me which has been subjected to the wrath and horns of the bull, and which the first dummy figure would not wish to call its own"). And yet it is precisely the function of the *pila* to be thrown before bulls.

7 *Agenoreas ... lacernas:* Along with Sidon (**2.16.3**), Tyre, home of the mythical figures Agenor and Cadmus, was known for its purple dye. For brightly colored clothing as a sign of wealth, see on **2.29.3**.

The *lacerna* was a cloak fastened at the shoulder and worn over other clothing (14.131, 133, 135; Marquardt 1886: 568–569; Potthoff 1992: 128–131); beautifully colored *lacernae* are again associated with wealth at **2.46.3**.

8 *nummis ... tribus:* Literally meaning "coins," *nummi* often specifically refers to sesterces (*OLD* s.v. 3). The (negligible) amount may be contextualized as follows. In **2.57** we read of a man who has pawned a ring for barely 8 sesterces in order to pay for dinner; a copy of a book of Martial's epigrams costs 4 sesterces but could also be had at the discounted price of 2 sesterces (12.3); 20 *asses,* or 5 sesterces, for an amphora of wine is a low price, as is 1 sesterce (4 *asses*) for a measure of wheat (12.76); a quick sexual encounter could cost as little as 2 *asses* (a half-sesterce, **2.53.7**), or even 1 *as* (a quarter-sesterce, the price of a chickpea dish, 1.103.10). See Ramirez Sabada 1987 for monetary figures in Martial in general.

8 *coccina nostra:* As Collesso notes, *coccina* must be ironic; for the use of the neuter plural, compare *coccina* and *ianthina* at **2.39.1** and *tua candida* at **2.46.5**.

9–10: Round tabletops (*orbes*) of various types were placed on legs of various kinds of material. Here a particularly expensive combination is imagined: a tabletop of citrus wood from northern Africa (cf. 14.91.2) on legs of Indian ivory (cf. 1.72.4, 5.37.5; for the phrase *Indus dens,* see Catull. 64.48, Stat. *Silv.* 3.3.94, and cf. *Libycus dens* at 14.3.2). In 10.98 Martial describes the same kind of table ("citrum vetus Indicosque dentes," 6) as being beyond his means, again attributing it to a rich friend who has young slaves who are sexier even than Ganymede and at whom Martial cannot help gawking; in 14.3 a table made of citrus wood and African ivory is an image of luxury. Such furniture is here (and later at Juv. 11.117–127; Colton 1991: 397 argues for a direct influence) contrasted with Martial's simple beech-wood tabletop propped up on potsherds, much as Hecale replaces one of her simple table's broken legs with a potsherd (*testa*) in order to keep the tabletop level at Ov. *Met.* 8.661–662.

11–12: Laurens 1989: 233 traces a thread through Latin literature, from Lucilius 1235 Marx (a huge sturgeon) to Hor. *Sat.* 2.2.39, 2.8.42–43 (with the addition of the platter) to Pers. 5.182–183 through this passage to Juv. 5.80–85.

As their name indicates, *chrysendeta* are dishes inlaid with gold; compare **2.53.5**, 6.94.1, 11.29.7, 14.97 with Leary ad loc., and note the visual contrast between Candidus' gold-inlaid dishes and Martial's lobster-colored crockery. For *mulli* see on **2.37.4**. Although lobster (*cammarus*) today is generally considered a delicacy and is even a symbol of luxury, Martial clearly views it as a simple and uninteresting food in comparison with the prized mullet fish. At Juv. 5.84 it is likewise cited as an inexpensive seafood, contrasted with a *squilla;* see Plin. *N.H.* 32.148 for the *cammarus* and other shellfish.

13–14: Wealthy households often featured troupes of attractive slaves; see Cic. *Verr.* 2.1.91–93, *Fin.* 2.23, *Tusc.* 5.61, *Amic.* 55, *Q. Fr.* 1.1.8; Nep. *Att.* 13.4; Tac. *Ann.* 3.53. Here and elsewhere (e.g., 10.98, 12.66) Martial assumes that handsome slave boys were there to be enjoyed as sexual objects; he again compares them to Ganymede at 9.73.6, 10.98.2, 11.22.2. By contrast, the speaker at Juv. 11.142–161 boasts that he does *not* have slaves like this; see on **2.37** for related contrasts. Colton 1991: 183 notes a similarity to Juv. 5.52–60, with its ironic reference to an unattractive slave from North Africa as *Gaetulus Ganymedes.*

13 *Iliaco . . . cinaedo:* An irreverent reference to Ganymede, the handsome young Trojan prince who attracted Zeus' attention and was consequently carried off by him to Olympus to serve as his cupbearer and sexual partner. He was a standard image in ancient literature and art for a beautiful young man in general and slave boy in particular; see Weinreich 1928: 31, Kempter 1980, Sichtermann 1988, Williams 1999: 56–59. For Martial's use of mythological paradigms, see on **2.14.3–4**. Not surprisingly, Ganymede makes frequent appearances in Martial's epigrams: 3.39, 7.50, 8.46, 9.11, 9.16, 9.25, 9.36, 9.73, 10.66, 11.22, 11.26, 11.43, 11.104. Martial again uses the phrase *Iliacus cinaedus* at 10.98.2 (elsewhere the less insulting *minister:* 11.104.19, 12.15.7; cf. 10.66.7): the phrase is nowhere else attested and is quite probably a coinage of Martial's. For *cinaedus,* see on **2.28.1**, and for its use with reference to a slave, see 9.90.7: "uni tibi sit puer cinaedus."

14 *at mihi succurrit pro Ganymede manus:* For a body part conceived as standing in for a slave, compare 14.65.2 ("pro puero pes erit ipse sibi"). Here we find a cleverly constructed double entendre, noted already by Collesso. "My hand is my Ganymede" in that it, rather than a handsome slave boy, (*a*) pours out my wine and (*b*) sexually satisfies me (i.e., I will have to content myself with masturbation; cf. 11.73.3–4: "cum frustra iacui longa prurigine tentus, / succurrit pro te saepe sinistra mihi"). For the self-pitying stance and the joking reference to masturbation as a response to the absence of sexual partners, see also 11.58 with Kay ad loc. Ignoring these two epigrams, Sullivan 1991 takes the joking condemnation of masturbation in 9.41 too seriously; see further Williams 1999: 330 n. 34 and, for ancient references to masturbation in general, Krenkel 1979.

15 *veteri fidoque sodali:* The phrase recurs at 5.19.9 and as a variant reading at **2.30.3**. For the collocation *vetus sodalis,* frequently found in Martial, see on **2.30.3**.

2.44

Emi seu puerum togamve pexam
seu tres, ut puta, quattuorve libras,
Sextus protinus ille fenerator,
quem nostis veterem meum sodalem,
ne quid forte petam timet cavetque,   5
et secum, sed ut audiam, susurrat:
"septem milia debeo Secundo,
Phoebo quattuor, undecim Phileto,
et quadrans mihi nullus est in arca."
o grande ingenium mei sodalis!   10
durum est, Sexte, negare cum rogaris;
quanto durius antequam rogeris!

Whether I've bought a slave boy or a brand-new toga or, say, three or four pounds of silver, right away that moneylender Sextus—you all know him: my old friend—is afraid that I might ask for a loan. So he takes his precautions, whispering to himself, but loudly enough for me to hear: "I owe seven thousand to Secundus, four thousand to Phoebus, eleven thousand to Philetus, and there's not a single coin in my money chest." How clever my friend is! It is harsh enough

to say no when you are asked, Sextus; how harsh it is to say no
even before you are asked!

Themes.   There are clear continuities between this epigram and its immediate predecessor: both directly concern the narrator (a fact made clear by
the first word of the present epigram), describe a rich but stingy friend, lament the betrayal of the ideal of sharing in friendship, and use the tag *vetus
sodalis*. After the monodistich **2.45** on Glyptus, who has had himself castrated, the theme will return in **2.46**.

For the widespread practice of loans and moneylending in general, necessary in a society lacking a formalized banking system, see on **2.3**. Particularly amusing in conjunction with the present epigram is 4.15, where Caecilianus
asks Martial for a loan and Martial refuses, explaining that he does not have
the money—thus placing himself in the position of Sextus! Usually, however,
Martial portrays himself as the one who is seeking (and only sometimes ob-
taining) a loan: see on **2.30**. In Juvenal 3.171–181 ("commune id vitium est,
hic vivimus ambitiosa / paupertate omnes") Umbricius complains bitterly about
people who borrow money in order to buy expensive clothing, that is, more
or less what Martial portrays himself as doing in the present epigram. See on
2.37 for contrasts between the two poets' personae.

Since the implication is that Sextus' excuse is invented and he could
easily afford to make the loan, this epigram can also be seen in conjunction
with those on rich but stingy friends; see on **2.24** and compare 4.67, where
Gaurus asks his old friend for a loan and is refused. Truthful or not, Sextus'
excuse illuminates an important aspect of moneylending among Romans,
comparable to the potentially problematic aspect of *clientela* that Martial has
already pointed to in **2.18**: a man who lends out money to others may himself need to borrow from others.

Structure.   The epigram lends itself to a bipartite analysis: 1–9 constitute
the introductory narration of Sextus' behavior, and 10–12 give the narrator's
commentary, culminating with a *sententia* marked by repetitions of the words
durum and *rogare*. The first part itself consists of three sense units of two
verses each (1–2, 3–4, 5–6), followed by a three-line quotation. Compare
2.30 both for subject matter and for the structural feature of shifting in the
final verses from a third-person narrative to a second-person address (for
which see on **2.16**).

1 *emi:* Such an omission of *si* is frequent in Martial (Friedlaender cites
3.38.8, 3.44.11–16, 3.46.5, 3.46.9, 5.56.8).

1 *puerum:* See on **2.37.8**. Garrido-Hory 1981: 108 and Obermayer 1998:
30–32 understand the present allusion to be to a slave as sexual partner, but

there is no reason to believe that when Martial says *emi puerum,* his Roman readership will have automatically assumed that he was buying a concubine.

1 *togamve pexam:* One whose wool has been freshly combed, that is, a brand-new toga. A *toga pexa* can thus be contrasted with a worn-out item: see, for example, **2.58**, where Martial's toga is *trita* and he is too poor to own a *pexa*. See further on **2.29.4**.

2 *ut puta:* For the phrase, see *OLD* s.v. *puto* 9b ("introducing an example or illustration"); for the shortening of the final *-a,* compare 3.26.5, 9.95b.5, 11.95.2, and see on **2.18.1**.

2 *libras* (sc., *argenti*): This must refer not to unworked silver but rather to silver vessels whose value was indicated by their weight (Strong 1966: 19–20). Martial's other allusions to *librae* of silver—some of them likewise omitting the genitive *argenti*—include **2.76**, 3.62, 8.71, 10.57, 11.105, 12.36, 14.97. From these passages it is clear that three or four pounds was hardly an astronomical amount of silver. An example of true extravagance is provided by Pliny the Elder (*N.H.* 33.143): Seneca's father-in-law, Pompeius Paullinus, brought 12,000 pounds of silver with him when he went to Germany in A.D. 58 as military commander.

3 *Sextus:* See on **2.3.1** for this name.

3 *ille fenerator:* The demonstrative both signifies "that one whom you know" (cf. the following line) and lends a contemptuous tone ("that infamous one"): *OLD* s.v. 4. A *fenerator* was someone who made money by lending money at interest (*fenus*); see Andreau 1999. While the verb *fenerare* is found at 1.76.6 and 1.85.4, this is the only occurrence of the noun in Martial, a fact which perhaps heightens its intensity here. The term is in any case anything but flattering: compare Cic. *Off.* 1.150 ("ii questus, qui in odia hominum incurrunt, ut portitorum, ut feneratorum") and Valerius Maximus' disparaging phrase "avara et feneratoria Gallorum philosophia" (2.6.11). The translation "capitalist" (Shackleton Bailey) is much broader in scope than *fenerator* and introduces anachronistic implications.

4 *veterem meum sodalem:* See on **2.30.3** for this phrase, characteristic of Martial.

7 *septem milia:* The omission of the unit of currency (here *sestertium*) is fairly common: see also **2.65.5**.

7 *Secundo:* The name appears elsewhere in Martial, sometimes referring to a real man (1.2 [a freedman who sells Martial's books], 5.80 [perhaps the younger Pliny], 7.84), sometimes to an apparently fictional character: in 7.92, as in the present epigram, he is a moneylender; in 12.75 he is a desirable boy.

8 *Phoebo quattuor, undecim Phileto:* The line is neatly divided by the caesura into two self-contained halves, each of which contains exactly two words: the creditor's name and the amount he is owed. It is almost as if

Sextus were reading a list from an account book, though the chiastic arrangement reminds us that *we* are reading a carefully crafted epigram.

The name *Phoebus* occurs sixteen times in Martial, with a few thematic clusters adhering to it: see on **2.35.2**. Most relevantly to the present epigram, the name is again associated with moneylending in 6.20, 9.92, and 9.102.

The name *Philetus* occurs only here in Martial.

9 et quadrans mihi nullus est in arca: A *quadrans* is a coin having the value of one quarter of an *as,* and because it was the coin of the lowest denomination in circulation, the term is often used generically to refer to a minimal amount of money: see Hor. *Sat.* 2.3.93; Phaedr. 4.20.22; Petr. *Sat.* 43.1. In **2.51.1** ("unus saepe tibi tota denarius arca") the denomination mentioned is much larger—in Martial's day a *denarius* was worth 16 *asses*—but as it represents a man's entire savings, the effect is the same: the image of a specific coin in a money chest (*arca*) concretely illustrates a man's poverty.

For Martial's negative phrase, comparable to the American "I don't have a dime" or the Italian "non ho una lira," see also 5.32.1 ("quadrantem Crispus tabulis, Faustine, supremis / non dedit uxori"), 7.10.12 ("quadrantem nemo iam tibi credit"). Colton 1991: 286 argues that Juv. 7.8 ("nam si Pieria quadrans tibi nullus in umbra / ostendatur") combines the present verse with Mart. 9.84.3 ("haec ego Pieria ludebam tutus in umbra").

11–12 durum est, Sexte, negare cum rogaris; / quanto durius, antequam rogeris: This is an example of one of the types of *sententiae* discussed by Quint. *Inst.* 8.5.5: *per exclamationem* (Barwick 1959: 40). With the paradoxical ending *negare antequam rogeris* ("to say no before you are asked") compare the endings of **2.25** ("iam rogo, Galla, nega") and, again in conjunction with the name Phoebus and the theme of moneylending, of 6.20 ("iam rogo, Phoebe, nega").

2.45

Quae tibi non stabat praecisa est mentula, Glypte.
   demens, cum ferro quid tibi? gallus eras.

Glyptus, that dick of yours that never stood up has now been cut.
Are you out of your mind? Why did you take up the knife? You
were a eunuch already.

Themes. Coming between two longer poems in two different meters on unhelpful friends, this monodistich makes a simple joke that returns us to the realm of the sexual. Previously impotent and thus no better than a eunuch, Glyptus has taken the drastic but redundant step of surgery (most likely castration: see on 1 below). The joke is uttered in the voice of a man proud of his own intact virility and has a touch of locker-room humor: *mentula* is a blunt obscenity. Comparable is the pun in 11.74, where a surgical procedure on his penis is said to turn a man from Raetia into a *Gallus*.

Structure.   The structure is as straightforward as the content: the first line lays out the situation, identifying Glyptus by name, and the second line offers the speaker's commentary, first with an emotive rhetorical question and then with a sarcastically dismissive statement (*gallus eras*). The two lines display markedly different rhythms: the first is taken up by an entire sentence and punctuated by the vocative; the second falls into three parts (exclamatory vocative; question; statement).

1 *quae tibi non stabat:* Allusions to impotence in Roman literature include Mart. 3.75 (also with *stare*), 8.31, 9.66, 10.91, 11.25 (*stare*), 11.46, 11.71, 12.86; Ov. *Am.* 3.7; Tib. 1.5, 1.39; *Priap.* 83; Petr. *Sat.* 132; see Obermayer 1998: 255–330. In Greek epigram impotence tends to be the occasion not of satire but of self-pity (*A.P.* 5.46, 11.30, 12.11, 12.216, 12.232; Prinz 1911: 66), as also in some Latin texts (Ov. *Am.* 3.7, Petr. *Sat.* 132).

1 *praecisa est:* Does Martial's reference to "cutting" refer to castration (as most scholars take it) or circumcision (Verdière 1969: 105, Barié and Schindler)? The verb itself might suggest both (*OLD* s.v. 1: "to cut or break the tip off; shorten by cutting or sim. action, cut back, lop"; Cato, *Agr.* 40.2: "quem ramum insiturus eris, praecidito"; Plin. *N.H.* 11.228: "[pinnae] praecisae non crescunt, evulsae renascuntur"). But a reference to circumcision, which Glyptus would presumably have undergone as part of a conversion to Judaism, seems unlikely: the tone of Martial's other allusions to circumcision is gently mocking (see 7.30, 7.35, 7.82), hardly so intense as to liken the procedure to castration, and at the same time he would probably have taken the opportunity to make an explicit jab at the Jews. A reference to castration is more likely; compare 9.2.13: "i nunc et miseros, Cybele, praecide cinaedos." As Shackleton Bailey puts it, having been practically a *gallus* before, Glyptus has now "joined the fraternity."

1 *mentula:* This is the first occurrence in Book II of this extremely blunt word. As opposed to such metaphors as *penis* (originally denoting "tail"), it is the obscene *vox propria* for the penis and survives in such Romance derivatives as regional Italian *minchia;* see Adams 1982: 9–12. Cic. *Fam.* 9.22.3 implies that, like *cunnus,* it cannot be spoken in polite company, and it has rightly been called "il termine osceno per eccellenza" (Citroni ad 1.35.5; cf. 3.69, 11.15). Not surprisingly, *mentula* is by far the most frequent of all sexual terms in Martial, whether obscene or not, occurring forty-nine times: it is followed by *moechus* (twenty-nine), *cunnus* (twenty-seven), *cinaedus* (twenty-two), and *pedicare* (eighteen).

1 *Glypte:* An ironically significant name: γλύφω, "to carve." For other such names see on **2.34.1**. It occurs only here in Martial and is listed neither in *PIR* nor in Solin and Salomies 1994.

2 *demens, cum ferro quid tibi?* For the insulting *demens,* see Opelt 1965: index s.v. For the tone of (mock-?) horror in the face of castration, compare 7.95, where Martial speaks of a freshly castrated eunuch priest (*Gallus recens*) as a frightening figure, comparable to a hundred *cunnilingi.*

2 *gallus:* The term refers to a eunuch priest of the Asian mother goddess, a real-life correspondent to the mythic archetype Attis, who is the subject of Catull. 63 (see on **2.86.4–5**). Martial's other allusions to *galli* include 3.81, 3.91, 4.43, 5.41, 7.95, 9.2, 11.72 with Kay ad loc., 11.74, 13.63–64, 14.204 with Leary ad loc. See also Lucr. 2.600–680, Sen. *Dial.* 7.13.3, Juv. 6.511–516, Apul. *Met.* 8.24–30, with Nocks 1925, Lane 1996, Taylor 1997: 330–337. For a comparison between the *galli* and the Indian *hijra,* see Roscoe 1996.

Of course, Glyptus was not literally a *gallus* previously—otherwise, he would not have to undergo surgery now—but rather, because impotent, was to all intents and purposes a eunuch. But seemingly taking Martial's phrase literally, or else misled by the fact that *Gallus* is also a man's name, MS L transmits this epigram with the lemma *Ad Gallum.*

2.46

Florida per varios ut pingitur Hybla colores,
    cum breve Sicaniae ver populantur apes,
sic tua subpositis conlucent prela lacernis,
    sic micat innumeris arcula synthesibus,
atque unam vestire tribum tua candida possunt,   5
    Apula non uno quae grege terra tulit.
tu spectas hiemem succincti lentus amici,
    pro scelus, et lateris frigora trita tui.
quantum erat, infelix, pannis fraudare duobus—
    quid renuis?—non te, Naevole, sed tineas?   10

Just as flowering Hybla is decorated with various colors when the Sicilian bees plunder the brief spring, so your clothespresses gleam with cloaks, your storage chest shines with countless dinner clothes, and your white togas, produced by more than one Apulian flock, are enough to clothe one whole tribe of Roman citizens. You impassively look upon your scantily clad friend's wintry state—oh, the shame!—and upon your companion's threadbare chill. You wretch, would it be too much to take two rags—why do you refuse?—not from you, Naevolus, but from the moths?

Themes.   We pass from the obscenity of the preceding epigram to a lovely evocation of a meadow in the spring which turns out to function as an image for a rich man's colorful clothing. With the fourth couplet we come to the poem's central theme: the failure to live up to ideals of friendship on the part of a wealthy but cheap friend. As opposed to earlier poems on this theme (**2.24**, **2.43–44**), here Martial does not explicitly identify himself as Naevolus' unfortunate friend (*amici* and *lateris tui* in 7–8 are vague enough), but the possibility subtly suggests itself. If we accept the emendation of *times* to *mei* in 8 (see below for the textual problem), the identification is explicit.

Structure.   The opening couplet consists of a vividly poetic description of a colorful field in a Sicilian spring (note the striking image *ver populantur* again at 9.13.2: "cum breve Cecropiae ver populantur apes"), but its syntax (*ut . . .*) hints that more is to follow. With the following couplet (*sic . . .*) we learn that what has preceded is a simile for Naevolus' wardrobe, whose depiction continues into the following couplet (5–6), where *unam tribum* is contrasted with *non uno grege*. With the asyndetic *tu spectas* (7) the subsequent couplet introduces a contrast with Naevolus' unfortunate friend (*hiemem . . . amici* vs. *ver*), while the final couplet (9–10) meditates on the difference (*pannis . . . duobus* vs. *innumeris . . . synthesibus*) and sharpens the point with a sarcastic twist in the last word (*tineas*). The final note is thus brutally prosaic, in contrast with the elaborate opening couplet. For the first appearance of the vocative in the final line, see on **2.30.6**.

1 *florida . . . Hybla:* Hybla in Sicily was famous for its flowery meadows, bees, and honey and is paradigmatic in Martial: see 5.39.3 ("Hyblaeis madidas thymis placentas"), 7.88, 9.11, 9.26, 10.74, 11.42, 13.104–105 with Leary. In fact, there were three cities bearing the name in Sicily: the Hybla in question, known as Ὕβλα μείζων, was located about 15 kilometers northwest of Syracuse (see *RE* s.v.). To judge by Strabo 6.2.2, the town no longer existed in Martial's day, but the name remained famous precisely because of its honey. Martial's epithet for the city may be Ovidian in inspiration, as it is attested only here and at Ov. *Trist.* 5.6.38: "florida quam multas Hybla tuetur apes" (Zingerle 1877: 34).

1 *pingitur:* See on **2.29.8**.

2 *Sicaniae . . . apes:* The phrase recurs at 11.8.8, describing the fragrance of his boy's kisses: "quod qui Sicanias detinet hortus apes."

3–5: Each line refers to a different item of clothing. For the *lacerna* see on **2.43.7**. The *synthesis* was a set of loose-fitting clothes worn on festive occasions, such as the Saturnalia or parties in general (5.79, 14.1.1, 14.142; Marquardt 1886: 570–571; Wilson 1938: 169ff. with fig. 51; Potthoff 1992: 191–193). For the *toga* see on **2.29.4**. For colorful clothing in general, see **2.29.3**, **2.43.7**, **2.57.2**, and 6.59 with Grewing.

3 *prela:* The word refers to a press, whether for olives or grapes (1.26, 13.111) or, as here and in 11.8, clothes.

4 *arcula:* Schneider 1909: 44 points out that the diminutive contradicts the required sense; its usage here is probably encouraged by metrical considerations.

5: It seems easy enough to understand the unanimous MS reading *unam* in the sense "an entire." See *OLD* s.v. *unus* 6 ("forming a single whole, one single") with Plaut. *Miles* 584 ("nam uni satis populo impio merui mali," though the reading is doubtful), Mela 3.2 ("si . . . unum animal est [mundus]"), and Apul. *Met.* 9.31 ("unum larem varie dispergit"). Yet Shackleton Bailey takes the rare step of obelizing, noting various conjectures in his apparatus (his own *plusque unam;* Postgate's *atque omnem;* Håkanson's *atque tuam;* we might add Watt 1984's proposal *et quam non vestire . . . tulit?*).

5 *tua candida:* Neuter plural: "your whites" (i.e., your white togas). For the usage, compare **2.39.1** (*coccina, ianthina*) and **2.43.8** (*coccina nostra*). *TLL* 3.243.68 erroneously takes *candida* to refer to *prela*.

6: For high-quality Apulian wool, see on **2.43.3**.

7 *hiemem:* Literally, "winter"; for the usage (Friedlaender: "das Frieren"), compare Ov. *Met.* 2.827: "sic letalis hiems paulatim in pectora venit."

7 *succincti:* See on **2.1.3**. Here the word may suggest that the friend only wears his girt-up tunic and no toga (Collesso detects the image of a man about to set out on a journey: "hoc est, paene nudi et quasi ad iter capessendum accincti").

8 *pro scelus:* *Pro facinus* and *pro pudor* occur on one other occasion each in Martial (1.90.6 and 10.68.6 respectively) and frequently elsewhere, and *scelus* is found in other exclamations (11.91.3, *ah scelus;* 11.93.3, *o scelus*), but this is the only attestation of *pro scelus* in extant Latin literature.

8 *et lateris frigora trita tui:* For *latus* (literally, "side" or "flank"), figuratively denoting a companion, that is, one who protects or guards another's flank, compare 6.68.4 ("Eutychos ille, tuum, Castrice, dulce latus") with *OLD* s.v. 4b, *TLL* 7.1026.40–62. For the association of clothing, cold, and poverty (often in turn associated with a lack of generous patrons), compare 3.38.9, 6.50.1–2 ("cum coleret puros pauper Telesinus amicos, / errabat gelida sordidus in togula"), 7.92.7, 10.76.5 ("pullo Mevius alget in cucullo").

The universal MS reading *et lateris frigora trita times* seems to contain an error and is accepted by no modern editor other than Lindsay. Reeve 1983 thus cites the line as one among several passages in which all three MS families agree in transmitting a significant error, a point which suggests that the tripartite division cannot be traced back to revisions by Martial himself; see also **2.praef.**, **2.84.4**, and perhaps **2.53.7**. Accepting the MS reading, Lindsay glosses, "you express polite apprehension in case your client should feel the cold with his thread-bare coat" (Lindsay 1903b: 51); *times,* he argues, has the sense of *timorem exhibes* or *dicis te timere*. But why would Naevolus "express polite apprehension"? As Shackleton Bailey observes, this fits poorly with *spectas . . . lentus*. Friedlaender's emendation *et lateris frigora trita tui* [sc., *lentus spectas*] has won general acceptance; *frigora* would be metonymic for "cold clothing." In his 1619 edition, Schryver proposes *lateris frigora trita mei,* "the thread-bare cold of my own flank," which would explicitly identify Martial himself as the suffering friend.

9 quantum erat: Literally, "How much would it be?" (*erat* for *sit:* see KS 2.1.171 and cf. *poteram* for *possim* at **2.1.1**). The sense, as in the case of the exclamations at *Sp.* 15.2 ("quanta est Carpophori portio") and Ov. *Met.* 9.561 ("quantum est quod desit"), is "How little it would be!" Salanitro 1991 suggests punctuating the sentence as an exclamation rather than a question: "What a great thing it would have been!" (cf. 6.59.7: "quanto simplicius, quanto est humanius illud").

10: Family α reads *quid metuis,* family β *quid renuis,* and family γ *quid/ quod renuis*. Lindsay 1903a: 24 includes this passage in a list of 106 examples of ancient variants among which "the choice is often extremely uncertain"; see also **2.30.3**, **2.40.1**, **2.61.1**. He himself prefers *renuis* to *metuis,* but only tentatively, and the decision is indeed difficult. *Renuis,* printed by most modern editors, would signify "Why do you refuse my request?" (see on **2.14.14**); *metuis,* printed by Ker and Shackleton Bailey, would have the sense "Why are you afraid of granting me the request?" (cf. Stat. *Silv.* 4.9.44–45: "aut unam dare synthesin—quid horres?—/ alborum calicum atque caccaborum").

10 Naevole: The name appears again in 1.97, 3.71, 3.95, and 4.83. Tanner 1986: 2672–2673 proposes a synthesizing reading of all this character's appearances, though the premise is questionable; see further on **2.32.2**. The name famously appears in Juvenal 9, where it refers to a client who both metaphorically and literally prostitutes himself to his patron.

10 *tineas:* The larva of a moth or beetle, destructive of clothes, books, and other materials (*OLD* s.v.). Other allusions to *tineae* in conjunction with clothes include Cato *Agr.* 98.1, Hor. *Sat.* 2.3.119, Plin. *N.H.* 27.52.

2.47

Subdola famosae moneo fuge retia moechae,
    levior o conchis, Galle, Cytheriacis.
confidis natibus? non est pedico maritus.
    quae faciat duo sunt: irrumat aut futuit.

Stay clear of the notorious adulteress' treacherous nets! I'm warning you, Gallus, smoother than Venus' conch shells. Are you relying on your buttocks? Her husband is not a buttfucker. There are two things he does: he fucks mouths or cunts.

Themes.   After the preceding epigram's complaint regarding unfulfilled ideals of friendship between men, this epigram offers ironic, coarse commentary (*pedico, irrumat,* and *futuit* are obscenities) on the possible consequences of a traditionally disapproved type of relationship between men and women, *adulterium.* A brief series is here introduced: with the exception of **2.48** and **2.53**, epigrams **2.47–54** all contain obscene references to sexual practices or bodily features, and **2.51–53** all play with the notion of spending money.

The effeminate Gallus (whose name is singularly appropriate: see on **2.45.2**) is willing to run the risk that the husband of the woman in question, if he discovers the affair, will take his revenge by the traditional means that Martial elsewhere calls the *puerile supplicium,* that is, anal rape; see on **2.60**. The implication—itself a passing swipe—is that Gallus might actually enjoy this. Martial then reveals that the unnamed husband will not be interested in exacting this sort of revenge but instead prefers oral or vaginal penetration; the ticking off of various possible sexual roles recalls **2.28**. The conclusion is that Gallus, if caught, will be "irrumated" by the husband (compelled to perform fellatio) and thereby placed in a role represented elsewhere in Martial and other texts as being even more demeaning than that of being anally penetrated: see Obermayer 1998: 193–195, Williams 1999: 201–203. A similar thematic complex recurs two poems later (**2.49**) and again in **2.60**; in **2.83** *irrumatio* and adultery are likewise linked. For the image of an effeminate man who takes pleasure both in intercourse with women and in being anally penetrated, see also **2.49**, **2.62** with Williams 1999: 142–153; effeminacy is independent from any specific sexual role.

Boswell 1990: 79 takes the final remark to mean that the husband is not interested in sexual contact with males, an unconvincing interpretation also suggested by Ker's translation: "Do you trust in your own charms? The husband is not of that sort: there are two things he can do, and neither is what you offer." Kuppe 1972: 114 interprets *irrumat aut futuit* similarly, drawing the necessary conclusion that the poem ends weakly ("nach der so hoch gespannten Erwartung also ein Umbruch ins Triviale!"). Scherf 2001: 47 comes to the peculiar conclusion that the husband of the present epigram, like that of **2.60**, will castrate Gallus or even kill him (so Schmidt 1989: 65); this also misses the point.

Manuscript T, belonging to the family that Lindsay describes as descending from an ancient edition *in usum elegantiorum,* omits the second couplet, with its intractable obscenities, in its entirety. The result is a simple and fairly uninteresting monodistich warning Gallus to stay away from a *moecha.*

Structure. There is a smooth progression of thought from one syntactically self-contained line to another: stay away from the adulteress (1); you are effeminately soft (2); if you expect to pay the usual punishment, you are mistaken (3); worse will await you (4). The point is cleanly brought home with the final sentence: *irrumat aut futuit.* Note, too, the shift from syntactic units occupying the entire line (1–2) to lines divided into two units each (3–4).

1 subdola ... retia: The phrase is also found at **2.40.3**; see further on **2.27.1** (*retia tendit*).

1 famosae ... moechae: See on **2.39.1**.

1 moneo: Parenthetical *moneo* is a fairly frequently occurring colloquial feature of Martial's language; Hofmann 1951: 198 compares *scio, sentio,* and *video.*

2 levior o conchis ... Cytheriacis: For the phrase *levior conchis,* compare 5.37.3 ("concha Lucrini delicatior stagni"), 8.64.5–6 ("levior ... / tritis litoris aridi lapillis"), 10.37.10 ("quosque tegit levi cortice conchia brevis"), and 14.209 ("levis ab aequorea cortex Mareotica concha"). The image may be Ovidian in inspiration (Zingerle 1877: 320), as a search of the PHI disk for *lev-* and *conch-* turns up only the passages from Martial and Ov. *Met.* 13.792: "levior assiduo detritis aequore conchis."

For the gendered quality of *levis,* compare Ov. *Ars am.* 3.437–438: "femina quid faciat, cum sit vir levior ipsa, / forsitan et plures possit habere viros?" Conch shells were traditionally associated with Venus or Aphrodite (one of whose cult titles was Κυθέρεια, perhaps because an important sanctuary of the goddess was found on the Aegean island of Cythera: see *RE* s.v.) since she was said to have risen from the waves in such a shell (cf. [Tib.] 3.3.34: "et faveas concha, Cypria, vecta tua"; Stat. *Silv.* 1.2.118, 3.4.5). But conch and other shells seem also to have been associated, thanks to a visual similarity, with the female genitalia (Adams 1982: 82), and indeed there was a type of shell called the *veneria* (Plin. *N.H.* 9.103, 32.151).

2 *Galle:* The name (also occurring in 1.108, **2.56**, 3.27, 3.92, 4.16, 7.55, 10.56, 10.82, 12.46) does not consistently refer to any single character and invites two different kinds of puns, both of which Martial naturally exploits. As here, it may pun on *gallus,* a castrated priest of the mother goddess (see on **2.45.2**), or on *Gallus* in the sense of "inhabitant of Gaul"; see 11.74 for a combination of both.

3 *confidis natibus?* For the implication both here and in **2.60** that the young adulterer might actually enjoy his punishment, compare the fine paradox at *Priap.* 64, where the god threatens to punish an intruder who steals "out of love of the punishment" (*amore poenae*) by *not* punishing him.

3 *non est pedico maritus:* For *pedico,* an obscenity designating a man who plays the insertive role in anal intercourse with either male or female partners, see on **2.28.3**.

4 *quae faciat duo sunt: irrumat aut futuit:* For the verbs *irrumare* (to orally penetrate) and *futuere* (to vaginally penetrate), see Adams 1982: index s.v. and Williams 1999: 161–162. It might seem peculiar that a man who enjoys oral and vaginal penetration regardless of the sex of his partner in the first case should be totally uninterested in anal penetration, but the poem may be read less as a realistic documentation of a man's sexual tastes than as a witty epigram aiming to deliver an effective zing.

2.48

Coponem laniumque balneumque,
tonsorem tabulamque calculosque
et paucos, sed ut eligam, libellos;
unum non nimium rudem sodalem
et grandem puerum diuque levem   5
et caram puero meo puellam:
haec praesta mihi, Rufe, vel Butuntis,
et thermas tibi habe Neronianas.

An innkeeper, a butcher, and a place to bathe; a barber, a game board and its pieces; a few books of my own choice; one companion, not too uncouth; a full-grown slave boy who will long remain smooth and a girl dear to my boy. If you give me all of this, Rufus, even in Butunti, you can keep the Neronian baths to yourself!

Themes. There is a shift from coarse commentary on sexual relations to an idealizing evocation of the simple life in the country or a small town, a traditional theme in Roman literature. Two of the most famous treatments are Horace's parable of the country mouse and city mouse (*Sat.* 2.6) and the protracted invective of Juvenal 3; consider also two epigrams attributed to Seneca (*A.L.* 433, 444 Riese). Here, rather than offering explicit criticism of life in the city as he does in 10.12, 10.30, 10.74, 12.praef., 12.57, and 12.68, Martial concentrates on the blessings of life in the country. For other celebrations of life in the country or in a small town like his native Bilbilis, see 1.49, **2.90**, 3.38, 3.47, 3.58, 4.5, 4.55, 4.66, 7.39, 10.12, 10.30, 10.58.6, 10.70, 10.74, 10.96, 12.praef., 12.57, 12.68. The most renowned of Martial's meditations on "the good life" (*vita beata*) is set, not coincidentally, outside the city (10.47.4–5: "non ingratus ager, focus perennis; / lis numquam, toga rara, mens quieta"). But we should not forget Martial's capacity to enjoy the pleasures of urban life: see, for example, 5.20 (with a loving list: "gestatio, fabulae, libelli, / campus, porticus, umbra, Virgo, thermae," 9–10), not to mention the expressions of regret in 12.praef. ("illa quae delicati reliquimus desideramus quasi destituti"), written some time after Martial had returned to Spain.

Structure. The entire epigram consists of a single sentence, largely made up of a series of nouns in the accusative, a notable example of the technique of *cumulatio* that creates the expectation of a verb that will be satisfied only in 7 (*praesta*). We begin (1–2) with a bare list of nouns (for the technique, see **2.37**) connected by means of repetitions of *-que* in the same metrical position. Thereafter, the items are given more specificity: not just any books, but those which he has chosen; not just any friend, but one who is fairly cultivated; etc. With the final dismissal of Rome's elegant public baths (*thermas Neronianas*), echoing the opening request for a simple private bath (*balneum*), a ring-composition is created.

1–2: Other examples of two juxtaposed lines listing items with the same metrical shape include 3.44.6–7, 3.53.2–3, 5.24.5–6, 9.57.5–6; see Siedschlag 1977: 41.
1 *coponem laniumque balneumque:* A *copo* (or *caupo;* see Citroni ad 1.26.9 for the difficulty of choosing between the two spellings) was one who kept a tavern or inn (1.26.9, 1.56.2, **2.51.3**, 3.57.1, 3.59.2, 7.61.9, 13.11.2);

a *lanius* was a butcher or slaughterer. The two appear together again, along with a *tonsor* (2) and the *cocus,* as features of the urban landscape at 7.61.9–10. At **2.51.3** a *copo* and a pastry chef (*pistor*) are cited as people on whom a Roman might easily spend his money.

A *balneum* was a private bathing facility, here contrasted with *thermas Neronianas* in the epigram's final line. See further on **2.14.11–13**.

For *-que . . . -que* see on **2.41.7**.

2 tonsorem: For *tonsores,* who cut hair and shaved or trimmed beards and who are often the object of satire, see 6.52 with Grewing, 6.57, 7.64, 7.83, 8.52, 11.58, 11.84; Plin. *N.H.* 7.211.1–6; Nicolson 1891. For Roman shaving practices, see on **2.36.3**. For a female *tonstrix,* see **2.17**.

2 tabulamque calculosque: Game boards (*tabulae*) and game pieces (*calculi*) appear among the Saturnalian gifts catalogued in Book XIV (14.17, 14.18 with Leary); see Marquardt 1886: 831–832.

3 paucos, sed ut eligam, libellos: See on **2.1.3** for *libelli*; for *sed*, see on **2.6.6**.

4 non nimium rudem: For *rudis* in the sense "unlettered, uncouth, in-experienced" (*OLD* s.v. 4), compare Quint. *Inst.* 1.10.20; Vell. 1.13.4; Stat. *Ach.* 1.846: "heu simplex *nimiumque rudis.*" Shackleton Bailey understands the adjective in another sense: "one friend not too new."

5–6: Martial is typically Roman in imagining the possession of slaves as a central trait of "the good life"; see further on **2.32.5**. But how exactly would the slave boy and girl mentioned here contribute to Martial's happiness? The detail *diuque levem* suggests that the slave boy is a potential sexual partner, as is surely also the slave girl; the point is made explicitly at 9.90.7–8 ("sic uni tibi sit puer cinaedus / et castissima pruriat puella"). But the detail *caram puero meo* has perplexed some. Why is it important that she be "dear" to the boy? Collesso suggests that because of his desire for the girl, the slave boy will always stay home ("amore irretitus domi assiduus esset"). Sullivan 1991: 166 wonders if Martial intends to mate the two to produce new slaves. Obermayer 1998: 18–20, 173–174, argues that the narrator himself has a sexual interest in both slaves and envisions a ménage à trois, perhaps one in which he might simultaneously be penetrated by the slave boy and penetrate the girl. An allusion to simultaneous copulation is hardly unthinkable in Martial (cf. 9.32.4: "hanc volo quae pariter sufficit una tribus"), but the euphemistic, even sweet language of the present epigram does not invite such a reading. Moreover (*pace* Obermayer 1998 and Lorenz 2002), it is extremely unlikely that Martial would have placed himself even implicitly in the role of the penetrated. In short, Martial may view each slave singly as a sexual object, and the two slaves may themselves be imagined as having an attachment to each other, but these possibilities hardly imply a ménage à trois, let alone simultaneous copulation.

5 *grandem puerum:* The noun *puer,* the most commonly occurring of all in Martial (see on **2.37.8**), clearly refers to a slave boy, but what is the implication of the adjective *grandis?* Since it is immediately followed by the qualification *diuque levem,* it does not seem to mean "fully mature" in the sense "bearded adult." Instead, it probably means "sexually mature," that is, having attained puberty (*TLL* 6.2180.34–49); a *grandis puer* is not, for example, an eight-year-old. For the sense of sexual ripeness implicit in *grandis,* see 3.58.40 ("grandes proborum virgines colonorum"), 7.10.4 ("poscit iam dotem filia grandis"), 7.62.1 ("grandes percidis"), 8.3.16 ("grandis virgo bonusque puer"), 11.43.4 ("ille tamen grandi cum Ganymede iacet"), 12.49.12–13 ("formosos, niveos, pares, gemellos, / grandes, non pueros, sed uniones"); Pl. *Aul.* 191 ("virginem habeo grandem"); Cic. *Clu.* 11 ("grandem . . . et nubilem filiam"). Obermayer 1998: 54 unconvincingly argues that *grandis* means the boy has a large penis.

5 *diuque levem:* Most translations understand *levis* to refer specifically to smooth cheeks; that is, Martial's ideal boy will long remain beardless; see on **2.61.1**. But the adjective often refers to the absence of body hair in general or hair on the buttocks in particular: compare **2.47.2–3** ("levior o conchis, Galle, Cytheriacis. / confidis natibus?"), 10.65.8 ("levis dropace tu cotidiano"), 14.205.1 ("sit nobis aetate puer, non pumice levis"); Catull. 64.322 ("levia . . . bracchia"); Ov. *Ars am.* 3.437 ("femina quid faciat cum sit vir levior ipsa?"). See also 4.7.3, where the boy Hyllus (see on **2.51.2**) appeals to his beard and body hairs as a sign that he ought no longer to play the receptive role in sexual encounters with the poet. For smoothness in general and the adjective *levis* in particular as markers of sexual attractiveness in young men, see 11.22.5, 11.43.10, and 11.63.2–3. Obermayer 1998: 65 takes *levis* to signify an absence of pubic hair, but this is quite unlikely, as prepubescent boys are not generally represented as objects of desire in Martial or elsewhere in Roman literature.

7 *Rufe:* Friedlaender identifies him with Canius Rufus, but it is hard to be certain which Rufus is meant here; see on **2.11.1**. As often, the addressee functions as little more than a prop.

7 *Butuntis:* Located in Calabria, Butunti (modern Bitonto) is emblematic of the distant, uninteresting small town both here and, again in the final line, in 4.55: "haec tam rustica malo quam Butuntos."

8 *thermas tibi habe Neronianas:* Along with those of Agrippa and Titus, the *thermae Neronianae* were one of the three great complexes of public baths in Martial's day. They were located in the Campus Martius near the present site of the Church of S. Agostino and were emblematic of the pleasures of city life; see on **2.14.13** and compare 3.25.4, 7.5, 7.34.5 ("quid thermis melius Neronianis?"), 12.83.5; Stat. *Silv.* 1.5.62; G. Ghini in Steinby 1993–2000: s.v. For *tibi habe,* see on **2.10.4**.

2.49

Uxorem nolo Telesinam ducere. "quare?"
moecha est. "sed pueris dat Telesina." volo.

> I do not want to marry Telesina.—Why not?—She is an adulteress.—
> But Telesina does it with boys.—I want her.

Themes.   We move from a fairly leisurely exploration of an ideal situation involving, among other things, a slave boy (*puer,* **2.48.5**) to a swift,
pointed joke that ends up expressing desire for boys in general (*pueri,*
2.49.2). In a tight monodistich that requires some thought on the part of
the reader to decipher, Martial intertwines the motifs of the *moecha,* or
adulteress (**2.39**, **2.47**), and his own sexual tastes or experiences (**2.31**;
Obermayer 1998: 41–42 discusses the present epigram in the context of
Martial's allusions to ways in which he might acquire young male sexual
partners). The reason for Martial's about-face here is clear only if we are
aware of the Roman tradition which he elsewhere calls (significantly) the
supplicium puerile: if a husband caught his wife in flagrante delicto, he
had the right to take his revenge on her partner by anally penetrating him;
see **2.47** and **2.60**. The joke in this case is that revenge would be sweet;
compare the tale narrated in Apul. *Met.* 9.28, and see Schmidt 1989, Halperin
2002: 38–41. The epigram thus has a strong element of macho boasting:
the speaker has the power to decide what kind of wife he wants and makes
his decisions based on the amount of sexual pleasure he might obtain from
her and others. At the same time there is a more subtle element of self-
mockery: no self-respecting Roman man would knowingly take a wife who
was likely to betray him. Or would he?

Tanner 1986: 2674 describes **2.49–52**, like **2.60–62**, as a sequence characterized by "a cynical coarseness of tone . . . which doubtless suited the tem-
per of [the book's] probable originally intended recipient, the delator Regulus."
The suggestion is presumably inspired by **2.93** but is not convincing.

Structure.   In the absence of *inquis, quaeris,* or similar verb, it is difficult
to decide whether this epigram is a dialogue like **2.21**, 6.51, 6.54, 6.56, 8.10,
and others or rather an internal monologue (Laurens 1989: 262–264). I have
tentatively punctuated the epigram as a dialogue between Martial and an
unidentified interlocutor, but whether dialogue or monologue, the epigram
has a particularly tight and lively rhythm, as there are four changes of speaker
or perspective in two lines.

1 *Telesinam:* The name (perhaps significant: Kay ad 11.97.2 translates "Little Fulfillment") occurs only here in Martial, at least in modern editions: some MSS read *Telesina* instead of the generally accepted *Telesilla* in 6.7 (also attacked as an *adultera*), 7.87, 11.97 (rejected as a sexual partner). For the masculine *Telesinus* see 3.41, 6.50, 12.25, and Schulze 1904: 526.

2 *moecha:* See on **2.39.1**.

2 *pueris dat:* The noun need hardly have the specific sense "slave boys" (Izaac, Ceronetti); the point is that Telesina tends to young male partners in general. For *dat* see on **2.9.1**. Presumably misled by Ker's euphemistic translation (Telesina "is kindly to boys"), Kurmally 1971: 77 misinterprets the point to mean that Martial wishes to marry Telesina because she is "willing to overlook the homosexual interests of her husband."

2 *volo:* With two related but distinct senses: *volo Telesinam* and *volo uxorem ducere.* For the technique of bringing the point home with a single, particularly charged word, see on **2.17.5**.

2.50

Quod fellas et aquam potas, nil, Lesbia, peccas.
qua tibi parte opus est, Lesbia, sumis aquam.

When you give head and drink water, Lesbia, you do no wrong.
Precisely where you need it, Lesbia, is where you're washing up.

Themes. The sexual thematic continues, and we shift from a statement of the speaker's own desire to a description of a woman's behavior. In both the preceding and the present epigram, a named woman is exposed for her sexual practices: Telesina is a *moecha;* Lesbia, a *fellatrix*. Here Martial voices with exemplary clarity a prejudice attested throughout Latin literature: that fellatio and cunnilinctus pollute the mouths of those who practice them. See among many others 1.94, **2.42**, **2.61**, **2.70**, 3.75, 6.50, 9.63, 14.70, with Krenkel 1980 and 1981, Richlin 1992: 26–30, Williams 1999: 197–203. Such attacks on those who practice oral sex are rather less frequent in Greek literature, though certainly not unheard of: see Aristoph. *Knights* 1281ff., *Peace* 883ff., *Wasps* 1280ff.; *A.P.* 9.554, 11.221–223; Lucian, *Pseudolog.* 28, 31; *Rhet. praec.* 23. The thematic juxtaposition of washing and oral sexual practices likewise characterizes **2.42**, **2.70**, 3.87, 6.69.

Structure.   Each line of the monodistich contains a complete sentence, a common technique (see on **2.3**). For the technique of setting out a situation by means of a *quod*-clause and then moving on to commentary in the main clause (*nil peccas*), see on **2.10.1**. For the repetition of the vocative *Lesbia* in each of the two lines, see on **2.25**.

1 *quod fellas et aquam potas:* A brutal opening, as *fellare* is a direct obscenity; at **2.33.4** the verb has a similarly striking effect as the epigram's final word. For the phrase *aquam potas,* again in conjunction with fellatio, compare 6.69.1 ("non miror quod potat aquam tua Bassa") with Grewing. If, as the anonymous reader for Oxford University Press suggests, there is some echo of Horace's *aquae potores* (Hor. *Epist.* 1.19.3), the phrase offers an amusing paradox—Lesbia is both *fellatrix* and abstemious—explained in the second line: her unusual preference for water has a practical function.

1 *Lesbia:* "The name Lesbia, with its Catullan reminiscences and its overtones of λεσβιάζειν (to fellate), is appropriate for one who practices fellation (**2.50**), is an exhibitionist (1.34), sexually aggressive (6.23) and an old hag (10.39) who has to pay for sex (11.62)" (Sullivan 1991: 246). Horace also uses the name in a sexual context (*Epod.* 12.15). Swann 1994: 78–81 argues that while six of Martial's thirteen uses of the name clearly refer to Catullus' Lesbia, the remaining seven occurrences, including the present epigram, refer to a prostitute. But there is no hint at this in the present case, and a *fellatrix* is not necessarily a *meretrix.*

2 *sumis aquam:* Not an impossible way to refer to the act of drinking water (cf. *OLD* s.v. *sumo* 3), but the phrase *aquam sumere* elsewhere describes the act of washing up after a sexual encounter: Ov. *Am.* 3.7.84 ("dedecus hoc *sumpta* dissimulavit *aqua*"), *Priap.* 30.3 ("quarum si carpseris uvam, / cur aliter *sumas,* hospes, habebis *aquam*"); compare Cic. *Cael.* 34 (Ap. Claudius Caecus' damning apostrophe to Clodia: "ideo aquam adduxi ut ea tu inceste uterere?"). See also Mart. 7.35.8 with Galán Vioque. Ceronetti brings out the point by translating into modern idiom: it is Lesbia's mouth that needs a bidet.

2.51

Unus saepe tibi tota denarius arca
  cum sit et hic culo tritior, Hylle, tuo,
non tamen hunc pistor, non auferet hunc tibi copo,
  sed si quis nimio pene superbus erit.

infelix venter spectat convivia culi   5
  et semper miser hic esurit, ille vorat.

Though you often have only one *denarius* in your whole money
chest, Hyllus, and it is more worn out than your own asshole, it is
not the baker or the innkeeper who will take it away from you, but
rather someone proud of his huge penis. Your unhappy belly looks
upon your asshole's banquets; the one, poor thing, goes hungry while
the other feasts.

Themes.   The crude sexual invective of the preceding epigram continues,
but the barb is now aimed at a male target and the focus shifts from the
mouth (*qua parte,* **2.50.2**) to the anus (*culo tuo,* **2.51.2**). Indeed, Hyllus is
the object of several insults simultaneously: he is penniless (cf. 1.92, 3.48,
3.82, 6.77, 10.31, 11.21.9, 11.32, 12.76, 12.87–88); he squanders what little
money he has by way of satisfying his sexual desires (cf. **2.34**, **2.63**); and
these desires are themselves exposed in unmistakable terms (MS L transmits
the poem with the lemma *In Hyllum Cinaedum*). The lively antithesis between Hyllus' stomach (which normally takes in, but in his case goes without) and his anus (which normally expels, but in his case eagerly takes in)
makes the clear point that Hyllus not only enjoys being penetrated but has
a strong appetite for it. Furthermore, in view of the fact that Hyllus *pays* his
penetrators—whether these are prostitutes to whom he gives cash or other
partners upon whom he lavishes gifts is left unstated—there may be a hint
of invective against "the paying *pathicus*" (Obermayer 1998: 181, 252; cf.
9.63 and Juv. 9).

Structure.   The epigram's sequence of thought is structured around its three
couplets, which in turn break down neatly into single lines. You have but a
single *denarius* (1) and it is more worn out than your anus (2); you spend
it not on culinary delicacies (3) but on your sexual partners (4); your stomach is unhappy with this arrangement (5) and suffers while your other ori-
fice satisfies its own desires (6). The structure can thus be described as
tripartite: the statement that Hyllus is poor and a *pathicus* (1–2); the criticism that he spends his money on sexual pleasures (3–4); a summary medi-
tation structured around antithesis and paradox (5–6: note the contrasts
between *venter* and *culus, infelix* and *convivia, hic esurit* and *ille vorat,* as
well as the paradoxical expressions *convivia culi* and *ille* [sc., *culus*] *vorat*).

    1 *unus... denarius:* The *denarius* was the principal Roman silver coin
from about 211 B.C. until the third century A.D. As its name suggests, it was
originally worth 10 *asses,* but with the monetary reforms of ca. 130 B.C. it

was revalued at 16 *asses,* though maintaining its name. A *denarius* would be an absurdly small amount to have as one's entire savings—note the emphatic contrast between *unus denarius* and *tota arca*—yet "a single *denarius*" is not meant literally but is rather a way of referring to a small amount of money; compare **2.44.9** ("quadrans mihi nullus est in arca"). Ramirez Sabada 1987: 154–155 takes Martial's phrase literally, including this in his list of prices for sexual pleasures; see on **2.53.7**.

2 *culo tritior . . . tuo:* For the motif of the *culus tritus,* or "worn-out anus," see also 3.98, 6.37, and 9.57 with Obermayer 1998: 178–183. It has particular point if one considers the fact that coins and other objects are worn down by being handled by many different people; compare 8.3.4 ("*teritur* noster ubique liber") and 11.3.4 ("a rigido *teritur* centurione liber").

Culus refers specifically to the anus but is often generalized to refer to the buttocks; see Adams 1981, 1982: 110–112, 134–135, 220, 226. To judge by its distribution, the word was an obscenity on a level with *mentula* and *cunnus:* Ausonius, for example, never uses *mentula, cunnus, futuo, pedico,* or *culus* but does use *podex* (see on **2.42.1**) and *fello.*

2 *Hylle:* Martial uses the name elsewhere to refer to an attractive, effeminate young man. In **2.60** he also enjoys sexual relations with women; in 4.7 he has been Martial's receptive partner but now wants to put an end to the relationship, pointing to his newly grown beard and body hairs; in 9.25 the name is applied to the desirable *mollis minister* of Martial's friend Afer. See on **2.33.1** and **2.35.2** for the possible continuity of names across book divisions. In Greek myth the name most famously designates the son of Herakles and Deianeira: might his appearance as a youth in Sophocles' *Trachiniae* have inspired Martial?

3 *pistor, copo:* Anticipating *venter* in 5, both terms evoke the pleasures and expenses of dining: a *pistor* is a baker (6.39, 8.16, 11.31, 12.57, 13.10, 14.222–223), and a *copo* (see on **2.48.1**) is the keeper of an inn or tavern.

4 *nimio pene superbus:* For the widespread value placed on impressively large penises, whether, as in Hyllus' case, as a source of sexual pleasure or as a token of masculine power, see Williams 1999: 86–91. Priapus' self-satisfied remark that even *matronae* like to look at a large penis (*Priap.* 8.4–5: "nimirum sapiunt videntque magnam / matronae quoque mentulam libenter") is, in a Roman context, something more than self-delusion. In Martial see also 1.58, 1.96, 3.73, 11.63, 11.72.

While Cic. *Fam.* 9.22.2 says "at hodie 'penis' est in obscenis," the noun *penis* was not actually an "obscenity" in the strict sense of the English term. As Adams 1982: 35–36 observes, "the fact that [Cicero] cites it openly implies that it was a milder term than *mentula,* which he alludes to only in a roundabout way," and historians like Calpurnius Piso (fr. 40) and Sallust (*Cat.*

14.2) use the term as well. Translations like those of Shackleton Bailey ("cock") and Obermayer 1998: 181 ("Schwanz") thus strike the wrong tone.

5–6: Note the comic effect achieved by the pathetic allusion to Hyllus' belly (*infelix, miser*) and the personification of his body parts achieved by the verbs *spectat* (the verb is used at **2.46.7** to refer to someone looking upon an extreme situation passively or helplessly) and *vorat*. For the image of the hungry anus, Adams 1981: 249 compares 12.75.3 ("pastas glande natis habet Secundus") and Catull. 33.4 (*culo voraciore*), as well as other examples of the attribution of oral characteristics to the anus, such as the speaking anus at Sen. *Apoc.* 4.3, Aug. *Civ.* 14.24.

2.52

Novit loturos Dasius numerare: poposcit
mammosam Spatalen pro tribus. illa dedit.

Dasius knows how to count his customers at the baths. He asked the big-breasted Spatale to pay the entrance fee for three. And she did!

Themes.   With this return to the monodistich format of **2.49** and **2.50**, the tone shifts from coarse invective to ironic commentary and from a male back to a female target. Is it coincidental that the preceding poem ends with the two-word sentence *ille vorat* and the present with *illa dedit?* Compare the similar endings of 1.43 ("sed tu ponaris cui Charidemus apro") and 1.44 ("bis leporem tu quoque pone mihi").

Imagining a scene that will have been extremely familiar to his readers, Martial makes fun of a woman's excessive bustiness; for the centrality of bathing establishments in Roman life, see on **2.14.11–12**. For jokes at the expense of overly large breasts, which generally do not seem to have been considered desirable, see also 14.66, 14.134 with Leary, 14.149; *A.P.* 11.250 (Pertsch 1911: 16–19). Compare Martial's comments on such other peculiarities as Phoebus' bowleggedness (**2.35**) or Sextus' distorted face (**2.87**).

Structure.   The epigram falls naturally into three parts corresponding to its three sentences, which follow each other swiftly in asyndeton. The point is spread out over the two latter sentences: Spatale's breasts are enormous, and she cannot deny it. Barwick 1959: 9 cites this epigram as an example of a type where the second half of the bipartite structure is missing: the epigram contains "only a brief report" ("nur einen kurzen Bericht"). But this particular report already implies subjective commentary.

1 *loturos:* This, the reading universally transmitted by the MSS, is a generic masculine plural, reminding us of the fact that baths were often mixed; see 11.47 with Kay, Nielsen 1990, Yegül 1992, Fagan 1999. Some Italian humanists unnecessarily emended to the feminine *loturas*.

1 *Dasius:* The Latin form of a Messapic name from southern Italy (see *RE* s.v.), the name occurs again only in 6.70, where it refers to a doctor. Here Dasius is presumably the owner or manager (*conductor*) of the baths who collects the entrance fee; see the next note.

1 *poposcit:* Money taken in as an entrance fee went either to the state, in which case it was known as a *vectigal,* or to the private franchisers, in which case it was called a *balneaticum.* Generally the fee for men was a *quadrans,* or one-fourth of an *as,* a low price indeed (3.30.4; Hor. *Sat.* 1.3.137; Sen. *Epist.* 86.9). A passage from Juvenal (6.445–447) implies that women normally paid a higher fee, and the post-Hadrianic *lex metalli Vipascensis* found inscribed on a bronze tablet in Lusitania explicitly mentions a charge of one-half of an *as* for men but a full *as* for women (*CIL* 2.5181.22). Young children were exempt from the fee (Juv. 2.152 with scholia), and among the various acts of largesse or generosity that an emperor or other important figure might indulge in was to grant free admission to a bath (Marquardt 1886: 273–274).

2 *Spatalen:* The name occurs only here in Martial. Van Stockum 1884: 57 considers it significant (σπατάλη, "wantonness, luxury") since Spatale is a "lustful woman" (*mulier libidinosa*). But the epigram tells us nothing about Spatale other than the fact that she is extremely busty, and there is no evidence for a Roman association between large breasts and lustfulness.

2 *pro tribus:* The number has been the occasion of some dispute, not to say hairsplitting. Following Collesso, Friedlaender explains that Spatale is so big-breasted that she is as big as three ordinary women: "weil sie so viel Raum einnimmt wie drei gewöhnliche Badende." Housman 1907: 234 harshly criticizes Friedlaender (as on **2.8.8**, **2.14.12**, **2.77.2**, et al.) as "not merely wrong but obviously and perversely wrong, and wrong where earlier interpreters were right": he has "has missed the force of *tribus,*" which is that Spatale and her two breasts occupy the space of one normal woman *each.* Greenwood 1990, while agreeing that the point of Martial's joke is that "her breasts are each charged separately, as it were," defends Friedlaender: he understood the joke, but "the conservatism of a German scholar of the—albeit late—nineteenth century led him to omit explicit reference to the woman's breasts."

2 *illa dedit:* The point has already been made, but with these words it is lent additional sharpness: Spatale herself acknowledges that Dasius' request is justified. The *variorum* commentary sees a play on the sexual sense of *dare* ("ambigiturque an nummos dederit, an potius ipsam se"; see on 2.9.1): the second meaning would be that Dasius demands the price for three and Spatale pays not with money but with her sexual favors.

2.53

Vis fieri liber? mentiris, Maxime, non vis:
    sed fieri si vis, hac ratione potes.
liber eris, cenare foris si, Maxime, nolis,
    Veientana tuam si domat uva sitim,
si ridere potes miseri chrysendeta Cinnae,   5
    contentus nostra si potes esse toga,
si plebeia Venus gemino tibi vincitur asse,
    si tua non rectus tecta subire potes.
haec tibi si vis est, si mentis tanta potestas,
    liberior Partho vivere rege potes.   10

Do you want to become free? You're lying, Maximus, you don't want to. But if you *do* want to become free, you can do so in the following way. You will be free, Maximus, if you refuse to dine out; if the Veientine grape quenches your thirst; if you can laugh at the gold-inlaid dishes of the wretched Cinna; if you can be satisfied with my toga; if you win over an ordinary Venus for two *asses;* if you don't mind stooping as you enter your home. If you have this power, if you have such strength of mind, you can live more freely than the king of Parthia.

Themes. The poem's opening three words signal a marked elevation in tone and subject matter from what has preceded. Addressing a certain Maximus, who has evidently been leading a life of fairly luxurious pleasures, Martial adopts a preachy tone: if you want to live in "freedom" (here he is inspired by philosophical and especially Stoic language: see on 1 below), you will not be a "slave" to various physical comforts. At the same time, the poet sets himself up as already living up to most of these standards of "freedom": explicitly in 6 ("contentus *nostra* si potes esse toga") and implicitly elsewhere, as in 3, which recalls Martial's mockery of Selius in **2.11**, or in 8, which reminds us of Martial's own modest dwelling (1.108 and 1.117 with Citroni, 8.67). The concrete imagery of this epigram is characteristic of Martial's poetry in general and Book II in particular—the *cena* (**2.11**, **2.14**, **2.18–19**), dishes (**2.43.11**), the toga (**2.29**, **2.43–44**), prostitutes (**2.63**)—and metaphors of freedom and slavery characterize a number of Martial's reflections on social relations and on finding happiness; in Book II alone see **2.18**, **2.32**, **2.68**, and see also Sullivan 1991: 126–127, Fitzgerald 2000: 71–77.

Scherf 2001: 41 suggests that **2.18** and the present epigram form a thematic pair. If we read the opening question as echoing a statement that Maximus himself has made, it may be that Maximus, who is described in **2.18** as unconsciously servile with regard to his own patrons, has now recognized his situation and declares that he wishes truly to be "free." For his part, Spiegel 1891: 73 cites this epigram among others (3.38, 4.5, 5.13, 5.60, 6.61, 7.81, 10.45, 10.58, 11.42) as evidence substantiating his defense of Martial on charges of servility and hypocrisy.

The ideal outlined here is not to be confused with asceticism, as is clear from the examples of wine and sex (4, 7). There is no suggestion that one ought to renounce drinking wine entirely: it is enough to drink ordinary wine. There is no need to renounce sexual pleasures as a whole, or even to restrict them to your wife for the purpose of procreating, as Musonius Rufus 86.4–14 Lutz preaches: it is enough to visit an ordinary, inexpensive prostitute. See further Williams 1999: 38–56.

Structure.   An opening couplet both expresses Martial's doubts that Maximus truly wishes to be "free" and introduces the body of the epigram, in which various concrete examples of how he might gain this freedom are listed. Each line of the following three couplets is dedicated to a different topic, the first three (dining, drinking, dishes) being closely related to each other. For the accumulative effect created by the sequence of subordinate clauses (here protases of conditional sentences), see on **2.11**. Variety is achieved by the positioning of the conjunction *si:* sometimes at the beginning of its line, sometimes after the principal caesura. The final couplet begins with a summary phrase (*haec tibi si vis est*) and ends with a striking metaphor for freedom; *liberior* (10) points back to the opening *liber* (1, 3).

1–2: For the repetition, with syntactic variation, of the key verb (*vis? ~ non vis. ~ si vis*) see Laurens 1989: 273, who detects a "dialectique critique." Note that the homophonic noun *vis* reappears in the epigram's concluding couplet.

1 *fieri liber:* This use of the language of "freedom" is a philosophical commonplace, particularly characteristic of Seneca: see *Epist.* 8.7 (an Epicu-

rean dictum: "philosophiae servias oportet, ut tibi contingat vera libertas"),
37.4 ("sapientia, quae sola libertas est"), 47 passim, 51.9, 75.18. See also
Hor. *Sat.* 2.7, Pers. 5 passim, Juv. 5.161 ("tu tibi liber homo et regis conviva
videris") with Heilmann 1984. In Martial, see also 1.67, **2.32.8**, 4.42.12
("liberior domino saepe sit ille suo"), 4.83.4, 9.9.4 ("liber non potes et gulosus
esse"), 9.87.4.

1 *Maxime:* See on **2.18.1**.

2 *hac ratione:* For *ratio* in the general sense of "way," see 1.85.5 ("quae
ratio est igitur"), 1.97.3 ("hac ratione potest nemo non esse disertus"), 6.51.2
("inveni noceam qua ratione tibi").

3 *cenare foris:* For the centrality of dining out in Martial's world see
on **2.11**. The implicit message here, made explicit in **2.69**, is that one ought
not to act like Selius.

4 *Veientana . . . uva:* Wine from Veii, in Etruria, is cited again in 1.103
and 3.49 as undesirable and presumably inexpensive (cf. 1.26.6; Hor. *Sat.*
2.3.143; Pers. 5.147), as are also wines from the Vatican Hill (1.18, 12.48.14)
and from the territory of the Paelignians in Italy (1.26.5, 13.121, 14.116) and
the Laletanians in Spain (1.26.9). For desirable wines, including the famous
Falernian, see on **2.40.5–6**.

5 *miseri chrysendeta Cinnae:* For luxurious dishes in general and
chrysendeta in particular, see on **2.43.11–12**. The name *Cinna* appears in
thirteen other epigrams and describes a wide variety of figures. Here the
adjective *miseri* adds a touch of philosophical distance, even superiority: Cinna
is to be pitied for his attachment to or dependence on material signs of luxury.

6: For the importance of the toga, see on **2.29.4**. Depending on his argumentative needs, Martial cites his own toga sometimes as a sign of his
poverty or inadequate compensation (**2.43**) and sometimes, as here (cf. **2.58**),
as an emblem of his decently simple lifestyle.

7 *gemino . . . asse:* In itself, the remark's value as evidence that an encounter with an inexpensive prostitute might cost as little as 2 *asses* is limited, as this could be a case of satiric hyperbole. But we have confirmation
in the form of graffiti from Pompeii specifying the prices of prostitutes of
both sexes in precisely this range (Lais fellates for 2 *asses,* Felix for 1; Eutychis
and Meander are available at 2 *asses* each: *CIL* 4.1969 add. p. 213; 4.5408;
4.4024; 4.4592). See Ramirez Sabada 1987: 154–155 for a survey of the various prices for sexual services mentioned by Martial, ranging from 1 *as*
(1.103.10) to 2 *denarii,* or 32 *asses* (9.32). He distinguishes this lower range,
affordable by most Romans, from a second, much higher range of prices
(100,000–200,000 sesterces: **2.63**, 3.62, 7.10); but these refer to prices for
purchasing slaves as opposed to a one-time fee. See further on **2.63.2**.

7 *tibi vincitur:* For the dative of agent, see on **2.1.7**. The verb *vincitur,*
handed down by all MSS, is, if correct, highly ironic, as one normally has no

need of "conquering" or "winning over" a paid partner. Heinsius emended to *iungitur* (cf. [Tib.] 3.19.2: "hoc primum iuncta est foedere nostra Venus"; Ov. *Ars am.* 2.679: "Venerem iungunt per mille figuras"; Ov. *Rem. am.* 407: "Venerem quoque iunge figura"), a reading printed by Ker and Shackleton Bailey. Reeve 1983 also takes *vincitur* to be an error, citing this line along with **2.46.8** as instances in which all three MS families agree in transmitting an error.

8: An apartment with a low ceiling would be located in an attic or an upper story, always considered less desirable. Compare Martial's description of his own dwelling at 1.108.3 ("at mea Vipsanas spectant cenacula laurus") with Citroni ad loc., 1.117.7; Juv. 3.201–202.

9 *haec tibi si vis est:* Like Shackleton Bailey, Ceronetti, and Scandola, I understand the clause independently (*vis* = "strength"). Others perceive an *apo koinou* structure, such that *vis* is completed by *mentis* ("strength of mind").

10 *liberior Partho vivere rege potes:* Inhabiting a zone south of the Caspian Sea in what is now northeastern Iran, the Parthians were an archetype of the foreigner or barbarian and represented one of the greatest threats to the Roman Empire in the east. We cannot know if Martial is referring to some (now lost) proverbial expression regarding Parthian kings, as neither Otto 1890 nor the PHI disk offers any relevant passages. But the fact that Persian and Parthian kings referred to themselves as *reges regum* (Plin. *N.H.* 30.2, Suet. *Cal.* 5) is suggestive. The *variorum* commentary reminds us that the Parthians fought tenaciously and successfully to remain free of Roman domination. For the Parthians and Persians in general, see Dalby 2000: 186–191. See on **2.18.5** for the common use of *rex* as a *negative* paradigm.

2.54

Quid de te, Line, suspicetur uxor
et qua parte velit pudiciorem,
certis indiciis satis probavit,
custodem tibi quae dedit spadonem.
nil nasutius hac maligniusque.   5

What your wife suspects about you, Linus, and in which part of your body she wishes you were more chaste than you are, she has sufficiently demonstrated with clear signs: she has assigned you a eunuch as a guardian! Nothing is sharper than she, nothing more spiteful.

Themes.   We return to the realm of the sexual in this, the first epigram of Book II to touch on relations between husband and wife; Martial's satiric pieces on married relations include 1.73, 4.69, 8.12, 8.35, 8.43, 9.15, 9.78, 9.80, 10.16, 10.41, 10.43, 10.63, 11.23, 11.71, 12.91, 12.96, 12.97. Linus' wife suspects that he derives pleasure from being sexually penetrated and thus, in an amusing reversal of the elsewhere attested practice of husbands putting eunuch guardians over their wives (see on 4), she assigns a castrated slave to watch over him. We thus find yet another exposure of a *pathicus* (cf. **2.51** and see Obermayer 1998: 237–243), with an added swipe at the man as entirely subject to his wife's power and, perhaps worse still, put under the guardianship of an unmanned slave. At the same time, the poet strikes a note of (ironic?) sympathy for the poor husband: *nil hac malignius*. Martial later recasts the scenario of a wife assigning guardians to her husband in 10.69, an epigram whose emphasis lies on the husband's paradoxical subjugation to his wife: "Custodes das, Polla, viro, non accipis ipsa. / hoc est uxorem ducere, Polla, virum." (Polla, you assign guardians to your husband but take none for yourself. This, Polla, means taking a husband as wife.) One might be tempted to ask how usual it was for Roman wives to place *custodes* over their husbands, but the whole scenario may well be an exercise in imagination.

Scherf 2001: 44 suggests that the present epigram forms a thematic pair with **2.38** and thus sheds light on the earlier poem. There, Martial is glad not to see Linus; here, we learn the reason, namely that he is a *pathicus*. This seems out of keeping with Martial's persona, as he is perfectly willing to make fun of *pathici* but hardly finds them as repellent as Scherf's reading suggests.

Structure.   The epigram's structure is pleasingly simple: each line is syntactically self-contained, and each builds upon its predecessor. The epigram might have begun by giving the crucial information in an opening *quod*-clause (see on **2.10.1**) but instead postpones this until 4: "custodem tibi quae dedit spadonem." Thus, the point is made not in the final but in the penultimate line, while the last line adds an ironic note of sympathy. Alternatively, one might argue that the final line itself constitutes the point: see below.

  1 *Line:* See on **2.38.1**.
  2 *qua parte velit pudiciorem:* Since *pudicitia* and *impudicitia,* when predicated of men, regularly refer to the ideal of masculine impenetrability (Williams 1999: 172–174), the decorous phrase makes its point clearly: *qua parte* is euphemistic for the anus. See Adams 1982: s.v. *pars,* and compare **2.50.2**, where *qua parte* refers to the mouth in a sexual context.

4 *custodem:* For guardians, sometimes but not always eunuchs, charged with protecting women and especially wives from sexual advances, see 1.73; Prop. 1.11.15, 2.6.37; Ov. *Am.* 2.2–3, 2.19, 3.4, *Ars am.* 2.635–638, 3.601– 602; Juv. 6.O.29–33; Tac. *Ann.* 11.35; Apul. *Met.* 9.17.

4 *spadonem:* In some legal texts *spado* designates those impotent since birth or through illness, while *eunuchus* refers to those artificially castrated (D. 1.7.2, 23.3.39), but the distinction is not maintained with any regularity in literary texts; see Grewing ad 6.2. References to eunuch slaves abound in Roman literature (in Martial alone, see 3.58.32, 3.82.15–17, 5.41.1, 7.80.10, 8.44.15; Maas 1925; *RE* s.v. "Eunuchen"), as do allusions to women's use of eunuchs as sexual partners (6.2, 6.39, 6.67, 10.91, 11.81; Juv. 6.366–378). Martial puts it bluntly enough at 6.67.2 ("vult futui Gellia nec parere"), re- minding us thereby that some eunuchs were capable of erection. Linus' wife will have chosen one who was not.

5 *nil nasutius hac maligniusque:* Until this final line, Martial's word- ing has focused on what Linus' wife *suspects* to be the case, but when he says that she is *nasuta* and *maligna,* he implies that these suspicions were well founded. The adjective *nasutus* (literally, "having a long nose") can mean "witty, satirical, sharp" (*OLD*), as at 12.37.1 ("nasutus nimium cupis videri") and 13.2.1–5 ("nasutus sis usque licet . . . / non potes in nugas dicere plura meas / ipse ego quam dixi"), but the nose was also understood as the organ of scorn: see 1.3.6 ("et pueri nasum rhinocerotis habent") with Howell and Phaedr. 4.7.1 ("tu qui nasute scripta destringis mea"). Linus' wife is "sharp" in both senses: clever enough to have figured out what Linus likes and nasty enough to deprive him of this pleasure (so too the *variorum* commentary: "nasutius ad avertendum; malignius ad coercendum"). Obermayer 1998: 243 interprets the adjectives differently: she is *nasuta* because of the efficiency of the measure she has taken, *maligna* because she has exposed her hus- band to ridicule.

The formula "nothing is more X than Y" was a common figure of speech (Siedschlag 1977: 17–18) and not to be taken literally; see Hofmann 1951: 89–90, 195, for examples of the expression applied to people. Its sheer frequency and range of application in Martial are remarkable: see 1.35.15 ("gallo turpius est nihil Priapo"), 3.69.3 ("nihil est te sanctius uno"), 4.30.5, 4.56.3 ("sordidius nihil est, nihil est te spurcius uno"), 4.66.2 ("qua nihil omnino vilius esse potest"), 4.78.9–10 ("deformius, Afer, / omnino nihil est ardalione sene"), 4.83.1, 5.50.6 ("improbius nihil est hac, Charopine, gula"), 5.63.3 ("nihil est perfectius illis"), 6.24.1 ("nil lascivius est Charisiano"), 6.33.1 ("nil miserabilius, Matho, pedicone Sabello") with Grewing, 7.20.1 ("nihil est miserius neque gulosius Santra"), 8.6.1 ("archetypis vetuli nihil est odiosius Aucti"), 8.59.3 ("nihil est furacius illo"), 9.57.1 ("nil est tritius Hedyli lacernis"), 10.71.8 ("improbius nihil his fletibus esse potest"), 10.77.1 ("nequius a caro nihil umquam, Maxime, factum est"), 10.83.11 ("calvo turpius est nihil comato"), 12.63.12–13.

2.55

> Vis te, Sexte, coli; volebam amare.
> parendum est tibi: quod iubes, coleris.
> sed si te colo, Sexte, non amabo.

You want respect, Sextus; I wanted to give you my affection. Your wishes must be met; you will have the respect you ask for. But if I respect you, Sextus, you won't have my affection.

Themes.   After a series of poems offering ironic commentary on or aiming invective against others (**2.50–54**), Martial is once again directly involved in the scenario depicted. In a brief, tightly structured epigram we find two intertwined themes central to his poetry: affectionate relationships between men known as *amicitia* (see on **2.5**, **2.24**, **2.43**) and the openly hierarchical relationship between patrons and clients known as *clientela,* in which Martial usually takes the stance of the junior partner (see on **2.18**).

The distinction between *colere* and *amare,* which structures a later epigram (10.58) as well, is often aligned in modern scholarship with that between *clientela* and *amicitia.* White 1978: 81 observes that the noun *cultor* is a less bald version of *cliens,* and that the verb *colere* is used "where the distinction of persons is to be observed"; Spisak 1998a: 246 explains *colere* as "cultivate, court, i.e., cater to," and *amare* as "love, esteem," adding that "Martial clearly shows that he himself is quite aware of the sometimes subtle distinction between an actual *amicus* and a *cliens.*" But what "an actual *amicus*" is in Roman terms is notoriously hard to say.

At first glance Martial's retort seems ineffectual, since Sextus implies that he is not interested precisely in the emotional aspects of their relationship; but the epigram has a sharper point if the implication is that Sextus will sooner or later regret his stance since he will have missed the opportunity for a closer relationship with Martial. A similar contrast underlies a remark by Seneca to the effect that certain patrons keep clients not for the sake of friendship but rather for display (*De brev. vit.* 7.7: "ille potentior amicus, qui vos non in amicitiam sed in apparatum habet"). See also Sen. *Ben.* 6.35: we often end up not only not loving but positively hating those whose favor we court. Thus, Martial's *non amabo* may suggest *odero.*

Structure.   Each of the first two lines falls into two distinct, syntactically independent halves, while the third line constitutes a syntactic whole, though still falling into two halves (protasis and apodosis) separated by the vocative *Sexte.* At the same time, the thought progresses line by line, each containing at least two verbs, the contrast between which forms the substance of this brief poem: *vis ~ volebam; parendum est ~ iubes; colo ~ amabo.*

1 *vis te, Sexte, coli: volebam amare:* Note the contrast between the present tense *vis* and the imperfect *volebam:* the battle of wills has already been decided. For this sense of the verb *colere,* compare 3.38.11 ("atria magna colam"), 6.50.1 ("cum coleret puros pauper Telesinus amicos"), 12.68.2 ("atria, si sapias, ambitiosa colas"). For the name *Sextus,* extremely common in Martial, see on **2.3.1**.

2: MSS of family γ read *colere;* those of family β, *coleris.* Both readings have found supporters. On the one hand, it is easy to imagine an original *coleris* being changed to *colere* under the influence of *amare* in the preceding line (Shackleton Bailey), and Heraeus 1925: 334 argues that endings in *-re* are otherwise found only where metrically necessary (e.g., **2.60.3**, *castrabere*). On the other hand, Gilbert and Friedlaender argue for *colere* precisely because of the rhyme with *amare* in the preceding line.

3 *sed si te colo . . . non amabo:* This seems to represent the two terms as mutually exclusive (Laurens 1989: 277, Spisak 1998a: 246), and yet the fact that Martial has to make the point explicitly suggests that the two are not always and *necessarily* mutually exclusive. Representing them as such in this case serves Martial's argumentative purposes.

2.56

Gentibus in Libycis uxor tua, Galle, male audit
   immodicae foedo crimine avaritiae.
sed mera narrantur mendacia. non solet illa
   accipere omnino. quid solet ergo? dare.

Among the peoples of Libya your wife, Gallus, has gained a reputation for the indecent offence of uncontrolled greed. These are pure lies! She is not at all in the habit of receiving favors. What, then, is her habit? To give them.

Themes.   Returning to the theme of husband-wife relations (**2.54**) and to the exposure of a *moecha* (**2.49**), this gossipy piece makes its point with its final word, *dare,* which stands in contrast with *accipere.* Ostensibly defending the wife of a Roman official in North Africa on a charge of having abused her position, Martial uses the delightfully ambivalent verb *dare:* she does not "take" (*accipere*) anything from the locals but rather "gives." On the surface this suggests financial generosity, but thanks to the secondary meaning of the verb (see on **2.9.1**), Martial ends up refuting one charge in order to impugn something worse: she is free with her sexual favors, with non-Romans at that. For the technique of denying one accusation in order to level another, graver one, compare 4.43 ("non dixi, Coracine, te cinaedum . . . / dixi te, Coracine, cunnilingum") with Williams 1999: 201–202, and for this function of double entendre in epigrammatic wit see Plass 1985. At the same time, the epigram insults Gallus as well, calling into question his masculine honor by exposing his wife as a *moecha* (cf. 3.26.6: "uxorem sed habes, Candide, cum populo"; 7.10.13: "uxor moecha tibi est").

Whether or not Roman provincial officials ought to bring their wives and daughters with them was a long-debated issue; the traditional practice was to leave them at home (Sen. *Contr.* 9.2.1–2, Tac. *Ann.* 3.33). Ulpian (D. 1.16.4.2) observes that it is permissible but not advisable for the wife to accompany the official to the province, citing a decree passed in A.D. 24 according to which the magistrate will be held responsible for any wrongdoings committed by his wife (cf. Tac. *Ann.* 4.20.6: "provincialibus uxorum criminibus proinde quam suis plecterentur").

The epigram well illustrates the centrality of gossip to Martial's world: the Libyans talk about Gallus' wife (*male audit*), and Martial joins in on the game with a riposte that is typical in its rejection of others' version of the story (*mera narrantur mendacia*) and its seemingly blunt denial of the charge (*non solet illa accipere omnino*), which is in turn capped off with a new and more devastating insinuation. For Martial's language of gossip in general, see Greenwood 1998a.

Structure.   The first couplet reports Gallus' wife's reputation, and the second couplet responds to it. At the same time a buildup in tension is signaled by an increasing simplicity and brevity of sentence structure, from the first sentence, which occupies the entire first couplet, to the three-word question "quid solet ergo?" to the single-word reply with which the poem ends.

1 *Galle:* See on **2.47.2** for this name, frequently appearing in Martial but not clearly associated with any single personality. Interestingly, in **2.25** we find the feminine *Galla* associated with the sexual sense of *dare.*

1: For the expression *male audire* (cf. κακῶς ἀκούειν), see *OLD* s.v. *audio* 5b.

2: Instead of *foedo crimine avaritiae,* MSS of family β read *foede* (i.e., *foedae*) *crimine avaritiae.* But, although the adjective *foedus* elsewhere modifies *avaritia* (Cic. *Leg.* 1.51.9: "quid enim foedius avaritia?"; Plin. *Epist.* 7.31.2), modern editors unanimously print *foedo crimine.*

3–4: I have borrowed from Ker's translation of the final line and a half. Barié and Schindler see a particularly sharp final point: Gallus' wife takes money to commit adultery with non-Romans. Yet Martial hardly implies that Gallus' wife prostitutes herself; on the contrary, "non solet illa / accipere omnino."

3 *mera narrantur mendacia:* Not surprisingly, *narrari* occurs in several of Martial's allusions to gossip: see **2.72.1**, 3.9.1 ("versiculos in me narratur scribere Cinna"), 5.77.1 ("narratur belle quidam dixisse, Marulle") with Greenwood 1998a: 298. For the phrase *mera mendacia,* see Plaut. *Pseud.* 943 ("mera iam mendacia fundes") and Sen. *Apoc.* 6.2 ("mera mendacia narrat").

4 *quid solet ergo? dare:* For the technique of posing a question at the epigram's end and then answering it with a word or phrase that brings home the point, see on **2.7.8**. For a final question with *ergo* leading into an unexpected conclusion, see on **2.28.5**. For single-word points (*dare*), see on **2.17.5**.

2.57

Hic quem videtis gressibus vagis lentum,
amethystinatus media qui secat Saepta,
quem non lacernis Publius meus vincit,
non ipse Cordus alpha paenulatorum,
quem grex togatus sequitur et capillatus   5
recensque sella linteisque lorisque,
oppigneravit modo modo ad Cladi mensam
vix octo nummis anulum, unde cenaret.

This man whom you all see walking in leisurely fashion with a slow step, cutting through the midst of the Saepta in amethyst-colored clothes; who is outdone in coats not even by my friend Publius, nor even by Cordus, that alpha among the cloak-wearing pack; who is followed by a flock of toga-clad clients and long-haired slave boys, his litter freshly adorned with linen curtains and leather thongs: he has just now pawned his ring at Cladius' shop for barely eight sesterces in order to pay for his dinner.

Themes.   Ironic social commentary continues, and the meter switches to choliambics, for which see on **2.11**. The poem is reminiscent of **2.29**, in which the portrait of a man who leads an ostentatiously luxurious life is likewise drawn over the course of a single sentence built around a series of relative clauses capped off with the revelation that all is not as it seems. There, the truth is that the man was born in slavery; here, that he is in such financial difficulty that he is reduced to pawning a ring in order to pay for his dinner. The theme recurs in **2.74**; Burnikel 1980: 88–94 and Scherf 2001: 39 treat them as a separated pair: see also **2.65**, **2.76**, and perhaps also **2.18**, **2.53**. Typically, the practice of borrowing in order to lead an extravagant life (something Martial's own persona seems to do in **2.44**) provokes a rather more bitter complaint in Juvenal: see 11.9–13 and 11.42–43, where a man sells his ring as a desperate last measure. For the display of wealth, see also **2.58**, **2.74**, 3.51, 4.33, 4.37, 4.61, 5.47, 6.14, 6.77, 6.84, 6.94, 12.69.

Structure.   The structure is closely comparable to that of **2.11** and **2.29**, although here the effect is even more striking, as the entire epigram consists of a single sentence. A sequence of subordinate, mostly relative, clauses referring to the opening deictic *hic* (see on **2.11** for such accumulations) culminates with the main clause (*oppigneravit*) in the last two verses. The relative clauses in which the detail is accumulated display variation. Each of the three opening lines contains the relative pronoun (1, *quem*; 2, *qui*; 3, *quem*); 4 continues the syntax of 3, just as 6 continues that of 5. At the same time there is a thematic sequence from colorful images of how the man walks (1) and what his clothing looks like (2–4) to a description of his entourage (5–6) to a revelation of the harsh reality lying behind appearances (7–8).

1 *hic quem videtis:* See on **2.29.1** for such deictic openings. The plural *videtis* is of note, since such deictic openings most often have singular verbs: compare *vides* in **2.11.1**, **2.29.1**. As in **2.23** ("non dicam, licet usque me rogetis"), the opening remark takes the form of a public comment and thus has the function of exposing a figure who is nonetheless so vaguely described that there cannot have been a single recognizable real man lying behind him.

1 *gressibus vagis lentum:* The point of *gressibus vagis* is that he does not take a straight path but wanders seemingly aimlessly. Together with *lentum,* this makes the point that he is trying to be seen by as many people as possible; see further on 2 (*secat*) and compare Ov. *Ars am.* 1.99: "spectatum veniunt, veniunt spectentur ut ipsae."

2 *amethystinatus:* For expensive, amethyst-colored clothing, see 10.49.1, 14.154 with Leary. At 1.96.7 a moralizer dismisses such clothing as effeminate ("amethystinasque mulierum vocat vestes"), and for general suspicion of brightly colored clothing on men, see on **2.29.3**.

2 *media qui secat Saepta:* The Saepta Julia in the Campus Martius was a favorite strolling ground and social showcase: see on **2.14.5**. The verb *secat* suggests that he is making his way through a crowded area (*OLD* s.v. 5: "to cleave a path through"), a detail that builds on the preceding line's evocation of his strategy to be seen by as many as possible.

3 *Publius meus:* A common praenomen, though found in Martial on only four other occasions (1.109, 7.72, 7.87, 10.98). The use of *meus* creates a tone of friendly familiarity (*OLD* s.v. 2b.), and this detail, together with the complimentary tone overall, raises the possibility that the Publius of the present epigram is a real man whom Martial flatters in passing. He may or may not be the same Publius described in 1.109 and 7.87, who has a portrait painted of his beloved puppy.

4 *Cordus:* In 5.23 and 5.26 a man named Cordus is again described as possessing a large number of colorful, expensive cloaks; in 3.15 he is said not to be wealthy; in 3.83 he advises Martial to write shorter epigrams (cf. **2.77**). Friedlaender thus distinguishes between a wealthy real man and a poor fictional character. Howell ad 5.26 likewise suggests that the Cordus of that poem, and thus also of the present epigram, was a real man, but that in view of Martial's declared practice of not attacking real people by name, the joking allusions to his cloaks must have been "intended as no more than a mild joke." Alternatively, Cordus may have been a pseudonym for a real man or else an entirely fictional character whom Martial resurrects in Book V. Compare the case of Selius (**2.11.1**, **2.69.6**).

4 *alpha paenulatorum:* The *paenula* was a close-fitting, hooded cloak made of weatherproof material (Marquardt 1886: 564–565). It was worn by all types of people: workers and slaves who were active outdoors but also upper-class men when traveling or in inclement weather: see Cic. *Att.* 13.33.4, *Mil.* 29, 54; Sen. *N.Q.* 4b.6.2; Tac. *Dial.* 39.1. Martial refers to the garment on several other occasions: 1.103.5, 13.1.1, 14.84.1, 14.128.2, 14.130, 14.145.

Martial's interesting phrase ("the alpha of the cloak-wearers"; my translation draws on the metaphor of the "alpha dog" in a pack) is nowhere else attested but has an obvious meaning: Cordus is chief among cloak-wearers. Otto 1890: 15 tentatively cites this usage of *alpha* as proverbial but adds that it may simply be an ad hoc joke since the figurative usage of the word *alpha* is not otherwise attested until Christian Latin texts inspired by the famous New Testament phrase "ego sum alpha et omega" (Rev. 1.8, 22.13). Martial makes use of other Greek letter names in **2.93** (*iota*), 5.26 (*alpha* and *beta*), 7.37 (*theta*); for his use of entire Greek phrases or sentences, see on **2.43.1**.

The phrase is once again applied to Cordus in an epigram published about four years later: "Quod *alpha* dixi, Corde, *paenulatorum* / te nuper, aliqua cum iocarer in charta, / si forte bilem movit hic tibi versus, / dicas licebit beta me togatorum" (5.26). Martial occasionally refers back to specific earlier epigrams (3.50 refers to 3.44 and 3.45; 3.97 to 3.83 and 3.87; 6.65 to 6.64; 9.49 to 8.28 and other earlier epigrams), but this case is remarkable for the great distance separating the earlier from the later poem. Burnikel 1980: 91 thus describes the pair **2.57**/5.26 as an extreme example of the "reaction" or "reply" type (cf. 1.34/35, 1.39/40, 1.44/45, 1.109/110, **2.21–22/23**, 3.16/99, 4.71/81); see **2.91–92** for another type of continuation sequence, and **2.22** for a reference back to an earlier epigram (**2.10**).

5–6: The image of a man aiming to impress by means of his entourage and litter recurs at Juv. 7.141–143: "respicit haec primum qui litigat, an tibi servi / octo, decem comites, an post te sella, togati / ante pedes." Colton 1991: 317–318 assumes a direct imitation.

The phrase *grex togatus . . . et capillatus* refers to a throng of dependents, both freeborn clients (*grex togatus:* cf. on **2.18.5**) and young male slaves (*grex capillatus*). For this use of *grex,* see Cic. *Att.* 1.18.1 (*gregibus amicorum*), Sen. *De brev. vit.* 7.6 (*clientium greges*), Juv. 1.46 (*gregibus comitum;* Colton 1991: 35–36 sees the influence of Martial). For the toga as symbol of the client, see especially **2.74**, where toga-clad clients (*amici et greges togatorum*) are again imagined escorting a pretender to wealth; and 1.108.7, 3.46.1 (*operam togatam*), 6.48 (*turba togata*), 9.100.1, 10.47, 10.82.2, 14.125; Juv. 1.96 (*turba togata*). For long hair as the emblem of attractive young male slaves, see 3.58.30–31 (*lascivi capillati*), 12.18.24–25, 12.49 (*crinita turba*), 12.70 (*comati*), 12.84, 12.97 (*comati*); Juv. 8.128 (*acersecomes*); Obermayer 1998: 94–144. The cutting of their hair upon achievement of manhood was an event charged with symbolism: see 1.31 with Citroni ad loc., 7.29.3. Contrasted with them as an emblem of simplicity were *tonsi ministri:* 10.98.9, 11.11.3, 12.18.25, 14.158.1.

6 *sella:* Literally "seat," here referring to a chair in which one could be carried around by slaves, a convenient way of getting around the crowded city streets since daytime wheeled traffic had been generally forbidden since the *lex Julia municipalis* of 45 B.C. Martial's references to *sellae* include 3.36, 4.51, 5.14, 5.61, 6.84, 9.22, 9.100, 12.77; for *lecticae,* or litters in the form of a couch or bed on which one could recline, see **2.81**. At Juv. 1.32–33 ("causidici *nova* cum veniat *lectica* Mathonis / plena ipso") a new litter is similarly the sign of ostentation (Colton 1991: 31).

6 *linteisque lorisque:* See on **2.30.3** for *-que . . . -que.*

7 *modo modo:* "Just now" (*OLD* s.v. 5; cf. Petr. *Sat.* 37.3: "et modo modo quid fuit?"), an example of expressive gemination especially characteristic of colloquial speech (Hofmann 1951: 59–60, 190); compare Italian *ora ora* and Modern Greek τώρα τώρα.

7 ad Cladi mensam: MSS of family β read *Gladi,* while those of family γ read *Claudi.* The latter is impossible metrically, and the former presents an otherwise unattested name. All modern editions have adopted Salmasius' emendation *Cladi.* But is this the genitive of *Cladus* or *Cladius?* Commentators and translators, along with *PIR* and *RE,* give both forms, but Solin and Salomies 1994 are able to cite only inscriptions with the form *Cladius.*

A *mensa* was a table or counter on which one did business, especially monetary transactions (in which case the phrase *mensa nummularia* is also used); compare Modern Greek τράπεζα, "bank."

8 octo nummis: That is, 8 sesterces, a negligible amount (see on **2.43.8**). For the correption of the final vowel of *octo,* see on **2.9.2**.

8 unde cenaret: For this use of *unde* ("from which," denoting source, material, or the like: *OLD* s.v. 10), compare Pl. *Mil.* 687 ("eme . . . lanam unde tibi pallium . . . conficiatur") and Tac. *Ann.* 11.20 ("recluserat specus quaerendis venis argenti, unde tenuis fructus . . . fuit").

2.58

> Pexatus pulchre rides mea, Zoile, trita.
> sunt haec trita quidem, Zoile, sed mea sunt.

In your brand-new toga you laugh at my worn-out clothes, Zoilus.
To be sure, they are worn out, Zoilus, but they are mine!

Themes. The character Zoilus returns, as does the narrator's direct involvement in the scenario described (**2.55**), and the focus on clothing constitutes a thematic link with the preceding epigram (**2.57.2–4**). Once again Martial points to his less-than-ideal toga (see on **2.29.4**, **2.44.1**), though now with complacency.

In what sense will Zoilus' toga not have been "his"? One possibility is that he has stolen it, though elsewhere there are no clear hints at Zoilus' being a thief. Another possibility is suggested by Sullivan 1991: 244. Zoilus had borrowed the money to buy the clothes but has not repaid the loan, and perhaps he never will: in this sense they are not fully his. For loans and defaulters, the latter sometimes including Martial himself, see on **2.44**, where Martial depicts himself as seeking to borrow money precisely to buy, among other things, a *toga pexa*. Similarly in 6.94, Calpetianus uses gold-inlaid dishes that are not his (4: "non habet immo suum"; for points executed by means of a possessive, see on **2.20.2**). Grewing ad loc. suggests that he has borrowed them, bought them on credit that he will never be able to repay, or even simply stolen them.

Yet another possibility is that Martial is referring to the toga as sign of Roman citizenship. Elsewhere he makes it brutally clear that Zoilus was born a slave and was moreover a runaway, and that while he is now a citizen, he belongs to the socially ambivalent category of *libertini,* or freedmen (3.29, 11.12, 11.37, 11.54; see on **2.29**). The final words of this epigram may thus constitute a proud reminder that the toga is Martial's by birth, a privilege Zoilus cannot claim; compare the bitter expostulations at Juv. 3.81–85.

Structure.   As often with monodistichs, the structure is as straightforward as the content. In the first line we learn of the situation, and the two items of clothing are kept distinct at the beginning and end of the line (*pexatus pulchre ~ mea trita*); in the second line we hear Martial's reaction. The repetition of the vocative in each of the two lines is a fairly frequent feature of monodistichs: see **2.25**, **2.38**, **2.42**, **2.50**.

1 *pexatus pulchre:* Fresh togas were described as *pexae*, that is, with their wool neatly combed; see on **2.44.1**. Hofmann 1951: 71, 192, sees *pulchre* as an example of a colloquial tendency to exaggeration, the adverb being essentially equivalent to *bene;* compare 1.77.1: "pulchre valet"; 12.17.9: "cum recubet pulchre." Yet the full meaning of *pulchre* is also active in this case.

1 *Zoile:* Zoilus is a frequently recurring target of Martial's barbs; see on **2.16.1**. His relationship to clothing is the subject of a later epigram, in which he is said to change his dinner clothes eleven times in the course of an evening (5.79).

2 *sunt haec trita quidem:* For the technique of granting an opponent's or interlocutor's claim, see on **2.8.7**.

2.59

Mica vocor; quid sim cernis: cenatio parva.
    ex me Caesareum prospicis ecce tholum.
frange toros, pete vina, rosas cape, tinguere nardo:
    ipse iubet mortis te meminisse deus.

I am called the Speck. You can see what I am: a small dining hall.
Look! From me you have a view of the Caesars' rotunda. Crush the
couches' cushions, call for wine, take roses in your hand, anoint
yourself with nard! The god himself bids us be mindful of death.

Themes.   This is one of the few epigrams in Book II that do not satirize a
specific person, type, or social behavior. It is instead of an epideictic nature,
being an abbreviated version of an *ecphrasis,* or description of an object or
place. References to specific buildings or sites in Rome abound in Martial
(in the present book alone see **2.14**, **2.17**, **2.29**, **2.63**, **2.74**), but this epigram exemplifies the rarer technique of making the monument itself central
to the poem; compare *Sp.* 2 and 8.65.

The description of the dining hall (for its precise identity see on 2 below)
is accompanied by a traditional Epicurean message. Just as the nearby tomb
reminds us that we must all die one day, the dining hall offers an opportunity to enjoy life while we have it; see in general Heilmann 1984, 1998.
Martial repeats the lesson in a later epigram that likewise refers to a banquet held, presumably in the same *Mica,* near the Mausoleum of Augustus:
"tam vicina iubent nos vivere Mausolea, / cum doceant ipsos posse perire
deos" (5.64.5–6). This response to the mortal condition is one of the most
famous themes of ancient literature, expressed in lapidary form in Horace's
"carpe diem" (*C.* 1.11; see also *C.* 1.4, 2.3, 2.11, 2.14, 2.29, 4.7); in Martial,
see also 1.15, 4.54, 5.58, 5.64, 7.47, 8.44, 8.77, 13.126; in Greek epigram,
see *A.P.* 5.72, 11.56 (Pertsch 1911: 30–31). As Petronius' Trimalchio puts it:
since we know we are going to die, why should we not live? (Petr. *Sat.* 72:
"ergo cum sciamus nos morituros esse, quare non vivamus?"). The theme
had a particular association with banquets: depictions of skeletons were
sometimes placed in or near dining rooms, and see *A.P.* 9.439, 11.38 with
Prinz 1911: 14–15, along with Petr. *Sat.* 34 and such epitaphs as *CLE* 84,
190, 485, 1084. The point that even the emperors, destined to become gods,
are subject to death is also explored in *A.P.* 7.8; *CLE* 90, 971, 1068; and especially Sen. *Cons. Marc.* 15.1.

The epigram was imitated by Robert Louis Stevenson (*Collected Poems,*
ed. Janet Adam Smith, [London, 1950]):

Look round: You see a little supper room;
But from my window, lo! great Caesar's tomb!
And the great dead themselves, with jovial breath,
Bid you be merry and remember death.

Scherf 2001: 68–69 observes that **2.59** introduces a sequence of five poems
with symmetrically arranged verse lengths (4, 4, 8, 4, 4); compare on **2.4**, **2.9**.

Structure.   The epigram falls into two halves corresponding to its two couplets: the first sets the scene, and the second draws a lesson. There is a pleasingly varied rhythm. The first couplet begins with a pointed, two-word
sentence that brings us directly to the subject matter (*mica vocor;* cf. **2.16.1**,
Zoilus aegrotat) and that is followed by two increasingly long sentences
explaining what the *mica* is and where it is located. The second couplet's
first line presents a rapid sequence of imperative clauses efficiently describing a banquet, each consisting of only two words (verb and object); its second line gives the theoretical justification, making at the same time a larger
spiritual point. The asyndetic sequence contributes to the swiftness and tightness of the whole.

1 *mica vocor:* The noun *mica* denotes a grain of salt or a crumb of
some other substance but was used figuratively to refer to tiny objects;
Valentinian ironically used the term to describe a pet bear inclined to eating
human beings (Ammian. Marc. 29.3.9), and it was also applied to a structure
on the Janiculum (Platner 1929, Richardson 1992 s.v.); see on 2 below for
the *Mica Aurea* on the Caelian. There have been varied suggestions about
precisely what form Martial's *Mica* had. Friedrich 1910: 590–591 imagines a
palatial residence (*Schloß*) containing a dining room; P. Liverani in Steinby
1993–2000 suggests some kind of private pavilion ("un padiglione privato");
Lorenz 2002: 135 n. 94 thinks of it, improbably, as a type of fast-food stand
("Imbissbude"). Prinz 1911: 14–15 wonders if it ever existed at all.

The technique of having an object speak up in the first person is characteristic of epigram from its beginnings, as in the case of the famous cup
from late-eighth-century B.C. Ischia whose inscription begins, "I am the cup
of Nestor, lovely to drink" (*CEG* 1.454: Νέστορος ἐ[μι] εὔποτον ποτέριον;
Pavese 1996; Edmunds 2001: 6–7).

1 *cenatio:* The correption of *o* is a common feature in Latin verse (see
on **2.9.2**), especially, as here, in the fifth foot of the hexameter.

2 *ex me Caesareum prospicis ecce tholum:* In view of 5.64, which
locates a dining hall near the *Mausolea,* this must refer to the Mausoleum of
Augustus, which served as tomb for all emperors (Tac. *Ann.* 3.9 calls it
tumulus Caesarum) until the completion of the *templum gentis Flaviae* several years after Book II was first published (9.1). The *Mica* will thus have
been a small dining room with a view of this structure; Castagnoli 1993: 110
and Coarelli (Steinby 1993–2000: s.v.) suggest a location on the Pincian.

We know of a *Mica Aurea* on the Caelian, but this was hardly in sight of
the Mausoleum of Augustus and in any case seems to have been built after
Book II was first published (Jerome, *A. Abr.* 2110e dates it to A.D. 94–95).
Attempts to identify the dining hall described here with the structure on the
Caelian (Richardson 1992: 253, Scheithauer 2000: 149) must assume not only

that Jerome's dating is off (as it admittedly often is) but also that this epigram was first published in a putative second edition of Book II appearing around A.D. 93 and, even more boldly, must interpret *Caesareum tholum* to refer to some structure other than the Mausoleum of Augustus (Richardson proposes that the Arch of Titus is meant, though it is hard to see how that structure could be called a *tholus*). Yet the parallel with 5.64 remains compelling, such that the present epigram almost certainly has nothing to do with the *Mica Aurea* of the Caelian (*pace* Grimal 1989).

3 *frange toros*: The phrase appears again at 4.8.6 and nowhere else in extant Latin; the cushions or the bed itself will be worn down or even eventually broken from constant use. For the use of *torus* to refer to a bolster on a dining couch, compare 4.8.6, 14.136; at **2.16.3** and elsewhere it refers to a bed on which to rest or sleep.

3 *rosas cape, tinguere nardo*: *Nardus* refers to the oil extracted from the plant of the same name, used to add fragrance to hair and associated with banquets or feasts: compare 3.65.8 ("madidas nardo passa corona comas"), 4.13.3, 13.51. For the combination of roses and nard unguent, see 5.64.3–4, 10.20.19–20, 13.51.

4 *mortis . . . meminisse*: One is reminded of the famous phrase *memento mori* (e.g., Shakespeare, *1 Hen. IV* 3.3.34). Although there are no extant attestations of that phrase in classical Latin, see Heilmann 1998: 205–210 for the thought.

2.60

Uxorem armati futuis, puer Hylle, tribuni,
 supplicium tantum dum puerile times.
vae tibi, dum ludis, castrabere. iam mihi dices
 "non licet hoc." quid? tu quod facis, Hylle, licet?

You are fucking the wife of a military tribune, boy Hyllus, as long as you fear only the boyish punishment. But you're in trouble: while you're playing around you'll be castrated. Now you'll tell me, "That's not allowed!" What? Is what *you're* doing allowed, Hyllus?

Themes. The contrast between the final line of the preceding epigram and the blunt obscenity of this poem's opening words could hardly be greater. This epigram introduces a brief cluster of poems (**2.60–63**) on sexual themes, as well as a sequence offering commentary in the second person (**2.60–64**).

In its subject matter the epigram recalls **2.47** (where Gallus too seems to take pleasure in the "punishment") and **2.49** (where Martial indirectly imagines the pleasures of exacting it), while the name Hyllus brings us back to **2.51**. Elsewhere described as soft and effeminate and finding pleasure in being penetrated, the young Hyllus here is having an affair with a married woman; LaPenna 2000: 91 suggests that he might be her slave (see on 1 below). For the image of an effeminate male who enjoys both intercourse with women and being penetrated, see on **2.47** and **2.62**.

Traditional Roman folk justice provided various kinds of harsh punishments for an adulterer caught in the act. Val. Max. 6.1.13 and Hor. *Sat.* 1.2 provide an overview ranging from extortion to anal rape to castration to murder; see **2.83** for yet another punishment. Juv. 10.314–317 ("exigit autem / interdum ille dolor *plus quam lex ulla dolori / concessit:* necat hic ferro, secat ille cruentis / verberibus, quosdam moechos et mugilis intrat") suggests that while such extreme punishments went beyond what the law allowed, they were sometimes carried out nonetheless.

Structure.   The opening line lays out the situation with notable clarity, its obscenity (*futuis*) resolutely bringing home the point that Hyllus is engaging in an adulterous affair. The subordinate clause in the second line introduces the detail upon which the rest of the epigram is built: Hyllus is willing to suffer the *supplicium puerile*. The second couplet complicates the scenario (*castrabere*) and ends on a note not of resolution but of challenge, marked by the pointed repetition of the key verb *licet*. The pace is lively throughout: consider the obscenity *futuis,* the exclamation *vae tibi,* the brief dialogue introduced with *iam mihi dices,* and the pointed rhetorical questions at the end. For the structural device of positioning the vocative (*Hylle*) in the second half of the first and last lines respectively, see on **2.10**.

1: With Collesso, Izaac, Norcio, Ceronetti, Scandola, and LaPenna 2000: 91, I take *armati tribuni* to be a periphrasis for *tribuni militaris* or *tribuni militum* (as opposed to *tribuni plebis*). Ker, Shackleton Bailey, and Barié and Schindler translate the phrase literally ("an armed tribune"). In any case, the adjective may be anticipating the type of punishment the tribune will exact.

Instead of the obscene *futuis,* MSS of family α read the metrically equivalent *tractas* (Ker euphemizes in his own way: "you have relations with"). See on **2.31.1** for the tendency of family α to present euphemizing emendations and Lindsay's theory of an ancient edition *in usum elegantiorum*.

For *Hyllus* see on **2.51.2**. Garrido-Hory 1981: 59 identifies the character of the present epigram as a slave, as also in 4.7 and 9.25; but note that the name seems to refer to a free man in **2.51**.

2: The text as given above is universally printed by modern editors but is not transmitted in this form by any of the extant MSS, which offer unsatisfying readings: *supplicium tantum dum* (or *nec* or *num*), *puer Hylle* (*hille* or *ille*), *times*. The reading *puerile* (easily corrupted into *puer ille* or *puer Hylle*) represents one of the few emendations by Italian humanists that have won acceptance among modern editors; see also *versibus* in **2.praef**.

The phrase *supplicium puerile* (which echoes *puer Hylle* in the preceding line: Schmidt 1989: 66) reflects an association of anal intercourse with *pueri* that is amply attested in both Greek and Roman sources; see Williams 1999: 50–51, 185–188. Martial himself describes anal intercourse with a woman as *illud puerile* (9.67.3) and speaks of the anus and anal intercourse as *mascula nomina* (11.43.11); a Plautine joke refers to *puerile officium* (*Cist.* 657: cf. Adams 1982: 193), and Apuleius speaks of *puerile corollarium* (*Met.* 3.20). In *A.P.* 5.49 φιλόπαις is the equivalent of *pedico* just as γυναικομανής is of *fututor* and φιλυβριστής of *irrumator;* anal intercourse with a female is described as ἀρσενόπαις Κύπρις in *A.P.* 5.54 and as τὰ παιδικὰ κέρδη in *A.P.* 6.17. Ceronetti misinterprets Martial's *supplicium puerile* to refer to the kind of punishment one gives small children, a slap on the wrist as in Tac. *Ann.* 5.9 ("posse se puerili verbere moneri"). But, as Shackleton Bailey and Barié and Schindler observe, the parallels with **2.47** and **2.49** make the reference unmistakable.

3 *ludis:* For the sexual overtones of this verb, and of *iocari,* see Adams 1982: 161–163.

3 *castrabere:* For the ending in *-re*, here metrically necessary, see on **2.55.2**.

3–4 *iam mihi dices / "non licet hoc":* Probably in A.D. 82–83 (perhaps hence Martial's *iam*), Domitian issued a prohibition against castration: compare 5.2, 6.2 with Grewing, 9.5, 9.7; Stat. *Silv.* 4.3.13–15; Suet. *Dom.* 7.1; Dio 67.2.3; Philostr. *Vit. Apoll.* 6.42; Amm. Marc. 18.4.5; Grelle 1980. The fact that it was renewed by later emperors (Dio 68.2.4 [Nerva]; D. 48.8.4.2 [Hadrian]; cf. Just. *Novell.* 142) suggests that the prohibition was as ineffective as Domitian's revival of the *lex Julia de adulteriis.*

For the technique of anticipating or imagining an interlocutor's response or comment with a verb of saying (*dices, inquis, respondes*), see on **2.21.2**; the formula *iam dices* is found again at **2.63.4** ("'non amo' iam dices") and 7.86.11 ("iam dices mihi 'vapulet vocator'").

4 *tu quod facis, Hylle, licet?* By engaging in sexual relations with the wife of a Roman citizen, Hyllus is committing *adulterium,* among sexual offences perhaps the most threatening to a patriarchal society (Edwards 1993: 34–62, Williams 1999: 113–119). With the Augustan *lex Julia de adulteriis coercendis,* for which see especially Raditsa 1980, *adulterium* became an offense capable of being prosecuted in the public courts; for Domitian's revival of the law see Mart. 5.75, 6.2, 6.4, 6.7, 6.22, 6.45, 6.91, and Grelle 1980. Martial's allusions to *adulterium,* which most often take the form of a condemnation of a *moecha* or *adultera,* are too numerous to be listed here; in Book II alone see **2.17, 2.25, 2.31, 2.34, 2.39, 2.47, 2.49, 2.56, 2.83.**

For the final question, unanswered and pointed, compare the end of **2.62** ("cui praestas, culum quod, Labiene, pilas?"), **2.72** ("quid quod habet testes, Postume, Caecilius?"), and **2.89** ("vitium, dic mihi, cuius habes?"). Otherwise, pointed questions at the end of epigrams are followed by an answer of one kind or another: see **2.7, 2.11, 2.28–29, 2.31, 2.39.**

2.61

Cum tibi vernarent dubia lanugine malae,
   lambebat medios improba lingua viros.
postquam triste caput fastidia vispillonum
   et miseri meruit taedia carnificis,
uteris ore aliter nimiaque aerugine captus   5
   adlatras nomen quod tibi cumque datur.
haereat inguinibus potius tam noxia lingua:
   nam cum fellaret, purior illa fuit.

While your cheeks were still in their spring, covered with their tentative down, your shameless tongue licked men's groins. Now that your grim head has earned the disgust of the paupers' undertakers and the aversion of the wretched executioner, you use your mouth in other ways: overcome with maliciousness, you snarl at whatever name is given to you. May so destructive a tongue bury itself instead in other people's groins: when it was sucking dick, it was actually cleaner.

Themes.   The sexual thematic continues. After a first line whose gentle evocation of youthful beauty stands in contrast with the preceding poem's opening obscenity (*futuis,* **2.60.1**) and at the same time echoes its allusion to the *puer* Hyllus, we are then bluntly told of an unnamed boy's penchant for fellatio, which complements Hyllus' predilection for being anally penetrated. The point of this epigram is particularly sharp and lent special emphasis by the paradoxical final line: as filthy as this man's mouth was when he was young, it is much worse now that he is in the habit of indiscriminately "bad-mouthing" others (perhaps prosecuting in the law courts: see on 6 below).

The blending of oral sex and "bad-mouthing," together with a focus on the *lingua,* recurs in 7.24, where someone who attempts by his mischievous words to disrupt Martial's friendship with Juvenal receives this curse: "hoc tibi pro meritis et talibus imprecor ausis, / ut facias illud quod, puto, lingua, facis" (7–8). Elsewhere Martial represents a figure comparable to the figure of the present epigram as nasty but pitiable (5.28). In 7.10 Martial again makes the point that sexual misdeeds, no matter how much they may be worthy of ridicule, are in the end less grave than other social offenses.

To be sure, Martial himself constantly engages in gossip, but such examples as **2.4**, **2.17**, or **2.20** presumably do not qualify as venomous or "barking" talk because they use pseudonyms or do not refer to real people. In this regard a somewhat unusual feature of the present epigram is worth noting: the addressee, who is also the subject of the poem, remains unnamed. Usually when there is no vocative addressee, the epigram describes some other person or thing, as in **2.57**. By directly addressing but refusing to name this malicious gossip even with a pseudonym, it is as if Martial is showing that he will not stoop to his level.

Structure.   The first three couplets lay out the situation, both past and present, and the final couplet offers commentary. There is also a crescendo effect. In the first couplet we read that when this man was young (1) he practiced fellatio (2), but his current behavior is spread out over two couplets: now that he is a repulsive old man (3–4) he speaks badly of others (5–6). There is a progression too from the opening line's poetic image for youth, to a blunt but still euphemistic reference to fellatio (*lambebat medios improba lingua viros*), to an equally blunt allusion to the man's old age, to the direct *fellaret* in the final paradoxical line.

1 *cum tibi vernarent dubia lanugine malae:* This line presents a poetic image for that period of male adolescence sometimes called the *flos aetatis* (Williams 1999: 77), when the full beard has not yet grown, but a fuzz has begun to make itself known. Zingerle 1877: 23 detects Ovidian reminiscences in the phrase, comparing *Met.* 9.398 ("paene puer dubiaque tegens lanugine malas") and 13.754 ("signarat teneras dubia lanugine malas"), and indeed a search of the PHI disk for the combination of *dubia lanugine* and *malas* brings up only these passages. But there may also be some Virgilian influence: compare the hexameter clausulae "tenera lanugine mala" (V. *Ecl.* 2.51) and "prima lanugine malas" (V. *Aen.* 10.324; Wagner 1880: 8). Friedlaender also points to Lucr. 5.889: "et molli vestit lanugine malas." For the metaphorical use of *vernare,* compare Prop. 4.5.59: "dum vernat sanguis, dum rugis integer annus."

Instead of *dubia,* which the *variorum* commentary glosses as "barely perceptible to the eye" ("quae vix oculis percipitur"), the MSS of family β read *tenera,* yielding a phrase closely reminiscent of the Virgilian "tenera lanugine mala" (V. *Ecl.* 2.51). Lindsay 1903a: 24 identifies this as an example of ancient variants between which "the choice is often extremely uncertain" (see also **2.30.3, 2.40.2, 2.46.10**), and yet all modern editors print *dubia.* Indeed, Schmid 1984: 426 sees *tenera* as one among several examples of a late-antique editor's conscious intervention in the text ("erläuternde, verdeutlichende, umschreibende oder stilistisch normalisierende Kleininterpolation").

2 lambebat medios ... viros: For the blunt but euphemistic expression, compare 3.81.2 ("haec debet medios lambere lingua viros"), 7.67.15 ("medias vorat puellas"), 11.61.5 ("mediumque mavult basiare quam summum"); Catull. 80.6 ("medii tenta vorare viri"); *Priap.* 74 ("Per medios ibit pueros mediasque puellas / mentula, barbatis non nisi summa petet"). Auson. *Epigr.* 66.1 ("lambere cum vellet mediorum membra virorum") may well be inspired by Martial's phrase.

3–4: For ridicule of old men, see also 4.78, 10.83, and 11.81 with Kay. For the combination of *vispillones* or *vespillones* (those who bury the poor who cannot pay for their own funerals: 1.30, 1.47) and *carnifices* (public executioners) as embodiments of disreputable figures, compare Juv. 8.175, where we read that among the low types frequenting a tavern are *carnifices* and *fabri sandapilarum* (for *sandapilae* see on **2.81.2**). Since sexual contact with such figures was considered debasing in the extreme (Catull. 59.4–5, 97.11–12; cf. Mart. 3.93.15, *bustuaria moecha*), this remark is particularly insulting: not even *they* are interested in the addressee's services.

For the spondaic line and the four-syllable final word *vispillonum,* see on **2.29.5**.

For *caput* in the context of allusions to oral sexual practices, see on **2.42.2**.

5–6: Criticism of a malicious gossip is found also in 1.89, 3.28, 3.63, 5.61. For *aerugo,* literally "copper rust," or verdigris, as a metaphor for a malevolent attitude, see also 10.33.5 ("viridi tinctos aerugine versus"); Hor. *Sat.* 1.4.101, *A.P.* 330.

The verb *adlatrare* (literally, "to bark toward") is attested only in its transferred sense: see Colum. 1.praef.9 ("sed ne caninum quidem, sicut dixere veteres, studium praestantius locupletissimum quemque adlatrandi . . ."), and compare Lact. *Div. inst.* 6.18.26 (Cicero is guilty of *canina eloquentia*). Consider also the joke reported by Cic. *De orat.* 2.220 and Quint. *Inst.* 6.3.81: "Quid latras?—Furem video." Martial uses *adlatrare* on one other occasion, and it is in a similar context: "adlatres licet usque nos et usque / et gannitibus improbis lacessas" (5.60.1–2).

6 *nomen quod tibi cumque datur:* In other words, any name that comes his way he will gladly besmirch. The anonymous reader for Oxford University Press raises the more specific possibility that this man has become a *delator*, that is, indiscriminately prosecutes anyone whose name is given to him (by an enemy?).

7 *baereat inguinibus:* The phrase is reminiscent of Seneca's scandalized description of Hostius Quadra: "cum caput merserat inguinibusque alienis obhaeserat" (*N.Q.* 1.16.4).

7 *tam noxia lingua:* For the image of the destructive or evil tongue, compare Catull. 7.12 (*mala lingua*), Ov. *Am.* 1.14.42 (*invida lingua*) with Galán Vioque ad 7.24.2 (*perfida lingua*).

8 *cum fellaret, purior illa fuit:* In Roman terms this is a marked paradox, since fellatio and cunnilinctus were said to befoul the mouth or tongue or, precisely, to make one's mouth *impurum:* compare **2.50**, **2.70**, 3.75, 6.50, 9.63, 11.61 with Kay ad loc., 11.95, 14.70; and see Adams 1982: 199, 213; Richlin 1992: 26–30; Williams 1999: 197–203. For final paradoxes, see on **2.12.4**.

The demonstrative force of *illa* is quite weak here, hinting at the origins of the Romance personal pronouns (*elle, ella*).

2.62

Quod pectus, quod crura tibi, quod bracchia vellis,
   quod cincta est brevibus mentula tonsa pilis:
hoc praestas, Labiene, tuae—quis nescit?—amicae.
   cui praestas, culum quod, Labiene, pilas?

You pluck your chest, your legs, and your arms, and your dick has a neatly trimmed fringe of hairs around it. You do all this, Labienus, for your girlfriend: who doesn't know that? But for whom, Labienus, do you depilate your asshole?

Themes. The focus remains on masculine sexuality, and corresponding to the opening image of the man's fuzzy cheeks when he was a boy in **2.61.1** is this epigram's opening description of depilation, a practice last mentioned in **2.36**. The crude tone of *fellaret* in the final couplet of **2.61** is continued with the open obscenity *mentula* in this epigram's opening couplet.

The poem ends in a manner reminiscent of **2.28**: in both cases a lead-ing question is left unanswered, but the implication of less than fully mascu-line behavior is clear. There, Sextillus is exposed as a *fellator* and *cunnilingus;* here, Labienus is revealed to be a *pathicus.* For the exposure technique compare 1.24, 1.96, 7.62, 9.27, 9.47, 11.88; and see Obermayer 1998: 237–243, Williams 1999: 188–189. Ausonius' imitation of this poem brings out its implications in a brutally explicit way. The addressee depilates his genital region for the sake of female prostitutes (*lupae*), and the reason he depilates his anal region is explained in unmistakable terms: "you are a woman be-hind, a man in front" (*Epigr.* 93.6: "tergo femina, pube vir es").

Labienus disregards Ovid's advice to men interested in attracting women: you should trim your hair, beard, nose hairs, and fingernails and see to it that neither your breath nor your underarms smell, but do not artificially curl your hair or depilate your legs (*Ars am.* 1.505–524). That Labienus does so in order to gratify his girlfriend gives us an interesting glimpse into women's possible tastes or, rather, into men's ideas about women's tastes; compare Sen. *Contr.* 2.1.6: "incedentem ut feminis placeat femina mollius," with Williams 1999: 142–153. The final line, framed as an innocent question, makes the direct insinuation that Labienus has a male sexual partner who penetrates him. But since there is no hint that Labienus' relationship with his *amica* is ungenuine or a pretense (though see on 3 below), we once again encounter the assumption that such a combination of sexual tastes is neither peculiar nor anomalous; see also **2.47**, **2.60**. Indeed, allusions to men like Labienus recur in the ancient sources in such a way as to imply that they were a normal feature of the landscape, even if a minority: see Ov. *Ars am.* 3.437–438 ("femina quid faciat, cum sit vir levior ipsa, / forsitan et plures possit habere viros?"), *Am.* 1.8.68; Williams 1999: 203–209.

Structure.   The first two lines describe Labienus' depilatory practices, and the third line specifies his aim. There is a crescendo effect: a tripartite first line, each segment containing *quod* and a body part, is followed by a longer *quod*-clause that occupies the whole of the second verse (for the accumula-tion of detail by means of subordinate clauses, see on **2.11**, and for the tech-nique of opening with a *quod*-clause, see on **2.10.1**) and finally the main clause in the third verse. The fourth verse, beginning with an echo of the immediately preceding line (*hoc praestas ~ cui praestas*) and echoing in its second half the vocative *Labiene* found in the first half of the preceding line, brings the point home with a challenging question.

1 *pectus:* Other allusions to men who depilate their chests are hard to find, but for the hairy chest as potent symbol of masculinity see **2.36.5–6**.

1 *crura:* Specifically, the shins (Shackleton Bailey), or, via synecdoche, the legs as a whole (most other translators). Martial explicitly refers to men's depilation of their shins or legs at 5.61.6 (see Howell ad loc.), 9.27.4, 10.65, 12.38 (*crure glaber*), implicitly in **2.36** and 6.56.

1 *bracchia:* For depilation of the arms, see on **2.29.5–6**.

2 *cincta est brevibus mentula tonsa pilis:* Literally, "your shorn dick is encircled by short hairs." Being a coarse obscenity, *mentula* effects a shift in tone. Martial again refers to a man who depilates his pubic region at 9.27.1–2: "cum depilatos, Chreste, coleos portes / et vulturino mentulam parem collo" (cf. Pers. 4.35–36). In both cases the penis is described in humorous terms using animal imagery: here a shorn sheep (cf. *OLD* s.v. *tondere* 2), there a vulture's neck.

3 *Labiene:* Martial uses the name several times, but with little thematic coherence. In 5.49 he is ridiculed for his baldness; in 7.66 he complains about how little he has inherited from a friend; in 12.16 and 12.33 he has purchased some slave boys as sexual partners.

3 *quis nescit?* It is just possible that the question is ironic: Labienus' actions are all a farce and everyone sees through them; that is, he has no *amica* (Williams 1999: 130 with n. 18, LaPenna 2000: 109). Yet some men did actually depilate in order to please women, and even if we read the epigram ironically, the cultural implications remain the same, insofar as Labienus expected to be able to convince others that he had an *amica* for whom he depilated.

3 *amicae:* See on **2.34.5**.

4: For the technique of ending with a pointed question, see on **2.60.4**. For *culus,* see on **2.51.2**, and for the depilation of the anal region as the sign of a *pathicus,* see 6.56 and 9.27.3 with Obermayer 1998: 117–119.

2.63

Sola tibi fuerant sestertia, Miliche, centum,
    quae tulit e Sacra Leda redempta Via.
Miliche, luxuria est si tanti dives amares.
    "non amo," iam dices. haec quoque luxuria est.

You only had a hundred thousand sesterces, Milichus, and you gave it all to buy Leda from the Sacra Via. Milichus, it would be an extravagance to spend so much on love even if you were rich. But now you'll say, "I don't love her!" This, too, is an extravagance.

Themes. The satiric focus on sexual experiences continues in yet another poem directly addressing its target, as do **2.60**, **2.61**, and **2.62**; we move from Labienus and his unnamed *amica* in the final couplet of **2.62** to Milichus and Leda in the opening couplet of the present epigram. The image of a man who has only a small amount of money but who spends it to satisfy his sexual desires, and the criticism this arouses, recall **2.51**; see also **2.34**, 4.9, 4.28, 8.5, 9.2; LaPenna 2000: 97. The question is whether Milichus spends the money for encounters with Leda in a brothel in the Sacra Via (Norcio) or whether he buys her outright (Friedlaender and others). The latter seems much more likely in view of the verb *redempta* and the high price cited: 100,000 sesterces is a steep but not unheard-of price to pay for a slave, but an impossibly high amount to have spent on visits to a prostitute. See further on 1 and 2 below.

Structure. The opening line quickly paints a familiar portrait—Milichus has a specific and fairly limited amount of money—and the second line tells us that he has spent it all on a sexual partner. The second couplet then meditates on what Milichus has done, adding an unexpected twist ("non amo"), which then prompts the final comment. The sentences become increasingly brief, progressing from the opening two-line sentence with relative clause (1–2), to a one-line conditional sentence (3), to two simple sentences in asyndeton, each occupying a half-line (4). Also of note is the chiastic arrangement of the key concepts of *amor* and *luxuria* in the final couplet ("Miliche, *luxuria* est si tanti dives *amares*. / 'non *amo*' iam dices: haec quoque *luxuria* est") and the framing technique in the same couplet (*Miliche, luxuria est ~ haec quoque luxuria est*).

   1 *fuerant:* For the pluperfect see on **2.41.3**.
   1 *sestertia ... centum:* The sum of 100,000 sesterces (see on **2.30.1** for the ellipsis of *millia*) is mentioned several times by Martial as the price of a desirable slave: 1.58.1, 3.62.1, 7.10.3, 11.70.1. For legal purposes, slaves were usually assumed to have the value of 2,000 sesterces, but actually attested prices range from 725 to 700,000 sesterces (Kay ad 11.38.1). Plin. *N.H.* 7.129 cites the record sum of 50,000,000 sesterces paid for a eunuch, an exorbitant price indeed.
   1 *Miliche:* The name occurs only here in Martial.
   2 *e Sacra Leda redempta Via:* The Sacra Via was an important street in the center of Rome, running through the Forum from the Arch of Titus to the Temple of Saturn; here triumphal processions made their way to the Capitoline. See Steinby 1993–2000: s.v., with detailed discussion of the debate over the precise length and path of the street. A large structure from the Republican period located northwest of the Arch of Titus has been iden-

tified as a *lupanar*, or brothel, and if the identification is correct, Martial might be alluding to this building in particular (Castagnoli 1993: 110). On the other hand, a porticus was later built over this structure, and it is possible that this had taken place by Martial's day.

Martial does use the verb *redimere* elsewhere to refer to payment for a sexual encounter (9.32.3: "hanc volo quam redimit totam denarius alter"), but **2.34.1** ("cum placeat Phileros tota tibi dote redemptus") reminds us of the literal sense of purchasing outright, which is clearly at stake here; so too Garrido-Hory 1981: 108. A price of 100,000 sesterces would be impossibly high for a sexual encounter. The next highest figure cited in Martial is the 10,000 sesterces mentioned in 4.28 and 11.27 as gifts to a sexual partner; see on **2.53.7** for the significantly lower prices for encounters with prostitutes.

The name *Leda* appears again at 3.82.3, 4.4.9, and 11.61.4, designating a prostitute; in 11.71 she is a woman married to an impotent old man. The name makes ironic reference to the mythic figure to whom Zeus came in the form of a swan and who bore Helen, Clytemnestra, and the Dioscuri.

3 luxuria: Extravagance was always a ready topic for Romans wishing either to moralize in general or to attack a specific individual; consider Valerius Maximus' chapter *De luxuria et libidine* (9.1). Other epigrams on men who lead a luxurious lifestyle include 1.37, **2.16**, **2.29**, **2.43**, 11.11, 11.70, 12.17; the theme is not characteristic of Greek epigram (Prinz 1911: 79). At 11.70.11 Martial claims that to buy slave boys at the price mentioned here (100,000 sesterces each) is *luxuria,* and even more so to sell them for that price!

3 si tanti . . . amares: A rare but easily understandable use of the genitive of price or value, usually found with verbs signifying the act of evaluation (e.g., *aestimo, facio*); KS 2.1.457–460. Compare Front. *Amic.* 2.7.19, "quanti sperabit."

4 "non amo" iam dices: For the correption of the final vowel in *amo*, see on **2.9.2**. For the formula *iam dices,* see on **2.60.3–4**.

2.64

Dum modo causidicum, dum te modo rhetora fingis
    et non decernis, Laure, quid esse velis,
Peleos et Priami transit et Nestoris aetas
    et fuerat serum iam tibi desinere.
incipe, tres uno perierunt rhetores anno,   5
    si quid habes animi, si quid in arte vales.

si schola damnatur, fora litibus omnia fervent,
    ipse potest fieri Marsua causidicus.
heia age, rumpe moras! quo te sperabimus usque?
    dum quid sis dubitas, iam potes esse nihil.   10

While you are training sometimes to be a courtroom lawyer, sometimes to be a teacher of rhetoric, and you can't figure out which
one you want to be, Laurus, the lifetime of a Peleus, a Priam, or a
Nestor has gone by, and by now it would be late for you to retire.
Get moving—three rhetoricians have passed away in just one year!—
if you have any resolve, if you have any ability at all in the craft. If
you reject the schools, the fora are all buzzing with court cases, and
Marsyas himself could become a courtroom lawyer. Come on,
enough delaying! How long will you keep us hoping? While you
take your time deciding what to be, you could at any moment be
nothing.

Themes.   We leave the realm of the sexual, but ironic second-person commentary on a specific man's behavior continues. Laurus is criticized for his
inability to decide between the two related professions of teacher of rhetoric and courtroom pleader. The epigram sarcastically retools the traditional
themes *carpe diem* and *memento mori,* applying them to an individual rather
than offering them as a generic encouragement to live life fully, as in **2.59**.
Here our mortal condition becomes an implement used to prod Laurus into
action. Prinz 1911: 82 detects a close relationship to Epictetus *Diss.* 3.15.5,
and the theme is central to Seneca's *De brevitate vitae* (cf. 3.5: "quam serum
est tunc vivere incipere, cum desinendum est").

    Characteristic is the concreteness achieved by the use of personal names
to make hyperbolic statements: three mythic figures to emphasize the
passage of time, and a statue's name to emphasize the frenzied activity in
the fora. Indeed, the language of the epigram as a whole creates an urgent
tone: observe the imperatives (*incipe; rumpe moras*), the hyperbolic imagery in 3 and 8, the challenging conditions (*si quid habes animi; si quid
in arte vales*), and the flattering but pressing question (*quo te sperabimus
usque?*).

Structure.   The first two couplets set the stage clearly, naming the principal character. The rest of the poem presents Martial's commentary, beginning with the strong imperative *incipe* (5). A sudden exclamation (*heia age,
rumpe moras!*) followed by an ironically flattering question leads to the wry
point.

1: A *causidicus* is one who exercises his rhetorical knowledge by plead-ing cases (*causas dicere*) in the courtroom; a *rhetor* teaches the art in itself. Juv. 7.105–177 includes precisely these two professions among those who must lead an ostentatious life in order to attract customers. The contrast between *causidicus* and *rhetor* is reflected below in that between *fora* and *schola* (7).

1 *te ... fingis:* Most likely in the sense "you are shaping yourself," that is, training yourself (cf. V. *Aen.* 8.365: "te quoque dignum finge deo" with *OLD* s.v. *fingere* 5); so Ker, Shackleton Bailey, Izaac, Ceronetti, Scandola. Others (Norcio, Barié and Schindler) understand *fingis* in the sense "to visu-alize, imagine" (*OLD* s.v. 8).

2 *Laure:* The name recurs in only one other epigram, where he is like-wise an aging man, said to have been an avid ball player when young (10.86). Readers of the tenth book, whose first edition was published about ten years after Book II, will surely not recall the name from this epigram; still, it may be that Martial resurrected the pseudonym for an aging man, or just possibly that Laurus was a real person.

3: Martial cites three mythological figures associated with the Trojan War cycle as archetypical long-lived men: Achilles' father, Peleus; the Tro-jan king Priam; and the Greek hero Nestor (the last, not coincidentally, known for his rhetorical abilities from *Il.* 1.249 onward). See Otto 1890: 242, Sonny 1896: 71, Sutphen 1901: 253, Szelinski 1904: 155 for numerous appearances of *Nestor* as the archetype of the old man in poets ranging from Tibullus to Juvenal; in Martial alone, see 4.1, 5.8.5, 6.70.12 with Grewing, 7.96.7, 8.2.7, 8.6.9, 8.64.14, 10.24.11, 10.38.14, 13.117.1. For *Priam*, see Otto 1890: 287, Sonny 1896: 74, Sutphin 1901: 364, Szelinski 1904: 316; in Martial, see 5.58.4, 6.70.12 with Grewing, 6.71.3, 8.64.14. Martial cites the two together again at 5.58.5, 6.70.12, 8.64.13, 10.67.1, 4. The only other attestation of *Peleus* as a symbol of old age I have been able to find is Juv. 10.256, where, immedi-ately after a description of Nestor, he is cited along with Priam and Laertes as examples of those who have lived to see their sons die. Nestor and Priam are cited together at Juv. 6.326 and Stat. *Silv.* 3.4.104; Nestor and Tithonus at Prop. 2.25.10; Nestor, Priam, and Tithonus at *Priap.* 76.4.

The contraction of *transiit* to *transīt*, here metrically useful, is of a type frequently found throughout Latin literature. In Martial alone, see *Sp.*16.1, 3.75.1, 10.48.2, 10.75.3, 10.77.2, 10.86.4, 10.90.8, 11.7.4, 11.25.2, 11.38.1, 11.82.3.

4 *et fuerat serum:* The *variorum* commentary humorously explains: "Unless you're thinking of pleading courtroom cases in the underworld" ("nisi cogites de causis apud inferos agendis"). For the indicative *fuerat* standing for a subjunctive, see on 2.1.1 (*poteras*).

6 *si quid habes animi, si quid in arte vales:* A challenging double condition, divided neatly between the two halves of the pentameter; compare **2.53.9**: "haec tibi si vis est, si mentis tanta potestas."

7 *schola:* A Greek borrowing, originally denoting "an exposition by a teacher of his views on a subject" and then "a place or establishment in which a teacher expounds his views," that is, a school—often, as here, specifically a school of rhetoric (*OLD* s.v.).

7 *fora litibus omnia fervent:* Perhaps this phrase echoes Sen. *Dial.* 6.26.4: "fora litibus strepere" (Fletcher 1983: 406–407). The fora of Rome and of other Italian cities and towns were centers not only of trade but also of legal business—hence the label *genus forense* for courtroom oratory and the use of *forum* as a metonymy for its practice. See 1.76.12, 3.38.3–4, 5.20.6–7 ("nec litis tetricas forumque triste / nossemus"), 7.28.5, 7.64.4, 12.praef., 14.136 ("nec fora sunt nobis nec sunt vadimonia nota"); Stat. *Silv.* 4.9.45. Martial's phrase *fora omnia* reminds us that various fora existed in the Rome of his day: the ancient *forum Romanum* and the three imperial fora of Julius Caesar, Augustus, and Vespasian. See also 7.65 (*fora tria*), 10.51 (*fora iuncta quater*), and Citroni ad 1.2.8 (*Palladium forum*).

8: Even a lifeless statue could learn to be a lawyer simply by hanging around the fora. A statue of Marsyas, the satyr flayed alive by Apollo after having challenged him to, and lost, a musical contest, was located in the Forum Romanum (in the western part of the Comitium near the praetorian tribunal) and was a meeting place for lawyers and businessmen: see Hor. *Sat.* 1.6.120, Juv. 9.2; Platner 1929, Richardson 1992, and Steinby 1993–2000: s.v. *statua Marsyae*.

The meter requires the Latinized nominative singular *Marsua* without the final *-s*, whereas in 10.62.9 we find the Greek form *Marsyas*. As for the internal vowel, upsilon was originally represented by Latin *u*, but by Cicero's day the practice of using the borrowed *y* had taken hold (KS 1.10–11). Yet uniformity was never achieved, and we consequently find both *Marsua(s)* and *Marsyas* in Latin texts.

9 *heia age, rumpe moras:* This is the only occurrence of the interjection *heia (age)* in Martial; exclamatory *age* is found again at 8.67.5 and 10.87.1. See on **2.1.12** for other interjections. Although *(h)eia age* is attested elsewhere (Colum. 10.68, Stat. *Silv.* 1.2.266), as is *rumpe moras* (V. *Geo.* 3.42–43, *Aen.* 9.13, Ov. *Met.* 15.583, Lucan 2.525, Sil. Ital. 8.214–215, Plin. *Epist.* 5.10.2), the phrase *heia age, rumpe moras* is found only here and at V. *Aen.* 4.569: a Virgilian echo and correspondingly bathetic effect are thus quite likely.

10 *esse nihil:* Playing off *quid sis,* this is a slightly peculiar way of referring to death, though compare *CIL* 6.26003: "n[i]l sumus et fuimus mortales; respice, lector / in nihil ab nihilo quam cito recidimus."

2.65

Cur tristiorem cernimus Saleianum?
"an causa levis est?" inquis. "extuli uxorem."
o grande fati crimen! o gravem casum!
illa, illa dives mortua est Secundilla,
centena decies quae tibi dedit dotis?   5
nollem accidisset hoc tibi, Saleiane.

Why do we see Saleianus so dejected? "Do you think there's no good reason?" you say. "I've buried my wife." O grievous crime of fate! O grim misfortune! That woman, the wealthy Secundilla, is dead, the one who gave you a million in dowry? I wish this hadn't happened to you, Saleianus.

Themes. A fairly long string of epigrams in elegiac couplets (**2.58–64**) is broken by a poem in choliambs, and the second-person address of the previous five epigrams is replaced by a third-person reference to Saleianus in the first line, which, however, immediately shifts to a second-person address in the second line. The poem begins on a serious note, narrating Saleianus' loss and adding a pathetic exclamation (1–3), but the following sentence, beginning with the equally emotive repetition *illa, illa,* raises our suspicions, as does the information that his wife was rich. The final line, in all its ambiguity ("I wish you hadn't lost your wife" or "I wish your wife hadn't come with a million in dowry, which is now yours"), invites us to consider the possibility— raised more than once by Martial (5.37, 9.80, 10.16), Juvenal (6.136–141, 12.111–120), and elsewhere—that Saleianus had married Secundilla principally or exclusively for her money. As often, Martial's perspective on the phenomenon is not rigidly uniform: his own persona elsewhere implies that he would be interested in marrying an old woman if she were rich (10.8).

Burnikel 1980: 88–94 and Scherf 2001: 39 treat this epigram and **2.76** as a pair dedicated to the theme of successful and unsuccessful legacy hunting; see **2.57** and **2.74**, and perhaps also **2.18** and **2.53**, for other examples of paired but separated poems in Book II. Gerlach 1911: 17 praises the poem for its successful combination of ambiguity, irony, and ἀπροσδόκητον (an unexpected ending): "est carmen argutissimum et Martialis arte dignissimum."

Structure. There is an effective line-by-line progression. Saleianus is sad (1); he has lost his wife (2); Martial punctuates the news with an exclamation of sympathy (3); an equally emotive repetition introduces a line informing us of the wife's name and of the crucial fact that she was wealthy (4), where-upon the reader's suspicion may already be aroused; in the next line we are given the impressive figure of a million sesterces (5). Finally Martial makes another comment, this time laden with ambivalence, and the second occur-rence of Saleianus' name after the opening line effects a ring-composition structure (6). The technique of shifting from a third-person narrative (*Salei-anum*) to a second-person address (*inquis*) appears again in the immedi-ately following epigram (**2.66**); see on **2.16**.

1: How are we to interpret the comparative *tristiorem?* Ker, Norcio, and Izaac take it literally ("sadder" than usual); Shackleton Bailey, Ceronetti, Scandola, and Barié and Schindler take it more loosely ("rather sad").

The name *Saleianus* occurs only here in Martial.

3: The double expression of grief, each half introduced with *o*, is remi-niscent of Catullus's expostulation on the defunct *passer* in a poem likewise permeated with irony (3.16: "o factum male! o miselle passer!"). The phrase *o grande fati crimen* is noticeably elevated in tone, associated as it is with expressions of funerary lamentation: compare 10.61.2 ("crimine quam fati sexta peremit hiems") along with Lucan 9.143–144 ("quaecumque iniuria fati / abstulit hos artus, superis haec crimina dono"), *CLE* 1061.5 ("pro superum crimen, fatorum culpa nocentum"), and numerous epitaphs with phrases like *invidia fati* (*CLE* 386.4, 974.1, 1059.2, 1311.3, 2072.2).

4 *illa, illa dives . . . Secundilla:* Note the echoing effect created by the repeated *illa* at the beginning of the line and the diminutive *Secundilla* at its end. For the pronominal gemination, a mainly post-Augustan but always somewhat rare technique, compare 3.63.13 ("hoc est, hoc est homo, Cotile, bellus?"), [V.] *Catal.* 2.2 ("iste, iste rhetor"), Pers. 4.27, Lucan 1.203 and 2.317, Juv. 8.147–148 ("et ipse, / ipse rotam adstringit sufflamine mulio consul"); and see Wills 1996: 77–78.

The name *Secundilla,* like that of her husband, occurs only here in Martial.

5 *centena decies:* Literally, "ten times a hundred (sesterces)," mean-ing "ten times a hundred thousand (sesterces)," that is, a million. For *centena* in the sense *centena milia,* see on **2.30.1**; for the omission of *sestertium,* compare **2.44.7**.

5 *dotis:* Roman dowry regulations were complex in all respects, includ-ing the question as to what happened to the dowry if the wife predeceased the husband; see *RE* s.v. *dos,* Treggiari 1991. The husband did not automati-cally inherit his wife's dowry, and indeed, in some cases, it was returned to the wife's father (the so-called *dos profecticia*). But Martial is apparently referring to the type known as *dos adventicia,* which the husband might retain upon his wife's death.

6 *accidisset:* The double meaning is focused on this verb: either *mors uxoris* or *dos* might be its implied subject (Joepgen 1967: 84).

2.66

Unus de toto peccaverat orbe comarum
  anulus, incerta non bene fixus acu.
hoc facinus Lalage speculo, quo viderat, ulta est,
  et cecidit saevis icta Plecusa comis.
desine iam, Lalage, tristes ornare capillos,   5
  tangat et insanum nulla puella caput.
hoc salamandra notet vel saeva novacula nudet,
  ut digna speculo fiat imago tua.

A single curl out of her whole head of hair went astray: an unsteady hairpin had not kept it in place. Lalage took revenge for this crime using the mirror with which she had witnessed it. She struck Plecusa, who fell victim to the cruel locks. Stop adorning your grim hair, Lalage, and let no slave girl touch your frenzied head. Instead, may a salamander leave its mark or a harsh razor shave it, so that your reflection may be worthy of your mirror.

Themes.   The initial contrast with the previous epigram's subject is noteworthy: we move from the death of Saleianus' wife to Lalage's peevish outburst, described in humorously elevated language. Some have found the tone of this epigram to be unusually bitter, approaching a Juvenalian note (Prinz 1911: 46–47), but the intensity of Martial's final comment is mitigated by its openly comic nature: the worst he can wish for Lalage is that she become bald!

For the mistreatment of slaves in general, and women's abuse of their hairdressers in particular, see also Ov. *Am.* 1.11–12, 2.7–8, *Ars am.* 3.239–242; Sen. *Epist.* 47, *De ira* 3.32, 3.35, *De const. sap.* 4, *De clem.* 1.18, *Ben.* 3.22.3; Juv. 6.219–224. Juvenal's narrative of the punishment of an *ornatrix* named Psecas at 6.490–496 may have been influenced by the present epigram (Colton 1991: 263–266). According to Sullivan 1991: 164–165, Martial implies that women "are more prone to mistreat their hapless slaves," but we must also keep in mind the horrifying abuse of a slave by a man that is depicted in **2.82**. Note, too, that Seneca denounces men who lose their tempers when their hair falls out of place (*De brev. vit.* 12.3: "quomodo excandescunt si quid ex iuba sua decisum est, si quid extra ordinem iacuit, nisi omnia in anulos suos reciderunt").

Structure.   The epigram falls neatly into two halves: the first two couplets describe Lalage's outrageous behavior in a third-person narrative, where-upon the phrase *desine iam, Lalage,* marks a switch to the second-person address and commentary in the third and fourth couplets. For the switch from third to second person, also characterizing the preceding epigram, see on **2.16**. The bipartite structure is reflected in the verbs: the narrative contains past indicatives (*peccaverat, viderat, ulta est, cecidit*), while the subsequent reaction contains imperatives and subjunctives (*desine, tangat, notet, nudet, fiat*) expressing the poet's wishes. For the technique of ending with a curse or negative wish, see on **2.24.8**.

1 *peccaverat:* The ambiguities of this word are exploited here. At first glance, the verb seems to have its directly physical sense ("to fall out of its proper place"), for which compare 14.111.1–2 ("peccant / securae nimium sollicitaeque manus"), Manil. 1.189, Stat. *Theb.* 8.688 with *TLL* 10.886.1–9. But there is surely also an ironic exploitation of the sense "to commit a moral offence, do wrong" (*OLD* s.v. 3); compare *facinus* in 3.

2 *incerta non bene fixus acu:* For Roman hairpins, many of which have survived from antiquity, see 14.24 with Leary. The verb *figere* appears there, as also at Ov. *Ars am.* 3.240; the description of a petulant woman assaulting her *ornatrix* in the latter passage may well have exerted influence on Martial.

3 *facinus:* Based on the root of the verb *facere,* this noun originally meant a "deed" in a neutral or even positive sense (see Plaut. *Aul.* 587: "hoc est servi facinus frugi"), but it came to be used especially in the negative sense "misdeed, outrage, crime" (see 1.90.6: "pro facinus!"; 11.93.3: "o scelus, o magnum facinus crimenque deorum"). Here it is used ironically to describe the hairdresser's carelessness.

3 *Lalage:* The name ("babbling one") occurs only here in Martial but appears in a famous Horatian ode (*C.* 1.22; cf. *C.* 2.5) as well as at Prop. 4.7.45. Both here and at *Priap.* 4.3, where she dedicates tablets with ob-scene images to Priapus and asks to imitate them, a bathetically humorous effect is achieved by the use of this lovely name with its poetic associations.

3 *ulta est:* For the metrical pattern, see on **2.28.5**.

4 *cecidit saevis icta Plecusa comis:* The phrase has received vary-ing interpretations. Izaac, Scandola, Shackleton Bailey, and Barié and Schindler take *saevis comis* as dative, as at 12.90.4 ("ut caderet magno victima grata Iovi"); Shackleton Bailey thus translates, "Plecusa fell smitten, victim of the cruel tresses." Friedlaender and Ker take the phrase to be an ablative (Ker: "Plecusa, smitten, fell because of those cruel locks"), while Norcio argues that *saevis comis* stands for Lalage and takes it as ablative of means: Plecusa was struck *by* the cruel tresses ("colpita dalla inesorabile chioma"). Housman 1907: 265 cites with approval Markland's drastic measure of emending *saevis* to *sectis* and *comis* to *genis* (Plecusa fell smitten, her cheeks having been cut).

The name *Plecusa* is found only here in Latin literature. The participle of πλέκω, this is a fine example of a *redender Name,* or significant name (see on **2.34.1**): "the one who braids."

6 insanum: For the ambivalence of *sanus/insanus,* compare **2.16.2, 6**, and Sen. *De brev. vit.* 14.3: "isti qui per officia discursant, qui se aliosque inquietant, cum bene insanierint. . .." *Insanus* often functions as an insult: see Opelt 1965: index s.v.

7 salamandra: For the depilatory properties of a fluid emitted by the salamander, see Petr. *Sat.* 107.15, Plin. *N.H.* 10.188, 29.116. For baldness in women as especially unattractive, see **2.33** and 12.6, and compare Seneca's moralizing outrage in *Epist.* 95, on masculine women who suffer from masculine diseases like baldness and gout. This will have been one reason why some Roman women wore wigs, often made from northern European women's hair (5.68, 6.12, 12.23, 14.26–27).

8: The reflection of your face "will be smooth like the mirror, but with the further implication that the cruel mirror deserves an ugly reflection" (Shackleton Bailey).

2.67

Occurris quocumque loco mihi, Postume, clamas
    protinus, et prima est haec tua vox: "quid agis?"
hoc, si me decies una conveneris hora,
    dicis: habes, puto, tu, Postume, nil quod agas.

No matter where you run into me, Postumus, you shout right away—
and it's the first thing you say: "What's up?" Even if you meet me
ten times within an hour, this is what you say. It seems to me,
Postumus, that nothing's up with you.

Themes.   We move from a female stereotype (the woman who abuses her slave) to a male stereotype (the idle busybody) with a long history in Roman literature. A famous predecessor is Horace's bore (*Sat.* 1.9), who likewise greets the narrator with an eager "Quid agis?" (1.9.4). The figure appears again in Martial in 1.79 (also with a play on the verb *agere*) and 4.78; the theme is not characteristic of Greek epigram (Prinz 1911: 79). For the name *Postumus*, memorably describing a man with repulsive kisses in the earlier part of the book (**2.10, 2.12, 2.21–23**), see on 1 below.

The wordplay of this poem illustrates what Freud describes as a play on the "full" and "empty" senses of a word or expression. The example he offers (Freud 1992: 64–65 = 1960: 34) likewise plays on the literal sense of a standard greeting. "How's it going?" said the blind man to the cripple. "As you see," replied the cripple. ("Wie geht's?" fragte der Blinde den Lahmen. "Wie Sie sehen," antwortete der Lahme dem Blinden.) Other examples of the technique in Martial include 1.17, 1.67, 3.13.3–4 ("tamquam omnia cruda / attulerit; numquam sic ego crudus ero"), 3.90, 4.80, 5.61.14 ("res non uxoris, res agit iste tuas"), 9.87; see also Siedschlag 1977: 88.

The wordplay is cleverly rendered in English by Michie: "Whenever, Postumus, you meet me / You rush forward and loudly greet me / With 'How do you do?' Even if we meet / Ten times in an hour you still repeat / 'How do you do?' How does one do / As little with one's time as you?"

Structure. The narrative of Postumus' behavior occupies the first three verses as well as the beginning of the final verse (*dicis*), and the poet's subsequent commentary is brief and to the point, taking up merely the remainder of the last verse. The technique of placing a vocative of the addressee toward the end of the first line and again in the last line is quite common in Martial: see on the closely similar **2.10**, whose first and last lines contain the vocative in the same metrical position (*Postume, labro; Postume, dimidium*) as in the present epigram (*Postume, clamas; Postume, nil quod agas*).

1 *occurris quocumque loco mihi:* Compare the openings of 1.117 ("occurris quotiens, Luperce, nobis") and of 3.44 ("occurrit tibi nemo quod libenter").

1 *Postume:* Although here he is not associated with oral sex, we need hardly conclude that this is a character entirely distinct from the figure appearing earlier in the book, as many scholars do (Barwick 1958: 300; Burnikel 1980: 89: "nichts zu tun"). Burnikel argues further that the Postumus of **2.72** is yet another character and that Martial separated these two later poems so widely from the earlier Postumus poems precisely in order to distinguish among the characters. But we will see that **2.72** may imply that Postumus is a *fellator*. See also the discussion of the variant *Postume* at **2.18.8**.

2 *quid agis?* Literally, "What are you doing?" this is an ordinary form of greeting (Hor. *Sat.* 1.9.4, Plin. *Epist.* 3.20.11) more or less empty of its literal content, as are also Modern Greek τι κάνεις; and English "How do you do?"

4 *puto:* See on **2.41.2** for parenthetical *puto* and on **2.9.2** for the shortening of the final vowel.

4 *Postume:* For the vocative in the second half of the final pentameter, see on **2.18.8**.

4 *nil quod agas:* It may be that Postumus' constant repetition of the question gave it an increasingly literal sense, such that *quid agis?* came to convey insistent curiosity: no longer "How are you doing?" but "*What* are you doing?" In any case, the frequent repetition provokes the exasperated remark that Postumus himself must have nothing better to do than to waste his time plaguing people like Martial.

2.68

Quod te nomine iam tuo saluto,
quem regem et dominum prius vocabam,
ne me dixeris esse contumacem:
totis pillea sarcinis redemi.
reges et dominos habere debet   5
qui se non habet atque concupiscit
quod reges dominique concupiscunt.
servum si potes, Ole, non habere,
et regem potes, Ole, non habere.

Because I now call you by your own name, though I previously called you Lord and Master, do not say that I am arrogant. I have bought the cap of freedom with all of my possessions. Lords and masters are for those who do not master themselves, for those who desire what lords and masters desire. If you can do without a slave, Olus, you can do without a lord, Olus.

Themes. The meter switches to hendecasyllabics but the focus remains on masculine social relations and greeting practices in particular: Postumus greets Martial with *quid agis?* whereas Martial salutes Olus by name. The second line makes it clear that, as in **2.18**, **2.32**, and **2.53**, the poet is offering critical commentary on the patron-client relationship. Again he uses the imagery of slavery, now announcing that he has given up the stance of the abject client in his relationship with Olus. Nor is this the first time that Martial has raised the possibility of calling a patron by his name rather than using honorific terms of address: compare 1.112 ("Cum te non nossem, dominum regemque vocabam. / nunc bene te novi: iam mihi Priscus eris"). The thematic combination characterizing the present epigram—calling a patron by name and the representation of ending a patron-client relationship as "purchasing one's freedom"—reappears in a later piece (6.88).

A poem by Robert Louis Stevenson (*Collected Poems,* ed. Janet Adam Smith [London, 1950]) inspired by the present epigram ends on this grand note: "Those only who desire palatial things / Do bear the fetters and the frowns of Kings; / Set free thy slave; thou settest free thyself."

Structure. The opening two lines lay out the situation with Martial's usual clarity, and the remainder of the poem presents and varies the poet's reflections on the situation; a punctuating *sententia* is spread out over the final two lines. At the same time there is a subtle progression from the remark that Martial refers to his patron by name (*nomine tuo*) instead of calling him *rex* and *domine,* to a repetition of the key terms *rex* and *dominus,* to a final revelation of the patron's name. The epigram is also noteworthy for the recurrence of key words in the same or juxtaposed lines—*rex* and *dominus* (paired in 2, 4, 6; cf. *servus* and *rex* in 8–9), *habere* (4, 5), *concupere* (6, 7)—and for the close parallel between lines 8 and 9. For such repetitions, see on **2.4.**

1: For the technique of opening with a *quod*-clause, see on **2.10.1.**

2 regem et dominum: For the use of this collocation in the context of a patron-client relationship, see 1.112.1, 4.83.5, 10.10.5, 12.60.14, and Juv. 8.161; and compare, singly, *rex* at **2.18.8** and *dominus* at **2.32.8.** The phrase was used in other contexts as well, perhaps by analogy; compare 1.60.5: "nemorum dominum regemque"; Cic. *Verr.* 2.3.70: "aratorum dominum ac regem"; Terent. Maur. *De litt.* 1834: "rex et dominus prior ipse est." More generally, Sen. *Epist.* 3.1 observes that *domine* was a term of address useful to someone who had forgotten a name, and in 1.81 Martial plays with the ambiguity of the term: a son might call his father *domine,* but so also might a slave call his master.

4 totis pillea sarcinis redemi: The point is made more explicitly at 6.88.3–4: "quanti libertas constat mihi tanta, requiris? / centum quadrantes abstulit illa mihi." In other words, having given up being Olus' client, Martial will forfeit the *sportula* and will make up for the lost income by selling his possessions (Collesso; for *sarcinae* see on **2.11.8**). The *pilleus* or *pilleum* was a felt cap worn at the Saturnalia (11.6.4 with Kay ad loc.; 14.1) but also, more relevantly here, by newly manumitted slaves (*OLD* s.v. b); hence, the expression *ad pilleum vocare* means "to set free from slavery" (Liv. 24.32.9).

6 *qui se non habet:* For *habeo* in the sense "have under control," see *TLL* 6.2430.77–2432.32 (Ov. *Met.* 1.197: "qui fulmen, qui vos habeoque regoque"). Martial's phrase is influenced by philosophical and perhaps particularly Senecan language of self-control: compare Sen. *Epist.* 42.10 ("qui se habet nihil perdidit: sed quoto cuique habere se contigit?"). This pregnant sense of *se habere,* as opposed to its frequent usage with an adverb to mean "to be in a . . . state" (*TLL* 6.2451.59–2452.13), is otherwise barely attested.

8 *servum si potes, Ole, non habere:* The second person both refers to Olus and has a generic function: whoever can live without slaves or riches can live without the *dominus* from whom he might hope to obtain such things (Collesso). The name *Olus* occurs again in 3.48, 4.36, 7.10 (where he is the recipient of some of Martial's most memorable advice: see on **2.61**), and 10.54, without any obvious thematic continuity.

2.69

Invitum cenare foris te, Classice, dicis:
  si non mentiris, Classice, disperam.
ipse quoque ad cenam gaudebat Apicius ire;
  cum cenaret, erat tristior ille, domi.
si tamen invitus vadis, cur, Classice, vadis?   5
  "cogor" ais. verum est; cogitur et Selius.
en rogat ad cenam Melior te, Classice, rectam.
  grandia verba ubi sunt? si vir es, ecce, nega.

You say you eat out against your will, Classicus: if you're not lying I'll be damned, Classicus. After all, Apicius himself enjoyed going to dinner and was gloomier when he dined at home. But if you really go out against your will, Classicus, why do you go at all? You say, "I have no choice." That's true: Selius has no choice either. But look at this! Melior is inviting you to a formal dinner. Where are those grand words of yours now? If you're a man, come on: say no.

Themes.   Client-patron relations and invitations to dinner: this and the preceding epigram illustrate two of the central features of Martial's urban landscape. Classicus protests that he cannot avoid eating at other people's homes, but Martial reminds us that he could, after all, refuse, thus implying that

Classicus is little better than the memorable Selius. The exposure of the hollowness of a man's high-sounding words (*grandia verba*) by contrasting what he says (*dicis*) with what he does (*vadis*) is reminiscent of **2.43.1–2**: "haec sunt, haec sunt tua, Candide, κοινά, / quae tu *magniloquus* nocte dieque *sonas?*"

Structure. The opening couplet simultaneously lays out the situation and expresses the poet's attitude; the rest of the poem expands on the possibility raised in the second verse. The unusual number of repetitions of the addressee's name (*Classice* appears four times) adds a tone of urgency, as does the lively variation in syntax, especially in 5–8: pointed question; imagined response; three brief sentences in a single line; *en* and *ecce* in the final couplet. A crescendo effect is achieved by the positioning of complete sentences in the first line of each couplet throughout the poem and in the second line of its first two couplets, whereas the second lines of the final two couplets each break down into smaller syntactic units.

1 *cenare foris:* As opposed to *cenare domi:* see further on **2.11.10**. For *cenare* in the first line, see on **2.18.1**. The phrase appears in a similar context at **2.53.3**: "liber eris, cenare foris si, Maxime, nolis."

1 *Classice:* The name occurs in Martial only here, in **2.86**, and in 12.47; in the latter two he delivers an opinion on literary matters. This might be coincidence, but it is also just possible that Classicus was a real man.

2 *si non mentiris . . . dispeream:* Literally, "May I perish if you are not lying"; again at 1.39.8 (see Citroni ad loc.), 9.95b.4, 10.11.3, 11.90.8. The phrase is similar in sense to *ne valeam si . . .* (**2.5.1**); note the comparably bold opening of **2.53.1**: "vis fieri liber? mentiris, Maxime, non vis."

3 *Apicius:* M. Gavius Apicius, who lived during the reigns of Augustus and Tiberius, became a proverbial figure apparently even in his own day, an emblem of one who enjoys good food and plenty of it. As the scholiast on Juv. 4.23 succinctly puts it: "fuit nam exemplum gulae." Compare **2.89.5**, 3.22.5 ("nihil est, Apici, tibi gulosius factum"), 10.73.3; Sen. *Epist.* 120.19 ("modo Licinium divitiis, Apicium cenis . . . provocant"); and see Otto 1890: 20, *PIR* G91.

4 *tristior:* As at **2.65.1**, the comparative might be taken strictly ("gloomier" than when he ate out: Ker, Shackleton Bailey, Izaac, Scandola) or loosely ("rather gloomy": Barié and Schindler, Norcio, Ceronetti). The former seems more likely in view of the explicit contrast between *ad cenam ire* and *cum cenaret domi*.

6 *"cogor" ais:* For the technique of imagining an interlocutor's response and marking it with a verb of saying (*ais, inquis, dicis*), see on **2.21.2**. Note the ironic effect achieved by the balanced positioning of *cogor* and *cogitur* at the beginning of each of the two halves of this verse, the verbs being used in different senses: Classicus claims that he is compelled by external social forces (cf. Cic. *Att.* 5.21.3 with Shackleton Bailey), while Martial implies that Selius is compelled by internal forces.

6 *verum est:* For the granting of an interlocutor's argument, see on **2.8.7.**

6 *cogitur et Selius:* For Selius, see on **2.11.1.** Barwick 1958: 301 claims that since he appears here as a well-known hunter for dinner invitations, the name must correspond to a real person whose identity will have been clear to Martial's contemporary readership. This is possible, but Selius could just as well be a personage invented by Martial, a paradigmatic character resident not so much in the Rome of the 80s A.D. as in Book II of Martial's epigrams. In this case the allusion to Selius in the present epigram would be referring back to the Selius of the earlier epigrams in the book (so too Damon 1997: 157), just as *Chione* at 3.97 refers back to the Chione of 3.83 and 3.87 regardless of whether or not a real woman lies behind the name. Other such back-references in Martial include 5.26 and **2.57**; 4.81 and 4.71; 9.49 and 8.28.

7 *cenam ... rectam:* A regular, or "proper," meal as contrasted to the *sportula,* or token amount of food or money given by a patron to a client instead of the expected meal (*OLD* s.v. *rectus* 8b); compare 8.49.10: "promissa est nobis sportula, recta data est"; Suet. *Dom.* 7.1.

7 *Melior:* The present epigram gives no clue about who this man is, other than that he is wealthy enough to put on abundant formal dinners (so too at 4.54.7–8). But almost certainly the reference is to Atedius Melior, celebrated as a generous patron by both Statius (*Silv.* 2.1, 2.3) and Martial (4.54, 6.28–29, 8.38). See Nauta 2002: general index s.v. for his relationship to the two poets, both of whom lament the death of his beloved slave Glaucias (Stat. *Silv.* 2.1, Mart. 6.28–29; see further Henriksén, pp. 96–99).

8 *grandia verba:* A striking phrase, recurring at 9.27.7–8 and 9.32.5 but not unique to Martial: see Pers. 3.45 and Petr. *Sat.* 5.1.20, and compare Sen. *Suas.* 6.12 ("grandia loquitur"), Sen. *Epist.* 48.11 ("grandia locuti").

8 *si vir es:* The Roman language of masculinity is frequently applied to individual men so as to encourage or discourage, praise or blame. Here the desired result is a stereotypically masculine self-control; see further Williams 1999: 132–135. The phrase *si vir es* (*si viri estis*) is so widespread that Otto 1890: 373 includes it in his catalogue of proverbs; see further Weyman 1893 and 1904; Sonny 1896: 79; Sutphen 1901: 250, 388; Szelinski 1904: 636. Examples include Cic. *Fam.* 9.18.3 ("veni igitur, si vir es"), Sall. *Cat.* 40.3 ("si modo viri esse voltis"), Hor. *Epod.* 15.12 ("si quid in Flacco viri est"), Ov. *Fast.* 6.594 ("si vir es, i, dictas exige dotis opes"), Sen. *Dial.* 7.20.2, Apul. *Met.* 2.17.

2.70

Non vis in solio prius lavari
quemquam, Cotile. causa quae, nisi haec est,
undis ne fovearis irrumatis?
primus te licet abluas, necesse est
ante hic mentula quam caput lavetur.   5

You do not want anyone else to bathe in the tub before you, Cotilus.
The only reason for this can be that you want to avoid soaking in
water that has had dick in it. You can bathe first, but you have to
wash your dick before your head.

Themes. We return to coarse sexual themes, verbal obscenity (*irrumatis,
mentula*), and the hendecasyllabic meter, as well as to imagery of bathing
and cleanliness (**2.42**, **2.50**), in an epigram whose interpretation requires
some thought. Cotilus' disinclination to bathe after others derives from his
desire not to be exposed to water that has been irrumated, that is, has been
made unclean by other men's penises. Yet even if Cotilus is the first to bathe
in the tub, he will necessarily place his penis in the tub before his head, and
so cannot avoid the problem. Thus, "you are as great a source of pollution
as the others you complain of" (Ker, Shackleton Bailey). But if this were all
there were to the epigram, the joke would be weak, and it is tempting to
look for an ambiguity or double meaning. The phrase *necesse est* provides
it. Not only will Cotilus necessarily bathe his penis before his head, but he
ought to do so, because his head is actually dirtier than his penis. That is,
despite his affected horror of unclean water, he is himself *irrumatus*. Thus,
what seems at first to be well-meant advice ends up being an exposure of
Cotilus (Obermayer 1998: 220–221), and we detect a thematic continuity with
2.69: pretense is exposed. The same joke is made more explicitly later, in
an epigram whose punch line reads: "You wash your head; I would prefer
you washed your groin" (6.81.4: "et caput ecce lavas: inguina malo laves").

For the complex of imagery surrounding bathwater, penises, mouths or
heads, and cleanliness, see also **2.42**, **2.50**, and 11.95, with Obermayer 1998:
220–222.

Structure. There is a tripartite structure corresponding to the poem's three
sentences: Cotilus' refusal to bathe; the ostensible reason for it; Martial's
pointed commentary. Variety is achieved by the use of diverse verbs refer-

ring to the act of bathing (*lavari, fovearis, abluas, lavetur*), and a ring-composition effect is created by the positioning of *lavari* and *lavetur* as the final words in the first and last lines respectively. Throughout, the relationship between syntactic and metrical structure is somewhat less straightforward than usual: sentences and clauses spill over from one line to the next.

1 *solio:* See on **2.42.1**.

2 *Cotile:* A speaking name (κωτίλος, "chattering, babbling") occurring on only one other occasion in Martial: 3.63, where he is mocked as a *bellus homo* (for which see on **2.7**).

3 *undis ne fovearis irrumatis:* A striking phrase that combines the poetic *undis* with the sensual *fovearis*—a verb specifically associated with warm baths at 1.62.4 ("Baianis saepe fovetur aquis," with Citroni ad loc.), 7.35.2 ("calidis . . . foveris aquis"), *A.L.* 119.8 Riese ("membra fovebit aquis")—and concludes with the brutal *irrumatis,* for which see on **2.47.4**.

4 *necesse est:* For the possible double sense of the concept "it is necessary," see *OLD* s.v. 2 ("inevitable") and 1 ("indispensable").

5 *mentula:* For this basic obscenity, which gives the final line a particular sharpness, see on **2.45.1**.

5 *caput:* For the overlap between mouth (*os*) and head (*caput*) in allusions to those who practice oral sex, see on **2.42.3**.

2.71

Candidius nihil est te, Caeciliane. notavi,
   si quando ex nostris disticha pauca lego,
protinus aut Marsi recitas aut scripta Catulli.
   hoc mihi das, tamquam deteriora legas,
ut conlata magis placeant mea? credimus istud.   5
   malo tamen recites, Caeciliane, tua.

You are the ultimate in kindliness, Caecilianus. I have noticed that whenever I read a few couplets from my work, you right away recite either from Marsus or from Catullus. Do you do this for me as if reading verses worse than mine, so that mine may be more pleasing by comparison? I believe it. But in that case I would rather you recited your own verses, Caecilianus.

Themes.   The exposure of a man's pretense or hypocrisy continues, and
Martial returns to one of his favorite themes: his own poetry (see on **2.1**).
Martial's unexpected insult of Caecilianus' poetry invites further thought, as
does his perhaps exaggerated *credimus istud.* What lies behind the epigram's
final point is that Martial sees through Caecilianus' practice: he is reading
from Marsus and Catullus not to pay Martial a compliment but rather so that
the latter's verse may suffer by comparison. For Martial's technique of reporting others' criticism of his own work and then replying to it by attacking
his attackers, see on **2.8**. For attacks on other poets in particular, see 1.91,
2.20, **2.77**, **2.86**, **2.88–89**, 3.9, 3.44, 12.43, among others; precedents in Greek
epigram include *A.P.* 11.127, 129, 133–135, 137, 185, 218, 394 (Pertsch 1911:
25, Prinz 1911: 34–37).

Structure.   The poem's opening lines gradually present pieces of information. First we find a complimentary address to Caecilianus (1); then learn
that when Martial recites some of his work (2), Caecilianus responds by
reciting Marsus or Catullus (3), presenting them as inferior to Martial (4) by
way of paying a compliment to the latter (5). Martial's ironic *credimus istud*
introduces his brief, pointed reaction (6). The syntactical variety is typical:
short, simple sentence (1); longer complex sentence (1–3); rhetorical question followed by a reply (4–5); two-word sentence (5) leading up to the
final point (6). For the framing technique of positioning the vocative of the
addressee in the second half of the first and last lines respectively, see on
2.10.

   1 *candidius nihil est te:*   The adjective literally means "bright" or "clear"
(cf. *candeo, candesco, candor*) and, when applied to persons, "fair" and thus
"beautiful," but also, as here, "good-natured, kind" (*OLD* s.v. 8). The latter
sense is found at 13.2.9–10 ("si candidus aure / nec matutina si mihi fronte
venis"), Ov. *Trist.* 1.11.35 ("his debes ignoscere, candide lector"), Petr. *Sat.*
129.11 ("animumque eius candida humanitate restitue"). See further on **2.24.6**.
   For formulations of the type "nothing/no one is more X (than)," see on
2.54.5.
   1 *Caeciliane:*   See on **2.37.11**. Five-syllable names such as Caecilianus,
Gargilianus, Tongilianus, and Caedicianus are found in Martial almost exclusively in the second half of the pentameter; see Giegenack 1969: 158ff.
   2 *lego:*   See on **2.20.1**.
   3 *aut Marsi . . . aut . . . Catulli:*   Martial again names these two poets
together as his models in 7.99, adding Pedo (for whom see on **2.77.5**) at
1.praef. and 5.5.5–6. Domitius *Marsus* (*RE* 66; cited again by Martial in **2.77**,
4.29, 7.29, 8.55) composed a collection of satirical epigrams called *Cicuta,*

presumably because they were as venomous as hemlock. He also wrote an epic *Amazonis* (Mart. 4.29.8), and a prose work, *De urbanitate* (Quint. *Inst.* 6.3.102ff.). Surviving fragments of his work include an epigram on the death of Tibullus and two on Atia, the mother of Augustus. See Fogazza 1981; *FLP* 300. It is interesting that C. Valerius *Catullus* should be cited as a master not of elegy or epyllion but of epigram, and indeed Martial seems to consider him one of the greatest practitioners of the genre: see 10.78.16 ("uno sed tibi sim minor Catullo") with Offermann 1980. This is the starting point of Swann 1994.

5 credimus istud: For this affirmation, which may arouse suspicion by its intensity and which in fact turns out to be ironic, compare **2.72.7** ("vis hoc me credere? credo."), 7.88.10 ("credam iam, puto, Lause, tibi"), and 11.107.3–4 ("omnia legisti. credo, scio, gaudeo, verum est. / perlegi libros sic ego quinque tuos").

6 malo: See on **2.9.2** for the shortening of the final vowel (also with this verb at **2.21.2**).

6 Caeciliane, tua: Maaz 1992: 81 observes the metrical parallel with 1.65.4 (*Caeciliane, tuos*), 1.73.2 (*Caeciliane, tuam*), **2.78.2** (*Caeciliane, tuis*), 4.51.6 (*Caeciliane, tibi*), 9.70.10 (*Caeciliane, tui*), and Godfrey of Winchester, *Epigr.* 119.2 (*Caeciliane, tuam*).

2.72

Hesterna factum narratur, Postume, cena
    quod nollem (quis enim talia facta probet?):
os tibi percisum quanto non ipse Latinus
    vilia Panniculi percutit ora sono.
quoque magis mirum est, auctorem criminis huius   5
    Caecilium tota rumor in urbe sonat.
esse negas factum. vis hoc me credere? credo.
    quid quod habet testes, Postume, Caecilius?

People are talking about something that happened at dinner last night, Postumus, something that I hope didn't happen. After all, who could approve of such things? It is said that you were smacked in the face even more loudly than Latinus slaps Panniculus' vulgar face in the mimes. More remarkably still, the whole city is alive with gossip to the effect that Caecilius was the doer of the deed. You deny that it happened. Do you want me to believe that? Fine, I believe it. But, Postumus, what of the fact that Caecilius has his witnesses?

Themes.   Malicious second-person commentary continues as the scene shifts from a recitation of poetry to gossip about a dinner party. Socially significant speech (*recites* in the final line of **2.71** and *narratur* in the opening line of the present epigram) constitutes a thematic link, and the similarity of the names *Caecilianus* (**2.71**) and *Caecilius* (**2.72**) is worth noting. For the ever-present *cena* evoked in the opening line, see on **2.11** and 1 below.

Having recently appeared in **2.67**, the name Postumus now recurs in a piece indulging in a sexual pun or two. While on the surface this is a straight-forward piece of gossip—rumor has it that Caecilius had slapped Postumus, and there are witnesses—the phrases *os percisum* (3) and *habet testes* (8) together suggest the secondary meaning that Caecilius irrumated Postumus, that is, orally penetrated him, thus playing the role of a "real man" endowed with testicles; so too Joepgen 1967: 63–65 and, more tentatively, Shackleton Bailey. See on **2.67.1** for the weak argument that this Postumus is totally unrelated to the man ridiculed for his repulsive kisses earlier in Book II; the earlier implication that Postumus is a *fellator* or *cunnilingus* is surely relevant to the present epigram (Joepgen 1967: 64).

Prinz 1929: 114–116 sees an ambiguity in *habet testes* but denies any sexual double meaning in *os tibi percisum,* noting that 3–4 unambiguously refer to a noisy slap in the face ("sie gehen unzweideutig auf eine schallende Ohrfeige"). Caecilius' action is indeed compared to Latinus' loud blows, but the comparison is based on the sound (*quanto . . . sono*) and hardly excludes a sexual double meaning. Entirely ignoring the possibility of double mean-ings, Colton 1991: 206–207 argues that Juv. 5.170–173 draws on the language of this epigram.

Pace Adams 1982: 212, however, this secondary scenario is surely not being presented as actually having happened. It is highly unlikely that we are to imagine Postumus fellating Caecilius in front of guests at a dinner party. The epigram is an elaborate verbal witticism.

Structure.   The opening couplet quickly creates a tone of suspense, not to say voyeurism: rumor has it that something happened at dinner last night, something that Martial hopes is not true. This statement is immediately fol-lowed by a rhetorical question typical of a gossip: Who, after all, could approve of such things? The following couplet (3–4) satisfies our curiosity, laying out the scenario with a phrase that suggests a sexual double meaning (*os tibi percisum*); the next couplet (5–6), again using the language of the scandalmonger (*quodque magis mirum est*), adds the name of the perpetra-tor, punctuating the revelation with an appeal to authority: the whole city is talking about it. There follows a line divided into three brief sentences (statement; rhetorical question; answer) that leads into the final verse with its clear double entendre (*habet testes*), jabbing vocative, and meaningful juxtaposition of *Postume* and *Caecilius.*

1 hesterna ... cena: See Siedschlag 1977: 35 for Martial's technique of introducing an incident by anchoring it in a specific point in time (as here, 1.27–28, 4.15, 11.8) or a specific place (**2.17**). Dinners are a favorite setting: see on **2.18.1**.

1 narratur: See on **2.56.3** for this verb in the context of gossip and rumor.

3 os tibi percisum: The noun *os* may refer either to the mouth (*OLD* s.v. 1–2) or to the face (*OLD* s.v. 6–10). The verb *percidere*, literally to "slap or hit hard" (*OLD* s.v. 1), is also used metaphorically to refer to sexual, albeit usually anal, penetration (*OLD* s.v. 2, *TLL* 10.1205.8–23, Adams 1982: 136–137). Thus, *os percisum* suggests both "slapped in the face" (as at Pl. *Cas.* 404, Sen. *N.H.* 4b.4.1) and "screwed in the mouth," that is, *irrumatus.* The same double entendre is found at Pl. *Pers.* 282–284 (to a boy: "caedere hodie tu restibus.—tua quidem, cucule, caussa! / —non hercle, si os perciderim tibi, metuam, morticine— / video ego te: iam incubitatus es") and is further suggested by Martial's insinuation earlier in Book II that Postumus practices fellatio and/or cunnilinctus; see on **2.10**.

3–4: *Latinus* was a renowned actor in mimes favored by the emperor Domitian, whom he also served as an informer; see Juv. 1.36, 6.44; Suet. *Dom.* 15; *RE* s.v. 3. Martial several times cites him as the mime actor par excellence and as a *derisor,* or one who scorns others: 1.4.5 (*derisoremque Latinum*), 3.86.3, 5.61.11, 9.28, 13.2.3 ("et possis ipsum tu deridere Latinum"). A scene in which he slapped a character named *Panniculus,* whose name suggests the rags, or *panni,* of a clownlike figure (Apul. *Apol.* 13), seems to have become proverbial: compare 5.61.11–12. Panniculus and Latinus are named together again at 3.86.3 as embodiments of the mime.

5 magis mirum: Why is it surprising that Caecilius should be the author of the deed? Martial's other uses of the name (see on next verse) offer no help, but the context suggests that he had the reputation of being a weak or ineffectual man.

6 Caecilium: The name appears again in 1.41 (he likes to think of himself as *urbanus* but is not), 11.31.1 (he is fond of gourds and tries to present them as an elegant dish); in 7.84 the name refers to the younger Pliny.

6 tota rumor in urbe sonat: Similar expressions are found in 3.73 (*rumor negat*), 3.80 (*rumor ait*), 3.87 (*narrat rumor*), 4.16 (*rumor erat*), 4.69 (*rumor negat*). In many of these cases, given the sexual context, there just might be a sound-play on *rumor* and *irrumatio* (Adams 1982: 212). For the power of gossip in general, compare **2.82.2** (*populum loqui*), 6.56.5 ("scis multos dicere multa"), and 7.10; and see Laurens 1989: 223, Greenwood 1998a.

7 vis hoc me credere? credo: See on **2.71.5** (*credimus istud*) for this ironic affirmation. The brusque paratactic rhythm suggests not only colloquial speech but "une dialectique essentiellement aggressive" (Laurens 1989: 258).

8 quid quod habet testes? Puns on *testes* (literally, "witnesses," used to refer to the testicles because they testify to a man's manhood: Plin. *N.H.* 11.263, Suet. *Nero* 28.1; Adams 1982: 67–68) are found also at Pl. *Cur.* 30–31 ("quod amas amato testibus praesentibus"), *Mil.* 1414–1426; Phaedr. 3.11.5; *Priap.* 15.4–7 (again with *percidere*). The double meaning is thus that (*a*) Caecilius has witnesses to the event, and (*b*) Caecilius "has balls," is a "real man" (cf. Petr. *Sat.* 44.14: "si nos coleos haberemus, non tantum sibi placeret"; Pers. 1.103–104: "haec fierent si testiculi vena ulla paterni / viveret in nobis?").

For the final question, unanswered and pointed, see on **2.60.4**.

2.73

Quid faciat vult scire Lyris. quod sobria: fellat.

Lyris wants to know what she is doing. The same thing she does when sober: she sucks dick.

Themes.   While the preceding poem ends with a pun on *testes* and probably hints that Postumus is a *fellator,* the present epigram undeniably imputes the practice, now to a woman, with the blunt *fellat.*

All extant MSS present a single-line epigram, but many scholars argue that the poem originally consisted of two lines, one of which fell out of the MS tradition at an early stage; see below. In any case its point is brutally clear: Lyris is both a *fellatrix* and a lush, indeed so drunk as not to know what she is doing. The stereotype of the drunken woman recurs in 1.87, 5.4, and 14.63; compare also the repulsive depiction at Juv. 6.425–433. For another accusation of fellatio directed against a woman, see **2.50**.

Whether it originally consisted of two lines or one, the poem's dactylic meter is fairly unusual in Latin epigram. The only other poems of Martial in the meter are 1.53, 6.64, and 7.98, and at 6.65 he defends its use. See further Marina Sáez 1998: 273–275.

Structure.   The MSS transmit this epigram as a single line, and this is most likely how Martial wrote it (Siedschlag 1977: 130–131, Sullivan 1993: 229, Scherf

2001: 117). The poem is hardly incomplete in sense, and monostichs, though

232   *Epigram 2.74*

2001: 117). The poem is hardly incomplete in sense, and monostichs, though rare, are certainly to be found elsewhere in Martial: see 7.98 (also a dactylic hexameter) and 8.19 (a choliamb), as well as other epigrammatists, both Latin and Greek (e.g., *A.P.* 1.51, 9.402, 9.491, 16.76; *A.L.* 89, 495–506; Ennod. 207— is it only coincidental that almost all of these postdate Martial?). Nonetheless, Italian humanist readers felt that something was missing and offered the following reconstructions of an original second line: *gaudeo. quid faciet ebria facta Lyris?* or *gaudeo. quid facies ebria facta, Lyris?* (I'm glad. What will she/ you do when she's/you're drunk?). But this seems incompatible with the obvious assumption of the extant line that Lyris is already drunk. Munro proposed that the epigram's *first* line had fallen out of the tradition, and he reconstructs it as follows: *quid faciat se scire Lyris negat ebria semper* (When drunk, Lyris always says she doesn't know what she's doing). This addition is supported by both Housman 1925 and Shackleton Bailey.

Others have emended the existing line. Zicàri 1963 suggests *quid faciat volt scire Lyris. quod sobria: fellet.* (Lyris wants to know what she ought to do. She should do what she does when she is sober: suck dick.) Greenwood 1996 proposes *quid faciat, vis scire, Lyris? quod sobria: fellat* (You want to know what Lyris is doing? What she does when sober: she is sucking dick.), observing that formulas of the type "you want to know" (*scire cupis/vis*) occur elsewhere in Martial (3.20.21, 3.44.4, 10.68.9, 11.8.13–14) and that if we emend the present epigram to read *vis scire,* 50 percent of the occurrences of *scire* in Martial are in the context of this formula. The argument is not compelling enough to justify emending a MS reading that makes perfect sense.

1 Lyris: The name is nowhere else attested, but Greek women's names like *Chione, Thais,* and *Ias* often designate prostitutes. See 1.34, 1.92, 3.30, 3.34, 3.83, 3.87, 3.97, 11.60, and Juv. 3.136 for *Chione;* 3.8, 3.11, 4.12, 4.50, 4.84, 5.43, 6.93, and 11.101 for *Thais;* 1.34 for *Ias* and *Chione* together.

1 fellat: For the execution of the final point by means of a single word, see on **2.17.5**. Here the blunt obscenity lends the point particular sharpness.

2.74

Cinctum togatis post et ante Saufeium,
quanta reduci Regulus solet turba,
ad alta tonsum templa cum reum misit,
Materne, cernis? invidere nolito.

comitatus iste sit precor tuus numquam.   5
hos illi amicos et greges togatorum
Fuficulenus praestat et Faventinus.

Saufeius is preceded and followed by clients in their togas, the kind
of crowd that escorts Regulus home when he sends the freshly shaven
defendant to give thanks at the lofty temple. Do you see him,
Maternus? Don't envy him, though. I pray you may never have such
a crowd of escorts. These friends, these flocks of toga-wearing clients, are provided to him by Fuficulenus and Faventinus.

Themes.   After the sexually colored gossip of the preceding epigrams, this
poem's opening lines bring us back to the streets of Rome, painting the portrait
of a man reveling in the signs of apparent success. Martial proceeds to ex-
pose the truth: Saufeius only has so many followers thanks to Fuficulenus
and Faventinus. Our understanding of the joke depends on the identity of
these two men, whom Martial never names again. The context clearly suggests that they were moneylenders, the point being that Saufeius has used
the money he borrowed from them, no doubt at high interest, in order to
"buy" himself a throng of attendants. In other words, he has used the money
to purchase the appurtenances of wealth and thus to attract clients (Kay).
Friedlaender and Barié and Schindler offer a slightly different explanation:
the former posits that Saufeius has borrowed money in order to pay his clients ("um seine Clienten zu bezahlen"), presumably with the *sportula;* the
latter that Saufeius needs to borrow from the moneylenders because he has
already spent his own money on his clients.
    See **2.57** for the theme of the show-off and for the possibility that the
two epigrams form a thematic unit. The image of the apparently successful
Saufeius surrounded by his clients may have inspired Juvenal's wry description of what people look for in a lawyer: not their ability but their wealthy
appearance (7.141–143: "respicit haec primum qui litigat, an tibi servi / octo,
decem comites, an post te sella, togati / ante pedes . . .").

Structure.   The opening line paints the picture clearly, naming its protago-
nist; the following two lines expand on the portrayal by means of the comparison to Regulus. The accusatives of the first line (*cinctum . . . Saufeium*)
create an expectation only met in the fourth line with the characteristic "opening" verb *cernis* (see on 4 below). There follows Martial's rejection of this
type of success as undesirable (4–5) and, after a transitional line that recalls
the poem's opening (*hos illi amicos et greges togatorum ~ cinctum togatis
post et ante Saufeium*), his characteristically compressed and concrete explanation. It is enough simply to name Fuficulenus and Faventinus.

1 *togatis:* See on **2.18.5** and **2.57.5**.

1 *Saufeium:* The name occurs only here in Martial (cf. *Saufeia* at 3.72) but is amply attested elsewhere. The comparison to Regulus in the next line may imply that he is a courtroom pleader aiming to give the impression of great success; so *RE* s.v. 9. Otherwise, he will simply be a man who wishes to give the appearance of financial and social success.

2: M. Aquilius *Regulus* is here cited as the paragon of the successful lawyer and appears elsewhere as a friend and patron of the poet; his invocation in this book's final epigram (**2.93**; cf. 1.111) gives him a degree of prominence. Regulus, whose career extended from around A.D. 67 to 100, has gone down in history as a merciless denouncer and prosecutor (*delator*): see Tac. *Hist.* 4.42 and the remarks of Regulus' adversary Pliny the Younger (*Epist.* 1.5 [where he quotes with approval a dictum of Modestus: "Regulus omnium bipedum nequissimus"], 1.20, 2.11, 2.20, 4.2, 4.7, 6.2), along with *RE* s.v. Aquilius 34. Here Martial flatters him as a successful defense attorney—not, it is worth noting, as a prosecutor—and elsewhere praises him for various virtues (1.111, 4.16). In 5.28 he is cited as the paragon of eloquence ("licet vincas . . . oratione Regulos"); in 6.64 Martial boasts that Regulus, along with Silius Italicus and the emperor himself, reads and appreciates his verse; in 1.12 and 1.82 the poet enthusiastically celebrates Regulus' miraculous escape from an accidental death. Before condemning Martial for hypocritical flattery of scoundrels, as Spiegel 1891: 59 seems to do, we ought to recall that Pliny's and Tacitus' portraits of Regulus are themselves hardly objective. It is of interest that Martial never mentions him after Book VII but gives no hint as to why.

3 *ad alta tonsum templa cum reum misit:* Note the sequence of *t*-sounds. The plural *templa* is most likely "poetic" (cf. 5.10.6: "Catuli vilia templa"), and the reference is probably to the Temple of Jupiter Optimus Maximus on the southern peak of the Capitoline Hill (5.10, 6.10, 10.51.14: "quaeque nitent caelo proxima templa suo"). After a fire in A.D. 80, Domitian had the temple rebuilt in a particularly splendid form; see Mart. 9.3.7, 13.74; Sil. Ital. 3.622–624; Stat. *Silv.* 1.6.101–102, 4.3.160–161.

Since defendants traditionally refrained from shaving their beards so as to give the appearance of mourning (see on **2.36.3**), Martial's phrase— "with trimmed beard" rather than, as Ker suggests, "with trimmed hair"— is a concise way of referring to a defendant who has been acquitted thanks to the efforts of his advocate and goes to the temple to offer a sacrifice of thanksgiving.

4 *Materne:* The name appears on two other occasions in Martial: in 1.96 he is a friend (*nostro Materno*); in 10.37 he is flattered as a skilled courtroom pleader. If all three refer to the same (real) man, which is not unlikely, the allusion to Regulus' success in the courtroom in 3 is particularly apt.

4 cernis? See on **2.29.1** (*vides?*) for this type of question, usually at the beginning of an epigram and often leading into the exposure of a hypocrite or pretender.

6 amicos et greges togatorum: The phrase refers to clients; see on **2.18.5**. For the overlaps between *amicitia* and *clientela*, see on **2.5**; at **2.32.7** a patron is called *amicus*. For *togati*, see on 1 above.

7 Fuficulenus, Faventinus: The names occur only here in Martial but are attested in inscriptions: see *CIL* 6.975, 7494, 18619, 18621 for the former, and Schulze 1904: 45, 113, 196, 524 for the latter. Either these were real men known to Martial's readers as moneylenders, or they are fictional names created ad hoc, the context implying their function.

2.75

Verbera securi solitus leo ferre magistri
    insertamque pati blandus in ora manum
dedidicit pacem subito feritate reversa,
    quanta nec in Libycis debuit esse iugis.
nam duo de tenera puerilia corpora turba,   5
    sanguineam rastris quae renovabat humum,
saevus et infelix furiali dente peremit.
    Martia non vidit maius harena nefas.
exclamare libet: "crudelis, perfide, praedo,
    a nostra pueris parcere disce lupa!"   10

A lion who had been accustomed to put up with the whippings of his fearless master, and who had tamely allowed hands to be inserted into his mouth, suddenly unlearned his peaceful behavior and returned to a savage state such as cannot have been his even in the mountains of Libya. Two boys in the crowd of young slaves raking clean the bloody arena floor—the cruel wretch killed them with his frenzied fangs. The Roman arena has never seen a greater outrage. One would like to cry out: "Cruel, treacherous criminal! Learn from our she-wolf how to spare boys!"

Themes. We return to the epideictic mode of **2.59** with an epigram largely taken up with a pathetic description of a gory incident in an arena, most likely the Colosseum. The lion's attack on the slave boys prompts a highly rhetorical response: first the hyperbolic assertion that no greater outrage (*nefas*) has ever occurred in a Roman arena, and second the apostrophe to the lion himself, urging him to take a lesson from the she-wolf who raised Romulus and Remus.

Public entertainment in the amphitheater provided rich material for epideictic epigram. Not only did Martial publish an entire book celebrating the opening of the Colosseum (*Liber de spectaculis*), but he composed a group of epigrams on the performance of a lion and a hare in the arena (1.6, 14, 22, 48, 51, 60, 104). One of these in particular shows some similarities to the present epigram: 1.48 begins with an allusion to a lion's mouth ("rictibus his tauros non eripuere magistri, / per quos praeda fugax itque reditque lepus") and ends with an emotive apostrophe to an animal ("lepus improbe"). The present epigram may also be described as forming a pendant to *Sp.* 18 (on a tiger) and *Sp.* 10 (on a lion): see Weinreich 1928: 87–88, 110. Other animal shows are mentioned at *Sp.* 5, *Sp.* 16, 1.44, 5.31, 5.65, 8.53; a related phenomenon was the public execution of criminals by throwing them before aggressive animals in the arena (*Sp.* 7–8, 21, with Coleman 1990).

Structure.   Barwick 1959: 8 cites this epigram as an illustration of his "objective"/"subjective" model: 1–8 constituting the first part, and the final couplet the second. Siedschlag 1977: 100 n. 1 rightly points out that on this scheme the "subjective" element actually begins in 8. The description of the event itself falls into two parts: an opening sentence (1–4) that piques our curiosity, and a second sentence that begins with explanatory *nam* (5–7) and reports the details. There follows a single-line, strongly worded commentary on the deed (8), punctuated by the even more rhetorically colored apostrophe to the lion (9–10) introduced by the emotive *exclamare libet*.

1 *leo:*   For tame lions, see the seven epigrams in Book I on the lion and hare (cited above), along with *Sp.*10, 9.71, and Stat. *Silv.* 2.5 (a lamentation on the death of a *leo mansuetus*). In 1.6 the tame lion is reverently cited as a symbol of the emperor's clement power (see Citroni ad loc.); here the emphasis is on the potential of reversion to his original state (*dedidicit,* 3), or even worse (4). See Keller 1909: 24–61, Toynbee 1973: 61–69. For the shortened second vowel of *leo,* see on **2.9.2**.

2:   The verse-final phrase *in ora manum* recurs in 3.19.4, describing an incident in which the beautiful slave boy Hylas inserts his hand into the mouth of a statue of a bear and is bitten by a viper.

4 *in Libycis ... iugis:*   The mountains of northern Africa were renowned in antiquity for their lions: see V. *Aen.* 5.351, Sil. Ital. 7.401.

5 *duo ... puerilia corpora:*   A periphrasis, here probably poetic in tone, for *duo corpora puerorum* or even more simply *duo(s) pueros*. Hofmann 1951:

160–161, 202, cites this as an example of a colloquial tendency to use such possessive adjectives as *erilis, muliebris,* and *puerilis* instead of the corresponding genitives (*eri, mulieris, pueri*), but the usage is found throughout Latin literature and indeed seems to be a fundamental characteristic of the language (LHS 2: 60–61), taking its tone from its context.

5 *tenera . . . turba:* The adjective implies that the entire group of slaves, not just the two victims, was young; compare *OLD* s.v. *tener* 2.

6: The slaves' task was to rake over the bloodstained sand which covered the center of the amphitheater so as to prepare for the subsequent event. The adjective *sanguineam* adds a poignant touch: the arena floor, already bloody from a previous fight, now unexpectedly became the scene of further bloodshed.

8 *Martia . . . harena:* Most translators render *Martia* literally, and Ker and Shackleton Bailey translate *harena* literally as well ("the sand of Mars" and "Mars's sand" respectively). But *Martia* is more likely metonymic for "Roman" (*OLD* s.v. 3): compare *Martia turba* at 1.3.4 and *Martia Roma* at 5.19.5; the usage is poetic and solemn (Citroni ad 1.3.4, Galán Vioque ad 7.6.6; cf. V. *Ecl.* 9.12 and Stat. *Theb.* 7.460: *tela Martia*). Similarly, *harena* may be taken as a synecdoche: "arena" rather than "sand"; compare *Sp.* 9.1, 8.53.5 ("in Ausonia . . . harena"), 14.53.1 ("in Ausonia . . . harena"); Cic. *Tusc.* 2.46; Sen. *Epist.* 99.13; *OLD* s.v. 3.

8 *non vidit maius . . . nefas:* For extreme statements of the type "the most X," see on **2.54.5**. *Nefas* is a strong term indeed, originally signifying "an offence against divine law, an impious act" (*OLD* s.v. 1) and hence "a wicked act, crime" (*OLD* s.v. 2) or "an unnatural event, portent, horror" (*OLD* s.v. 3). In Martial, see 1.12.6 (the collapsing porticus which nearly killed Regulus was almost guilty of *nefas*), 5.69.4 ("hoc admisisset nec Catilina nefas"), 6.39.14 (sexual intercourse with one's own son is *nefas*), 6.62.3, 9.70.2 (Catilina again), 14.75.1 ("flet Philomela nefas incesti Tereos"); ironically at 3.72.1–2 ("vis futui nec vis mecum, Saufeia, lavari. / nescio quod magnum suspicor esse nefas").

9–10: The emotive phrase *exclamare libet* underscores the rhetorical nature of the epigram's final point; the quotation itself opens with an asyndetic, partially alliterative tricolon. Weinreich 1928: 110 is not impressed: it smacks too much of "the unhealthy games of wit in the rhetorical schools" (schmeckt die Pointe doch sehr nach den ungesunden Geistreicheleien der Rhetorikschule). Laurens 1989: 364, by contrast, sees "un parallèle ingénieux."

The passionate address to the lion, with its suggestion that he learn from the she-wolf, is reminiscent of emotive apostrophes to the hare in the lion-and-hare cycle of Book I: see 1.22, 1.48.7, 1.51, 1.60 with Citroni. However formal the device may be, a certain anthropomorphism lurks in such addresses to animals; in this case the notion is that animals can and should behave according to human ideals. Compare *Sp.* 10 (a lion deserves punishment for having violated human standards of conduct), 17 and 29 (an elephant and a doe perceive the emperor's divinity); 1.104.22 ("norunt cui serviant leones"); 14.73 (a parrot has taught himself to say "Hail Caesar").

9 crudelis, perfide, praedo: For the use of these words (literally, "cruel," "traitor," "thief") as insults, sometimes devoid of their literal sense, see Hofmann 1951: 85–89, 194; Opelt 1965: index s.vv.

10: A proud allusion ("*nostra* lupa") to one of the central details of Rome's foundation myth: the twins Romulus and Remus, having been abandoned by their mother, were raised by a she-wolf. The tale is most famously narrated in Livy's first book, and the image of the she-wolf suckling the boys was and remains an important symbol of the city; see Toynbee 1973: 101–102. Weinreich 1928: 110 detects a parallelism between the two slave boys and the two mythical brothers. For the paradigmatic use of mythic figures, see on **2.14.4**. Citroni ad 1.62.6 observes that the technique often appears, as here, at the end of an epigram: 3.32 (Hecuba, Niobe), 3.76 (Hecuba, Andromache), 8.6 (Priam, Astyanax).

2.76

Argenti libras Marius tibi quinque reliquit,
cui nihil ipse dabas. hic tibi verba dedit.

Marius left you five pounds of silver; you yourself never gave him a thing. He has tricked you!

Themes. After the preceding epideictic epigram we return to the satiric mode in a finely pointed monodistich, the first since **2.58**, that brings us back to the theme of legacy hunting, for which see on **2.26**. Other than the fact that there is a play on the verb *dare* in 2 (first used literally, then in the idiomatic phrase *verba dare,* "to deceive, cheat, trick"), certainty regarding the point is denied us, since we may print the final sentence either as a statement or as a question. If, with Lindsay, Siedschlag, Izaac, and Norcio, we see a question ("Did he trick you?"), there are two interpretive directions we might take. Siedschlag 1977: 83 sees the question as riddling: on the one hand, the addressee has certainly *not* been cheated, as he has received more than he ever gave; on the other hand, he *has* been deceived, in that he will have expected more than five pounds of silver. Alternatively (Gilbert and

Friedlaender, who both erroneously identify the addressee as Marius), the question might be repeating and endowing with irony the addressee's disappointed reaction to the inheritance. He has complained *iste mihi verba dedit,* and Martial puts him in his place: did he really? If, on the other hand, with Ker, Izaac, Ceronetti, Shackleton Bailey, and Barié and Schindler, we print the sentence as a statement, the joke works rather differently. The addressee will have expected to receive nothing from Marius, since he himself had never given him anything. Thus, as Shackleton Bailey puts it, "the humor lies in turning upside down the stock situation in which a testator 'cheats' a legacy-hunter by leaving him out of his will."

The two possibilities are quite distinct. If we print the sentence as a question, the addressee will have *expected* to inherit something from Marius even though he had never given him anything; if we print it as a statement, he will *not* have expected to inherit and thus, in this ironic sense, has been "deceived" by Marius. On the former reading, the addressee is being held up for criticism and the tone is fairly grim; on the latter, the addressee is not the object of criticism and the tone is humorously ironic.

Yet another possibility is raised if, like Ker, Izaac, and Salanitro 1991, we punctuate as follows: "Argenti libras Marius tibi quinque reliquit. / cui nihil ipse dabas, hic tibi verba dedit." In this case the relative *cui* refers not to Marius in particular but makes a general statement that constitutes the point of the epigram: he who gives nothing cannot expect to receive anything.

Burnikel 1980: 88–94 and Scherf 2001: 39 argue that this epigram forms a pair with **2.65**, the theme being successful and unsuccessful legacy hunting; see **2.57** and **2.74**, and perhaps also **2.18** and **2.53**, for other examples of paired but separated poems in Book II.

Structure.   The structure is easily described as bipartite, but the two halves do not correspond to the two lines of the monodistich. The first line and a half, up until the caesura, constitutes a single sentence introducing the situation; the remainder of the second line offers ironic commentary. The pun in the second line is underscored by the parallel position of *dabas* and *dedit* at the end of each half-line.

For an unnamed addressee as the central subject of the epigram, see on **2.61**.

1 *argenti libras ... quinque:* See on **2.44.2**. This is a small bequest indeed; consider 12.36.1, where two or four pounds of silver is an example of an unsatisfying gift (Salanitro 1991).

1 *Marius:* The name is also found in 1.85, 3.28, 10.19. The fact that Marius is quite alive in Books III and X suggests that there is no single character behind the name.

2 *tibi verba dedit:* For this idiom, meaning "to deceive," see also 5.23.6, 5.50.8, 6.56.2, 8.22.2, 9.67.4. For the pun on the two senses of *dare* (Freud's "full" and "empty"), see on **2.67** and compare Joepgen 1967: 111–112.

2.77

Cosconi, qui longa putas epigrammata nostra,
  utilis unguendis axibus esse potes.
hac tu credideris longum ratione colosson
  et puerum Bruti dixeris esse brevem.
disce quod ignoras: Marsi doctique Pedonis   5
  saepe duplex unum pagina tractat opus.
non sunt longa quibus nihil est quod demere possis;
  sed tu, Cosconi, disticha longa facis.

Cosconius, you think my epigrams are long? You're good for oiling axles! On this principle you would consider the Colossus too tall and you would call the statue of Brutus' slave boy too short. Learn what you don't know: one piece by Marsus or the learned Pedo often takes up two pages. If you can't take anything away, it's not long. Meanwhile, you yourself write couplets that are long.

Themes.   After a fairly long sequence of satiric and epideictic pieces, we return to Martial's self-referential mode, recently encountered in **2.71**. As often, criticism of his poetic practice is presented and countered with a strong defense (Lausberg 1982: 46–47 observes that the traditional appeal to such other arts as architecture and sculpture contributes to the authoritative tone) coupled with a retort against the critic himself (see on **2.8**). Likewise characteristic is the citation of respected earlier poets (1.61, **2.71**, 4.14, 5.5, 7.29, 7.99, 8.18, 10.78), here invoked as setting precedent. For specific criticism of the length of Martial's epigrams, see 1.110, 3.83, 6.65, 10.59, with Szelest 1980. For attacks on other poets, see on **2.71**.

Pertsch 1911: 61 astutely observes that this epigram, treating the question of length, is preceded by one and followed by no fewer than five monodistichs, as if Martial were offering a further reply to Cosconius' criticism: "See, I can also write monodistichs!" Pertsch compares the following sequences: 1.34 (containing the obscenity *futui*) and 1.35 (Cornelius complains of Martial's obscene verses); 1.109 (an epigram of twenty-three lines) and 1.110 (Velox complains that Martial writes long epigrams); 3.82 (an epigram of thirty-three lines) and 3.83 (Cordus urges Martial to write shorter pieces).

Structure. This epigram is cleverly constructed so as to respond to Cosconius: we have before us a rhetorically and aesthetically satisfying piece. The syntax sweeps us quickly through Cosconius' criticism, summarized in the opening relative clause, and brings us directly to the poet's forceful commentary, introduced as it is with an insult: *utilis unguendis axibus.*

Martial's response is itself liable to further structural analysis. The opening insult is followed by a couplet parodying Cosconius' perspective: he would consider the (impressive) Colossus to be too tall and the (elegant) statue of Brutus' slave boy too small. To this (mis?)representation of his critic's beliefs the poet then adds a couplet that presents the authoritative citation of precedent (Marsus and Pedo) and is introduced by a brusque, indeed insulting, imperative: *disce quod ignoras.* The epigram is then rounded off by a final couplet that itself breaks into two halves, each occupying a line: the hexameter contains a *sententia* expressing a general truth, while the pentameter returns to a direct address of Cosconius (*sed tu, Cosconi;* for the repetition of the vocative in the first and last lines, see on 8) and to yet another insult. While aimed at essentially the same object, these insults are pleasingly varied: a broad attack on Cosconius' intelligence (2) is followed by more specific ridicule of his putative beliefs (3–4), a brief assertion of his ignorance regarding earlier epigrammatists (5), and finally concrete criticism of his poetic technique (8). Only with this final verse do we learn that Cosconius himself has tried his hand at Martial's craft.

1 *Cosconi:* The name appears again in 3.69, where Martial ironically praises him for writing epigrams so chaste that they can be read even by *pueri* and *virgines.* Friedlaender doubts that a real man lies behind the name; these two epigrams give us grounds neither for skepticism nor for confidence.

1 *qui longa putas epigrammata nostra:* Izaac, Lausberg 1982: 46–47, Shackleton Bailey, and Scandola translate *longa* here as "too long" to bring out the sense of Cosconius' criticism. See further on 3 (*longum*) and 4 (*brevem*).

2 *utilis unguendis axibus esse potes:* There is some disagreement over what this presumably proverbial phrase ("you can be useful for lubricating axles") actually means. It already led to confusion among Italian humanists, some of whom emended *unguendis* to *urgendis.* Following Collesso, Friedlaender explains that people suited for lubricating axles are those for whom nothing can move quickly enough: Cosconius wants everything to fly by. Housman 1907: 234 sharply dismisses this explanation, supporting instead the interpretation offered by the seventeenth-century commentator Ramirez de Prado: "Cosconius, if we boiled him down, would yield a large quantity of excellent axle-grease. *Pinguis* means stupid" (cf. Ov. *Met.* 11.148, Hor. *Sat.* 2.6.14–15). Ker, Shackleton Bailey, Merli, Watson and Watson, and, tentatively, Bridge and Lake consider this the most likely explanation of the phrase, but not everyone has been convinced. Izaac and Norcio understand the phrase to mean that Cosconius is so inept that he knows only how to lubricate axles, Izaac erroneously attributing the interpretation to Friedlaender. Lausberg 1982: 46–47 raises the attractive possibility that the expression is multivalent, suggesting *both* stupidity *and* an interest in speed and thus brevity, since, after all, a greased axle contributes to speed.

3 colosson: Although Martial refers elsewhere to a *colossus Augusti* (8.44.7) and to the Colossus of Rhodes, after which all the others were named (1.70.8, *Rhodium opus*), here he is almost certainly referring to the colossal statue of Nero in Rome, which had been altered under Vespasian to represent the sun god and which gave its name to the nearby Flavian Ampitheater, or "Colosseum." Martial also refers to this monument at *Sp.* 2.1 (*sidereus colossus*), 1.70.7–8 (*miri colossi*), and probably, likewise in a poem that plays with the idea of measurement, 8.60.1 (*Palatini colossi*).

3–4 longum, brevem: Ker translates the adjectives literally ("you would fancy the Colossus to be tall, and would describe Brutus' boy as short") but this potentially obscures Martial's point: by objective standards, after all, the Colossus *is* tall and Brutus' boy *is* short. Thus, like most translators, I have added the adverb "too." Barié and Schindler interpret *tu credideris* in an impersonal sense: one might consider the Colossus tall, Brutus' boy short. This is certainly a possible meaning of the second person in Latin, but in this context *tu* clearly refers to Cosconius in particular.

4 puerum Bruti: A statuette of a boy made by the sculptor Strongylio and admired by Brutus, the assassin of Caesar; see Plin. *N.H.* 34.82 ("idem fecit puerum, quem amando Brutus Philippiensis cognomine suo inlustravit"). Martial again uses the statuette as an image for his own work at 9.50.5 and elsewhere informs us that ceramic copies of the statuette were given as gifts at the Saturnalia (14.171).

Both Martial's phrase *puerum Bruti* and Pliny's brief notice have received two strikingly different interpretations. Ceronetti and Barié and Schindler (ad 9.50.5) understand Brutus to have loved the boy himself rather than the statuette; similarly the Loeb Classical Library editor of Pliny, H. Rackham, translates: "The same sculptor made the figure rendered famous by Brutus under the name of Brutus's Boy because it represented a favourite of the hero of the battles at Philippi." Others (Izaac, Ker, Norcio, Shackleton Bailey, Merli) understand Pliny to be saying that Brutus "loved," that is, admired, the statue, not the boy it represented. This is the more likely interpretation. The antecedent of *quem amando* is to be sure *puerum,* but in context this refers to the statue: it is, after all, the direct object of *fecit.* The same holds for Martial 14.171.2: "istius pueri Brutus amator erat."

5 *Marsi doctique Pedonis:* Martial again cites these two Augustan poets in 1.praef. and 5.5 as his predecessors and models in the art of epigram. For *Marsus,* see on **2.71.3**. Albinovanus *Pedo* is praised for his wit and skill at narrative at Sen. *Epist.* 122.15 and Quint. *Inst.* 9.3.61. Like Marsus, he also wrote an epic poem (a *Theseid* cited by Ov. *Pont.* 4.10.71) and a poem on Germanicus' North Sea expedition in A.D. 16, in which Pedo may have taken part personally; Sen. *Suas.* 1.15 quotes a passage. He was a friend of Ovid and an acquaintance of the younger Seneca: see Sen. *Contr.* 2.2.12; Sen. *Epist.* 122.15; *FLP* 315. Other than in 1.praef. and 5.5, Martial names Pedo again in 10.20.

Martial would have been gratified to find himself cited by the fifth-century A.D. bishop Sidonius Apollinaris along with Marsus, Pedo, and Tibullus in a catalogue of authors: "non Gaetulicus hic tibi legetur, / non Marsus, Pedo, Silius, Tibullus . . . / aut mordax sine fine Martialis" (*Carm.* 9.259–268); compare *Carm.* 23.163: "quid celsos Senecas loquar, vel illum / quem dat Bilbilis alta Martialem, / terrarum indigenas Ibericarum?"

Doctus ("learned") was a standard epithet in Martial's day for accomplished writers and especially poets. Martial applies it above all to Catullus (7.99.7, 8.73.8, 14.100.1, 14.152.1) but also to Potitus (10.70.2), Severus (11.57.2), Lucensis (1.2.7), Seneca (4.40.2), Secundus (5.80), Apollinaris (4.86.3), and even to the Muses themselves (1.70.15, 9.42.3, 10.58.5). Watson and Watson note the pointed contrast between *docti* and *ignoras* in the same verse.

6 *unum . . . opus:* Many translators (Ker, Izaac, Norcio, Ceronetti, Scandola) take the phrase to mean "a single theme," but *opus* surely refers to a single epigram of Marsus or Pedo, since that is precisely the concern of this poem (Friedlaender): compare 14.2.2 ("versibus explicitum est omne duobus opus"), where *omne opus* refers to each single poem of the book.

6 *pagina:* Although, like most translators, I have rendered *pagina* as "page," it should be kept in mind that the word refers to a column in a papyrus scroll: see on **2.praef.4**. Since a papyrus column regularly held between 25 and 45 lines of text (Kenyon 1951: 55–57), an epigram taking up two *paginae* would be "by any standards long" (Watson and Watson).

7–8: For the sequence of a general maxim followed by a specific allusion to the addressee in this light, compare the final couplet of **2.18**, where the order is reversed: Martial first complains about his relationship with Maximus and then offers a generalized *sententia.*

8 *Cosconi:* For the return in the final line to the vocative cited in the first line, a common practice in Martial, see on **2.10**; more often the vocative is placed in the second half of the final line. Here it is particularly effective, as it brings us back after general discussion of the history of epigram and a *sententia* to a direct attack on Cosconius. The pleasing tightness of form itself constitutes part of Martial's retort to Cosconius' criticism.

8 *disticha:* "Couplets," referring either to the individual metrical units of an epigram written in elegiac couplets (i.e., each couplet of Cosconius' is too long) or, as is more likely, to epigrams consisting of a single couplet (i.e., even the shortest imaginable poem by Cosconius is too long). For the former meaning of *distichon,* see 11.108.2 ("a me disticha pauca petis") and for the latter, 3.11.2 ("cur in te factum distichon esse putas," referring to the monodistich 3.8), 7.85. In any case, *disticha longa* is paradoxical (Joepgen 1967: 102–103, Watson and Watson); see on **2.12.4**.

2.78

Aestivo serves ubi piscem tempore quaeris?
in thermis serva, Caeciliane, tuis.

Where should you keep fish in the summertime, you ask? Keep it in your hot baths, Caecilianus.

Themes.   This poem introduces a striking sequence of five contiguous monodistichs, the longest such sequence in all of Martial, followed by **3.78–80** and **3.88–90**. It cannot be coincidental that this sequence is preceded by **2.77**, in which Cosconius complains that Martial's epigrams are too long. Scherf 2001: 64 observes that in each of these five monodistichs the central theme is a paradox or a contrast between surface and reality and that in each of them the contrast is distributed between the two lines, but these are frequently occurring characteristics of Martial's epigrams in general and monodistichs in particular.

The name Caecilianus, which we recently encountered in **2.71**, once again designates a man who is exposed to gentle mockery. The point of this distich is straightforward enough: Caecilianus' hot baths are actually so cold that even in the summer they could serve as a refrigerator to store fish. The remark is reminiscent of the dismissive allusion to the dark, drafty establishments of Gryllus and Lupus at **2.14.12** and plays on the etymological sense of *thermae;* see on 2 below. Greek epigrams criticizing baths as too cold or too hot include *A.P.* 9.617 and 11.411; Prinz 1911: 77–78 finds Martial "viel kürzer und sarkastischer."

Structure.   The monodistich gives the joke a particularly concentrated form. In the first line we read a seemingly innocent question, and in the second we find Martial's reply and simultaneously the name of the target. The reply itself introduces a sudden jab, executed with the final word *tuis.* Siedschlag 1977: 76 cites this epigram as an illustration of the close relationship between the two lines of a monodistich: the first creates a need for further information and the second satisfies it with a hyperbolic statement. For the technique of opening by repeating someone else's question (usually with *quaeris? vel sim.*) and then supplying an answer, see on **2.31.1.**

   2 thermis: Grewing 1998a: 339 observes that since *thermae* normally refer to large public facilities (but see on **2.14.13**) and that since a privately run facility is clearly meant here, the word calls attention to itself. In particular, he sees a play on its etymology ("hot baths"; cf. Isid. *Orig.* 15.2.39) and points to the vertical patterning (*aestivo* in 1, *thermis* in 2); compare 7.61 (*vicos/semita/via*), 3.25 (*balneum fervens/refugerat thermas*), 5.16 (*Roma/amor*).

   2 Caeciliane, tuis: See on **2.37.11** for the name, and **2.71.6** for the metrical pattern.

2.79

Invitas tunc me cum scis, Nasica, vocasse.
   excusatum habeas me rogo: ceno domi.

You invite me to dinner when you know that I have already invited others, Nasica. Please accept my apologies: I am having dinner at home.

Themes.   We move from baths to dinner parties, from *thermae* to the *cena:* two of the most important loci of social interaction in the world of Martial's epigrams. For dinner parties, see on **2.11**, and for further play with dinner invitations, see 6.51.

   As in **2.76**, a textual uncertainty gives rise to two different possibilities, though the overall tenor of the joke is clear. Nasica has invited Martial to dinner but the latter begs off in such a way as to make a swipe at Nasica, who has invited Martial only because he knows that the latter cannot come. The crux concerns *why* Martial cannot come: is he giving his own dinner party the same evening (*vocasse,* the reading of MS families α and β), or has he been invited elsewhere (*vocatum,* the reading of family γ)? See further below. In either case, the impoliteness of Martial's proffered excuse, *ceno domi,* is a sharp response to Nasica's ploy.

Structure. The distich has a fourfold rhythm, each line falling into two conceptual halves. You invite me to dinner; you know that I have another obligation; please accept my regrets; I am dining at home. The polite formulation of the penultimate element (*excusatum habeas me rogo*) stands in piquant contrast with the blunt formulation of *ceno domi.* The fact that each of the juxtaposed verbs *rogo* and *ceno* displays correption of its final vowel (see on **2.9.2**) speeds up the rhythm of the line.

1 *Nasica:* Martial uses the name, a cognomen traditionally associated with the Cornelii Scipiones, on one other occasion: in 11.28 he is an allegedly insane man who, reasonably enough, pounces on his doctor's attractive slave boy. Given the function of the nose as organ of discernment (see on **2.54.5**) the name may have an ironic function, just as in 11.28 it may imply a man "astute in his choice of boys" (Kay).

1 *vocasse:* The MS tradition is divided between *vocatum* (family γ) and *vocasse* (families α and β). The latter is printed by most modern editors, including Gilbert, Lindsay, and Shackleton Bailey, and I have tentatively followed them. The sense would be as follows. Nasica has invited Martial precisely because he knows that Martial has already planned a dinner gathering of his own. Martial's reply to the invitation ("I am dining at home") has received different interpretations. Shackleton Bailey explains in a note to his Loeb Classical Library edition: "The discourtesy of the excuse (he might have said 'I have guests coming') would show Nasica that his artifice had been detected"; similarly Barié and Schindler. But on this very reading Martial has already presented the desired excuse in the preceding line: *me scis vocasse.* The interpretation offered by Prinz 1911: 40–41 n. 3 is more satisfying: Nasica, knowing that Martial is giving his own dinner party, invites him in hopes of being in turn invited by Martial (cf. Plaut. *Stich.* 357ff.). In this case, Nasica is a typical *cenipeta* in Selius' mold (see on **2.11**), and Martial's excuse *ceno domi* disappoints Nasica's expectation, rudely dismissing the possibility of inviting Nasica himself.

The variant reading *vocatum* (family g, printed by Friedlaender and strongly favored by Schmid 1984: 416–417) would give the following sense. Nasica invites Martial in the knowledge that the latter has already been invited elsewhere; thus, Nasica is able to discharge a social duty without having to take on the responsibility of actually hosting Martial for dinner. And yet, although Martial has been invited elsewhere (*vocatum*), he says he would rather stay at home (*ceno domi*) than come to Nasica's dinner party, since he has seen through his pretense. In this case, Nasica is not being portrayed as a *cenipeta* and the rudeness of Martial's reply is even more pronounced.

2 *excusatum habeas me rogo:* This fairly elaborate phrase combines a polite request (*habeas rogo* for *habe; OLD* s.v. *rogo* 6) with the periphrasis *excusatum habeas* (cf. Ov. *Tr.* 4.1.1–2: "siqua meis fuerint, ut erunt, vitiosa libellis, / *excusata* suo tempore, lectore, *habe*"; *OLD* s.v. *habeo* 27).

2 *ceno domi:* See on **2.11.10**, where the phrase *domi cenat* likewise constitutes the epigram's point. A similar and equally surprising justification for refusing a request forms the punch line of a joke reported by Quintilian (*Inst.* 6.3.64). Having been asked if he might lend his cloak, Gabba replies that he cannot—because he is staying at home (*domi maneo*). This would normally be a good reason to be able to lend out a cloak, but Gabba's point is that his roof is leaky and he needs the cloak to protect himself.

2.80

Hostem cum fugeret, se Fannius ipse peremit.
    hic, rogo, non furor est, ne moriare mori?

As he was fleeing the enemy, Fannius took his own life. I ask you,
    is this not madness: dying in order not to die?

Themes. An incident that may or may not have really occurred (see below on 1, *Fannius*) inspires characteristically pithy narrative and pointed commentary in the form of a rhetorical question (*non furor est, ne moriare mori?*) whose paradoxical quality outdoes that of the preceding epigram's final "excuse" for refusing a dinner invitation (**2.79.2**). Martial's phrasing has antecedents in earlier Roman writers (Sen. *Epist.* 24.23 paraphrases a saying of Epicurus [fr. 497 Usener]: "tantam hominum imprudentiam esse, immo *dementiam,* ut quidam *timore mortis cogantur ad mortem*"; see further below), but he gives it a memorably concise form.

Taken out of context, Martial's pointed question (*non furor est?*) might be interpreted as a condemnation of suicide, yet elsewhere Martial praises brave acts of suicide: see 1.13 (Arria), 1.42 (Porcia), and 1.78 (the emperor's friend Festus). What prompts Martial's reaction in the present epigram, then, is not Fannius' act in itself but rather its motivation, just as in 6.32 he criticizes the emperor Otho's decision to kill himself at a moment when it was not yet clear that he would lose the battle he was fighting. Also at stake may

be a jab at Stoic pretensions: compare 11.56 with Kay, where Martial sar-
donically observes that it is easy enough for the Stoic Chaeremon to praise
death and scorn life because he lives in a state of wretched poverty; in 1.8
he similarly represents the act as too easy and almost cowardly, even dimin-
ishing the famous suicide of Cato Uticensis; see Citroni ad loc. For Stoic
thought on suicide, see above all Sen. *Epist.* 70, 78, 98, 104, and for general
discussion of ancient attitudes, see Ehrlich 1983 and Van Hooff 1990.

While some readers take this epigram quite seriously (Walter comments
that the "outraged question" expresses the poet's earnestness: "die entrüstete
Frage zu Beginn des zweiten Verses drückt aus, daß es Martial sehr ernst ist"),
the comment on Fannius' deed can also be seen as an exercise in wit. Bridge
and Lake, for example, cite a quotation from an Irish newspaper in the satirical publication *Punch:* "The speaker proceeded to refer to the sale of dis-
eased meat. A veterinary surgeon spoke of beasts killed to save their lives."

Nixon 1963: 142–143 traces later texts influenced by the present epigram.
Colton 1991: 448–449 cites Juv. 14.135–137, where the speaker describes the
miser's shabby manner of living as senseless: "sed quo divitias haec per tormenta
coactas, / cum *furor* haud dubius, cum sit manifesta phrenesis / *ut* locuples
moriaris, egentis vivere fato?"

Structure.   As Laurens 1989: 291 observes, this epigram illustrates Barwick's
bipartite scheme quite well: the first verse represents an "objective" situation,
and the second presents "subjective" commentary. The contrast between the
two is further marked by the distinction between a statement with past-tense
verbs (1) and a rhetorical question with present-tense verbs (2). At the same
time, there is a four-part rhythm, even more pronounced than that of **2.79**
since each line is divided into two syntactic units at the principal caesura.

1 *Fannius:* The name occurs again at 10.56.5, where he is a contemporary physician. Since these are the only two occurrences in Martial, and they
have no obvious thematic connection and appear in books published at least
ten years apart from each other, it is hard to imagine them as one and the
same person. Friedlaender identifies them as two distinct but real men, yet
there is no reason Martial might not have invented one or both of them.

Some commentators identify this Fannius with the Fannius Caepio who
was involved in a conspiracy in 22 B.C. against Augustus and was thereafter condemned to death: Suet. *Aug.* 19, *Tib.* 8; Dio 54.4–7; see *RE* Fannius
16 and *PIR* F117. But, *pace* Barié and Schindler and Norcio, Suetonius does
not say that Fannius Caepio committed suicide, and indeed Dio's language,
particularly the passive verb ἐσφάγησαν, implies that he was killed by
another's hand. Shackleton Bailey astutely observes that the noun *hostem,*
which usually signifies a wartime foe, suggests the scenario of a man on a

military campaign killing himself to avoid falling into enemy hands rather than that of a Roman citizen committing suicide. *PIR* reasonably distinguishes among various Fannii, including the man named in the present epigram (F114), the one named in 10.56 (F115), and Fannius Caepio (F117). In short, we can know nothing about this Fannius other than that he is almost certainly *not* Fannius Caepio (so too Walter). Watson and Watson wonder whether Martial is confusing Fannius with the Cestius who killed himself after having been proscribed (App. *B.C.* 4.26).

2 *hic, rogo, non furor est:* For the rhetorical question *non furor est,* compare 1.20.1 and 3.76.3. For other instances of parenthetical *rogo,* with no specific addressee and functioning more or less as an exclamation ("I ask [you]!"), see 3.76.3 (where the entire phrase is repeated, though in a very different context: "hic, rogo, non furor est, non haec est mentula demens?"), 4.84.4, 5.25.7 ("hoc, rogo, non melius?"), 13.58.2. For parenthetical *rogo* with a named addressee, see on **2.14.18**.

2 *ne moriare mori:* Heraeus 1925: 315 n. 1 traces this phrase's history (Ov. *Met.* 7.604–605: "mortisque timorem / morte fugant"; Sen. *Epist.* 70.8: "stultitia est timore mortis mori"), adding that "die prägnante Fassung" and "glückliche Zusammenpressung" are peculiar to Martial, who was himself later imitated (Claud. *Cons. Stil.* 1.341: "ne timeare times"). Friedrich 1910: 585–586 suggests that Martial found in the Senecan phrase an *Aufschluss* for which he composed an *Erwartung,* although Friedrich himself is not impressed ("nicht besonders gelungen"). For the play with two forms of the same word (*moriare, mori*), compare **2.18.8**: "qui rex est regem non habeat."

Quint. *Inst.* 8.5.6 observes that it is more striking to ask, "Is it really so dreadful to die?" (*usque adeone mori miserum est?*) than to state, "Death is not dreadful" (*mors misera non est*); see Barwick 1959: 40–41 for this *mutatio figurae.*

2.81

Laxior hexaphoris tua sit lectica licebit;
    cum tamen haec tua sit, Zoile, sandapila est.

Your litter may be roomier than those carried by six men, but since it is yours, Zoilus, it is a pauper's bier.

Themes. We shift from the weighty topic of suicide to a rather pettier comment on a man's ostentatious behavior, but the imagery remains connected with death. The nouveau riche freedman Zoilus, one of Martial's more memorable characters (see on **2.16**), is mercilessly mocked: his luxurious litter is actually no better than a bier used to transport the bodies of the penniless to the public gravesite. This reminds us of the contrast between Zoilus' origins as a slave and his present wealth, since the cadavers not only of paupers (9.2.12) but also of slaves (8.75) were borne on *sandapilae* to the funeral pyre. Some commentators have gone further: following Collesso, Friedlaender wonders if there is an allusion to Zoilus' (otherwise unattested) cadaverous appearance; Ker suggests that he is "such a worthless fellow (or, perhaps, so foul a man) that he is no better than a *vile cadaver*"; Norcio argues that he is "un essere inetto e inutile." See 6.77 for another epigram involving six-man litters and biers.

Structure.   The distich may be fruitfully compared to two nearby poems, **2.78** and **2.79**. In each case, the opening line sets out a situation, while the second line presents a reaction to it, and only with the epigram's final pointed word or words (*tuis; ceno domi; sandapila est*) is an invective tone established. Here we read in the first line that the addressee has a luxuriously capacious litter, while the second line recapitulates the situation (*cum tamen haec tua sit;* note the repetition and new emphasis on the possessive adjective, which had occurred unemphatically in the previous line), names the addressee, and delivers the barbed point.

   1 *hexaphoris:* The etymology of this Greek word is transparent: it denotes a litter borne by six men, a fairly pretentious way of traveling about the city (6.77; Juv. 1.64). The word is attested in this sense only in Martial (Vitr. 10.3.7 uses the word to refer to the six *bearers* of a litter) and might be a coinage on the poet's part (Grewing ad 6.77.10); see also 4.51.2, and compare *octaphoros* (6.84.1) and *hexaclinon* (9.59.9).

   1 *lectica:* A litter containing a couch or bed on which one might recline, and thus distinguished from the *sella,* a litter containing a seat; see on **2.57.6**, and for the two types, compare 10.10.7, 11.98.11–12 with Kay ad loc.

   2 *sandapila:* A wooden bier on which paupers' bodies were carried to their burial: see also 8.75.14, 9.2.12; Suet. *Dom.* 17.3; Juv. 8.175. At 8.75.9 we hear of a stripped-down version with four bearers, but the present epigram and 6.77 suggest that they too were normally borne by six men.

2.82

Abscisa servum quid figis, Pontice, lingua?
   nescis tu populum, quod tacet ille, loqui?

Why have you cut out your slave's tongue, Ponticus, and why now crucify him? Don't you know that what he keeps quiet, everyone is talking about?

Themes.   This is the final and most intense in a series of five satiric mono-distichs (**2.78–82**); its focus on what Ponticus has done to his slave consti-tutes an at least superficial thematic link with the preceding epigram's hint at Zoilus' servile origins. A parallel for the horrific scenario here described is found in Cicero (*Cluent.* 187): "nam Stratonem quidem, iudices, in crucem esse actum exsecta scitote lingua . . . [mulier amens] metuit ne condemnaretur extrema servoli voce morientis." Shackleton Bailey observes that Martial "may well have had in mind" the Ciceronian passage, although it is possible that the combination of mutilation and crucifixion was fairly widespread (for the latter, see on 1 below), whether in actual practice or at least in the popular imagination of what might happen to slaves, and thus that Martial is not specifically relying on Cicero.

Observing that *even if* his slaves keep quiet there will always be gossip about a rich man, Juvenal makes much the same point as Martial in the present epigram, though not imagining the extreme measure taken by Ponticus (Juv. 9.101–104). He goes on to claim that slaves will manufacture rumors about their masters by way of revenge for the beatings they have received and adds a *sententia* worthy of Martial: "the tongue is the worst part of a bad slave" ("lingua mali pars pessima servi," 9.121). On the other hand, Seneca (*Epist.* 47.4) speaks of owners who allow their slaves to speak openly in their presence, thereby gaining such loyalty that they remain silent even under torture. Martial 11.38 forms an interesting counterpoint to the present epi-gram: a deaf coach-driver is a desirable commodity!

Sullivan 1991: 164 cites this epigram as an illustration of how Martial "strongly criticises unjust or cruel behaviour on the part of masters and mis-tresses towards their slaves"; similarly, Szelest 1963: 186–187. To be sure, the implication of this epigram is that Ponticus has gone too far, and Martial does sometimes criticize excessive cruelty to slaves (see on **2.66**). Yet in the present epigram the poet does not actually voice any direct (let alone "strong") criti-cism of Ponticus' deed as an act of unjustifiable cruelty: rather, he emphasizes its futility. In fact, one might argue that the central theme here is not the master-slave relationship but rather the power of gossip; see on 2 below.

Structure.   Once again, the first verse describes a situation and the second presents a reaction to it. A special effect is obtained by casting both sen-tences as questions aimed at provoking an explanation or justification for the behavior described; Siedschlag 1977: 20 cites Greek and Latin predeces-sors. For the technique of opening with a *quid*-question, see on **2.42.1**.

1 *servum:* See on **2.11.8** for this noun.

1 *figis:* The verb is found only here in Martial in the sense "to crucify" (*cruci* or *in cruce* being understood). Elsewhere it refers to stabbing or piercing: *Sp.*12.2, 1.49.13, **2.66.2**, 9.56.3, 9.56.9, 10.16.1. In fact, this is the only pre-Christian attestation of *figere* in the sense "crucify" (see *OLD* and *TLL* s.v.). But the usage may have been a colloquialism (Friedlaender), and it may be a question of chance that no other attestations of the usage have survived. Perhaps precisely because of the rarity of this usage of *figere,* there is some MS confusion: families β and γ offer the readings *quod fugis* and *quid fingis* respectively (Collesso accepts *fingis* and glosses: "fingebat ab alio linguam fuisse servo abscisam"). Uniquely among modern commentators, Tanner 1986: 2671 understands Martial's *figis* to be referring to impalement.

A practice that the Romans may have taken over from the Carthaginians, crucifixion was a punishment most often inflicted on slaves (cf. Tac. *Hist.* 4.11: *servile supplicium*) but sometimes also on noncitizens. See *RE* s.v. *crux* and Hengel 1977.

1 *Pontice:* See on **2.32.2**.

2 *populum . . . loqui:* For the importance of gossip in Martial's world, see on **2.72.6**. Greenwood 1998a: 307 observes that here, as at 3.6.3 (*multi*), 5.77.1 (*quidam*), 7.6.3 (*auctor*), 7.72.12 (*quisquam malignus*), 10.3.5 (*poeta quidam clancularius*), the origin of a given rumor is suggestively represented as "unnamed and faceless." We might add that *populum* (as opposed to *multos;* cf. 6.56.5) has a particular force: the whole populace is talking about Ponticus' deeds.

2 *quod tacet ille:* Like Tanner 1986, Friedlaender assumes that all of Martial's references to Ponticus have to do with one and the same man, noting that none of the other epigrams mentioning him hints at the nature of the deed so shocking that he would take such measures to try to keep it secret. Focusing on the present epigram alone, Greenwood 1998b unconvincingly argues that, although *lingua* in verse 1 refers to the slave, there might be the implication that Ponticus is guilty of oral sexual practices.

2.83

Foedasti miserum, marite, moechum,
et se, qui fuerant prius, requirunt
trunci naribus auribusque vultus.

credis te satis esse vindicatum?
erras. iste potest et irrumare.   5

You have disfigured your wife's unfortunate lover, O husband: his
face, deprived of nose and ears, vainly seeks its former state. Do
you think you have sufficiently taken revenge? You're wrong. The
man can also fuck in the mouth.

Themes. As in the preceding epigram, the point is made that a violent
mutilation is not only pointless but will be avenged. After the rapid-fire sequence of elegiac epigrams **2.78–82**, each containing only two lines and
each naming a different man, the present epigram is longer, in hendecasyllabics, and does not name its subject, speaking generically of a *maritus* and
a *moechus*. At the same time we return to the sexual thematic and obscene
language last seen in **2.73**.

In fact, Martial here returns to one of his favorite satiric themes: adultery, in the Roman sense of the term *adulterium,* that is, sexual relations
between a married woman and someone other than her husband. In the first
two books alone, see 1.34, 1.62, 1.68, 1.74, 1.81, **2.17**, **2.25**, **2.31**, **2.34**, **2.39**,
2.47, **2.49**, **2.56**, **2.60**. Elsewhere, the poet constructs jokes or insults around
the risks accompanying such a relationship from the point of view of a married
woman's partner, the *moechus:* the cuckolded husband might rape or even
castrate him (**2.47**, **2.49**, **2.60**).

The present epigram reminds us of yet another form of revenge traditionally allowed the husband, namely the mutilation of the adulterer's face
by cutting off nose and ears, a punishment that was famously described in
the *Aeneid*'s narrative of the revenge exacted on Deiphobus (*Aen.* 6.497).
The joke here, repeated in a varied form at 3.85.3–4, is that this form of
revenge is not particularly effective since it leaves the offending member
intact: "nihil hic tibi perdidit uxor, / cum sit salva tui mentula Deiphobi"
(the phrase *tui Deiphobi* suggests that the mythic incident was well known).
The point is given particular sharpness in the present epigram by Martial's
rude comment that the adulterer can still, after all, irrumate or orally penetrate . . . whom? The addressee's wife, to be sure, but perhaps also the
addressee himself; see below on 5.

Structure. The poem moves relentlessly but smoothly forward in a familiar pattern. The first line sets out the situation with clarity and brevity,
and the following two lines add detail, all in a single sentence. The poet's
commentary on the situation is introduced by a second-person question

(*credis?*), followed by a reply (*erras*) that leads into the sharp point (see on 4 below).

1: Note the alliteration *miserum, marite, moechum,* and the suggestive juxtaposition of *marite* with *moechum.* The adjective *miserum* introduces a note of sympathy for the adulterer, while the vocative *marite,* unaccompanied by a name, lends the scene a paradigmatic character.

The noun *moechus,* a Greek borrowing equivalent to Latin *adulter,* usually designates the male lover of a married woman; see further on **2.39.1**. Thus, it might be translated "a/the adulterer" (Ker, Izaac, Norcio, Scandola) or, in view of the address to the *maritus,* "your wife's lover" (Shackleton Bailey, Barié and Schindler, Ceronetti). The noun is low, even vulgar in tone, occurring frequently in comedy and satire but very rarely in classical prose (Citroni ad 1.74.1).

2–3 *et se, qui fuerant prius, requirunt . . . vultus:* Note the highly rhetorical formulation that verges on the bizarre in a manner reminiscent of Ovid or Lucan. The reading, printed in all modern editions, represents an Italian humanist emendation of the nonsensical MS readings *e se qui fuerant prius requirunt* (family β) and *et si qui fuerant prius requirunt* (family γ).

3 *naribus:* Adams 1982: 35 n. 2 describes the mutilation of the nose here and at V. *Aen.* 6.497 as a castration symbol, pointing to parallels between penises and noses at 6.36.1 ("mentula tam magna est quantus tibi, Papyle, nasus") and Phaedr. 1.29.7–8.

4 *credis?* For the technique of following a question, often in the second person, with a reply near the end of an epigram, see on **2.7.8**. For such a question followed by a negation or denial of the addressee's claim or belief (*erras*), see on **2.1.11–12**.

5 *iste potest et irrumare:* The *et* is significant, as is the specificity of the verb *irrumare.* Not only can the adulterer continue to have vaginal intercourse (*futuere*) with the addressee's wife, but he can orally penetrate (*irrumare*) her as well. Yet the reference to this act seems only to have a point if the suggestion is that he might try to take his own revenge for what the husband has done to him by raping him orally (Adams 1983). For *irrumatio* as revenge, see Richlin 1981, Adams 1982: 127–129; for the notion that oral penetration is even more humiliating than anal penetration, see **2.47**, **2.60**; *Priap.* 28, 35; Williams 1999: 201–203.

Shackleton Bailey 1989: 133 claims that to imagine the husband as the implied object of *irrumare* is to "overshoot the mark" and that the joke is limited to the adulterer's relations with the speaker's wife. Richlin 1981: 46, followed by Obermayer 1998: 193–194, suggests emending the universal MS reading *irrumare* to *irrumari.* This would change the point considerably, as the speaker would now be urging the husband to take further revenge on the adulterer by irrumating him. The emendation seems unnecessary, particularly in view of the parallel with 3.85 (see above).

2.84

Mollis erat facilisque viris Poeantius heros:
vulnera sic Paridis dicitur ulta Venus.
cur lingat cunnum Siculus Sertorius, hoc est:
esse huic occisus, Rufe, videtur Eryx.

The hero Philoctetes was soft and readily gave himself to men: they say this is how Venus avenged Paris' wounds. The reason the Sicilian Sertorius licks cunt is this: it would appear, Rufus, that he was the one who killed Eryx.

Themes. Both the sexual thematic, with a focus on oral practices, and the crude language (*cunnum*) of the preceding epigram continues, and the ranking of sexual categories returns (**2.28, 2.47**). By means of a joking appeal to traditional myths, Martial suggests that a man's predilection for fellatio is even more objectionable than a predilection for being anally penetrated. If Philoctetes was cursed by Venus with a desire to be anally penetrated as punishment for having killed her favorite, Paris, then Sertorius' desire to perform cunnilinctus must have been inflicted upon him by the goddess for an even graver offense, namely for having killed her own son Eryx.

For Martial's use of mythological paradigms see on **2.14.3–4**; the effect is particularly piquant when, as here, myth is invoked in the service of obscene wit (Weinreich 1928: 30). See Kuppe 1972: 58–70 for discussion of this and other epigrams (1.62, 7.57, 8.6, 11.4) whose joke is based on a narrative of some kind of *exemplum*.

Structure. The epigram falls into two halves, the first couplet dedicated to Philoctetes and the second to Sertorius. Each couplet in turn is divided neatly into its two lines, the first describing the man's sexual taste, the second giving its etiology. There is a clear contrast between the periphrases of the first couplet, both euphemistic (*mollis facilisque viris*) and poetic (*Poeantius heros*), and the direct language of the second (*lingat cunnum; Siculus Sertorius*), as also between the mythic past (*erat*) and the present (*lingat*).

1: To say that a man is *mollis* is to label him as effeminate, but this in turn does not necessarily imply any single sexual identity, since the stereotype of the effeminate womanizer was alive and well in ancient Rome; compare Sen. *Contr.* 2.1.6 ("incedentem ut feminis placeat femina mollius") and see Pitcher 1993, Williams 1999: 127–129, 142–153. But *facilis viris* adds specificity: Philoctetes was inclined to play the receptive role in sexual intercourse with men. For the sexual coloring of *facilis* (present also in American slang: "easy"), compare 3.69.5 ("nequam iuvenes facilesque puellae") and 1.57.2 ("nolo nimis facilem [puellam]") with Howell ad loc.

The periphrasis *Poeantius heros* may be Ovidian in inspiration (*Rem. am.* 111, likewise a hexameter clausula). Philoctetes, son of Poeas, killed Paris with Hercules' bow and arrows. The peculiar legend about what happened thereafter is attested by the scholiast at Thuc. 1.12.2, who reports that because of Paris' death Philoctetes was inflicted with "the female disease" (τὴν θήλειαν νόσον) and, unable to endure the shame, left his homeland and founded a city that he named Malakia ("softness"). By contrast, Auson. *Epigr.* 75.2–3 jokes that Philoctetes' solitude on Lemnos led him to masturbate. Both traditions might have their origins in Greek comedy (Green ad Auson. loc. cit.).

2: More famous stories telling how Venus avenged slights by inspiring peculiar or destructive desires include those of Phaedra and her stepson Hippolytus and Pasiphae and the bull. The theme of the goddess' attachment to Paris is ancient, already found in *Iliad* 3, where she rescues him from certain death at the hands of Menelaus.

3 *lingat cunnum:* Examples of Martial's allusions to the practice include 1.77 (see Howell and Citroni ad loc.), **2.28**, 3.54, 7.67, 9.67, 9.92, 11.47, 11.61; see also Krenkel 1981 and Williams 1999: 199–203. Schneider 1909: 32 observes that the noun *cunnilingus* cannot be fitted into dactylic meter; the periphrasis occurs again at 7.67.17, 9.92.11, 11.47.8.

3 *Sertorius:* Martial uses the (fictitious) name on two other occasions, in both cases referring to an object of satiric commentary: he never finishes what he begins (3.79); he banquets until dawn (7.10).

3 *hoc est:* For the monosyllabic ending, found in eighty-six, or 2.59 percent, of Martial's hexameters and often being, as here, a form of *esse,* see Marina Sáez 1998: 153–158 and compare **2.28.5**, **2.66.3**. The technique was always fairly rare; it is found in 7.81 percent of Catullus' hexameters but only 0.24 percent of Statius.' Monosyllabic endings thus characterize a higher percentage of Martial's hexameters than of Virgil's (1.24 percent) or Ovid's (1.13 percent), but lower than those of Propertius (3.2 percent) or the *Priapea* (5.26 percent).

4 *esse huic occisus:* This is one of the few fairly desperate textual cruces in Martial (Heraeus 1925: 327), although luckily the sense is clear: Sertorius must have killed Venus' son Eryx. The MSS of both families β and γ (extant MSS of family α do not contain this poem) read *ab hoc occisus,* but this is impossible metrically; the only exception is C, which reads *ex hoc occisus,* a syntactic impossibility. There have been various attempts at emendation, none of them entirely satisfying. Lindsay prints the Italian humanists' *abs hoc occisus,* but in the classical period *abs* is found exclusively before consonants; only in late authors is it found before vowels and *h-* (Friedlaender); *TLL* 1.3.24–25 is able to cite only the fourth-century *Carmen adversus Marcionitas* ("abs ovibus," "abs alio").

Shackleton Bailey prints Delz's emendation *alter ab hoc caesus,* but this is inspired by the weak argument that Martial's contemporary Sertorius cannot literally have killed Venus' son since everyone knows Hercules did so (Delz 1971: 59): thus, Sertorius must have killed "a second Eryx" (whoever this might have been). This is to ignore the workings of hyperbolic epigrammatic humor: the remark that Sertorius must have been the one to kill Eryx, not Hercules, is not to be taken literally (LaPenna 2000: 92). Making a rare evaluative remark ("not one of Martial's better efforts"), Shackleton Bailey also suggests that *caesus* might introduce a sexual double meaning (= *paedicatus;* cf. Catull. 56.7): Venus punished Sertorius for having slain/penetrated a second Eryx.

Following Gilbert and Friedlaender, I have tentatively adopted Rooy's conjecture *esse huic occisus* (for the dative of agent, see on **2.1.7**). Other proposals include Heraeus' *acer ab hoc caesus* or *trux occisus ab hoc* and Helm's *certe occisus ab hoc.*

4 *Rufe:* See on **2.11.1**. Friedlaender and Schneider 1909: 50 identify him with Canius Rufus, but since the vocative here is little more than a prop, it is hard to say anything with certainty. For the first appearance of the vocative of the addressee in the epigram's final line, see on **2.30.6**.

4 *Eryx:* This son of Venus and either Butes or Neptune was killed by Hercules and buried on the mountain bearing his name, located in western Sicily above Drepana (modern Trapani); compare 5.65.4. Both the town Eryx (today Erice) and the nearby ancient sanctuary to a fertility goddess (Punic Astarte, Greek Aphrodite, Roman Venus) where temple prostitution was practiced were renowned in antiquity. For the mythic figure see Hdt. 5.42, V. *Aen.* 5.401ff., Ov. *Met.* 5.196, and for the site see Cic. *Verr.* 2.3 passim, Diodor. 4.83, Strabo 6.2.6, with *RE* s.v. and Kienast 1965.

2.85

Vimine clausa levi niveae custodia coctae:
   hoc tibi Saturni tempore munus erit.
dona quod aestatis misi tibi mense Decembri
   si quereris, rasam tu mihi mitte togam.

A flask for snow-cooled boiled water surrounded by light wicker-
work: this will be my gift to you at the Saturnalia. If you complain
that I have sent you in December a gift appropriate for the summer,
well, then, please send *me* a thin toga.

Themes. We shift from blunt exposure of a man's sexual tastes to gentler
commentary on gift exchange. Several themes familiar to readers of Martial
are here interwoven: gifts, the Saturnalia, clothing in general and togas in
particular (see on **2.29.4**). Gifts for the Saturnalia, and complaints regarding
them, are again the theme in 5.18, 5.59, 5.84; for the motif of gift exchange,
see 7.42, 7.53, 7.55, 7.78, and Spisak 1998a. For the toga as a gift, whether
at the Saturnalia or not, see below on 4 and compare **2.39.2**, 7.36, 7.86.8,
8.28.1, 10.15.7. The implication of Martial's final remark is that, because of
his relative poverty (see on **2.16**), he is happy to receive such a gift at any
time of the year.

For the central role played by an unnamed addressee, compare **2.61**,
2.76. Concerned to defend Martial on a charge of unseeming flattery or
hypocrisy, Spiegel 1891: 70–71 takes the absence of a name as a sign that
the poet wished to avoid giving offense, even though he has still gone too
far "by our standards" ("wenn er auch nach unsern Anschauungen überhaupt
zuweit gegangen ist"). White 1974: 41 considers this epigram, along with
several others, as an example of "poems in which a definite recipient is
envisioned but not named," but this is to take Martial too literally. It is not
clear that any specific, real-life recipient is at stake.

Structure. The structure corresponds to the division into couplets, each of
which contains an entire sentence. The first couplet in turn is neatly divided
between its two lines, the first describing the object, the second telling us that
this will be the poet's gift. The following line (3) introduces the contrast between this summer gift (*dona aestatis*) and the month of December (*mense
Decembri*), distributed between the line's two halves, but the syntax spills over
into the next line, thus bringing us to the final point.

1 *niveae ... coctae* (sc., *aquae*): Presumably, water that was boiled and then chilled with ice or snow, usually called *decocta,* was prized for its altered flavor; see 14.116 with Leary; Plin. *N.H.* 19.55; Juv. 5.49; Marquardt 1886: 333. According to Pliny (*N.H.* 31.40), it was an invention of Nero's; compare Suet. *Nero* 48.3.

2 *hoc:* Either, as translated (and punctuated) above, nominative, referring back to the preceding line, or, as Shackleton Bailey suggests, ablative: a flask will be my gift to you "at this time of Saturn."

2 *Saturni tempore:* A periphrasis, found again at 10.29.1, for the Saturnalia, which Martial elsewhere calls *Saturni quinque dies* (4.88.2), *Saturni septem dies* (14.72.2), or simply *Saturnalia* (4.46.1, 4.46.18, 5.84.11, 6.24.2, 7.53.1, 11.2.5, 14.71.1). Originally a farm celebration held on a single day, the Saturnalia had come to be the principal Roman holiday, and by Martial's time it lasted five (4.88.2, 7.53.2, 14.79.2) or sometimes seven (14.72.2) days beginning on December 17. By Catullus' time at the latest it had become customary to exchange gifts (Catull. 14), including but not limited to *sigillaria,* or miniature pottery or wax figures; the custom was continued in the Christian celebration of Christmas. Characteristic of the Saturnalia was a carnivalesque atmosphere: unrestrained gambling and drinking, sexual license, the wearing of the *synthesis* (see on **2.46.3–5**) rather than the toga, and a temporary and partial relaxation of role distinctions between slave and master. For an overview, see Leary 2001: 4–10. Martial had earlier published a book of couplets designed to accompany gifts exchanged at the Saturnalia (Book XIV) and was later to publish Book XI on the occasion of the festival, whose spirit dominates that book.

3 *misi tibi mense Decembri:* Similar language recurs in the opening lines of another epigram on the theme of gifts at the Saturnalia (5.18.1: "quod tibi Decembri mense . . .").

4 *si quereris ... tu mihi mitte togam:* Note the chiastically arranged alliterative pattern in *tu mihi mitte togam.* For the technique of ending with a suggestion to a dissatisfied interlocutor cast in the form of a conditional sentence, compare 1.44.3–4 ("nimium si, Stella, videtur / hoc tibi, bis leporem tu quoque pone mihi"), 5.26.3–4 ("si forte bilem movit hic tibi versus, / dicas licebit beta me togatorum"); and see Siedschlag 1977: 98.

4 *rasam:* "Shorn of their pile (and so thin or fine)" (*OLD*); compare Plin. *N.H.* 8.195 and Juv. 2.97, as well as **2.44.1** (*togam pexam*). Along with silver and gold, a toga and a cloak are cited in 13.48 as expensive gifts at the Saturnalia, albeit easier to give than a rare type of mushroom; see also 13.1, 14.124–125.

2.86

Quod nec carmine glorior supino
nec retro lego Sotaden cinaedum,
nusquam Graecula quod recantat echo
nec dictat mihi luculentus Attis
mollem debilitate galliambon: 5
non sum, Classice, tam malus poeta.
quid si per gracilis vias petauri
invitum iubeas subire Ladan?
turpe est difficiles habere nugas
et stultus labor est ineptiarum.   10
scribat carmina circulis Palaemon,
me raris iuvat auribus placere.

Because I do not exult in reverse poetry nor read the *cinaedus*
Sotades backward; because a Greek echo nowhere sings in answer,
nor does beautiful Attis dictate to me galliambic verse soft in its
weakness: I am not so bad a poet, Classicus. What if you were to
bid the runner Ladas to tread slender tightropes against his will? It
is absurd to make trifling poetry difficult, and hard work on frivolities is foolish. Let Palaemon write poetry for the crowds; I find pleasure in appealing to select ears.

Themes.   Martial returns to the theme of his own poetry, raised especially
toward the beginning of the book; see on **2.1**. Although there have been
various interpretations of some of the details (see below), Martial's central
message is clear enough. He distances himself from such flashy and popular metrical techniques as palindromes, echo poems, and galliambic meter
with the justification that his epigrams, being lightweight verse, are not suited
to such complexity. He would rather have a smaller number of appreciative
readers than a crowd easily swayed by metrical fireworks or "pedantic *tours
de force*" (Sullivan 1991: 75).

But this is hardly the only attitude Martial strikes. In 9.praef. ("maiores maiora
sonent: mihi parva locuto / sufficit in vestras saepe redire manus") and elsewhere, he is happy to reach a large audience, and in 9.81 he cares little about
other poets' criticism, preferring to please dinner guests (*convivae*) at the metaphorical banquet rather than fellow cooks (*coci*). Nor should we be misled by
Martial's statement into thinking that he entirely eschews striking metrical effects: see 5.24, 7.10, 9.57, 9.97, and below on *Graecula echo*. Still, the present

epigram informs us of his limits. The hesitance to claim a large readership may also be related to the fact that this poem was composed fairly early in the poet's career (Merli ad loc.); contrast the more confident assertions in later books (5.13.3: "toto legor orbe frequens"; 10.9.3–4: "notus gentibus ille Martialis / et notus populis") and in the opening of Book I (1.1.2: "toto notus in orbe"), often assumed to have been composed for a later, second edition.

For the application of the language of masculinity, effeminacy, and sexuality to poetry—perhaps with *supino* (1), certainly with *cinaedum* (2) and *mollem debilitate* (5)—compare 1.3, 1.35, 3.68–69, 11.5–6, and see Williams 2002b.

Structure.   The poem falls into several parts: an opening description of the metrical effects Martial avoids (1–5, an extended version of the technique of opening with subordinate clauses beginning with *quod,* for which see on **2.11**); a statement of self-defense, with vocative addressee (6); two sentences of two lines each announcing a general principle, by means first of a metaphor and rhetorical question (7–8) and then of a direct statement (9–10); finally, a closing contrast between another type of poet and his audience (11) and Martial's own aim, memorably expressed at the poem's end (12). The syntactic and rhetorical variety is especially appropriate in an epigram defending Martial's poetic practice.

1 *carmine . . . supino:* Various types of verse could be read backward in various ways; for this sense of *supinum,* compare Ov. *Pont.* 4.5.43: "flumina . . . in fontes cursu reditura supino." Martial's *carmen supinum* might refer to a line that is identical when read backward letter by letter, as with the verse cited at Sidon. Apollin. *Ep.* 8.11.5 ("Roma tibi subito motibus ibit amor"); a dactylic verse known as a *reciprocum heroicum,* which when read backward word for word produces a sotadean, such as "ire cupis si rus, mala vites omnia quaeso" or "astra tenet caelum, mare classes, area messem"; a *reciprocum iambicum,* which when read backward produces a pentameter, such as "micant nitore tecta sublimi aurea"; or a sotadean that when read backward produces an iambic trimeter, such as "caput exeruit mobile pinus repetita." According to the grammarian Diomedes, the *neoterici* introduced a particularly complex type of *versus reciprocus* in which two elegiac couplets can be read backward word for word but the metrical structure is preserved, as in the following example:

Nereides freta sic verrentes caerula tranant,
  flamine confidens ut Notus Icarium;
Icarium Notus ut confidens flamine, tranant
  caerula verrentes sic freta Nereides.

For these and other examples see Diomedes' survey of *versus recurrentes* at GLK 1.516–517, Servius' discussion at GLK 4.467.7–10, and Quint. *Inst.* 9.4.90.

The term *supinum* may secondarily evoke sexual imagery ("lying on one's back"): compare Catull. 28.9–10 ("bene me ac diu supinum / tota ista trabe lentus irrumasti"), Juv. 6.126 ("ac resupina iacens cunctorum absorbuit ictus"), Apul. *Met.* 8.29 ("nudatum supinatumque iuvenem execrandis oribus flagitabant"), Juv. 3.112 ("aviam resupinat amici"), and Juv. 8.176 ("resupinati cessantia tympana galli") with the scholiast ad loc. ("ebrii, turpia patientis").

2: Sotades of Maronea, active at Alexandria in the first half of the third century B.C., was notorious for his riddling verses making crude fun of great men; see Athen. 14.520f–621b, Plut. *Mor.* 11a. In a particularly daring example he attacked Ptolemy II Philadelphus for marrying his sister Arsinoe: "you are pushing the prick into an unholy hole." He seems to have been the first poet to write in a stichic ionic meter that later bore his name, the sotadean or sotadic (Servius at GLK 4.464.10–11 quotes the line "salpinx cane, tempus fugit, intende laborem"), in which he composed an *Iliad* and a *Descent to Hades*. Martial's *retro lego* suggests that Sotades also wrote verses that could be read backward; Ker, Izaac, and Barié and Schindler suggest that when read backward they yielded an obscene sense, but there is no concrete evidence for this (as Housman 1931b: 83 notes).

The epithet *cinaedus* (see on **2.28.1**) reminds us that Sotades and other reciters of a certain type of crude or risqué verse could be called *ionikologoi* or *kinaidologoi*. See Athen. 14.620e and Strabo 14.1.41, who provides a fascinating etiology for the term. A boxer named Cleomachus, having falling in love both with a *cinaedus* and with the latter's slave girl, began imitating the speech and other mannerisms of *cinaedi*. Sotades, followed by Alexander the Aetolian, then gave literary form to the practice.

3 *Graecula... echo:* Martial is obviously distancing himself from some kind of echoic verse, but the precise referent of his phrase is unclear. It probably does not refer to elegiac couplets in which the first words of the hexameter are repeated at the end of the pentameter for as many as seven syllables (a practice especially characteristic of Ovid), since Martial himself composed several poems using this technique: see **2.88** ("nil recitas ... nil recites"), 5.38.1–2 (*"Calliodorus habet* censum—quis nescit?—equestrem, / Sexte, sed et fratrem *Calliodorus habet"*), 5.61.1–2, 8.21.1–2, 9.97 (which consists of no fewer than six couplets, each beginning and ending *rumpitur invidia*), 11.70.1–2 and 11–12, 12.88. Wills 1996: 434 suggests instead that *Graecula echo* refers to echoing wordplay of the type exemplified in a famous epigram by Callimachus: Λυσανίη, σὺ δὲ ναιχὶ καλὸς καλός· ἀλλὰ πρὶν εἰπεῖν / τοῦτο σαφῶς, ἠχὼ φησί τις "ἄλλος ἔχει" (*A.P.* 12.43.5–6). But in 12.39 (admittedly in a much later book) Martial openly plays with echoing sounds: "Odi te quia bellus es, Sabelle. / res est putida, bellus et Sabellus,

/ bellum denique malo quam Sabellum. / tabescas utinam, Sabelle belle."
Another possible referent of *Graecula echo* is the type of line that Servius
defines as the *echoicum,* in which the final syllable rhymes with the
penultimate: "exercet mentes fraternas grata *malis lis"* (GLK 4.467.4–6).

4–5: Martial artfully blends mythic subject matter and poetic technique,
meter in particular. The story of Attis, kidnapped and castrated by the *galli,*
or priests of Cybele, is memorably recounted by Catullus in a poem (63)
composed in the meter bearing the name of those priests: galliambics. The
meter seems always to have been gendered as effeminate. Diomedes, for
example, speaks of a type of galliambic made *enervatius et mollius* by reso-
lutions (GLK 1.514.12–22), and most of the few extant examples of the meter
are in one way or another associated with effeminacy: at Petr. *Sat.* 23.3 a
cinaedus recites some bawdy verse in the meter, and, like Catullus, Maece-
nas composed verses on Cybele in galliambics (*FLP* 279–280). Martial's own
dismissal of the verse as *mollem debilitate* is unambiguously gendered: see
on **2.84.1.**

6 *Classice:* See on **2.69.1.**

6 *tam malus poeta:* This is the reading of all MSS, which Shackleton
Bailey emends to *iam malus poeta* for reasons that are not compelling
(Shackleton Bailey 1978: 275).

7 *petauri:* There is some confusion as to what exactly this object was,
but it was clearly a device used by acrobats or similar performers that was
singularly inappropriate for distance runners like Ladas. It is located in the
air at Lucil. 1298 Marx but on the ground at Manil. 5.439. Ker, Izaac, and
Norcio identify it as a springboard or trampoline, Shackleton Bailey as a tra-
peze, Barié and Schindler and Ceronetti as a tightrope, and Scandola as a
balancing beam. Alternatively, as Housman ad Manil. 5.439 proposes,
petaurus here may refer to the acrobat himself, otherwise called *petaurista*
or *petauristarius.* See further Kay ad 11.21.3.

8 *Ladan:* A famous Spartan runner and victor at the Olympian Games,
to whom Milo dedicated a statue (*A.P.* 16.54). Friedlaender, Izaac, and Barié
and Schindler identify him as an otherwise unknown contemporary of Martial's
bearing the same name. In any case, like Achilles (**2.14.4**), Ladas was clearly
proverbial for his swiftness; compare 10.100.5: "habeas licebit alterum pedem
Ladae."

10 *ineptiarum:* Like *nugae* in the preceding line (for which see on
2.1.6), this is a self-referential term found in "lighter" or "minor" literary genres
like epigram: compare 11.1.14 with Kay; Catull. 14b.1; Cic. *Att.* 12.24.2; Plin.
Epist. 4.14.8. Swann 1994: 50 strangely takes Martial here to be distancing himself from *ineptiae* and thus Catullus and argues that "almost 10 years
later [sc., in Book XI] Martial did come round to using *ineptiae* to describe
his own works in what had become by this time his usual pose of self-

deprecation." But this traditional pose is to be found throughout Martial's corpus (as Swann 1994: 51 n. 44 seems to acknowledge).

11–12: Note the contrast between *circulis* ("groups or rings of people assembled for conversation, as an audience, etc.," *OLD*) and *raris auribus:* between a mass phenomenon and individual readers. For this sense of *circuli* compare Liv. 3.17.10, Sen. *Ben.* 7 ("omnibus circulis narrant"), Petr. *Sat.* 27.3 ("duo spadones in diversa parte circuli stabant"). Ceronetti's "circhi letterari" and Sullivan's "cliques" (1991: 74) rather change the sense.

11 Palaemon: Q. Remmius (*RE* s.v. 4) Palaemon, a freedman and renowned *grammaticus* (see on **2.7.4**) who flourished in Claudius' reign, taught Quintilian and Persius, among others, and seems to have died before A.D. 76; see Plin. *N.H.* 14.49. He was the author of what was probably the first systematic Latin school grammar (Juv. 6.452 with scholiasts), and, along with some remarkable gossip regarding his sexual habits (for which see Baldwin 1995), Suet. *De gramm.* 23 informs us that Palaemon composed poetry in unusual meters: "nec non etiam poemata fecit extempore; scripsit vero variis nec vulgaribus metris." The present passage seems to confirm this. See further Kaster 1988: 55. Presumably because of the present-tense *scribat,* a number of scholars (Friedlaender, Ker, Norcio, Merli) have suggested that Palaemon was still alive when Martial composed this poem, which would therefore have been as many as ten years before the publication of Book II. Alternatively, Palaemon may already have been dead when the poem was written, and *scribat* is timeless. It is also possible that this is another Palaemon entirely.

12 raris ... auribus: The adjective suggests both "few" and "choice" (Ker), and the noun reminds us of the ideally aural nature of ancient verse in general and Martial's epigrams in particular, although of course private reading occurred as well. See Starr 1990–1991, Edmunds 2001: 108–132.

2.87

Dicis amore tui bellas ardere puellas,
    qui faciem sub aqua, Sexte, natantis habes.

You say that the pretty girls are on fire with love for you—you, Sextus, who have the face of someone swimming under water.

Themes. This straightforward monodistich makes a joke at the expense of someone's physical appearance. The humor is of a type common enough in Martial and elsewhere (cf. **2.35**), but the present epigram also draws on the piquancy of contrast: between Sextus' boast and the quite different reality but also between *ardere* and *sub aqua,* a technique also found at 1.62.4–5 ("dum Baianis saepe fovetur aquis, / incidit in flammas"). For jabs at the arrogant or boastful, compare 3.26, 3.95, 7.41, 7.76.

Structure.   Like most monodistichs, the poem falls into two halves corresponding to its two lines: Sextus' complacent boast (1) is followed by Martial's put-down (2). Laurens 1989: 297–298 calls attention to the opposition between *dicis* at the poem's beginning and *habes* at its end and helpfully compares 10.84: *"Miraris* quare dormitum non eat Afer? / accumbat cum qua, Caediciane, *vides."* (Do you wonder why Afer does not go to bed? You see the woman he is sleeping with, Caedicianus.)

1 *ardere:* Literally "to burn, to blaze," an ancient metaphor for erotic passion; compare 1.62.5 with Citroni, *OLD* s.v. *ardere* 7. Here its literal meaning provides the basis for a contrast with the image of water in the following line. For this type of wordplay (Freud's "empty" and "full"), see on **2.67.**

2 *faciem sub aqua . . . natantis:* There have been various attempts to explain this. Collesso suggests "pale and bloated" ("pallidam nempe et turgidam, ex eo quod, ut aiunt, sub aqua augescant omnia"); Ker and Norcio, "bloated and disfigured"; LaPenna 2000: 97 sees an allusion to pallor; and Prinz 1911: 75 to a cadaverous appearance. Citing Ov. *Met.* 6.376, on the Lycian farmers transformed into frogs ("quamvis sint sub aqua, sub aqua maledicere temptant"), Barié and Schindler propose that Sextus' face resembles that of a drunk or a frog, but the parallel seems strained. Shackleton Bailey cites with approval the suggestion of Housman 1931a that there is an allusion to underwater sexual practices of a kind mentioned by Suetonius (*Tib.* 44).

2 *Sexte:* For the name, frequently occurring in Martial but not attached to a single clear personality, see on **2.3.1.**

2.88

Nil recitas et vis, Mamerce, poeta videri.
quidquid vis esto, dummodo nil recites.

You offer no recitations, Mamercus, and yet you wish to be considered a poet. Be whatever you want, as long as you offer no recitations!

Themes.   In another pointed monodistich, Martial insults Mamercus' poetry. For Martial's jabs at fellow practitioners (or would-be practitioners) of
his craft, see on **2.71**. The epigram shares with its predecessor the use of
contrast: in **2.87** between Sextus' boast (*amore tui bellas ardere puellas*) and
his appearance (*faciem sub aqua natantis habes*); in the present epigram,
between Mamercus' behavior (*nil recitas*) and his desire (*vis poeta videri*)—
since, as *et vis* reminds us, offering recitations was generally a sine qua non
if one wished to have a reputation as a poet; see on **2.71.2**.

Structure.   Each of this monodistich's two lines—the first summarizing
Mamercus' practice and the second commenting on it—contains a paradox;
see below. Also of note is the repetition and distribution of forms of *recitare*
and *velle:* they are placed together in the first hemistich of 1 and distributed
between the two halves of 2. But perhaps the most striking structural feature of the epigram is the near-repetition of its opening words at its end (*nil
recitas . . . nil recites*); the reading of family α makes the echo exact. See
further on **2.43**.

   1: For the practice of reciting from one's work (*recitas*), see on **2.20.1**.
For this joke to work, Mamercus' desire to have the reputation of a poet
without engaging in recitation must be understood as paradoxical (Nauta
2002: 94). Compare 3.44.4 (an obnoxious reciter is *nimis poeta*), 8.20 ("Cum
facias versus nulla non luce ducenos, / Vare, nihil recitas. non sapis atque
sapis."), and Plin. *Epist.* 1.13.1.
   1 *Mamerce:* Martial uses the name on only one other occasion: in 5.28
he is a wretched man who maligns others, comparable to the addressee of
2.61.
   2: The tone of lighthearted exasperation leads to a second paradox,
evident in the logical contrast between the universal statement *quidquid vis*
and the proviso *dummodo*.

2.89

Quod nimio gaudes noctem producere vino,
    ignosco: vitium, Gaure, Catonis habes.
carmina quod scribis Musis et Apolline nullo,
    laudari debes: hoc Ciceronis habes.
quod vomis, Antoni; quod luxuriaris, Apici.   5
    quod fellas, vitium, dic mihi, cuius habes?

For taking pleasure in drinking too much wine well into the night, I can forgive you: Gaurus, you share Cato's bad habit. For writing poetry without Apollo and the Muses, you actually deserve praise: here you have Cicero's bad habit. Vomiting, you have Antony's; living extravagantly, Apicius.' Sucking dick: tell me, whose bad habit is that?

Themes. The insulting mode of the preceding two epigrams culminates with this, the last piece of invective in Book II. A passing thematic link is established by the joking allusion to Gaurus' bad poetry (3), comparable to the dismissal of Mamercus' work in **2.88**.

By means of a particularly effective example of the list technique, Martial manages to besmirch Gaurus with a series of practices or vices. The structure of the poem leads us to believe that the speaker is willing to forgive them all because they are associated with various well-known Romans; yet the final question, meant to be unanswerable, suggests that Gaurus can offer no such excuse for his predilection for fellatio. For the unstintingly negative attitude in Martial and other Roman writers toward those who practice fellatio and cunnilinctus, see on **2.28**. For the technique of listing famous predecessors in various behaviors, compare 5.28.3–6: "pietate fratres Curvios licet vincas, / quiete Nervas, comitate Rusones, / probitate Macros, aequitate Mauricos, / oratione Regulos, iocis Paulos." As Watson and Watson observe, such catalogues of *exempla*, both negative and positive, formed an important part of the rhetorical tradition: cf. Sen. *Contr.* 2.4.4, 9.2.19 ("in Gurgite luxuriam, in Manlio impotentiam . . . in Sulla crudelitatem, in Lucullo luxuriam"); Sen. *Dial.* 9.17.4. The present epigram seems to lie behind a piece by Claudian in which a list of vices is attributed not to famous predecessors but to astrological influence, and fellatio is replaced by cunnilinctus as the culminating vice (*Carm. min.* 44).

The humor of the present epigram is strongly reminiscent of a joke reported by Freud 1992: 85–86 (= 1960: 71). A certain man was said to have combined the qualities of the greatest men: he hung his head like Alexander the Great; was always playing with his hair like Caesar; drank coffee like Leibniz; sat back in his armchair and, ignoring food and drink, fell asleep like Newton; wore his wig like Dr. Johnson; always left a button on his pants open like Cervantes. This joke does not end with the sharp obscenity of Martial's, but the final detail does contain a sexual innuendo.

Structure. The poem displays an effective combination of two techniques: opening with a *quod*-clause (see on **2.10**) and accumulation (see on **2.7** and cf. **2.33**, **2.43**). For the buildup of subordinate clauses, see on **2.11**. Here each *quod*-clause presents a bad habit and each is balanced by a main clause identifying it with some famous predecessor. There is also a crescendo effect: the first two vices each take up a couplet, the vice being described in the first line, Martial's forgiveness declared and a renowned model named in the second; in the third couplet two different vices and models are named in the first line, each again with *quod* but with a compressed main clause (*Antoni* and *Apici,* sc., *hoc habes*); the final vice is expanded to occupy the entire final line so as to bring the point home. Smoothly parallel to all that has preceded, the brutal *quod fellas* comes as a shock.

1 *nimio...noctem producere vino:* Drinking well into the night or even until dawn was a sign of a luxurious lifestyle: see 1.28.2 ("in lucem semper Acerra bibit"), Suet. *Jul.* 52.1 ("convivia in primam lucem saepe protraxit"), Sen. *Epist.* 83.14 ("maiorem noctis partem in convivio exigebat").

2 *Gaure:* Martial uses the (fictitious) name again in 4.67, 5.82, 8.27, 9.50, but nowhere else attributes such a combination of traits to him. Thus, as often, the name does not seem to refer to a unified character, although in 9.50 he is said to write ponderous epic poetry (cf. "Musis et Apolline nullo" of the present epigram). Watson and Watson, following Howell ad 5.82 and Garthwaite 1998: 168–169, note that the name might suggest pomposity (cf. γαῦρος "haughty").

2: The reference is to Cato the Younger, also known as Cato Uticensis (great-grandson of Cato the Censor, who famously committed suicide in 46 B.C. rather than accept a pardon from Caesar and became thereby a symbol of resistance to tyranny). He was also known as a heavy drinker: compare Plut. *Cato Minor* 6, Cic. *Sen.* 46, Hor. *C.* 3.21.11–12 ("narratur et prisci Catonis / saepe mero caluisse virtus"), Sen. *Tranq. anim.* 17.4.9, Plin. *Epist.* 3.12 ("officia antelucana in quae incidere impune ne Catoni quidem licuit").

3 *Musis et Apolline:* The patrons of the arts in general and poetry in particular; see on **2.22.1** for the combination. As a parallel for Martial's sarcastic phrase, Watson and Watson aptly cite Var. *Men.* 52 Cèbe: "cum Quintipor Clodius tot comoedias sine ulla fecerit Musa."

4: Cicero wrote a good deal of poetry, but since antiquity he has suffered under the reputation of being as unsuccessful in this genre as he was brilliant in oratory. Quint. *Inst.* 11.1.24 wishes he had been more restrained and adds that Cicero's verse is constantly under attack; among the examples of Cicero's verse that he cites is the infamous verse *o fortunatam natam me consule Romam,* which Juvenal later ridicules (10.122–127). See Ewbank 1933: 27–39 and Allen 1956 for more sympathetic responses to Cicero's poetry.

5: In the course of his unstinting attacks on Marcus Antonius in the second of his fourteen *Philippics,* Cicero reports in scandalized tones and remarkable detail that, as a result of overdrinking the night before, Antony once vomited in a very public setting, while presiding over an assembly in his capacity as *magister equitum* (*Phil.* 2.63; cf. 2.76, 2.84, Plut. *Ant.* 9.6). Martial's brief allusion suggests that the incident became famous, just as Juvenal (10.122–127) claims that it was precisely the second Philippic that led to Antony's decision to place Cicero on the list of the proscribed, an act which directly lead to the orator's death.

For *Apicius,* legendary for his luxurious living and fondness for fine dining, see on **2.69.3**.

6: The climactic phrase *quod fellas* is all the sharper for the obscenity of the verb, an effect lost by such euphemizing translations as Ker's ("your beastliness"). The question is given a jabbing effect by the parenthetical *dic mihi,* for which see Citroni ad 1.20.1 ("locuzione affettiva di sapore colloquiale"), and is clearly meant to embarrass Gaurus, since he will have no ready answer. For the final unanswered question see on **2.60.4**, and see on **2.90** for Holzberg's argument that Martial's question might receive an answer in the immediately following poem.

2.90

Quintiliane, vagae moderator summe iuventae,
  gloria Romanae, Quintiliane, togae,
vivere quod propero pauper nec inutilis annis,
  da veniam. properat vivere nemo satis.
differat hoc patrios optat qui vincere census   5
  atriaque immodicis artat imaginibus.
me focus et nigros non indignantia fumos
  tecta iuvant et fons vivus et herba rudis.
sit mihi verna satur, sit non doctissima coniunx,
  sit nox cum somno, sit sine lite dies.   10

Quintilian, greatest of those who keep young men's vagaries in check! Quintilian, glory of the Roman toga! I am quick to enjoy life even though I am poor and hardly incapacitated by old age: please forgive me for this. No one can enjoy life quickly enough. The man who wishes to outdo his father's wealth and who packs his atrium with an extravagant number of ancestral images: let *him* put off living. Myself, I find pleasure in the hearth, a roof that does not disdain smoke and soot, a living spring of water, and fresh grass. May I have a homegrown slave who is never hungry, a wife who is not overly learned, nights with sleep, days without a lawsuit.

Themes.   As we head toward the book's ending, the tone becomes reflective and rather more serious after the fairly lighthearted **2.87** and **2.88** and the earthy invective of **2.89**. Indeed, there is a noteworthy contrast between the opening couplet of **2.89**, with its allusion to excessive drinking (*nimio vino*) and that of the present epigram, with its praise of Quintilian for his success in controlling the excesses of youth (*vagae moderator summe iuventae*).

Martial represents the great trainer of orators as having given some advice to the poet: presumably, like Titus in 1.17 and Gaius in **2.30**, he has suggested that Martial pursue a career in law (cf. *sit sine lite dies,* 10, with Szelest 1986: 2564–2565 and Sullivan 1991: 20). The poet here politely demurs, making a strong plea for the principle of "living" (*vivere*). For the pregnant sense of the verb, see below on 3, and compare a memorable formulation from Book I: "Believe me, it is not the sign of a wise man to say 'I shall live'; tomorrow's life is too late; live today" (1.15.11–12: "non est, crede mihi, sapientis dicere 'vivam': / sera nimis vita est crastina: vive hodie"). The epigram ends with Martial's vision of "the good life," an evocation of simple rural pleasures and an orderly home of a kind that he offers elsewhere; see on **2.48**.

Two scholars have recently commented on the juxtaposition of this epigram with **2.89**. Holzberg 2002: 82–83 proposes that since **2.89** ends with an unanswered question (*vitium . . . cuius habes?*) and since the other vices mentioned there are all associated with famous men, the implicit suggestion is that Quintilian is a *fellator*. Holzberg cites the appearance of Quintilian's great predecessor Cicero in **2.89.4** and observes that in Mart. 11.30 and Catull. 98 orators are associated with the *os impurum*. It is worth noting that the Catullan passage speaks generally of *verbosi* and *fatui,* not specifically of orators, but more important, it is highly unlikely that Martial would attribute, however indirectly or jokingly, the role of the *fellator* to so well known a figure as Quintilian by name (cf. 1.praef., 10.33.10). Moreover, **2.89** (q.v.) ironically plays with the tradition of citing *exempla,* i.e. precedents from the past: a contemporary figure like Quintilian hardly fits in.

Lorenz 2002: 20–21 argues that the tone of **2.89** makes it difficult to take seriously the statements in the present epigram regarding "the good life." But the juxtaposition of the obscene and the serious is hardly surprising in epigram, and in any case Martial elsewhere presents comparable images of "the good life" in contexts that invite being taken seriously. Compare 1.49, 1.55, **2.48**, and especially 10.47, where we find such details as field and hearth (4: "non ingratus ager, focus perennis"), an agreeable wife (10: "non tristis torus et tamen pudicus"), the absence of lawsuits (5: "lis numquam, toga rara, mens quieta"), and satisfying sleep (9: "nox non ebria sed soluta curis"; 11: "somnus qui faciat breves tenebras"). Whether or not Martial actually wished for himself such a life is an open question, but the seriousness of the imagery in the present poem seems undeniable.

Structure. The poem opens with a grand address to Quintilian: see below for its two formal features (epanalepsis of the vocative and an inserted apposition), and the phrases *vagae moderator summe iuventae* and *gloria Romanae togae* are lofty enough in themselves; other grand opening addresses are found in 1.15, 4.54, 7.47, 8.77. Thereafter, Martial describes his own behavior with characteristic concision (3), adding a request for understanding (*da veniam*) that introduces what amounts to a polite rejection of Quintilian's advice and a memorable enunciation of his ideal of living fully (*vivere*). The final couplet is noticeably balanced, consisting of four parallel clauses precisely corresponding to the hemistichs, each beginning with optative *sit*.

1 *Quintiliane:* The famed rhetorician M. Fabius Quintilianus was born, like Martial, in Spain, ca. A.D. 35. He was taught at Rome by the famous *grammaticus* Palaemon (for whom see on **2.86.11**) and, according to Jerome, was the first rhetorician to receive a salary from the public *fiscus,* an honor accorded him by Vespasian. He taught successfully for twenty years, and his pupils included Pliny the Younger and Domitian's two great-nephews and heirs. His most famous work, the *Institutio oratoria,* was probably not yet published at the time this epigram was written, but he was obviously already well known; he seems to have died in the 90s. The fact that Quintilian is mentioned here for the first and only time in Martial has led to speculation that the two never developed a relationship of friendship or patronage (Szelest 1986: 2580, Sullivan 1991: 20); see Arránz Sacristán 1987: 231 for an attempt at re-creating their relationship.

The positioning of the vocative of the addressee as the first word of the poem is not particularly unusual in Martial (in Book II alone see **2.3**, **2.29**, **2.42**, **2.77**), though Grewing ad 6.25.1 reminds us that it is also a feature of hymnic style. Combined with the other stylistic effects listed above, it may thus add a touch of solemnity; compare further Citroni ad 1.88.1. The repetition of the vocative in 2 (*Quintiliane . . . Quintiliane*) constitutes an example of epanalepsis, sometimes also called epanadiplosis or epanaphora: the "repetition of a word from a marked position in a line (at the beginning, at the end, or after the bucolic diaeresis) to a position at or near the beginning of the next" (Wills 1996: 124). The technique is especially characteristic of the neoteric and Augustan poets. In Martial, it is "an elevated figure to which the poet ascends only for lauded names" (Wills 1996: 169), as in the present epigram, 8.72.3–5 (Narbo), 9.99.1–4 (Marcus

Antonius), 11.80.1–2 (Baiae), 12.2.11–12 (Stella). The only exception is 5.8.4–6, where it is ironically applied to the pretentious Phasis.

1 *moderator:* Ker translates "trainer" and Shackleton Bailey "guide," but the noun has specific overtones of "restraining" and "checking" (*OLD* s.v. 3): compare Cic. *Fin.* 2.113 ("moderator cupiditatis pudor"), Liv. 26.48 ("non tam advocati quam moderatores studiorum fuerant"), Ov. *Met.* 7.561. Quintilian himself uses the term to describe the public figure who restrains a rebellious crowd in Virgil's famous simile found in the first book of the *Aeneid* (*Inst.* 12.1.27).

Quintilian's seriousness seems to have been well known, perhaps almost proverbial. Such is the implication of a sarcastic remark in Juvenal to the effect that women will fall for actors and singers but hardly for a Quintilian (6.75: "an expectas ut Quintilianus ametur?"; see also Juv. 7.186–189).

2 *gloria Romanae, Quintiliane, togae:* For the poetic figure of inserted apposition (also known as the *schema Cornelianum* or parenthetic apposition), see Solodow 1986, with many examples; in Martial, see 9.58.5 ("excipe sollicitos placide, mea dona, libellos"), 11.5.5 ("veteres, ingentia nomina, patres"), 14.89.1 ("felices, Atlantica munera, silvas"), 14.173.2 ("Oebalius, Phoebi culpa dolorque, puer"). Martial's phrase may have influenced Auson. *Profess.* 16.2.2: "alter rhetoricae Quintiliane togae." For the symbolic value of the toga in general, see on **2.29.4** and **2.57.5**; here it is metonymic for forensic oratory.

3 *vivere:* For the charged sense of *vivere* (*OLD* s.v. 7: "to live in the full sense of the word, really live"), see 1.103.12 ("aut vive aut decies, Scaevola, redde deis"), 6.27.10 with Grewing, 6.70.15, 8.44.3 ("at tu, miser Titulle, nec senex vivis"), 10.38.9, 12.60.6; Catull. 5.1 ("vivamus, mea Lesbia, atque amemus"); Sall. *Cat.* 2.9; Sen. *Brev. vit.* 7.10 ("non ille diu vixit, sed diu fuit") and passim, *CIL* 12.4548.9.

3 *pauper nec inutilis annis:* That is, Martial is not wealthy and is still young enough to work, and thus probably included in the group of *vaga iuventa* (1) over whom Quintilian exercises some influence. For his claims of poverty, which we must always evaluate with caution, see on **2.16**. The phrase *nec inutilis annis* (cf. 11.81.3: "et inutilis annis") is reminiscent of a Virgilian clausula: "et inutilis annos / demoror" (V. *Aen.* 2.647; Wagner 1880: 9).

4 *da veniam:* A formula characteristic of colloquial speech; see Hofmann 1951: 199 and compare 4.77.3: "paupertas, veniam dabis, recede."

5 *patrios ... census:* The *census* was, originally, the registration and classification of Roman citizens according to their property that was conducted every five years by the magistrate known as the *censor*. The term came also to be applied to the ensuing classification of a given individual or, even more generally, as here, to an individual's property or wealth. Zingerle 1877: 35 detects an echo of Ov. *Am.* 1.10.41: "census augere paternos."

6: The *imagines* mentioned here are the wax portrait-masks of those who had held higher magistracies; they were displayed in the atrium of their family homes and carried in funeral processions upon the death of a family member. Families having the right to display such *imagines* were called *nobiles;* thus, Juv. 8.1–23 likewise uses the *imagines* as a metonymy for aristocratic birth. There were various types of *imagines:* wax portrait-masks displayed in the atrium, portraits as part of a family tree painted either on a board or on the wall, other images with trophies located outside and around the entrance, and shield portraits. See Flower 1996 for detailed discussion.

7–8: A simple and direct evocation of a humble country abode with its hearth and smoke-blackened ceiling. The *focus* is an important element in Martial's picture of rustic or small-town bliss: see also 1.49.27 ("vicina in ipsum silva descendet focum") with Citroni, 1.55.8, 4.66.10 ("inculti rustica turba foci"). The phrase *nigros fumos* is a poetic plural of a type frequently found with nouns depicting comparable substances (*aquae, frondes, ignes, imbres*); KS 2.1.74.

9–10: The four climactic elements not only are balanced metrically and syntactically—each occupies a hemistich, each opens with an optative *sit*—but are endowed with a thematic balance. The first line speaks of human companions, one male and one female, one described as physically comfortable (*satur*), the other as endowed with an agreeable personality (*non doctissima*), while the second line offers overall images of well-being, a night *with* sleep and a day *without* the turmoil of the courtroom; note the chiastic structure *nox—cum somno—sine lite—dies*. The couplet is rendered thus by Robert Louis Stevenson: "A sturdy slave; a not too learned wife: / Nights filled with slumber, and a quiet life."

9 *sit mihi verna satur, sit non doctissima coniunx:* A *verna* is a slave who was born in the household rather than being acquired elsewhere; see Garrido-Hory 1981: 96–97, 119–120. This detail, along with the fact that he is well fed, adds to the comfortable, homey quality, as also at 3.58.22: "cingunt serenum lactei focum vernae." Collesso suggests a more practical detail: if the *verna* is well fed, he will be a better servant ("alacriter serviunt, nec conqueruntur, nec convivis invident"), a point perhaps implied at 3.58.43–44: "ebrioque non novit / satur minister invidere convivae." For the bias against overly learned wives, compare 11.19.1 ("quaeris cur nolim te ducere, Galla? diserta es") with Kay, Juv. 6.434–456 (Colton 1991: 261 sees Martial's influence). For Martial's wife, see on **2.91.5** and **2.92.3**.

Pointing to the parallelism between *verna* and *coniunx,* Obermayer 1998: 54 with n. 139 understands the slave boy to be the poet's sexual partner; yet a mere reference to a young male slave surely does not necessarily imply a sexual relationship (see on **2.44.1**). Holzberg 2002: 84 suggests that Martial desires a *non doctissima coniunx* because such a wife will not figure out what he is doing with the slave boy. But learning (*doctrina*) would hardly be relevant, especially since Martial often imagines himself and other men being brutally up front with their wives regarding their sexual relations with slaves: see 11.23, 12.96.

Martial's verse may well have inspired Paulin. Nolan. *C.* 4.15–17: "adsit laeta domus, epulis alludat inemptis / *verna satur* fidusque comes nitidusque minister / *morigera et coniunx* caraque ex coniuge nati" (Friedlaender).

10: For the combination of sleepless nights and days filled with business and legal woes as a characteristic of life in the city, see 1.49.35 ("non rumpet altum pallidus somnum reus") with Citroni, 5.20.6 (the *vera vita* is not characterized by *litis tetricas forumque triste*), 10.47 (above), and 12.68.5–6. The detail *sine lite dies* reminds us of Martial's expressions of distaste for the practice of forensic oratory; see on **2.30**.

2.91

Rerum certa salus, terrarum gloria, Caesar,
    sospite quo magnos credimus esse deos,
si festinatis totiens tibi lecta libellis
    detinuere oculos carmina nostra tuos,
quod fortuna vetat fieri permitte videri,   5
    natorum genitor credar ut esse trium.
haec, si displicui, fuerint solacia nobis;
    haec fuerint nobis praemia, si placui.

Sure salvation of the world, O glory of the earth, O Caesar! While you are safe, we believe that the great gods exist. If, on the many occasions when you have read my hastily composed books, some poems have caught your eye, grant that what Fortune has prevented from happening may seem reality: may I be considered the father of three children. If I have displeased, this will be my consolation; this will be my reward, if I have pleased.

Themes. The two themes marking Martial's book openings and beginnings—his own poetry and the emperor (see on **2.1**, **2.2**)—make a return and are intertwined in an epigram which, like its predecessor, opens with a couplet solemnly flattering its addressee, in this case Domitian. Here we have a foretaste of what is to follow in later books: see, for example, 5.8.1 (*dominus et deus*) and Sullivan 1991: 137–145. In a manner reminiscent of hymns and prayers to gods, the epigram follows high praise with a request; see Hom. *Il.* 1.39–42 for an early example. For the content of the request, see on 6 below. There follows the expected gesture of modesty, though the poet does allow himself to hope that his verse might have pleased the emperor. For Martial's relationship with Domitian, see on **2.2**.

Structure. The movement is smooth and elegant. After an opening honorific address to the emperor in the first couplet, the traditional prayer formula structures the following two couplets: the protasis of a conditional clause (3–4) and the apodosis, stating the request (5–6). The epigram's final couplet is structured around two alternatives, each of which is presented in a line beginning *haec*, and a chiastically arranged set of contrasted concepts (*si displicui, solacia; praemia, si placui*).

1–2: There are echoes of Horatian odes on Augustus and his relationship with Jupiter (*C.* 1.12.51–52: "tu secundo / Caesare regnes"; 3.1.5–6: "regum timendorum in proprios greges, / reges in ipsos imperium est Iovis"; 3.5.1–4: "Caelo tonantem credidimus Iovem / regnare: praesens divus habebitur / Augustus adiectis Britannis / imperio gravibusque Persis"). The formulation seems to have pleased Martial, and no doubt Domitian as well. The poet recycles it in another epigram combining flattery of the emperor with a delicate advertisement of the fact that he has probably read Martial: "o rerum felix tutela salusque, / sospite quo gratum credimus esse Iovem. / tu tantum accipias: ego te legisse putabo / et tumidus Galla credulitate ferar" (5.1.7–10). See also 7.60.2 ("quem salvo duce credimus Tonantem"), 8.66.6 ("rerum prima salus et una"). Two epigrams attributed to Seneca take the figure of thought present in 2 in the opposite direction, both of them using the phrase *credimus esse deos* at the end of the pentameter: since Licinus has a marble tomb but Cato none, how can we believe the gods exist? (*A.L.* 414, 414a Riese).

1 *rerum*: Many translators (Ker, Izaac, Norcio, Ceronetti) take this to be synonymous with *rei publicae,* that is, the state, but it more likely applies to the whole world: compare 6.64.14: "tanto dominus sub pondere rerum"; 8.2.6: "terrarum domino deoque rerum"; 8.66.6: "rerum prima salus et una Caesar"; and the famous Vergilian line quoted at 14.124.1: "Romanos rerum dominos gentemque togatam." In Martial's phrase *rerum certa salus* Fletcher 1983: 406–407 detects an echo of Sen. *Her. F.* 622: "certa . . . Thebarum salus."

3–4: Other statements regarding the emperor's knowledge and appreciation of Martial's work, not all of them so cautious, include 1.4.1 ("contigeris nostros, Caesar, si forte libellos"), 4.27, 5.1.9, 6.64.14–15 ("ipse etiam tanto dominus sub pondere rerum / non dedignatur bis terque revolvere Caesar"), 7.99. For the general question of Domitian as "literary patron" in Martial and Statius, see Nauta 2002: 327–440.

3 *festinatis . . . libellis:* Compare 10.2.1 ("festinata prior, decimi mihi cura libelli") and *Sp.* 31 ("festinat . . . qui placuisse tibi"). These *libelli* may be the earlier-published collections still extant (*Liber de spectaculis, Xenia, Apophoreta*); other, smaller collections that were circulated in various informal ways (White 1974, 1996); collections specifically intended for and dedicated to the emperor (Citroni 1988, Nauta 2002: 367); or any combination of these. Taking *libelli* to refer to the formally published *libri* that we have before us, Lehmann 1931: 25–29 argues that both the present epigram and **2.92** were written subsequently to the first edition of Book II and were first published in a later, revised edition of Books I–VII. Fowler 1995: 45 suggests another possibility: that *libelli* might refer to the earlier-published rolls whose contents were republished in the codex edition (1.1, 1.2) in which the (revised) version of Book II now before us first appeared. Shackleton Bailey avoids the issue by emending the text (see below). The anonymous reader for Oxford University Press makes the valuable suggestion that *libelli* here is playing with the sense "petition" (*OLD* s.v. 3b), and indeed the poem itself has this very function.

3 *tibi lecta:* Literally, "If my poems, often read by you in hurriedly gathered books, have ever detained your eyes." Shackleton Bailey 1978: 275 proposes emending the universal MS reading *tibi lecta* to *collecta* ("If my poems, often gathered in hurried books, have ever detained your eyes"), commenting on *tibi lecta,* "As though Martial could ever make such a public boast in his right senses!" and adding, "What is *tibi lecta* doing along with *si detinuere oculos tuos?*" He later acknowledges (1980: 69) that the first objection is invalid—Martial does indeed make such a boast at 4.27.1 ("saepe meos laudare soles, Auguste, libellos") and elsewhere—but nonetheless retains the conjecture in his Teubner and Loeb Classical Library editions. Yet it seems unnecessary, as the relationship of *tibi lecta* to the conditional clause is clear enough: the difference between merely reading his poetry (*lecta*) and dwelling on it (*detinuere oculos tuos*) is crucial to Martial's point.

4 *detinuere oculos carmina nostra tuos:* Probably an Ovidian reminiscence; compare Ov. *Trist.* 2.520: "saepe oculos etiam detinuere tuos." For the phrase *oculos detinere* see also Sen. *Epist.* 8.2 ("non vaco somno sed succumbo, et oculos vigilia fatigatos cadentesque in opere detineo"), Quint. *Inst.* 9.2.63 ("oculi diversarum aspectu rerum magis detinentur").

5 *quod fortuna vetat:* Watson and Watson, p. 3, interpret this phrase to mean that "Fortune had not granted him offspring, which suggests an infertile marriage, rather than a deliberate decision to remain single"; they compare Plin. *Epist.* 10.94.2, where Pliny requests the *ius trium liberorum* on behalf of Suetonius for similar reasons ("parum felix matrimonium expertus est, impetrandumque a bonitate tua per nos habet quod illi *fortunae malignitas denegavit*"). They thus conclude that, while Martial may well have been unmarried at the time of publication of Book II, he had previously had one or more unproductive marriages. See further on **2.92.3**.

6: This is a poetically phrased reference to the so-called *ius trium liberorum* (*natorum* for *liberorum, genitor* for *pater*). See further Daube 1976. Augustus' marriage laws of 18 B.C. (*lex Julia de maritandis ordinibus*) and A.D. 9 (*lex Papia Poppaea*) encouraged marriage and childbirth among Roman citizens by granting various legal privileges to the parents of three or more legitimate children. Men, for example, were exempted from acting as guardians (*tutores;* though some argue that this privilege was a second- or third-century addition), while women were freed from the necessity of having a legal guardian; thus, many epitaphs proudly announce that a woman is *ius liberorum habens.* Martial's request reminds us that the emperor had the ability to award the privilege to those who had not otherwise earned it, even to the unmarried. Well-known cases apart from Martial include Livia (Dio 55.2), Caligula (Dio 59.15), and Pliny the Younger (*Epist.* 2.13). Vestal Virgins were granted the privilege automatically (Dio 56.10). In general, see *RE* s.v. *ius liberorum* and Wallace-Hadrill 1981.

The privilege would have been particularly welcome to someone like Martial, since according to the *lex Julia de maritandis ordinibus,* an unmarried, childless man was automatically *incapax,* that is, prohibited from inheriting from others even if stipulated in their wills, while the married but childless (*orbi*) might take only half of any bequest. To be sure, a significant exception to this restriction was already built in to the system: relatives to at least the third degree and probably also to the sixth could always inherit, regardless of marital status (Wallace-Hadrill 1981). For Martial as potential *captator* of testamentary bequests, see on **2.26**.

7–8: Note the easy coexistence of plurals (*nobis*) with singulars (*displicui, placui*): see further on **2.3.1**. For the play on *placere* and *displicere,* compare *Sp.* 31: "Da veniam subitis: non displicuisse meretur, / festinat, Caesar, qui placuisse tibi." The future perfect forms (*fuerint*) are "used forcibly to express the certainty of a predicted result" (Watson and Watson); cf. 9.58.5–6 ("excipe sollicitos placide, mea dona, libellos: / tu *fueris* Musis Pegasis unda meis"), Cic. *Tusc.* 1.30 ("tolle hanc opinionem, luctum *sustuleris*").

2.92

Natorum mihi ius trium roganti
Musarum pretium dedit mearum
solus qui poterat. valebis, uxor.
non debet domini perire munus.

When I requested the privilege of three children, I was given the
reward for my Muses by the only one capable of doing so. Fare-
well, wife! Our lord's gift ought not to be wasted.

Themes.   This comes as a pendant to **2.91**, immediately revealing that Martial was successful in the request announced there. For this continuation
technique, see also 1.68 and 1.106; 5.21 and 5.24; 5.34 and 5.37; and perhaps **2.18** and **2.53**; Burnikel 1980: 91, Scherf 2001: 41. For juxtaposed poems
on related themes distinguished by meter, see **2.21/22/23**, 5.5/6, 5.11/12,
6.28/29; Merli 1993: 231, Scherf 2001: 62. The MSS of family β conflate this
epigram with its predecessor, even though the two poems are in different
meters; other instances of clearly mistaken conflation include **2.82** and **2.83**.
    Since Martial boasts that the emperor has granted him the privilege of
ius trium liberorum "as a reward for my poetry" (*Musarum pretium mearum*),
the alternative that Martial had politely offered in the preceding epigram—
if the emperor does *not* like his verse, at least let him grant him the privilege as a consolation prize (*solacium*)—is excluded. In short, we learn
that the hypothesis *si . . . detinuere* (**2.91.3–4**) is confirmed: Domitian
has indeed read Martial, taken pleasure in his verse, and rewarded him
amply (compare *praemia*, **2.91.8**, with *pretium*, **2.92.2**). See 3.95 for other
favors granted to Martial by Domitian, including an honorary tribunate
and the privilege of citizenship for the poet's clients or friends, along with
4.27.3–4: "quid quod honorato non sola voce dedisti / non alius poterat quae
dare dona mihi?" Thus, the first three lines of the epigram function as self-
advertisement on several levels, while the remaining one and a half lines
shift to a lighthearted dismissal of marriage.

Structure.   The sequence is clean-cut: the first line sets out the subject in
a lapidary but poetic form echoing the language of the previous epigram
(*natorum ius trium ~ natorum genitor trium*); the second line informs us
that he has obtained the benefit (*dedit*) as a reward for his poetry; the third
line identifies with flattering periphrasis (*solus qui poterat*) the man who has
given him this privilege. There follows an abrupt change in tone and syntax

with asyndeton (*valebis, uxor!*), and the ironic, teasing tone continues into the final line, with a passing return to flattery of the emperor (*domini*).

1 *natorum . . . ius trium*: As at **2.91.6**, a poetic rephrasing of the standard *ius trium liberorum*.

2 *Musarum . . . mearum*: As *Ceres* may signify bread or grain, *Bacchus* wine, and *Venus* sexual activity (**2.34.4**), so this phrase metonymically refers to Martial's poems; compare 7.46.5–6: "divitibus poteris Musas elegosque sonantes / mittere: pauperibus munera πεζά dato."

2 *dedit*: When exactly did Domitian grant him the privilege? The inclusion of this epigram in Book II might suggest that it had happened recently, perhaps in A.D. 85; but Martial's later allusions to the privilege (3.95.5–6, 9.97.5–6) reveal that "both Caesars" (*Caesar uterque*) had granted it to him. With near unanimity, scholars interpret that phrase to refer to Titus and his brother, Domitian, and indeed, according to Dio 67.2.1, upon his accession in A.D. 81 Domitian confirmed all the privileges that his brother and father had granted. But if, as it seems, this was an automatic process, why should Martial petition Domitian for the privilege, and why would he do so several years after Domitian's accession? As for the latter question, it may be that these two epigrams were actually composed soon after A.D. 81 and thus a few years before Book II was published (Merli). But why petition at all if the confirmation of Titus' acts was automatic? The most likely explanation is that epigrams **2.91** and **2.92** do not refer to an actual petition recently submitted to the emperor (*pace* Allen et al. 1969–1970: 345 n. 3) but rather advertise to the readership a privilege earlier received and at the same time offer public praise of the emperor for his generosity: see Nauta 2002: 336–337, Lorenz 2002: 121, Watson and Watson.

While it may well be true that the privilege was granted as a reward for Martial's poetry, this would have been Titus' motivation—perhaps as a reward for the *Liber de spectaculis* celebrating the Colosseum that he had brought to completion—rather than Domitian's, who would have confirmed it automatically.

3 *valebis*: "A formula of scornful dismissal to persons or things" (*OLD* s.v. 3d), in Martial again at 6.78.5 ("ridens Phryx oculo 'valebis' inquit") and 13.53.1 ("lactuca valebis"). In the present context *valebis* may well draw on the formal language of divorce: compare Pl. *Am.* 928: "valeas, tibi habeas res tuas, reddas meas."

3 *uxor*: Martial sometimes presents the persona of a husband (3.92, 4.24, 11.43, 11.104), sometimes of an unmarried man (**2.49**, 10.8, 11.19, 11.23), as suits the context. Here he plays the role of a married man who cavalierly can get rid of his wife now that he has no need of her (see on *valebis*, 3); alternatively, he is a bachelor and the phrase *valebis uxor* means that he is taking leave of the very idea of marriage.

We have no external evidence as to whether Martial ever in fact married, but most scholars today doubt he did. Sullivan 1991: 25–26, for example, observes the following. "Such a lowering of dignity [in obscene pieces like 11.43 and 11.104] would only be possible, given the natural tendency of the ancient audience to look for biography in even the most literary of works, if Martial were *known* to be unmarried. The request for the grant of the *ius trium liberorum* points in the same direction. It is not described as compensation for his own or his wife's (or wives') regrettable sterility, but as an honour which requires no apology. In another epigram (8.31) he chides a man for requesting this very privilege, since he has a wife and could therefore beget three children in the normal way; this implies that the opposite is his case." Likewise in 9.66 Martial argues that since Fabullus has a beautiful young wife, he ought not to ask the emperor for the *ius trium liberorum:* unless he is impotent, he can grant himself the privilege! For a different perspective on the question, see on **2.91.5**.

4 *domini:* A flattering usage, though less extreme than the later *dominus et deus* encouraged by the emperor himself; compare Suet. *Dom.* 13.2 and see Mart. 5.8.1, 7.34.8, 8.2.6, 9.66.3, 10.72.3. In itself, *dominus* no more necessarily implies divinity than does the English title "Lord" when applied to nobility, and indeed the term could be used to refer to one's patron; see on **2.32.8**. Nonetheless, the application of the title *dominus* to the emperor was often a sensitive question. Augustus, for example, had considered it a *maledictum* and *opprobrium* (Suet. *Aug.* 53; Sullivan 1991: 141).

2.93

"Primus ubi est" inquis "cum sit liber iste secundus?"
    quid faciam si plus ille pudoris habet?
tu tamen hunc fieri si mavis, Regule, primum,
    unum de titulo tollere iota potes.

"Where is the first book," you ask, "if this is the second?" What can I do if that book had more modesty? Still, if you want this to become the first book, Regulus, you can take away one of the two iotas from its title.

Themes. Having learned that Martial has been rewarded by the emperor for his poetry in general (**2.92.2**: *Musarum pretium mearum*), we now find an explicit reference to *this* book (*liber iste*). When, as here, he makes an explicit gesture of closure at the end of a book of epigrams, Martial's themes tend to be those of the book openings: the book itself or poetry in general (I–IV, VII–VIII, X–XI) and/or the emperor (VII–VIII). Other books (V–VI, IX, XII) end with epigrams that have no closing function, at least not at first glance (but see Fowler 1989).

This final epigram returns us to a familiar theme in a most concrete way. The topic is the very book of epigrams, in Martial's day a scroll probably labeled *LIBER II,* that we are holding in our hands and have just finished reading. The exact implications of Martial's pleasantry have been reconstructed in various ways (see on 1 below), but the basic point is clear: the present book labels itself "Book II" and Regulus asks where Book I is. Martial replies that if he wishes, he can simply remove an I from the label *LIBER II.* Explicit references to the number of books of one's own poetry are very rarely found before Martial (Ov. *Am.* 1.epigr., Ov. *Fast.* 1.723–724, and perhaps Prop. 2.13.25). It is a device the epigrammatist uses quite often: apart from the present epigram, see 5.1, 5.15, 6.1 with Grewing, 6.85, 7.17, 8.praef. with Schöffel, 8.3 (where the tone is again mock-modest), 10.2, 12.4. Compare also the prefaces to Books I, III, and IV of Statius' *Silvae.*

Structure. The line opens with a quotation marked as such by *inquis* (for the technique see on **2.21.2**, and for the opening question see on **2.31.1**), but we do not know who is the subject of this verb is until 3. With the second line and its first-person singular (*faciam*), the epigram takes on the quality of a dialogue between this yet-unnamed person and the poet himself; compare **2.21**, **2.49**, **2.60**, **2.66**. The third line, being the protasis of a conditional sentence, creates the expectation of an apodosis, which we find in the next and last line, with its mild joke.

1 *primus ubi est:* Regulus is surprised to see the present book calling itself "Book II" because he has not seen Book I. Why not? The first answer that comes to mind is that Martial never gave him a copy (Friedlaender, Barié and Schindler; Shackleton Bailey suggests unconvincingly that not only has Regulus not seen the first book, but Martial has no copy to offer him). The remark that the first *book* has more modesty (*plus ille pudoris habet*) would be a metonymic way of saying that *Martial* was not confident enough to present the first book to Regulus. This would be possible only if we take the reference to be to an earlier version of Book I that did not contain 1.1 and other confident poems found in the present version.

Lehmann 1931: 37–39 offers an unnecessarily complicated explanation, suggesting that the present Book II was actually the first book of epigrams published after the *Liber de spectaculis, Xenia,* and *Apophoreta,* and that the present Book I first appeared only in a later revised edition. The present epigram, along with others referring to the current book numbers (5.2, 5.15, 6.1, 6.85), would have been composed for the later, revised edition of Books I–VII, and Martial's point would have been that just as he himself has converted what was originally Book I into Book II, Regulus can change it back if he wishes. Another unconvincing explanation (Dau 1887: 85, Sage 1919: 174–175) is that when Martial released Book II he was holding on to the unpublished Book I, which he released shortly thereafter. Fowler 1995: 35 suggests yet another possibility, also fairly far-fetched. If the present Book II, including this epigram, was published in a revised codex edition of Martial (cf. 1.1, 1.2) containing all of Books I–VII, "one may . . . imagine that the title page of the codex contained only a general title, and that there was no *explicit* to Book One: the first reference to a book number would then be a 'II' at the opening of the second book." In this sense Regulus will not have seen a LIBER I.

The most convincing interpretation remains that proposed by Citroni 1975: xiv–xviii. The first book was "modest" in that it did not call itself LIBER I—a label which implies that more is to follow—but bore a simpler title, such as M. VALERII MARTIALIS EPIGRAMMATON LIBER. After all, Martial observes that the previous book had *more* modesty (*plus pudoris*)—more, presumably, than the present book, which calls itself LIBER II and thus leaves open the possibility that a LIBER III will follow.

1 *inquis:* Before we read the vocative *Regule* in 3, this second-person verb might suggest a generalized address to Martial's reader.

1 *liber iste:* For this use of the deictic *iste* to refer to the book we have before us, see on **2.8.1**.

2 *quid faciam:* Like such other formulas as *quid vis?* or *quid quaeris?* the phrase probably echoes colloquial speech; Hofmann 1951: 44–45, 189.

2 *plus ille pudoris habet:* However slightly, the phrase implies a personification of the book, a technique Martial exploits elsewhere at greater length: see 1.3 with Citroni, 1.35, 1.52, 11.15; Williams 2002b. In 3.4–3.5 and 10.1 the book actually speaks.

3 *Regule:* See on **2.74.2**. The fact that Martial addresses Regulus in this climactic poem, and associates him, however jokingly, with the book as such, gives him some emphasis as reader and patron. See Nauta 2002: 105–120 for the practice of presenting books to an individual.

4 *iota:* Greek names of letters of the alphabet appear again at **2.57.4** (*a*), 5.26 (*a*, *β*), 7.37 (*θ*). There certainly were Latin names for the letters (*ā, bē, cē, dē, ef, gē*, etc.; see Gordon 1973), but this passage implies that Greek names could also be applied to Latin letters, albeit perhaps controversially: see Lucil. 379 Marx, "s nostrum et semigraecei quod dicimus sigma."

Here *iota* is trisyllabic, with an elision between *tollere* and *iota,* for which see Birt in Friedlaender's introduction (33–34).

BIBLIOGRAPHY

This is not a complete bibliography of scholarship on Martial but rather a list of works cited in the present commentary. For further bibliography, see the commentaries listed below, along with Grewing 1998b.

A. Editions, Translations, and Commentaries

In the text, the following are cited by the editor's, translator's, or commentator's last name alone. See also the list of abbreviations (p. x).

Barié, Paul, and Winfried Schindler. *M. Valerius Martialis: Epigramme*. Zurich, 1999.
Bridge, R. T., and E. D. C. Lake. *Select Epigrams of Martial: Spectaculorum Liber and Books I–VI*. Oxford, 1908.
Ceronetti, Guido. *Marziale, Epigrammi*. Turin, 1964.
Citroni, Mario. *M. Valerii Martialis epigrammaton liber primus*. Florence, 1975.
Collesso, Vincentius. *M. Valerii Martialis epigrammata, paraphrasi ac notis variorum selectissimis ad usum serenissimi Delphini*. Amsterdam, 1701.
Friedlaender, Ludwig. *M. Valerii Martialis Epigrammaton Libri, mit erklärenden Anmerkungen*. Leipzig, 1886.
Galán Vioque, Guillermo. *Martial, Book VII: A Commentary*. Translated by J. J. Zoltowski. Leiden, 2002.
Giarratano, C. *M. Valerii Martialis epigrammaton libri*. Rev. ed. Turin, 1951.
Gilbert, W. *M. Valerii Martialis epigrammaton libri*. Rev. ed. Leipzig, 1893.
Grewing, Farouk. *Martial, Buch VI: Ein Kommentar*. Göttingen, 1997.
Henriksén, Christer. *Martial, Book IX: A Commentary*. Uppsala, 1999.

Heraeus, W. *M. Valerii Martialis epigrammaton libri.* Leipzig (Teubner), 1925. Revised by Iacobus Borovskij, Leipzig, 1976.

Howell, Peter. *A Commentary on Book One of the Epigrams of Martial.* London, 1980.

———. *Martial: The Epigrams, Book 5.* Warminster, 1995.

Izaac, H. J. *Martial, Epigrammes.* Paris, 1930–1933.

Kay, N. M. *Martial, Book XI: A Commentary.* London, 1985.

Ker, Walter C. A. *Martial, Epigrams.* London and New York, 1919.

Leary, Timothy J. *Martial, Book XIII: The* Xenia. London, 2001.

———. *Martial, Book XIV: The* Apophoreta. London, 1996.

Lindsay, W. M. *M. Valerii Martialis Epigrammata.* Oxford, 1929.

Michie, James. *Martial: The Epigrams, Selected and Translated.* London, 1973.

Norcio, Giuseppe. *Marziale, Epigrammi.* Turin, 1980.

Post, Edwin. *Selected Epigrams of Martial.* New York, 1908.

Scandola, Mario (translation), Mario Citroni (introduction), and Elena Merli (notes). *Marziale, Epigrammi.* 2nd ed. Milan, 2000.

Schneidewin, Friedrich Wilhelm. *M. Valerii Martialis epigrammaton libri.* 2nd ed. Leipzig, 1853.

Schöffel, Christian. *Martial, Buch 8. Einleitung, Text, Übersetzung, Kommentar.* Stuttgart, 2002.

Schrevelius, C. *M. Valerii Martialis epigrammata cum notis variorum.* Leiden, 1670.

Shackleton Bailey, D. R. *M. Valerii Martialis Epigrammata.* Stuttgart, 1991.

———. *Martial, Epigrams.* Cambridge, Mass., 1993.

Sullivan, J. P., and Peter Whigham, eds. *Epigrams of Martial Englished by Divers Hands.* Berkeley and London, 1987.

Walter, Uwe. *M. Valerius Martialis, Epigramme: Ausgewählt, eingeleitet und kommentiert.* Paderborn, 1996.

Watson, Lindsay and Patricia Watson. *Martial: Select Epigrams.* Cambridge, 2003.

B. Secondary Literature

In the text, the following are cited by the author's last name and year of publication.

Actas del simposio sobre Marco Valerio Marcial: Poeta de Bilbilis y de Roma. 1987. 2 vols. Zaragoza.

Adams, Andrew James. 1975. "The Nature of Martial's Epigrams." Diss., Indiana University.

Adams, J. N. 1981. "*Culus, Clunes,* and Their Synonyms in Latin." *Glotta* 59: 231–264.

———. 1982. *The Latin Sexual Vocabulary.* Baltimore.

———. 1983. "Martial 2.83." *Classical Philology* 78: 311–315.

Ahl, Frederick M. 1984. "The Rider and the Horse: Politics and Power in Roman Poetry from Horace to Statius." *ANRW* 2.32.1: 40–110.

Aldrete, Gregory. 1999. *Gestures and Acclamations in Ancient Rome.* Baltimore.

Allen, Walter, Jr. 1956. "*O fortunatam natam . . .*" *Transactions of the American Philological Association* 87: 130–146.

———, et al. 1969–1970. "Martial: Knight, Publisher, and Poet." *Classical Journal* 65: 345–357.

Anderson, W. S. 1982. "*Lascivia* vs. *Ira:* Martial and Juvenal." In *Essays on Roman Satire,* 362–395. Princeton.

André, J. 1981. *L'alimentation et la cuisine à Rome.* Paris.

Andreau, Jean. 1999. *Banking and Business in the Roman World*. Translated by Janet Lloyd. New York and Cambridge.

Arránz Sacristán, Felicísimo. 1987. "Hispania vista por Marco Valerio Marcial." *Actas del Simposio* 2.211–236.

Bakhouche, Béatrice. 2002. *L'astrologie à Rome*. Louvain.

Baldwin, Barry. 1995. "The Sexual Tastes of Remmius Palaemon." *Hermes* 123: 380–382.

Bannon, Cynthia J. 1997. *Brothers of Romulus: Fraternal* Pietas *in Roman Law, Literature, and Society*. Princeton.

Barrett, D. S. 1984. "Martial, Jews, and Circumcision." *Liverpool Classical Monthly* 9: 42–46.

Barton, Tamsyn. 1994. *Ancient Astrology*. New York and London.

Barwick, K. 1932. "Zur Kompositionstechnik und Erklärung Martials." *Philologus* 87: 63–79.

———. 1958. "Zyklen bei Martial und in den kleinen Gedichten des Catull." *Philologus* 102: 284–318.

———. 1959. *Martial und die zeitgenössische Rhetorik*. Berlin.

Binder, Gerhard. 1995. "Öffentliche Autorenlesungen: Zur Kommunikation zwischen römischen Autoren und ihrem Publikum." In *Kommunikation durch Zeichen und Wort*, edited by G. Binder and K. Ehrlich, 265–332. Trier.

Blanck, Horst. 1992. *Das Buch in der Antike*. Munich.

Blümner, H. 1911. *Römische Privataltertümer*. Munich.

Borgo, Antonella. 2001. "La *praefatio* del II libro di Marziale: La *brevitas* principio di poetica." *Bollettino di studi latini* 31: 497–506.

Boswell, John. 1990. "Concepts, Experience, and Sexuality." *Differences* 2: 67–87.

Bradley, Keith. 1987. *Slaves and Masters in the Roman Empire: A Study in Social Control*. New York and Oxford.

———. 1994. *Slavery and Society at Rome*. Cambridge.

Braund, Susanna. 1988. *Beyond Anger: A Study of Juvenal's Third Book of Satires*. Cambridge.

———. 1996. "The Solitary Feast: A Contradiction in Terms?" *Bulletin of the Institute of Classical Studies* 41: 37–52.

Brockmeyer, Norbert. 1979. *Antike Sklaverei*. Darmstadt.

Brown, Robert D. 1994. "The Bed-Wetters in Lucretius 4.1026." *Harvard Studies in Classical Philology* 96: 191–196.

Burnikel, Walter. 1980. *Untersuchungen zur Struktur des Witzepigramms bei Lukillios und Martial*. Wiesbaden.

———. 1990. "Zur Bedeutung der Mündlichkeit in Martials Epigrammbüchern I–XII." In *Strukturen der Mündlichkeit in der römischen Literatur*, edited by Gregor Vogt-Spira, 221–234. Tübingen.

Burzachini, G. 1977. "Filenide in Marziale." *Sileno* 3: 239–243.

Castagnoli, Ferdinando. 1993. "Roma nei versi di Marziale." In *Topografia antica: Un metodo di studio*, 1.107–14. Rome.

Cavallo, Guglielmo. 1975. *Libri, editori e pubblico nel mondo antico: Guida storica e critica*. Rome.

Champlin, E. 1991. *Final Judgments: Duty and Emotion in Roman Wills, 200 B.C.– A.D. 250*. Berkeley.

Citroni, Mario. 1968. "Motivi di polemica letteraria negli epigrammi di Marziale." *Dialoghi di archeologia* 2: 259–351.

————. 1969. "La teoria lessinghiana dell'epigramma e le interpretazioni moderne di Marziale." *Maia* 21: 215–243.

————. 1986. "Le raccomandazioni del poeta: Apostrofe al libro e contatto col destinatario." *Maia* 38: 111–146.

————. 1988. "Pubblicazione e dediche dei libri in Marziale." *Maia* 40: 3–39.

————. 1989. "Marziale e la letteratura per i Saturnali (poetica dell'intrattenimento e cronologia della pubblicazione dei libri)." *Illinois Classical Studies* 14: 201ff.

————. 1995. *Poesia e lettori in Roma antica: Forme della comunicazione letteraria.* Rome and Bari.

Claassen, Jo-Marie. 1999. *Displaced Persons: The Literature of Exile from Cicero to Boethius.* Madison, Wisc., and London.

Coleman, K. M. 1987. "The Emperor Domitian and Literature." *ANRW* 2.32.5: 3087–3115.

————. 1990. "Fatal Charades: Roman Executions Staged as Mythological Enactments." *Journal of Roman Studies* 80: 44–73.

Colton, Robert E. 1991. *Juvenal's Use of Martial's Epigrams: A Study of Literary Influence.* Amsterdam.

Conte, Gian Biagio. 1986. *The Rhetoric of Imitation: Genre and Poetic Memory in Virgil and Other Latin Poets.* Translated by Charles Segal. Ithaca.

Cramer, Frederick H. 1954. *Astrology in Roman Law and Politics.* Philadelphia.

Cristante, Lucio. 1990. "Un verso fantasma di Ovidio (*Inc.* 6, p. 143 Morel; 145 Buechner)." *Prometheus* 16: 181–186.

Dalby, Andrew. 2000. *Empire of Pleasures: Luxury and Indulgence in the Roman World.* London and New York.

Damon, Cynthia. 1997. *The Mask of the Parasite: A Pathology of Roman Patronage.* Ann Arbor.

D'Arms, John. 1984. "Control, Companionship, and *Clientela:* Some Social Functions of the Roman Communal Meal." *Classical Views/Echos du monde classique* 28: 327–348.

————. 1990. "The Roman *Convivium* and Equality." In *Sympotica: A Symposium on the* Symposion, edited by O. Murray, 308–320. Oxford.

————. 1991. "Slaves at Roman *Convivia.*" In *Dining in a Classical Context,* edited by William J. Slater, 171–183. Ann Arbor.

Darwall-Smith, Robin Haydon. 1996. *Emperors and Architecture: A Study of Flavian Rome.* Brussels.

Dau, Albrecht. 1887. *De M. Valerii Martialis libellorum ratione temporibusque.* Rostock.

Daube, David. 1976. "Martial, Father of Three." *American Journal of Ancient History* 1: 145–147.

Delatte, L., et al. 1981. *Dictionnaire fréquentiel et index inverse de la langue latine.* Liège.

Delz, Josef. 1971. "Kritische Bemerkungen zu Tibull, Ovid und Martial." *Museum Helveticum* 28: 49–59.

Deroux, Carl, ed. 1998. *Studies in Latin Literature and Roman History.* Brussels.

Duff, A. M. 1928. *Freedmen in the Early Roman Empire.* Oxford.

Eck, Werner, and Johannes Heinrichs, eds. 1993. *Sklaven und Freigelassene in der Gesellschaft der römischen Kaiserzeit: Textauswahl und Übersetzung.* Darmstadt.

Edmunds, Lowell. 2001. *Intertextuality and the Reading of Roman Poetry.* Baltimore and London.

Edwards, Catharine. 1993. *The Politics of Immorality in Ancient Rome*. Cambridge.

Ehrlich, Jerry Dell. 1983. *Suicide in the Roman Empire: An Historical, Philosophical, and Theological Study*. New York.

Elmore, J. 1912. "Notes on the Dramatic Element in Martial." *Transactions of the American Philological Association* 43: lxxi–lxxii.

Ewbank, W. 1933. *The Poems of Cicero*. London.

Fabre, G. 1994. "Affranchis et esclaves impériaux sous Domitien." *Pallas* 40: 337–355.

Fagan, Garrett G. 1999. *Bathing in Public in the Roman World*. Ann Arbor.

Fehling, Detlev. 1974. *Ethologische Überlegungen auf dem Gebiet der Altertumskunde*. Munich.

Ferguson, John. 1963. "Catullus and Martial." *Proceedings of the African Classical Association* 6: 3–15.

Fitzgerald, William. 2000. *Slavery and the Roman Literary Imagination*. New York and Cambridge.

Fletcher, G. B. A. 1983. "On Martial." *Latomus* 42: 404–411.

Flower, Harriet. 1996. *Ancestor Masks and Aristocratic Power in Roman Culture*. Oxford.

Fogazza, Donatella. 1981. *Domiti Marsi testimonia et fragmenta*. Rome.

Fontán Pérez, Antonio. 1987. "Estacio y Marcial: Dos vates contemporáneos, dos poéticas opuestas." *Actas del simposio* 2.339–355.

Forbes, R. J. 1955–1958. *Studies in Ancient Technology*. 6 vols. Leiden.

Fowler, Don P. 1989. "First Thoughts on Closure." *Materiali e discussioni per l'analisi dei testi classici* 22: 75–122.

———. 1995. "Martial and the Book." *Ramus* 24: 31–58.

Fraenkel, Eduard. 1960. *Elementi Plautini in Plauto*. Translated by Franco Munari. Florence.

Freud, Sigmund. 1992. *Der Witz und seine Beziehung zum Unbewußten*. Frankfurt am Main. (Orig. publ. 1905.) Translated by James Strachey as *Jokes and Their Relation to the Unconscious*, New York, 1960.

Friedrich, Gustav. 1909. "Zu Martial." *Philologus* 68: 88–117.

———. 1910. "Zu Seneca und Martial." *Hermes* 45: 583–594.

Garrido-Hory, Marguerite. 1981. *Martial et l'esclavage*. Paris.

———. 1984. *Index thématique des références à l'esclavage et à la dépendance: Martial*. Paris.

———. 1985a. "Enrichissement et affranchis privés chez Martial: Pratiques et portraits." *Index* 13: 223–271.

———. 1985b. "Le statut de la clientèle chez Martial." *Dialogues d'histoire ancienne* 11: 381–414.

Garthwaite, J. 1998. "Patronage and Poetic Immortality in Martial, Book 9." *Mnemosyne* 51: 161–175.

Gerlach, O. 1911. *De Martialis figurae ΑΠΡΟΣΔΟΚΗΤΟΝ quae vocatur usu*. Diss. Jena.

Giegengack, J. M. 1969. "Significant Names in Martial." Diss., Yale University.

Giulian, Antony A. 1930. *Martial and the Epigram in Spain in the 16th and 17th Centuries*. Philadelphia.

Gold, Barbara K., ed. 1982. *Literary and Artistic Patronage in Ancient Rome*. Austin.

Gordon, A. E. 1973. *The Letter Names of the Latin Alphabet*. Berkeley.

Gowers, Emily. 1993. *The Loaded Table: Representations of Food in Roman Literature*. Oxford.

Grasmück, E. L. 1978. *Exilium: Untersuchungen zur Verbannung in der Antike*. Paderborn.

Greenwood, M. A. P. 1990. "Housman on Friedlaender (Mart. *Epigr.* 2.52): An Unnecessary Criticism?" *Liverpool Classical Monthly* 15: 107–108.

———. 1996. "Martial's *Disiecta Membra* and the Text of *Epigrams*, 2.73." *Museum Helveticum* 53: 259–261.

———. 1998a. "Martial, Gossip, and the Language of Rumour." In Grewing 1998b: 278–314.

———. 1998b. "Talking Flamingos and the Sins of the Tongue: The Ambiguous Use of *Lingua* in Martial." *Classical Philology* 93: 241–246.

Grelle, F. 1980. "La *correctio morum* nella legislazione Flavia." *ANRW* 2.13: 340–365.

Grewing, Farouk. 1996. "Möglichkeiten und Grenzen des Vergleichs: Martials Diadumenos und Catulls Lesbia." *Hermes* 124: 333–354.

———. 1998a. "Etymologie und etymologische Wortspiele in den Epigrammen Martials." In Grewing 1998b: 315–356.

———, ed. 1998b. *Toto notus in orbe: Perspektiven der Martial-Interpretation*. Stuttgart.

Grimal, Pierre. 1989. "Martial et la pensée de Sénèque." *Illinois Classical Studies* 14: 175–183.

Halperin, David M. 2002. *How to Do the History of Homosexuality*. Chicago.

Harris, H. A. 1972. *Sport in Greece and Rome*. London.

Heilmann, Willibald. 1984. "'Wenn ich frei sein könnte für ein wirkliches Leben . . .': Epikureisches bei Martial." *Antike und Abendland* 30: 47–61.

———. 1998. "Epigramme Martials über Leben und Tod." In Grewing 1998b: 205–219.

Hengel, Martin. 1977. *Crucifixion in the Ancient World and the Folly of the Message of the Cross*. Philadelphia.

Heraeus, W. 1925. "Zur neueren Martialkritik." *Rheinisches Museum* 74: 314–336.

Herrero Inguelmo, M. C., and E. Montero Cartelle. 1990. "Filénide en la literatura grecolatina." *Euphrosyne* 18: 265–274.

Herter, Hans. 1959. "Effeminatus." *Reallexikon für Antike und Christentum* 4: 620–650.

Heyob, S. K. 1975. *The Cult of Isis among Women in the Graeco-Roman World*. Leiden.

Hirst, G. 1950. "Martial, II.14.18 (The Would-Be Diner Out)." *Classical Review* 64: 53.

Hofmann, J. B. 1951. *Lateinische Umgangssprache*. 3rd ed. Heidelberg.

Hofmann, W. 1983. "Martial und Domitian." *Philologus* 127: 238–246.

Holzberg, Niklas. 1986. "Neuansatz zu einer Martial-Interpretation. *Würzburger Jahrbücher für die Altertumswissenschaft* 12: 197–215.

———. 1988. *Martial*. Heidelberg.

———. 2002. *Martial und das antike Epigramm*. Darmstadt.

Hopkins, Keith. 1983. *Death and Renewal*. Cambridge.

Hopkinson, N. 1982. "Juxtaposed Prosodic Variants in Greek and Latin Poetry." *Glotta* 60: 162–177.

Housman, A. E. 1906. "Corrections and Explanations of Martial." *Journal of Philology* 30: 229–265.

————. 1914. "Greek Nouns in Latin Poetry from Lucretius to Juvenal." *Journal of Philology* 33: 54–75.

————. 1925. Review of Heraeus. *Classical Review* 39: 199–203.

————. 1931a. "Praefanda." *Hermes* 66: 402–412.

————. 1931b. Review of Izaac, vol. 1. *Classical Review* 45: 81–83.

Hoyo Calleja, Javier del. 1987. "Lexico referente a la esposa de Marcial." In *Actas del simposio 1987*: 1.110–115.

Hudson-Williams, A. 1952. "Some Other Explanations of Martial." *Classical Quarterly* 46: 27–31.

Humez, Jean McMahon. 1971. "The Manners of Epigram: A Study of the Epigram Volumes of Martial, Harington, and Jonson." Diss., Yale University.

Hutchinson, G. O. 1993. *Latin Literature from Seneca to Juvenal: A Critical Study*. Oxford.

Immisch, Otto. 1911. "Zu Martial." *Hermes* 46: 481–517.

Jackson, Ralph. 1988. *Doctors and Diseases in the Roman Empire*. London.

Janson, T. 1964. *Latin Prose Prefaces: Studies in Literary Conventions*. Stockholm.

Joepgen, Ursula. 1967. *Wortspiele bei Martial*. Diss., Bonn.

Jones, Brian W. 1992. *The Emperor Domitian*. London and New York.

Jones, C. P. 1987. "*Stigma:* Tattooing and Branding in Graeco-Roman Antiquity." *Journal of Roman Studies* 77: 139–155.

Jordan, H. 1878. *Topographie der Stadt Rom im Altertum*. Berlin.

Kajanto, Iiro. 1965. *The Latin Cognomina*. Helsinki.

Kasher, Aryeh. 1988. *Jews, Idumaeans, and Ancient Arabs*. Tübingen.

Kaster, Robert A. 1988. *Guardians of Language*. Berkeley.

Keller, Otto. 1909. *Die antike Tierwelt*. Vol. 1. Leipzig.

Kelly, J. M. 1966. *Roman Litigation*. Oxford.

Kempter, Gerda. 1980. *Ganymed: Studien zur Typologie, Ikonographie und Ikonologie*. Cologne.

Kenyon, F. G. 1951. *Books and Readers in Ancient Greece and Rome*. 2nd ed. Oxford.

Ker, A. 1950. "Some Explanations and Emendations of Martial." *Classical Quarterly* 44: 12–24.

————. 1953. "Martial Again." *Classical Quarterly* 47: 173–174.

Kienast, Dietmar. 1965. "Rom und die Venus vom Eryx." *Hermes* 93: 478–489.

Kleberg, Tönnes. 1969. *Buchhandel und Verlagswesen in der Antike*. 3rd ed. Darmstadt.

Kleijwegt, Marc. 1998. "*Extra fortunam est quidquid donatur amicis:* Martial on Friendship." In Grewing 1998b: 256–277.

Konstan, David. 1995. "Patrons and Friends." *Classical Philology* 90: 328–342.

————. 1997. *Friendship in the Classical World*. Cambridge.

Krenkel, Werner. 1979. "Masturbation in der Antike." *Wissenschaftliche Zeitschrift der Wilhelm-Pieck-Universität Rostock* 28: 159–172.

————. 1980. "*Fellatio* and *Irrumatio*." *Wissenschaftliche Zeitschrift der Wilhelm-Pieck-Universität Rostock* 29: 77–88.

————. 1981. "Tonguing." *Wissenschaftliche Zeitschrift der Wilhelm-Pieck-Universität Rostock* 30: 37–54.

Kruuse, Jens. 1941. "L'originalité artistique de Martial." *Classica et Mediaevalia* 4: 248–300.

Kuppe, E. M. W. 1972. *Sachwitz bei Martial*. Diss., Bonn.

Kurmally, Mohammed Yousouf. 1971. "Martial's Attitude towards Women." Diss., Ohio State University.

Lane, Eugene N., ed. 1996. *Cybele, Attis, and Related Cults: Essays in Memory of M. J. Vermaseren.* Leiden.

LaPenna, Antonio. 1999. "*Immortale Falernum:* Il vino di Marziale e dei poeti latini del suo tempo." *Maia* 51: 163–181.

———. 2000. "I cento volti dell'eros di Marziale." In *Eros dai cento volti: Modelli etici ed estetici nell'età dei Flavi,* 67–134. Venice.

Laurens, P. 1989. *L'abeille dans l'ambre: Célébration de l'épigramme de l'époque alexandrine à la fin de la Renaissance.* Paris.

Lausberg, Heinrich. 1973. *Handbuch der literarischen Rhetorik.* 2nd ed. Munich.

Lausberg, Marion. 1982. *Das Einzeldistichon: Studien zum antiken Epigramm.* Munich.

Lease, Emory B. 1898. "*I nunc* and *i* with Another Imperative." *American Journal of Philology* 19: 59–69.

Lehmann, E. 1931. *Antike Martialausgaben.* Berlin.

Lilja, Saara. 1972. *The Treatment of Odours in the Poetry of Antiquity.* Helsinki.

———. 1985. "Seating Problems in the Roman Theater and Circus." *Arctos* 19: 67–74.

Lindsay, Hugh. 1998. "Food and Clothing in Martial." In Deroux 1998: 10.318–327.

Lindsay, W. M. 1903a. *The Ancient Editions of Martial.* Oxford.

———. 1903b. "Notes on the Text of Martial." *Classical Review* 17: 48–52.

———. 1904. "The Orthography of Martial's Editions." *Journal of Philology* 29: 24–60.

Lorenz, Sven. 2002. *Erotik und Panegyrik: Martials epigrammatische Kaiser.* Tübingen.

Lucas, Hans. 1938. "Martial's *Kalendae nataliciae.*" *Classical Quarterly* 32: 5–6.

Lugli, Giuseppe. 1961. "La Roma di Domiziano nei versi di Marziale e di Stazio." *Studi romani* 9: 1ff.

Maas, E. 1925. "Eunuchos und Verwandtes." *Rheinisches Museum* 74: 439–441.

Maaz, Wolfgang. 1992. *Lateinische Epigrammatik im hohen Mittelalter: Literar-historische Untersuchungen zur Martial-Rezeption.* Hildesheim.

———. 2001. "Dekonstruierte Freundschaft: Zur Rezeption von Martial II 24, II 43, III 26 und III 46 bei Godefrid von Winchester." In *Mentis amore ligati: Lateinische Freundschaftsdichtung und Dichterfreundschaft in Mittelalter und Neuzeit,* edited by Boris Körkel et al., 293–303. Heidelberg.

Malnati, Thomas Peter. 1988. "Juvenal and Martial on Social Mobility." *Classical Journal* 83: 133–41.

Marina Sáez, Rosa Maria. 1998. *La métrica de los epigramas de Marcial: Esquemas rítmicos y esquemas verbales.* Zaragoza.

Marquardt, Joachim. 1886. *Das Privatleben der Römer.* 2nd ed. Leipzig.

Marshall, F. H. 1907. *Catalogue of the Finger Rings, Greek, Etruscan and Roman, in the Departments of Antiquities, British Museum.* Oxford.

Mateu Areste, Francisco-Javier. 1987. "Formas de proyección del enunciado gnómico en Marcial." In *Actas del simposio* 1987: 1.131–139.

McDonnell, Myles. 1996. "Writing, Copying, and Autograph Manuscripts in Ancient Rome." *Classical Quarterly* 46: 469–491.

Mendell, C. W. 1922. "Martial and the Satiric Epigram." *Classical Philology* 17: 1–20.

Merli, Elena. 1993. "Ordinamento degli epigrammi e strategie cortigiane negli esordi dei libri I–XII di Marziale." *Maia* 45: 229–256.

————. 1996. "Note a Marziale (8.50; 10.7; 11.90; 13.118)." *Materiali e discussioni per l'analisi dei testi classici* 36: 211–223.

————. 1998. "Epigrammzyklen und 'serielle Lektüre' in den Büchern Martials: Überlegungen und Beispiele." In Grewing 1998b: 139–156.

Miller, J. Innes. 1969. *The Spice Trade of the Roman Empire.* Oxford.

Nauta, Ruurd R. 2002. *Poetry for Patrons: Literary Communication in the Age of Domitian.* Leiden.

Nicolson, F. W. 1891. "Greek and Roman Barbers." *Harvard Studies in Classical Philology* 2: 41–56.

Nielsen, Inge. 1990. Thermae et Balnea: *The Architecture and Cultural History of Roman Public Baths.* 2 vols. Aarhus.

Nixon, Paul. 1963. *Martial and the Modern Epigram.* New York.

Nocks, A. D. 1925. "Eunuchs in Ancient Religion." *Archiv für Religionswissenschaft* 23: 25–33. Reprinted in Andreas Siems, ed., *Sexualität und Erotik in der Antike* (Darmstadt, 1988), 58–69.

Obermayer, Hans Peter. 1998. *Martial und der Diskurs über männliche "Homosexualität" in der Literatur der frühen Kaiserzeit.* Tübingen.

Offermann, H. 1980. *"Uno tibi sim minor Catullo." Quaderni urbinati di cultura classica* 34: 107–139.

Opelt, Ilona. 1965. *Die lateinischen Schimpfwörter und verwandte sprachliche Erscheinungen.* Heidelberg.

Otto, A. 1890. *Die Sprichwörter und sprichwörtlichen Redensarten der Römer.* Leipzig.

Parker, Holt N. 1992. "Love's Body Anatomized: The Ancient Erotic Handbooks and the Rhetoric of Sexuality." In *Pornography and Representation in Greece and Rome,* edited by Amy Richlin, 90–111. New York and Oxford.

Pascucci, Giovanni. 1957. *"Viden (ut)." Studi italiani di filologia classica* 29: 174–196.

Paukstadt, R. 1876. *De Martiale Catulli imitatore.* Diss., Halle.

Pavese, C. O. 1996. "La iscrizione sulla kotyle di Nestor da Pithekoussai." *Zeitschrift für Papyrologie und Epigraphik* 114: 1–23.

Peachin, Michael, ed. 2001. *Aspects of Friendship in the Graeco-Roman World.* Portsmouth, R.I.

Pertsch, E. 1911. *De Martiale Graecorum poetarum imitatore.* Berlin.

Peter, Hermann. 1901. *Der Brief in der römischen Literatur: Literargeschichtliche Untersuchungen und Zusammenfassungen.* Leipzig.

Peyer, Bernhard, and Hugo Remund. 1928. *Medizinisches aus Martial, mit Ergänzungen aus Juvenal und einem naturgeschichtlichen Anhang.* Zurich and Leipzig.

Pfohl, G., ed. 1969. *Das Epigramm: Zur Geschichte einer inschriftlichen und literarischen Gattung.* Darmstadt.

Pichon, René. 1902. *De sermone amatorio apud Latinos elegiarum scriptores.* Paris.

Pitcher, R. A. 1993. "The *mollis vir* in Martial." In Multarum artium scientia: *A "Chose" for R. Godfrey Tanner,* edited by Kevin Lee et al., 59–67. Auckland.

————. 1998. "Martial's Debt to Ovid." In Grewing 1998b: 59–76.

Pizzolato, Luigi. 1993. *L'idea di amicizia nel mondo antico classico e cristiano.* Turin.

Plass, P. 1985. "An Aspect of Epigrammatic Wit in Martial and Tacitus." *Arethusa* 18: 187–210.

Platner, Samuel Ball. 1929. *A Topographical Dictionary of Ancient Rome.* Revised by Thomas Ashby. London.

Potthoff, Anne. 1992. *Lateinische Kleidungsbezeichnungen in synchroner und diachroner Sicht.* Innsbruck.

Prinz, Karl. 1911. *Martial und die griechische Epigrammatik*. Vienna and Leipzig.
————. 1929. "Martialerklärungen II." *Wiener Studien* 47: 109–116.
Prior, R. E. 1996. "Going Around Hungry: Topography and Poetics in Martial 2.14." *American Journal of Philology* 117: 121–141.
Puelma, Mario. 1996. "Ἐπίγραμμα—*epigramma*: Aspekte einer Wortgeschichte." *Museum Helveticum* 53: 123–139.
Raditsa, L. F. 1980. "Augustus' Legislation concerning Marriage, Procreation, Love Affairs and Adultery." *ANRW* 2.13.278–339.
Ramirez Sádaba, J. L. 1987. "Utilidad de los datos cuantitativos transmitidos por Marcial para una historia economico-social." In *Actas del simposio*: 1.153–168.
Ransom, C. L. 1905. *Couches and Beds of the Greeks, Etruscans and Romans*. Chicago.
Reeve, M. D. 1983. "Martial." In *Texts and Transmission: A Survey of the Latin Classics,* edited by L. D. Reynolds, 239–244. Oxford.
Reinhold, M. 1970. *The History of Purple as a Status Symbol in Antiquity*. Brussels.
————. 1971. "Usurpation of Status and Status Symbols in the Roman Empire." *Historia* 20: 275–302.
Richardson, L., Jr. 1992. *A New Topographical Dictionary of Ancient Rome*. Baltimore and London.
Richlin, Amy. 1981. "The Meaning of *Irrumare* in Catullus and Martial." *Classical Philology* 76: 40–46.
————. 1992. *The Garden of Priapus: Sexuality and Aggression in Roman Humor*. Rev. ed. New York and Oxford.
Rives, J. B. ed. 1999. *Tacitus:* Germania. New York and Oxford.
Rodón Binué, Eulalia. 1987. "La expresividad léxica en Marcial." In *Actas del simposio* 1987: 2.291–300.
Roman, Luke. 2001. "The Representation of Literary Materiality in Martial's *Epigrams*." *Journal of Roman Studies* 91: 113–145.
Roscoe, Will. 1996. "Priests of the Goddess: Gender Transgression in Ancient Religion." *History of Religions* 35: 195–230.
Rosen, Klaus. 1995. "Römische Freigelassene als Aufsteiger und Petrons *Cena Trimalchionis*." *Gymnasium* 102: 79–91.
Rutledge, Steven H. 2001. *Imperial Inquisitions: Prosecutors and Informants from Tiberius to Domitian*. London.
Sage, Evan T. 1919. "The Publication of Martial's Poems." *Transactions of the American Philological Association* 50: 168–176.
Salanitro, Maria. 1991. "Il sale romano degli epigrammi di Marziale." *Atene e Roma* 36: 1–25.
————. 1998–1999. *"Non bene olet qui bene semper olet*: Marziale (2,12,4) ma non Petronio (fr. XXIIII)." *Orpheus* 19–20: 395–401.
Salemme, Carmelo. 1976. *Marziale e la "poetica" degli oggetti*. Naples.
————. 1987. "Alle origini della poesia di Marziale." *Orpheus*, n.s., 8: 14–49.
Saller, R. P. 1982. *Personal Patronage under the Early Empire*. New York and Cambridge.
————. 1983. "Martial on Patronage and Literature." *Classical Quarterly* 33: 246–257.
————. 1989. "Patronage and Friendship in Early Imperial Rome: Drawing the Distinction." In Wallace-Hadrill 1989: 49–62.
Scheithauer, Andrea. 2000. *Kaiserliche Bautätigkeit in Rom: Das Echo in der antiken Literatur*. Stuttgart.

Scherf, Johannes. 1998. "Zur Komposition von Martials Gedichtbüchern 1–12." In Grewing 1998b: 119–138.

———. 2001. *Untersuchungen zur Buchgestaltung Martials.* Munich and Leipzig.

Schmid, D. 1951. *Der Erbschleicher in der antiken Satire.* Tübingen.

Schmid, Wolfgang. 1984. "Spätantike Textdepravationen in den Epigrammen Martials." In *Ausgewählte philologische Schriften,* edited by Hartmut Erbse and Jochem Küppers, 400–444. Berlin.

Schmidt, V. 1989. "Ein Trio im Bett: *Tema con variazioni* bei Catull, Martial, Babrius und Apuleius." *Groningen Colloquia on the Novel* 2: 63–73.

Schneider, Georg. 1909. *De M. Valerii Martialis sermone observationes.* Bratislava.

Schulze, Wilhelm. 1904. *Zur Geschichte lateinischer Eigennamen.* Berlin.

Schumacher, Leonhard. 2001. *Sklaverei in der Antike: Alltag und Schicksal der Unfreien.* Munich.

Sebesta, J., and L. Bonfante, eds. 2001. *The World of Roman Costume.* Madison, Wisc.

Seel, O. 1961. "Ansatz zu einer Martial-Interpretation." *Antike und Abendland* 10: 53–76. Reprinted in Pfohl 1969: 153–186.

Shackleton Bailey, D. R. 1978. "Corrections and Explanations of Martial." *Classical Philology* 73: 273–296.

———. 1980. "Martial 2.91 and 10.20." *Classical Philology* 75: 69–70.

———. 1989. "More Corrections and Explanations of Martial." *American Journal of Philology* 110: 131–150.

Sichtermann, Hellmut. 1988. "Ganymedes." In *Lexicon iconographicum mythologiae classicae,* 4.154–169. Zurich.

Siedschlag, Edgar. 1972. "Ovidisches bei Martial." *Rivista di filologia e di istruzione classica* 100: 156–161.

———. 1977. *Zur Form von Martials Epigrammen.* Berlin.

———. 1979. *Martial-Konkordanz.* Hildesheim.

Siems, K. 1974. *Aischrologia: Das Sexuell-Häßliche im antiken Epigramm.* Diss., Göttingen.

Sittl, Carl. 1890. *Die Gebärden der Griechen und Römer.* Leipzig.

Slater, William J., ed. 1991. *Dining in a Classical Context.* Ann Arbor.

Solin, Heikki. 1982. *Die griechischen Personennamen in Rom: Ein Namenbuch.* Berlin and New York.

Solin, Heikki, and Olli Salomies. 1994. *Repertorium nominum gentilium et cognominum Latinorum.* 2nd ed. Hildesheim.

Solodow, J. B. 1986. "*Raucae, tua cura, palumbes:* Study of a Poetic Word Order." *Harvard Studies in Classical Philology* 90: 129–153.

Sonny, Adolf. 1896. "Zu den Sprichwörtern und sprichwörtlichen Redensarten der Römer." *Archiv für lateinische Lexikographie und Grammatik* 9: 53–80.

Spiegel, P. Gebhard. 1891. *Zur Charakteristik des Epigrammatikers M. Valerius Martialis.* Innsbruck.

Spisak, Art L. 1998a. "Gift-Giving in Martial." In Grewing 1998b: 243–255.

———. 1998b. "Martial's Special Relation with His Reader." In Deroux 1998: 8.352–363.

Sposi, F. 1997. "Archeologia e poesia in due epigrammi di Marziale (2,14; 7,73)." *Atene e Roma* 42: 16–27.

Stambaugh, J. E. 1978. "The Function of Roman Temples." *ANRW* 2.16.1: 573–596.

Starr, Raymond J. 1987. "The Circulation of Literary Texts in the Roman World." *Classical Quarterly* 37: 213–223.

————. 1990–1991. "Reading Aloud: *Lectores* and Roman Reading." *Classical Journal* 86: 337–343.

Steinby, Eva Margareta, ed. 1993–2000. *Lexicon topographicum urbis Romae.* 6 vols. Rome.

Stone, Shelley. 2001. "The Toga: From National to Ceremonial Costume." In Sebesta and Bonfante 2001: 13–45.

Strong, D. E. 1966. *Greek and Roman Gold and Silver Plate.* London.

Stumpp, Bettina Eva. 1998. *Prostitution in der römischen Antike.* Berlin.

Sullivan, J. P. 1979. "Martial's Sexual Attitudes." *Philologus* 123: 288–302.

————. 1991. *Martial: The Unexpected Classic.* Cambridge.

————, ed. 1993. *Martial.* New York and London.

Sutphen, Morris C. 1901. "A Further Collection of Latin Proverbs." *American Journal of Philology* 22: 1–28, 121–148, 241–260, 361–391.

Swann, Bruce W. 1994. *Martial's Catullus: The Reception of an Epigrammatic Rival.* Zurich and New York.

————. 1998. "*Sic scribit Catullus*: The Importance of Catullus for Martial's Epigrams." In Grewing 1998: 48–58.

Szelest, Hannah. 1963. "Martial und die römische Gesellschaft." *Eos* 53: 182–190.

————. 1974a. "Martial und Domitian." *Eos* 62: 105–114.

————. 1974b. "Die Mythologie bei Martial." *Eos* 62: 297–310.

————. 1980. "*Ut faciam breviora mones epigrammata, Corde:* Eine Martial-Studie." *Philologus* 124: 99–108.

————. 1986. "Martial, eigentlicher Schöpfer und hervorragendster Vertreter des römischen Epigramms." *ANRW* 2.32.4: 2563–2623.

Szelinski, V. 1903. "Zu den Sprichwörtern der Römer." *Rheinisches Museum* 58: 471–475.

————. 1904. "Zu den Sprichwörtern der Römer (II). *Rheinisches Museum* 59: 149–157, 316–317, 477–478, 635–638.

Tanner, R. G. 1986. "Levels of Intent in Martial." *ANRW* 2.32.4: 2624–2677.

Taylor, Rabun. 1997. "Two Pathic Subcultures in Ancient Rome." *Journal of the History of Sexuality* 7: 319–371.

Tennant, Peter M. W. 2000. "Poets and Poverty: The Case of Martial." *Acta Classica* 43: 139–156.

Teuffel, W. S. 1882. *Geschichte der römischen Literatur.* 4th ed. Leipzig.

Thompson, E. A. 1965. *The Early Germans.* Oxford.

Toynbee, J. M. C. 1971. *Death and Burial in the Roman World.* London.

————. 1973. *Animals in Roman Life and Art.* London.

Tracy, V. A. 1980. "*Aut captantur aut captant.*" *Latomus* 39: 399–402.

Treggiari, Susan. 1969. *Roman Freedmen during the Late Republic.* Oxford.

————. 1991. *Roman Marriage: "Iusti Coniuges" from the Time of Cicero to the Time of Ulpian.* Oxford.

Turner, Eric G. 1987. *Greek Manuscripts in the Ancient World.* 2nd ed. London.

Van Hooff, Anton J. L. 1990. *From Autothanasia to Suicide: Self-Killing in Classical Antiquity.* London and New York.

Van Stockum, Gulielmus Jacobus Machiel. 1884. *De Martialis vita ac scriptis commentatio.* The Hague.

Verdière, Raoul. 1969. "Notes critiques sur Martial." *Acta Classica Universitatis Scientiarum Debreceniensis* 5: 105–110.

Vessey, D. W. 1976. "Philaenis." *Revue belge de philologie et d'histoire* 54: 78–83.

Wagner, Ernestus. 1880. *De Martiale poetarum Augusteae aetatis imitatore.* Diss., Königsberg.

Wallace-Hadrill, Andrew. 1981. "Family and Inheritance in the Augustan Marriage Laws." *Proceedings of the Cambridge Philological Society* 27: 58–80.

———, ed. 1989. *Patronage in Ancient Society.* London and New York.

Walter, Uwe. 1998. "Soziale Normen in den Epigrammen Martials." In Grewing 1998b: 220–242.

Watson, L. C. 1983. "Three Women in Martial." *Classical Quarterly* 33: 258–264.

Watson, Patricia A. 1982. "Martial's Fascination with *Lusci.*" *Greece and Rome* 29: 71–76.

Watt, W. S. 1984. "Notes on Martial." *Liverpool Classical Monthly* 9: 130–131.

Weaver, P. R. C. 1972. *Familia Caesaris: A Social Study of the Emperor's Freedmen and Slaves.* Cambridge.

Weber, Marga. 1996. *Antike Badekultur.* Munich.

Weeber, Karl-Wilhelm. 1995. *Alltag im alten Rom: Ein Lexikon.* Zurich.

Weinreich, O. 1928. *Studien zu Martial: Literaturhistorische und religionsgeschichtliche Untersuchungen.* Stuttgart.

Weyman, Carl. 1893. "Zu den Sprichwörtern und sprichwörtlichen Redensarten der Römer."*Archiv für lateinische Lexikographie und Grammatik* 8: 23–38, 397–411.

———. 1904. "Zu den Sprichwörtern und sprichwörtlichen Redensarten der Römer." *Archiv für lateinische Lexikographie und Grammatik* 13: 253–270, 379–406.

Whipple, Thomas King. 1925. *Martial and the English Epigram from Sir Thomas Wyatt to Ben Jonson.* Berkeley.

White, Peter. 1972. "Aspects of Non-Imperial Patronage in the Works of Statius and Martial." Diss., Harvard University.

———. 1974. "The Presentation and Dedication of the *Silvae* and Epigrams." *Journal of Roman Studies* 64: 40–61.

———. 1975. "The Friends of Martial, Statius, and Pliny, and the Dispersal of Patronage." *Harvard Studies in Classical Philology* 79: 265–300.

———. 1978. "*Amicitia* and the Profession of Poetry in Early Imperial Rome." *Journal of Roman Studies* 68: 74–92.

———. 1996. "Martial and Pre-Publication Texts." *Classical Views/Echos du monde classique* 40: 397–412.

Williams, Craig. 1992. "Homosexuality and the Roman Man: A Study in the Cultural Construction of Sexuality." Diss., Yale University.

———. 1999. *Roman Homosexuality: Ideologies of Masculinity in Classical Antiquity.* New York and Oxford.

———. 2002a. "Ovid, Martial, and Poetic Immortality: Traces of *Amores* 1.15 in the *Epigrams.*" *Arethusa* 35: 417–433.

———. 2002b. "*Sit nequior omnibus libellis:* Text, Poet, and Reader in Martial's Epigrams." *Philologus* 146: 150–171.

———. Forthcoming. "*Paelignus, puto, dixerat poeta:* Martial 2.41 and the Art of Allusion."

Wills, Jeffrey. 1996. *Repetition in Latin Poetry: Figures of Allusion.* Oxford.

Wilson, Harry. 1898. "The Literary Influence of Martial upon Juvenal." *American Journal of Philology* 19: 193–209.

Wilson, L. M. 1938. *The Clothing of the Ancient Romans.* Baltimore.

Wiseman, T. P. 1970. "The Definition of *eques Romanus* in the Late Republic and Early Empire." *Historia* 19: 67–83.

Yegül, Fikret K. 1992. *Baths and Bathing in Classical Antiquity.* New York.

Zicàri, M. 1963. "Note a Petronio e a Marziale." In *Lanx satura: Nicolao Terzaghi oblata miscellanea philologica,* 343–354. Genoa.

Zingerle, A. 1877. *Martial's Ovid-Studien.* Innsbruck.

INDICES

These are selective indices. Fictional characters' names that occur only once and are never discussed elsewhere in the commentary are omitted here; for full indices of names, readers are referred to Shackleton Bailey's Teubner and Loeb Classical Library editions. The Index of Passages lists only those texts which receive some discussion and stand in a close relationship to an epigram of Martial's.

NAMES AND SUBJECTS

accumulation (*cumulatio*), 45, 59, 69, 107, 113, 125, 137–138, 173, 184, 193, 207, 267–268
adultery and adulteresses, 143–144, 171, 176–177, 201, 203, 253
See also Index of Latin words s.v. *moecha, moechus*
alliteration, 53, 61, 62, 94, 105, 131, 144, 254, 259
Ammianus, 35, 82
Apicius, M. Gavius, 223, 269
apo koinou structure, 28, 72, 96
Apollo, 95–96, 132, 268
Atedius Melior, 4, 8, 224
Augustus, Mausoleum of, 69, 199–200

baldness in women, 129, 218
Bastard, Thomas, 11

baths and bathing, 60, 72–74, 148, 155–156, 174, 182, 225–226, 244–245
See also Index of Latin words s.v. *balnea, solium, thermae*
beards and shaving, 81, 135–136, 174, 234
book format, 5, 20, 24, 40–41, 281–282
brevity, as virtue in epigram, 26, 240–244

Caecilianus, 101, 141, 227, 229, 245
Caesar
most frequently occurring personal name in Martial, 60
as title, 29

LATIN WORDS

PASSAGES